DICTATORSHIP AS EXPERIENCE

DICTATORSHIP AS EXPERIENCE

TOWARDS A SOCIO–CULTURAL HISTORY OF THE GDR

SHL
WITHDRAWN

Edited by Konrad H. Jarausch
Translated by Eve Duffy

Berghahn Books
New York • Oxford

First published in 1999 by

Berghahn Books

Editorial offices:
55 John Street, 3rd Floor, New York, NY 10038, USA
3 NewTec Place, Magdalen Road, Oxford OX4 1RE, UK

Library of Congress Cataloging-in-Publication Data

Dictatorship as experience: towards a socio-cultural history of the GDR
/ edited by Konrad H. Jarausch and translated by Eve Duffy.
   p.   cm.
The essays in this collection originated in a conference on "The
GDR—a modern dictatorship?" held in Potsdam, December 1997
   Includes bibliographical references and index.
   ISBN-1-57181-181-8 (hardback)
   ISBN-1-57181-182-6 (paperback)
   1. Dictatorship—Germany (East) Congresses. 2. Communism—Ger-
many (East)—History Congresses. 3. Germany (East)—Social condi-
tions Congresses. 4. Germany (East)—Social policy Congresses. 5.
Political culture—Germany (East) Congresses. I. Jarausch, Konrad
Hugo.
DD283.D54   1999   99-35667
943'.1087—dc 21   CIP

British Library Cataloguing in Publication Data

A catalogue record for this book is available from the British Library.

Printed in the United States on acid-free paper.

CONTENTS

Preface   ix

List of Abbreviations   xi

Introduction

Beyond Uniformity: The Challenge of Historicizing the GDR   3
Konrad H. Jarausch

The Theoretical Problem of Dictatorship

1. The GDR: A Special Kind of Modern Dictatorship   17
   Jürgen Kocka

2. Modernization and Modernization Blockages in
   GDR Society   27
   Detlef Pollack

3. Care and Coercion: The GDR as Welfare Dictatorship   47
   Konrad H. Jarausch

Mechanisms of Political Repression

4. From Dismantling to Currency Reform: External Origins
   of the Dictatorship, 1943–1948   73
   Jochen Laufer

5. Foreign Influences on the Dictatorial Development of
   the GDR, 1949–1955   91
   Michael Lemke

6. Repression and Tolerance as Methods of Rule in Communist
   Societies   109
   Mario Keßler and Thomas Klein

Means of Social Control

7. Creating State Socialist Governance: The Case of the
   Deutsche Volkspolizei   125
   Thomas Lindenberger

8. Food Supply in a Planned Economy: SED Nutrition Policy
   between Crisis Response and Popular Needs   143
   Burghard Ciesla and Patrice G. Poutrus

9. The Myth of Female Emancipation: Contradictions
   in Women's Lives   163
   Leonore Ansorg and Renate Hürtgen

10. The Socialist Glass Ceiling: Limits to Female Careers   177
    Dagmar Langenhan and Sabine Roß

Cultural Dimensions of Domination

11. Dictatorship as Discourse: Cultural Perspectives on
    SED Legitimacy   195
    Martin Sabrow

12. The Fettered Media: Controlling Public Debate   213
    Simone Barck, Christoph Classen and Thomas Heimann

13. Criticism and Censorship: Negotiating Cabaret
    Performance and Book Production   241
    Sylvia Klötzer and Siegfried Lokatis

14. The Pivotal Cadres: Leadership Styles and Self-Images
    of GDR-Elites   265
    Arnd Bauerkämper and Jürgen Danyel

Temporal Transformations

15. Stagnation or Change? Transformations of the Workplace
    in the GDR   285
    Peter Hübner

16. The Hitler Youth Generation in the GDR: Insecurities,
    Ambitions and Dilemmas   307
    Dorothee Wierling

17. Reforming Socialism? The Changing of the Guard from
    Ulbricht to Honecker during the 1960s   325
    Monika Kaiser

18. Mobility and Blockage during the 1970s   341
    Ralph Jessen

Postscript

19. Rethinking the Second German Dictatorship   363
    Christoph Kleßmann

Selected Bibliography   373

Notes on Contributors   379

Index   383

PREFACE

This volume presents to an English-speaking public some of the recent, increasingly sophisticated work on the GDR, conducted at the Zentrum für Zeithistorische Forschung. Growing out of the Forschungsschwerpunkt Zeithistorische Studien, this Center for Research on Contemporary History was founded in 1996, partly as a home for scholars of the former GDR Academy of Sciences whose projects had been evaluated positively and partly as a spur to inter-disciplinary innovation in the humanities and social sciences within the united Germany. Initially the institute proved highly controversial, since East German dissidents and West German Cold Warriors claimed that historians who had been active in the previous regime ought to be barred on moral and scholarly grounds, while Eastern postcommunists and Western radicals resented its probing analyses of the flaws in "real existing socialism" (see also Mary Fulbrook, "New *Historikerstreit*, Missed Opportunity, or New Beginning?" *German History* 12 [1994]: 203-7). Under its founding director Jürgen Kocka and his successor Christoph Kleßmann as well as myself, the ZZF has tried hard to develop an intermediary line of interpretation that would analyze the dictatorial character of the GDR comparatively, but at the same time acknowledge some of the normalcy of daily lives in the SED state.

The essays in this collection originated in a conference on "The GDR – A Modern Dictatorship?" held in Potsdam during early December of 1997 (see Anette Weinke, "Eine moderne Diktatur? Jahrestagung des ZZF" *Deutschland Archiv* 31 [1998]: 461-64). To advance the theoretical discussion beyond the totalitarianism paradigm M. Rainer Lepsius contributed a preview of his study of the GDR bureaucracy, Juan Linz commented on "post-totalitarianism" based on his book on democratic transition and Klaus von Beyme provided an overview of Stalinism in Eastern Europe (published in the *Potsdamer Bulletin für Zeithistorische Studien* 13 [July 1998]: 8-22). The symposium also centered on the presentation of new empirical studies from the ZZF's four research projects on "Sovietization", the transformation of elites, the interplay of repression and self-assertion in ordinary lives and finally the role of history in legitimizing the regime. In order to include a broad selection of works within a limited space, some authors have graciously combined their efforts in a joint text. As session chairs Sigrid Meuschel, Hans-Günter Hockerts, Adelheid von Saldern, and Manfred Görtemaker and as concluding panelists Inga Markovits, Dietrich Mühlberg, Joachim Petzold, Peter Steinbach, Rüdiger Thomas and Heinrich August Winkler contributed to a spirited discussion. Christa Schneider of the organizational staff of the institute, Eve Duffy as translator of many of the texts, Rosalie Radcliffe as their copyeditor and Cora Granata who prepared the index also deserve the warmest thanks.

This collection also hopes to provide fresh research impulses and interpretative direction for the rapidly expanding Anglo-American discussion of the GDR. Through the accessibility of its records and the political controversies surrounding its legacy, the second German dictatorship has become a popular subject, especially for dissertations, some of which are unfortunately directed by scholars who themselves have not been able to work on East German materials. An impressive body of English-speaking work is overcoming the polarization of Cold War stereotypes and utopian sympathies through methodological innovation, comparative perspective and political openness. But sometimes outside researchers need further guidance on the complicated internal German discussions, arcane structures of the GDR, or the indecipherable prose of the SED. Both the members of the ZZF and its many Anglo-American guests such as Mitchell Ash, Mary Fulbrook, Georg G. Iggers, Charles S. Maier, Voitech Mastny, Norman Naimark, and Eric Weitz, just to mention a few of the established scholars, have therefore benefited from interacting with each other. Reflecting my own involvement in both academic cultures, this volume is an effort to strengthen this transatlantic working relationship by encouraging especially younger scholars to look to the Center for consultation and support.

Potsdam and Chapel Hill,   *Konrad H. Jarausch*
September 1998

LIST OF ABBREVIATIONS

ABF	Workers and Peasant Faculties
ABV	Police Section Commissioner
CDU	Christian Democratic Union
COMECON	Council for Mutual Economic Assistance
COMINFORM	Communist International
CPSU	Communist Party of the Soviet Union
DEFA	German Film Studio
DSF	Society for German-Soviet Friendship
EKD	Protestant Church of Germany
FDGB	Free German Trade Union Federation
FDJ	Free German Youth
FRG	Federal Republic of Germany
GDR	German Democratic Republic
KIM	Industrial Feeding Farm
KPD	Communist Party of Germany
LPG	Agricultural Production Cooperative
MfS	Ministry for State Security (Stasi)
MTS	Machine Tractor Station
NAPOLA	Nazi Elite School
NÖSPL	New Economic Planning and Guidance System
NSDAP	National Socialist Workers Party
SAG	Soviet Stock Company
SBZ	Soviet Occupied Zone
SCC	Soviet Control Commission
SED	Socialist Unity Party of Germany
SPD	Social Democratic Party of Germany
SRK	State Radio Committee
SVAG	Soviet Military Administration of Germany

USSR	Union of Soviet Socialist Republics
VEB	People Owned Factory
VEG	People Owned Estate
VVB	Union of People Owned Companies
ZK	Central Committee of the Communist Party
ZPKK	Central Party Control Commission

INTRODUCTION

BEYOND UNIFORMITY

THE CHALLENGE OF HISTORICIZING THE GDR

Konrad H. Jarausch

Though public interest in the GDR may be starting to wane, scholarly concern is, if anything, still increasing a decade after the collapse of the second German dictatorship. The parliamentary commission of inquiry into the SED state has wound up its debates by creating a foundation for former Eastern dissidents.[1] In the 1998 election campaign, CDU posters portraying the historic handshake between Pieck and Grotewohl so as to tarnish the current cooperation between SPD and PDS have frightened fewer voters than four years before. Nonetheless, dissertations on the defunct GDR are multiplying so quickly that a Mannheim survey of the mid-90s counted about 759 German projects alone, making it a more popular research field after its demise than during its lifetime. The extraordinary opportunity of working on recent documents of the secret police, party or state, the surprising nature of the collapse of communism and the disorientation of losing a utopian alternative may have something to do with this academic boom.[2] While first syntheses are beginning to appear, agreement on the basic features of the second German dictatorship is not yet in sight.[3]

One leading school of commentary focuses on the politics of repression and portrays the GDR as an *Unrechtsstaat,* a fundamentally illegitimate regime. Motivated by anti-Communism, these after-the-fact critics emphasize the Soviet origins and the continued dependence of the East German state, picturing it as a kind of occupation regime that was supported largely by Red Army tanks after the abortive June 1953 uprising. Contrasting the SED regime to the free elections of the Federal Republic, they stress its fundamental lack of democratic legitimacy and argue that it could control its population only through the building of the Wall and the construction of a large-scale secret police apparatus, the feared Stasi. This stark interpretation takes communist propaganda claims largely at face value, and considers East German society thoroughly politicized, organized by subsidiaries of the ruling party so as to leave no space for a normal private life. The theoretical foundation of this indictment rests on a revived totalitarianism theory which sees most Nazi mechanisms of repression repeated in the ostensibly anti-Fascist GDR.[4] Not surprisingly, such a moralizing view appeals especially to former Eastern dissidents and to Western champions of the Cold War.

At the opposite end of the interpretative spectrum, a more benign picture of the GDR as a "failed experiment" seeks to recover the noble aims of socialism from the debris of its admittedly imperfect realization. An essential part of a positive view is the "legend of the good beginning," i.e. a somewhat nostalgic portrayal of the founding of the GDR as a radical humanist effort to create a better Germany that would never again repeat the Nazi crimes. This sympathetic stance supports in retrospect the expropriation of the large landowners, the nationalization of key industries, the empowerment of workers and peasants, the food, transportation and housing subsidies, the welfare provisions of pensions and inexpensive health-care, the liberation of women through industrial employment, free child-care, and so on. The conceptual difficulty which a more positive interpretation faces is, however, finding an explanation of what went wrong, when things ceased to work out and who was responsible for the mistakes that eventually brought down the Ulbricht–Honecker regime.[5] Feeding on memories of positive experiences, this effort to rehabilitate socialism resonates especially with post-communists in the East and the old Left in the West.

Though less vehement due to their physical distance, Anglo–American views on the other Germany nonetheless polarize along similar ideological lines. To most outside observers, the East German state remained an indistinct country, overshadowed both by the hegemonic power of the Soviet Union over its own bloc and by the larger size and economic influence of its Western twin, the Federal Republic. It is no wonder, that Cold War images taken from the June 1953 uprising or the building of the Wall still govern many public statements about the GDR, especially in political references to the defunct regime. Yet for many Western intellectuals East Germany was also an object of ideological sympathy as a "better Germany," untarnished by the Nazi past, and as an exemplar of a more egalitarian society, free from capitalist exploitation and suffering.[6] While negative media representations color the vague perceptions of the public, better informed academics are more ambivalent in their appraisals of the former GDR, mixing strictures about the lack of human rights with praise for an elaborate system of social provisions, impossible under capitalism.

The stakes of the debate about the nature of the GDR continue to be considerable, even if they no longer involve jobs and resources. The completion of the academic restructuring of East Germany has removed one layer of self-interest from the discussion and thereby created space for somewhat more dispassionate assessments.[7] But the public struggle between the hard and soft views of the GDR continues, since it revolves around a clash of different memories, depending upon whether one was a protagonist, a victim or merely a bystander of the SED regime. Moreover, the controversy also concerns the future orientation of political culture within united Germany, with one side demanding an anti-totalitarian consensus as an essential foundation of democracy while the other calls for an anti-capitalist egalitarianism as a necessary basis for political reform. Both of these views are couched in highly moral terms and use the GDR merely as evidence in what amounts to an ideological contest for the soul of the country, without being particularly interested in what the second German state was really like. Reverse mirror images of each other, these black or white interpretations reduce the paradoxes of the SED state to a clear-cut reality with a single political message for the future.

For more discerning historians the challenge consists of coming to terms with the contradictions of the GDR experience so as to recover the various shades of gray, characteristic even of life under a dictatorship. This goal requires a conscious effort to historicize the subject, that is, to accept the second German state as something that has become part of the past, although its legacy continues to trouble the present. Comparisons not just to the Third Reich but also with other Soviet bloc states will reveal a puzzling alterity of real existing socialism, especially for Western scholars without personal memories of the SED regime, who can only recover traces of a lost world in broken-down buildings, faded newspapers, and disturbing memories. However, such detachment does not mean suspending one's judgment and approving of everything that was done in the GDR. Criticism is not just legitimate but necessary, since the system was undeniably dictatorial – but strictures ought to depart from a clear understanding rather than from prior prejudice. That combination of interest and judgment is what the imperative of "critical historicization," which I have derived from Martin Broszat's term, is meant to suggest.[8]

Across various nuances of interpretation, the following essays are therefore united in an effort to construct a more differentiated picture of the East German past. The volume begins with a conceptual section focused on alternatives to totalitarianism theory that try to take seriously the dictatorial nature of the GDR, but also emphasize its contradictions as well as its limits. Although the SED system was quite bureaucratic, its social reality involved surprisingly complex negotiations between rulers and the ruled; even if Ulbricht's de-Stalinization remained half-hearted, the GDR gradually developed beyond its original Stalinism in its methods of governing; although the Stasi continued to grow cancerously, under Honecker the second German state became post-totalitarian, since it largely replaced brute force with indirect incentives.[9] Jürgen Kocka therefore sees the GDR as a special kind of modern dictatorship, and argues that its precise functioning cannot just be deduced from totalitarianism theory. Detlev Pollack investigates the many internal cleavages within East German society that limited its modernizing impulses through a number of unintended consequences. And by coining the new term *Fürsorgediktatur*, I want to suggest a conceptual label that attempts to capture both the egalitarian aspirations of socialism and its dictatorial practice.

An initial set of research examples explores in greater detail the various mechanisms of political repression that characterize the GDR as a modern dictatorship. Unlike the Third Reich which rested on a much larger base of internal approval, the SED system was imposed from without, a difference that is often ignored in totalitarianism theory.[10] On the basis of recently released Russian documents, Jochen Laufer analyzes the policies of the Soviet Military Administration in regard to the dismantling of industry and the reform of the Eastern currency which strengthened tendencies towards dictatorship and division, since they were supported only by a minority of Germans organized in the SED. From the vantage point of foreign policy, Michael Lemke similarly looks at the "Sovietization" of the GDR during the high-point of Stalinism and stresses the important role of external factors in the transformation of East Germany into a dictatorship, aggravated by the context of the East–West struggle during the Cold War. In order to show the basic ambivalence of the system, Thomas Klein meticulously investigates the cleansing of the SED of suspected social democrats, radical communists and the like while Mario Keßler finally scrutinizes the initial tolerance of the GDR towards the remaining Jews.

The next cluster of essays focuses on the social dimension of the East German experience, a realm both formed by, but also in some important ways remaining impervious to, the domination of politics.[11] From a perspective of everyday history, Thomas Lindenberger takes a closer look at the interaction between the lowest level of GDR state authority and the general population via local police officers (*Abschnittsbevollmächtigte*) and finds a contradictory pattern of societal compliance and resistance. In their contrasting stories of fast food restaurants, serving chicken and fish, Burghard Ciesla and Patrice Poutrus instead investigate the peculiarities of the East German version of consumerism that, in spite of some successes, could never quite match the life-style of the West. Such ambivalences also mark the conclusions of the investigation of women's work by Leonore Ansorg and Renate Hürtgen that shows, on the one hand a high degree of female involvement in the labor market, but on the other hand a continuing double bind, produced by older prejudices. A related essay on gender relations by Dagmar Langenhan and Sabine Roß comes to similar conclusions that reveal the contradictions between women's increased chances for pursuing independent careers and their unchanging exclusion from real positions of power in the GDR.

Another group of chapters addresses the paradox of SED support for and simultaneous control of intellectual and artistic endeavor which produced a cultural life of surprising intensity and variety.[12] From a Foucauldian perspective Martin Sabrow interprets dictatorship as a form of discourse that used verbal means and internalized thought patterns to orient professional scholarship, especially in the area of history, towards legitimizing the Communist project. In a similar vein Simone Barck, Christoph Classen and Thomas Heimann take a closer look at the manifold practices of party direction of and involvement in radio, television, film and literature that attempted to create public support for the SED regime. By contrasting cabaret criticism with book censorship, Sylvia Klötzer and Siegfried Lokatis establish the ironic interaction of satire and control in a regime that feared open debate but invariably tended to produce dissidence through repression. Finally, Arnd Bauerkämper and Jürgen Danyel analyze the cultural pattern of self-images, central values and leadership styles of East German elites which kept the system running for so long.

A last section of papers wrestles with the elusive issue of stagnation or change in the GDR that lies behind the paradox of seeming stability and sudden collapse.[13] Based on his research on labor history, Peter Hübner discusses the contradiction between organizational and ownership changes on the one hand and continuity of technical and attitudinal factors in the East German workplace that ultimately hindered modernization on the other. Through oral history interviews Dorothee Wierling recreates the personal experiences of the founding generation of the 1940s and 1950s which turned the success of rebuilding and professional advancement into loyalty to the Communist system. Monika Kaiser instead looks at the aging Ulbricht's efforts to make a post-Stalinist system more flexible through limited changes that were blocked by his star pupil Honecker with the help of the party apparatus and Soviet support. Ralph Jessen ultimately takes the generational discussion a step further by describing a structural blockage of social mobility during the 1970s and 1980s which contributed to the growing disillusionment of youth with a stagnating gerontocracy.

The picture of the German Democratic Republic which emerges from these essays is more complex and nuanced than either the totalitarian approach or nostalgic memories would allow. The perspective of individual experience which runs through many of the chapters of this volume suggests a considerable variety in actual lives beneath the normalizing uniformity of dictatorship. The range of individual fates comprises those who believed in the ideology and profited from the system, those who suffered from its rigidities and persecutions, and, beyond both, those untold people who just sought to get along and carve out meaningful lives as best they could. It is important to realize that the GDR could simultaneously be an exciting experiment in social engineering to advance human equality, a living hell of unjust persecution of ideological or class opponents, or the latest version of that German staple, the *Obrigkeitsstaat* that challenged its citizens to invent creative ways around its arbitrary rules. Instead of emphasizing just one of these qualities, historians would do well, by focusing on the actual East German people, to ponder their interrelationship, their shifting patterns and their precise implications.[14]

From the perspective of experience, the GDR dictatorship looks like a set of confusing ambivalences and irreconcilable antinomies. To Marxist sympathizers, the SED regime appeared like a heroic effort at modernization in industrial development, social services and gender equality; to Western visitors, it seemed hopelessly outdated in terms of technology, consumer goods, or personal lifestyles. For the Hitler youth cohort, the postwar rebuilding and class transformation was a dynamic experiment of social engineering; to their children, the stultifying gerontocracy of the later years presented the very picture of stagnation and immobility. Antifascist intellectuals considered the project of creating a "better Germany" not only legitimate but also necessary; a good part of the population saw the GDR as a Soviet occupation regime, resting on the bayonets of the Red Army. These selective readings of the East German past in personal memory and public commentary have led the satirist Peter Ensikat to ask provocatively: "Did the GDR exist at all?"[15] Unless one wants to dismiss these clashing recollections as willful misrepresentations, their differences can only be explained if one begins to distinguish beneath the gray uniformity of the SED regime a whole variety of contrasting shades in individual lives.

A more subtle reconstruction of the East German past therefore ought to be multidimensional and oriented towards a theoretical understanding that stresses complexity. Since the GDR was, indeed, to an extraordinary degree formed by Soviet occupation and by the SED's radical attempt to change institutions and thought patterns, politics must continue to play a central role in its analysis. However, Sigrid Meuschel's thesis of the dying away of society (*Entdifferenzierung*)[16] is refuted by many of the essays in this volume which indicate that the collapse of a self-organizing set of public structures led to a series of unanticipated replacements in semi-publics, in personal networks, in individual niches and the like. Because at the lowest level people could force the authorities to make compromises, the social dimension is essential in uncovering their *Eigen-Sinn*, the stubborn efforts to realize their own aims within and against the SED system.[17] Similarly the area of cultural production and practices reveals a highly ambiguous mixture of self-control via stereotyped language or ideological discourse and of ceaseless efforts at self-assertion via satire, jokes, double-entendre, split consciousness and the like. An ethnological perspective is therefore also crucially important in unlocking the seemingly uniform world of the GDR.[18]

The key ideological problem for any historian in studying the GDR lies in pondering the relationship between the emancipatory, antifascist rhetoric, and the repressive practice of the SED. Was the East German version of "real existing socialism" a fair test of socialist ideas, or was it hampered so much by Soviet occupation, Stalinism, bureaucracy, lack of material resources, etc. that it never had a chance? If the rhetorically humane Communist experiment – though its East German variant was not as brutal as some other regimes – also committed untold crimes against humanity, then how is a non-communist Left to recover some degree of moral credibility?[19] Or did the unsolved national question doom the GDR, since socialist internationalism served as too transparent a fig leaf for Soviet hegemony over Eastern Europe and – all the Third World rhetoric notwithstanding – there was no such thing as proletarian solidarity?[20] What finally of the involvement of historians in legitimizing the socialist experiment through the construction of a counter-narrative, was it an attempt to live up to enlightenment injunctions or a travesty of professional values?[21] Questions, upon questions for which there may be few clear-cut answers.

In order to move beyond ideological confrontation, several intellectual strategies promise to widen perspectives for future research on GDR history. Fresh approaches are necessary, since the utility of the totalitarianism theory which suggests results before actual research seems limited, and even a more open-ended comparison between the Nazi and Communist dictatorships appears to raise more questions than provide answers. First, the SED regime, both as a product of earlier historical legacies of the working class movement and an attempt at a radical break with traditions of bourgeois nationalism, must be seen as a political consequence of the catastrophic first half of the twentieth century. The GDR leadership tried hard to learn from the double trauma of the collapse of the Weimar Republic and the repression of the Third Reich, directing many of its policies such as collectivization of agriculture and nationalization of industry, not to mention its social measures, explicitly towards avoiding any repetition of such shocking experiences. Exploring such learning processes from the problematic antecedents which extended also to the population at large seems a promising avenue for future work.[22]

Second, the GDR should always be considered as part of the Soviet bloc since it was the keystone of a Russian hegemony over East Central Europe which left client states little freedom for independent decisions, even if national traditions somewhat blunted many centralizing impulses of Communism. Not only was the physical presence of the Red Army in the country unmistakable, but the political orientation of the SED towards the larger sister party in the East remained so strong that most important decisions involved appealing to Moscow for support. As a result of this dependency on the Soviet "friends," many of the SED policies and popular reactions were similar to those of other neighboring countries within the Russian orbit and can only be grasped by reference to general trends in the Warsaw Pact or the COMECON. Though rhetorically accepted as necessary, this intellectual injunction all too rarely guides research due to the considerable linguistic and cultural difficulties involved in the task of moving between the Slavic and Germanic worlds.[23]

Third, the emergence of East Germany ought not to be treated as a separate subject, but rather investigated as an integral part of a complex double development of two German states after 1945 that is characterized by surprising parallels, multiple interactions, and mutual projections. While the formal aspect of diplomatic confrontations and gradual establishment of more constructive relations between the two German successor states has been studied at some length, the informal competition for people's hearts and minds in popular culture or consumption is still largely unexplored. As some everyday historians of the GDR point out, the West was constantly present as a key referent in discussions in the East, whether as danger to be feared or as example to be emulated. Even if the FRG population was much less interested in its Eastern cousins, much Cold War rhetoric was nonetheless directed towards fending off the "Communist danger," thereby blocking certain potential avenues of reform. A sustained analysis of the asymmetrical relationship between these states and their people is the central subject of that double postwar history of the Germans that remains to be written.[24]

Finally, the GDR was also part of some more general developments of the twentieth century that crossed frontiers and were not directly related to its governing ideology. Even if the SED's boast that it was the "tenth biggest industrial state" of the world turned out to be rather hollow after 1989, East Germany tried to be a modern country that would provide an "alternate modernity" to the cyclical and employment problems of industrial capitalism. Constant references to a mythical "world standard" demonstrated that even behind the impenetrable Wall there was some consciousness that the GDR had to compete in a global market of goods and services if it were to survive. Its ultimate collapse had, to a considerable degree, also to do with the failure of smokestack socialism to meet the challenge of transition towards a postindustrial, information-based society.[25] Due to the regime's policy of *Abgrenzung* from the outside, placing the GDR in the wider perspective of crosscutting developments in the twentieth century may perhaps be the most difficult interpretative task of all.

Penetrating beneath the uniform surface of dictatorship constitutes the abiding challenge of historicizing the GDR. West German Cold War propaganda has painted East Germany as a monolithic system of Communist dictatorship over a reluctant people, and many Anglo–American observers have written off the second German state as the most loyal satellite of Moscow.[26] At the same time SED self-representations and the portrayals of some Western sympathizers have sought to create a more attractive picture of the GDR as an egalitarian social experiment, aiming to break with the pernicious traditions of German history.[27] Instead of striving to prove the correctness of one of these contending images, historians ought to address their interdependence, probe their relationship, and untangle their connection. Scholars digging through the mountains of archival evidence left by the disappearance of the East German state so as to expose the internal workings of the SED regime are finding more confusion, contradiction, and conflict than they had ever imagined. The GDR continues to be interesting, not simply because it proves the superiority of democratic capitalism, but because it represents a failed alternative, simultaneously attractive and flawed.

Notes

1. "Ost-West Distanzen auf der Spur. Historiker vermißt Perspektiven in der DDR-Aufarbeitung," *Frankfurter Rundschau*, 17 June 1998; and "Honeckers Unbewältigtes Erbe," *Süddeutsche Zeitung*, 18 June 1998.

2. Christoph Kleßmann and Martin Sabrow, "Zeitgeschichte in Deutschland nach 1989," *Aus Politik und Zeitgeschichte*, 1996, No. 39: 3–24. See also Hermann Weber, "Zum Stand der Forschung über DDR-Geschichte," *Deutschland Archiv* 31 (1998): 249–57.

3. For instance Mary Fulbrook, *Anatomy of a Dictatorship: Inside the GDR, 1949–1989* (New York, 1995). For a survey of materials see Ulrich Mählert, ed., *Vademecum DDR-Forschung. Ein Leitfaden zu Archiven, Forschungseinrichtungen, Bibliotheken, Einrichtungen der politischen Bildung, Vereinen, Museen und Gedenkstätten* (Opladen, 1997).

4. As example Klaus Schroeder, *Der SED-Staat. Partei, Staat und Gesellschaft 1949–1980* (Munich, 1998). For commentary see also Erhard Crome, "DDR-Perzeptionen. Kontext und Zugangsmuster," *Berliner Debatte. Initial* 9 (1998): 45–58; and Michael Thomas, "Die Entwicklung der DDR zwischen 'Klasse' und 'Individualisierung'. Erklärungsprobleme und Ansätze," *BISS public* 7 (1997): 167–87.

5. Dietmar Keller, Hans Modrow and Herbert Wolf, eds, *Ansichten zur Geschichte der DDR*, 11 vols. (Bonn, 1993–1998). See also Konrad H. Jarausch, "'Sich der Katastrophe stellen.' (Post-) kommunistische Erklärungen für den Zusammenbruch der DDR," in *Halbherziger Revisionismus. Zum postkommunistischen Geschichtsbild*, ed. Rainer Eckert and Bernd Faulenbach (Munich, 1996), 141–50.

6. Heinrich Bortfeld, *Washington, Bonn, Berlin. Die USA und die deutsche Einheit* (Bonn, 1993); and Konrad H. Jarausch, "Land im Schatten. Amerikanische Deutschlandbilder," (MS, Berlin, 1998).

7. Konrad H. Jarausch, "Creative Destruction – Transforming the East German Academic System: The Case of History," *Sociétés contemporaines* (forthcoming, winter 2000).

8. Konrad H. Jarausch, "The GDR as History in United Germany: Reflections on Public Debate and Academic Controversy," *German Politics and Society* 15 (1997): 133–48; and Mitchell G. Ash, "Geschichtswissenschaft, Geschichtskultur und der ostdeutsche Historikerstreit," *Geschichte und Gesellschaft* 24 (1998): 283–304.

9. See Theo Pirker, M. Rainer Lepsius, et al., *Der Plan als Befehl und Fiktion. Wirtschaftsführung in der DDR* (Opladen, 1995); Klaus von Beyme, "Stalinismus und Poststalinismus im Osteuropäischen Vergleich," *Postdamer Bulletin für Zeithistorische Studien* 13 (July 1998): 8-22; and Juan Linz and Alfred Stephan, *Problems of Democratic Transition and Consolidation: Southern Europe, South America and Post-Communist Europe* (Baltimore, 1996).

10. Eckhard Jesse, ed., *Totalitarismus im 20. Jahrhundert. Eine Bilanz der internationalen Forschung* (Baden Baden, 1996); and Alfons Söllner, et al., eds, *Totalitarismus. Eine Ideengeschichte des 20. Jahrhunderts* (Berlin, 1997). See also

Norman Naimark, *The Russians in Germany: A History of the Soviet Zone of Occupation, 1945–1949* (Cambridge, 1995), and Michael Lemke, ed., *Sowjetisierung und Eigenständigkeit in der DDR* (Cologne, 1999).

11. Richard Bessel and Ralph Jessen, eds, *Grenzen der Diktatur. Staat und Gesellschaft in der DDR* (Göttingen, 1996); as well as Hartmut Kaelble, et al., eds, *Sozialgeschichte der DDR* (Stuttgart, 1994). See also Thomas Lindenberger, ed., *Herrschaft und Eigen-Sinn in der Diktatur. Studien zur Gesellschaftsgeschichte der DDR* (Cologne, 1999).

12. David Pike, *The Politics of Culture in Soviet Occupied Germany, 1945–1949* (Stanford, 1992); and David Bathrick, *The Powers of Speech: The Politics of Culture in the GDR* (London, 1995). See also Martin Sabrow, ed., *Geschichte als Herrschaftsdiskurs. Fallstudien zum Umgang mit der Vergangenheit in der frühen DDR* (Cologne, 1999).

13. Peter Bender, *Episode oder Epoche? Zur Geschichte des geteilten Deutschland* (Munich, 1996); Charles S. Maier, *Dissolution: The Crisis of Communism and the End of East Germany* (Princeton, 1997). See also Peter Hübner, ed., *Eliten im Sozialismus. Studien zur Sozialstruktur des SED-Regimes* (Cologne, 1999).

14. Stefan Wolle, *Die heile Welt der Diktatur. Alltag und Herrschaft in der DDR 1971–1989* (Berlin, 1998) is beginning to move in a more differentiated direction than the prior volume with Armin Mitter, *Untergang auf Raten. Unbekannte Kapitel der DDR-Geschichte* (Munich, 1993).

15. Peter Ensikat, *Hat es die DDR überhaupt gegeben?* (Berlin, 1998).

16. Meuschel, *Legitimation und Parteiherrschaft. Zum Paradox von Stabilität und Revolution in der DDR* (Frankfurt, 1992), 10 ff.

17. Alf Lüdtke, *Eigen-Sinn. Industriealltag, Arbeitererfahrungen und Politik vom Kaiserreich bis zum Faschismus* (Hamburg, 1993). See also Alf Lüdtke and Peter Becker, eds, *Akten, Eingaben, Schaufenster. Die DDR und ihre Texte. Erkundungen zu Herrschaft und Alltag* (Berlin, 1997).

18. Dietrich Mühlberg, "Über kulturelle Differenzen in Ost und West. Entwurf einer Studie," (MS, Berlin, 1998)

19. Curiously the German edition of the controversial *Das Schwarzbuch des Kommunismus. Unterdrückung, Verbrechen und Terror* (Munich, 1998), edited by Stephane Courtois and others, required the addition of chapters by Joachim Gauck and Eberhard Neubert, since the French original omitted the GDR from the list of Communist crimes.

20. Christiane Lemke and Gary Marks, *The Crisis of Socialism in Europe* (Durham, 1992). See. also the debates in the journals *Utopie kreativ* and *Berliner Debatte. Initial*.

21. Georg Iggers, et al. eds, "Die DDR-Geschichtswissenschaft als Forschungsproblem," special issue Nr. 27 of *Historische Zeitschrift* (Munich, 1998). See also Martin Sabrow, ed., *Verwaltete Vergangenheit. Geschichtskultur und Herrschaftslegitimation in der DDR* (Leipzig, 1997).

22. Eric Weitz, *Creating German Communism, 1890–1990. From Popular Protest to Socialist State* (Princeton, 1997). For the more general point see Michael Geyer and Konrad H. Jarausch, *A Shattered Past: Reconstructing German Histories* (Princeton, 2000).

23. Hans-Günter Hockerts, "Zeitgeschichte in Deutschland. Begriff, Methoden, Themenfelder," *Aus Politik und Zeitgeschichte*, 1993, No. 29: 3–19. For one stellar example of such practice see the interesting work by John Connelly comparing the restructuring of the universities after 1945 in Poland, Czechoslovakia and the GDR.

24. Christoph Kleßmann, *Zeitgeschichte in Deutschland nach dem Ende des Ost-West-Konflikts* (Göttingen, 1998), vol. 5, *Stuttgarter Vorträge zur Zeitgeschichte*,

ed. Gerhard Hirschfeld. See also Arnd Bauerkämper et al., eds, *Doppelte Zeitgeschichte. Deutsch-deutsche Beziehungen 1945–1990* (Bonn, 1998), and Christoph Kleßmann et al., eds, *Deutsche Vergangenheiten – eine gemeinsame Herausforderung. Der schwierige Umgang mit der doppelten Nachkriegsgeschichte* (Berlin, 1999).

25. See Dieter Segert, "Was war die DDR? Schnitte durch ihr politisches System," *Berliner Debatte, Initial* 9 (1998): 5–21. See also Michael Geyer's essay on the GDR Economy in *Die DDR als Geschichte*, ed. Jürgen Kocka (Berlin, 1994); and Konrad H. Jarausch, "Zerfall oder Selbstbefreiung. Zur Krise des Kommunismus und Auflösung der DDR" in idem and Martin Sabrow, eds, *Weg in den Untergang. Der innere Zerfall der DDR* (Göttingen, 1999).

26. Rainer Eppelmann, et al. eds, *Lexikon des DDR-Sozialismus. Staats- und Gesellschaftssystem der DDR* (Paderborn, 1996); Henry Krisch, *The German Democratic Republic* (Boulder, 1985).

27. Heinz Heitzer, *DDR. Geschichtlicher Überblick* (Berlin, 1989). For a more serious treatment see Rolf Badstuebner, et al., *Die antifaschistische demokratische Umwälzung, der Kampf gegen die Spaltung Deutschlands und die Entstehung der DDR 1945–1949* (Berlin, 1989).

THE THEORETICAL PROBLEM
OF DICTATORSHIP

CHAPTER 1

THE GDR

A SPECIAL KIND OF MODERN DICTATORSHIP

Jürgen Kocka

A decade after the demise of the GDR regime, scholars cannot agree on how best to categorize it in historical or sociological terms. While few would argue that the GDR was a lawful, legitimate state, or a *Rechtsstaat,* many feel that the polemical term *Unrechtsstaat,* "unlawful," illegitimate state is too restrictive and distorts the true nature of the system. Most would even agree with the claim that the GDR should be considered a dictatorship. But what kind of dictatorship was it? Numerous adjectives have been suggested, such as totalitarian, modern, state socialist, communist, Stalinist, or post-Stalinist – and yet no consensus exists about their use. Often a nod towards comparison with the "Third Reich" or the label "second German dictatorship" is seen as sufficient. Recently, some scholars have introduced new terms such as "welfare dictatorship" (Konrad Jarausch) or "late totalitarian patriarchal and surveillance state" (Klaus Schroeder) into the debate. Others prefer to speak of real existing socialism, of a "Sovietized" socialist industrial society, of a "thoroughly ruled" (*durchherrschte*), "political," or "statist" (*verstaatlichte*) society, or a "tutelary state."

This variety should not be surprising. Certainly some terms overgeneralize and distort; others polemicize or affirm. Some categorizations are better, some worse. The processes of definition and classification involved in the choice of a concept are open for discussion, and change in the course of debate. But it is in principle legitimate to have a variety and range of categorizations. Because such terms are dependent on epistemological goals, they are influenced by the comparative perspective inherent in any given study, and are also linked, however indirectly, to the normative aims of those speaking and writing. It is imperative to uphold the right to conceptual diversity that is a direct result of such processes. Historians should be on their guard against any attempts to justify the use of "the correct" term (such as "totalitarian dictatorship"), or the proper "attitude." They should look skeptically at calls to "political correctness" when aimed at certain uses, such as the characterization of the GDR as a "modern dictatorship." The rules of discourse governing scientific debate are fundamentally different from those that define political campaigns.

Already in a 1993 article, I suggested the concept of a "modern dictatorship" as one way to characterize the GDR.[1] While this term has recently been called into question,[2] it also served as the title of the Potsdam conference on which this volume is based – albeit followed by a question mark. In the ensuing remarks, I will therefore attempt to defend the term, to limit its claims, and to supplement my argument with further considerations.

Classifying the political system of the GDR as a "modern dictatorship" underscores – in an ideal typical fashion – those characteristics of GDR society that result *ex negativo* from a comparison with the principles of modern, liberal-democratic, constitutional states. These attributes include: the systematic violation of human rights and citizens' rights, the open or thinly veiled rule of a single party with power restricted to a narrow circle of leaders, as well as the hegemonic claims of an institutionalized ideology. Further characteristics might also refer to the lack of any clearly demarcated limits to the state's power, the lack of autonomous social subsystems and their incomplete and unfinished nature, and related to this, the party and state's claims to complete control of the most varied areas of the economy, society, and culture, achieved by means of bureaucratic measures and propaganda, through both repression and mobilization alike.

It would be possible to add to this list, and differentiate these characteristics even further. We could compare them and explain them in historical and theoretical terms which would, among other things, highlight their relationship to theories of totalitarianism developed since the 1930s. These are characteristics which the GDR shares with other twentieth century European dictatorships, such as Hitler's Germany, Stalin's Soviet Union, Mussolini's Italy, as well as other "real socialist" neighbors to the East of the GDR[3] that were also part of the Soviet sphere of influence until 1989–90. These similarities make it possible to use such terminology as a categorical basis in a historical comparison of dictatorships. The legitimacy of such a comparative approach has seldom been questioned, and its usefulness has been proven by comparisons between the "first" and "second German dictatorship," or between Hitler's Germany and Stalin's Soviet Union. A broader comparative analysis with other countries in Eastern and Southeastern Europe remains in its early stages.[4]

Few challenge today the nature of the GDR as a *dictatorship*. This category seems acceptable to many historians across the East-West divide, allowing for a general agreement on terms, which is certainly a great advantage. But what benefits are to be had from calling the GDR a *modern* dictatorship in the face of knowledge of its ultimate fate – its role as a part of the stagnating and declining Eastern bloc, as a state that lagged behind the FRG and the superior West in terms of modernity, and as part of a united Germany whose attempts to modernize it seem doomed to fail?

It should be noted here at the outset that even in daily usage, "modern" is not synonymous with "democratic," "progressive," or "good." One does not have to ascribe to a tragic view of history to concede that in the twentieth century modernity can and has meant horrible devastation, terrible catastrophe, and tragic loss.

Ivan Berend argued recently that at least in parts of Eastern, Central, and Southeastern Europe, the dictatorial rule of state socialism also had modernizing effects in the economic, social, and cultural spheres that extended beyond its programmatic goals. In these countries – which were until the middle of the twentieth century in many cases only barely industrialized (excluding the Czech lands) and lagged behind international developments in the social sphere and in the process of state-building – communist and socialist policies resulted in developments that must be interpreted as steps towards modernization according to conventional standards. These include the reform of ineffective, socially unjust, often late-feudal agricultural property rights and social systems; increased industrialization, the growth of cities, as well as social and cultural urbanization; the establishment of an educational and training system for large segments of the populace; the extension of mobility to the lower two-thirds of the population; and the reduction of social inequalities as well as the creation of new functional elites and new, anti-traditional values and lifestyles. Ivan Berend emphasizes that these developments occurred even under conditions of dictatorial rule and foreign occupation. They were also often carried out – particularly in the first two decades – with brutal methods, and the advancement of some groups was bought at the price of the persecution, exclusion, and degradation of others. These modernizing elements were achieved at great cost. It is also evident that the authoritarian, repressive, and dictatorial strategy of modernization limited the system's internal dynamics and its chances of success at a most basic level. All too often methods were half-hearted, merely repeating patterns of the nineteenth and early twentieth century. By the 1970s at the latest, modernization in the East was lagging seriously behind the less fettered, more accommodating, dynamic, and generally superior developments in the West. All the same, the results appear mixed, at best, particularly if one does not lose sight of the *status quo ante*, with its mixture of backwardness and hopeless attempts to catch up, formed by a centuries-long dependence, especially at the periphery, and finally seriously damaged by foreign rule, persecution, and war.[5]

The GDR also experienced economic, social, and cultural modernization: economic growth, economic and technological innovation, industrial expansion, growth of cities, urbanization. Everyday life was punctuated with anti-traditionalist elements, whether in the area of family planning, competitive sports, gender relationships, or the modular apartment buildings of the suburbs. State and party rule established in the first two decades of the GDR's existence developed a remarkable measure of modernizing elan, a belief in progress, and a will to tackle problems. In many respects – land reform, social security, reforms in education and qualification – the GDR was able to achieve long-term modernizing accomplishments that deserve to be studied on their own merits.

But in retrospect, the destructive elements of the GDR's modernization remain more prominent: the persecutions, disempowerment and expulsion of functional elites, particularly from the middle classes; the violence of forced reforms; the destruction of the landscape and the cities; the manner in which civil society was crushed, and the stifling of innovation and dynamism. Retrospectively, one can make out limits and barriers to modernization that were specific to the GDR dictatorship: the authoritarian–repressive–patriarchal stranglehold of the state that stood in the way of the autonomy of social groups and hindered the self-regulation of society; the methods of control that invaded all spheres of life and hampered individualization, spontaneity and innovation, and adaptability; the way in which the system was completely controlled by the party and the manner in which the state blocked the development of autonomous, independent subsystems; the oppression of a functioning public sphere and a pluralistic society able to settle differences and reach new understanding by compromise. All of these elements seriously limited the modernity of the GDR according to definitions of modernization based on Western developments. They formed the basis of the modernization deficits *vis à vis* the Federal Republic, under which the GDR suffered and ultimately collapsed.[6]

Many reasons made the long-term achievements of modernization in the GDR seem less impressive, and the balance sheet between destruction and innovation, modernization and modernizing blockages less favorable than in the case of its Eastern neighbors. The greater degree of rigidity and lack of flexibility in the GDR, a country that lay at the Western edge of the empire and was confronted with a rival state of the same nationality meant that the GDR, unlike its neighbors, was constantly measured according to the standards of a Western state – the Federal Republic. But ultimately decisive was the fact that the authoritarian and dictatorial GDR regime was established in a Central European region that was historically relatively well-developed and – unlike many regions farther to the East – no longer in need of those limited modernizing effects that such a dictatorship could, in the best instance, achieve. In any case, this characterization of the GDR as a modern dictatorship is not based on the economic, social, and cultural modernizing achievements of SED policy, although these are worthy of consideration.[7]

Instead, the following three criteria form the basis of an understanding of the GDR dictatorship as modern:

1) Without a specific qualifying attribute, the term dictatorship is too general and heterogeneous to serve as the basis of precise historical research. The term "modern dictatorship" signals that it refers not to the dictatorships of Sulla or Caesar, Cromwell or Napoleon, Latin American or African military dictatorships, or the more traditional monarchical dictatorships of South-Eastern Europe in the interwar period, but instead, only to certain "modern" dictatorships of the twentieth century.[8]
2) What made the GDR dictatorship a modern one, what set it apart from older variants and tied it to other dictatorships of the twentieth century was:
   a) its bureaucratic administration (even if it was increasingly removed from the classical type of bureaucracy as defined by Max Weber);
   b) the modernity of its repressive measures of control and means of mobilization – extending from propaganda to the surveillance and subversive tactics of the state security system;
   c) the mass party with its claims to absolute control as ruler and means of rule;
   d) the regime's insistence on central control and direction of the system on behalf of party and state according to a binding, all-encompassing ideology.

It would not be difficult, were we to cast a comparative glance at the bureaucracies, mass parties, propaganda measures, and secret police of the last century, to define these phenomena as "modern," without which the – also modern – claims to central control of all areas of life by means of detailed political orders could not be realized.[9]

3) The fascist and communist dictatorships were born in the wake of serious socio–political crises related to democratizing movements that fundamentally shook the societies in which they occurred. The First World War, the revolutions and civil wars from 1917 to 1920, the mass mobilization and participation linked to these events, the crises of the inter-war years, the Second World War and its dislocations and resistance movements all had shattering effects. Insofar as the developing dictatorial movements and systems of rule attempted to find answers to these crises, they did so with modern means, among which can be counted propaganda, mobilization, mass parties, and repression, and not only the methods of a mere putsch or military dictatorship without broad, popular support. For the communist and fascist dictatorships of the twentieth century the rule was: the modernity of their methods and goals corresponded to the modernity of their causes.

If the choice of the term "modern dictatorship" can be adequately defended, it must be conceded that the concept cannot bear too much of an interpretative load. Classifying the GDR as a modern dictatorship does not communicate much about the nature of the regime. The term and considerations related to it may serve as a frame of reference, but they do not represent much more than a preliminary sketch of the landscape. For a closer examination, which would allow comparisons and enable historians to gain knowledge about change over time, further differentiation of the term is needed. Such refinement would allow scholars to distinguish between fascist and communist dictatorships, Stalinist and post-Stalinist variations of communist dictatorships, between totalitarian and non-totalitarian types of rule, as well as between totalitarian and post-totalitarian regimes of a more or less totalitarian nature.

The suggestions made above regarding modern dictatorships and the theoretical approaches associated with them owe much to discussions of totalitarianism that have been carried out for decades and that have recently reemerged with renewed intensity. What is here called a "modern dictatorship" is similar to *some* definitions of "totalitarian dictatorship," especially those put forward in Anglo-American works.[10] If we prefer the term "modern dictatorship" over "totalitarian dictatorship" to characterize and study the GDR, this choice does not imply that the latter should be rejected out of hand as useless for a comparison of "red" and "brown" dictatorships,[11] but it is rather based on the following reasons.

Despite all of the discussion surrounding the term "totalitarianism," and its theoretical frameworks, it is not generally realized – at least in Germany – that two different, conflicting definitions of the term have existed side by side. When applied to the GDR, these can lead to rather contradictory results. The first definition goes back to Hannah Arendt, and identifies as one of the central characteristics of totalitarian regimes their tendency to constant mobilization, permanent movement, and idiosyncratic loss of structure, as well as the resultant release of destructive energies directed both inwards and outwards – the presence of excessive force and terror that culminated in an aggressive dynamism, leading ultimately to self-destruction. With this definition Arendt most definitely had Hitler's Germany and Stalin's Soviet Union in mind; her analysis "fits" these two systems extremely well, and continues to do so to this day.[12]

But it is also certain that, judged by these criteria, the GDR cannot be considered totalitarian, at least since the 1970s. The regime neither ceased to be a modern dictatorship based on communist models, nor did it relinquish terror as a method of rule. But the extent and degree of violence and terror within the system were fundamentally different from that of National Socialist Germany or the Stalinist USSR. The problem of the late GDR was not permanent revolution, but the onset of arteriosclerosis. The GDR did not go down in the midst of a bloodbath that it had itself unleashed, but instead collapsed – almost without a sound – due to its increasing inability to change or grow.

A second definition of totalitarianism, which stands more in the tradition of Friedrich or Brzezinski, interprets attempts at or the relative success of efforts to control and plan all areas of life (carried out by the state and party based on a binding ideology by modern technical and organizational means) as *the* defining characteristic of totalitarian rule.[13] Based on this criterion, much evidence suggests that the GDR should be characterized as a "totalitarian dictatorship,"[14] especially if one concedes, as it has become common to do, that claims to total control and rule are never fully realized in any dictatorship – and were not in the GDR. But even this definition applies more fully to the early years of the GDR than to the development of its latter years.

The key problem lies in the almost unavoidable conflation of these two definitions of "totalitarianism." In my view, the term, at least in Germany, has been strongly influenced by the two extreme cases of totalitarian rule – National Socialist Germany and Stalinist USSR – which were similar in their murderous inhumanity, dictatorial violence, and excessive terror. This focus is understandable, since these regimes were responsible for the most catastrophic and traumatic experiences in twentieth century Europe, the memory of which still remains alive today and will continue to exert influence on shaping political and social language and thought. To the extent that the term "totalitarian" continues to live on, its use in other contexts of modern dictatorship that were by far less violent, less extreme, and less dismissive of human life – such as the post-Stalinist "People's Democracies," like the GDR – is problematic. These were – and this also holds true for the GDR in the 1970s and 1980s – in comparison to Nazi Germany and Stalinist USSR so much less totalitarian, that the term "post-totalitarian" seems to recommend itself. This concept points to the decline in violence and diminishing mobility as well as the lack of total control, characteristic of post-Stalinist systems, that was expressed either primarily as increasing inflexibility and stagnation (as in the GDR) or as development towards pluralism (in Poland or Hungary).[15] Only for the Stalinist phase of modern dictatorships of the Soviet type – up until the late 1950s and early 1960s, although the borders are fluid and different for different countries – is it preferable to use the adjective "totalitarian." In this manner, questions about the inner dynamics of the GDR and other modern dictatorships of the communist type will become more central.[16]

I would like to close with a reservation. I have argued that the term "modern dictatorship" could serve as a larger framework for understanding the GDR as a modern dictatorship of the communist type, and whose history can be seen as a transition from a totalitarian to a post-totalitarian stage (or whose history was marked by a decline in the degree to which it was totalitarian). Even when using this terminology, one looks "from above" and within the system down at GDR society. Although this is a legitimate perspective, it is merely one possibility among many. There were many aspects of life, daily experience, and socialization in the GDR that do not come into view from this angle. Even in the case of the GDR, complex historical realities can only partially be reconstructed if understood as objects of dictatorial and state rule. It is also necessary to consider the limits to dictatorial rule[17] and to open up the study of social structures and processes, perceptions, actions, and encounters which – although seldom entirely untouched by the dictatorship – nevertheless possessed their own inner logic, and often their own intrinsic value. The dictatorial approach has its limitations, even when it is not constrained by totalitarian theory.

Notes

1. Jürgen Kocka, "Die Geschichte der DDR als Forschungsproblem. Einleitung," in *Historische DDR-Forschung. Aufsätze und Studien,* ed. Jürgen Kocka (Berlin, 1993), 23f; see also the discussion in *"Aufarbeitung von Geschichte und Folgen der SED-Diktatur in Deutschland,"* Materialien der Enquete-Kommission, ed. Deutscher Bundestag (Baden-Baden, 1995), vol. IX, 590f.

2. Ibid.: 613; Wolfgang Schuller, "Modern und fürsorglich?" *Frankfurter Allgemeine Zeitung* (13 May 1998): 10.

3. This is less true for the "reform states" of Yugoslavia, Poland, and Hungary, but more applicable to Czechoslovakia, Bulgaria, and especially Rumania and Albania.

4. The viability of the comparison between National Socialism and the GDR is reviewed in Günther Heydemann and Christopher Beckmann, "Zwei Diktaturen in Deutschland, Möglichkeiten und Grenzen des historischen Diktaturenvergleichs," *Deutschland Archiv* 30 (1997): 12–40, with extensive notes on recent literature. See also esp. Ian Kershaw and Moshe Lewin, *Stalinism and Nazism: Dictatorships in Comparison* (Cambridge, 1997).

5. Ivan T. Berend, *Central and Eastern Europe 1944–1993. Detour from the Periphery to the Periphery* (Cambridge, 1996): ix–xvii, 182–221. For "modernization" as it is used here see Hans-Ulrich Wehler, *Modernisierungstheorie und Geschichte* (Göttingen, 1975), 11–17. Cf. Ilja Srubar, "War der reale Sozialismus modern? Versuch einer strukturellen Bestimmung," *Kölner Zeitschrift für Soziologie und Sozialpsychologie* 43 (1991): 415–32; Wolfgang Zapf, "Der Untergang der DDR und die soziologische Theorie der Modernisierung," in *Experiment Vereinigung,* ed. Bernd Giesen and Claus Leggewie (Berlin, 1991), 45f; Martin Kohli, "Die DDR als Arbeitsgesellschaft? Arbeit, Lebenslauf und soziale Differenzierung," in *Sozialgeschichte der DDR,* ed. Hartmut Kaelble et al. (Stuttgart, 1994), 34–38.

6. Konrad H. Jarausch, *Die unverhoffte Einheit, 1989–1990* (Frankfurt/M, 1995); Charles S. Maier, *Dissolution. The Crisis of Communism and the End of East Germany* (Princeton, 1997).

7. Although the first and second German dictatorships differed from each other in this regard, some interpretative impulses can be found in the debates regarding modernization and National Socialism. See Michael Prinz and Rainer Zitelmann, eds., *Nationalsozialismus und Modernisierung* (Darmstadt, 1991).

8. Concerning dictatorship see Ernst Nolte, "Diktatur," in *Geschichtliche Grundbegriffe* (Stuttgart, 1972), vol. 1, 900–24.

9. The literature on totalitarianism offers many starting points. See Eckhard Jesse, ed. *Totalitarismus im 20. Jahrhundert. Eine Bilanz der internationalen Forschung* (Baden-Baden, 1996); and more critical: Wolfgang Wippermann, *Totalitarimustheorien. Die Entwicklung der Diskussion von den Anfängen bis heute* (Darmstadt, 1997).

10. See for example, Juan J. Linz and Alfred Stepan, *Problems of Democratic Transition and Consolidation: Southern Europe, South-America and Post-Communist Europe* (Baltimore, 1996), 40.

11. See Jürgen Kocka, "'Totalitarismus' und 'Faschismus'. Gegen einen falschen Begriffskrieg," in *Totalitarismus und Faschismus. Eine wissenschaftliche und poltitische Begriffskontroverse. Colloquium im Institut für Zeitgeschichte am 24. November 1978* (Munich, 1978), 39–44.

12. Hannah Arendt, *Elemente und Ursprünge totaler Herrschaft* (München 1986): esp. 473ff. Similar Emil Lederer, *State of the Masses. The Threat of the Classless Society* (New York 1940); and Sigmund Neumann, *Permanent Revolution. The*

Total State in a World at War (New York 1942). See also Alfons Söllner, "Sigmund Neumanns 'Permanent Revolution.' Ein vergessener Klassiker der vergleichenden Diktaturforschung," in *Totalitarismus. Eine Ideengeschichte des 20. Jahrhunderts*, ed. Alfons Söllner et al. (Berlin, 1997), 53–73. Hans J. Lietzmann, "Von der konstitutionellen zur totalitären Diktatur. Carl Joachim Friedrichs Totalitarismustheorie," in *Totalitarismus. Eine Ideengeschichte des 20. Jahrhunderts*, 174–92, esp. 176f. supports the argument above and cites further authors who use *this* definition of "totalitarianism."

13. Carl J. Friedrich and Zbigniew Brzezinksi, *Totalitäre Diktatur* (Stuttgart, 1957); *idem*, "Die allgemeinen Merkmale der totalitären Diktatur," in *Wege der Totalitarismusforschung*, ed. Bruno Seidel and Siegfried Jenkner (Darmstadt, 1968), 600-17. Similar on this point, Martin Draht, "Totalitarismus in der Volksdemokratie. Einleitung," introduction to Ernst Richert, ed., *Macht ohne Mandat. Der Staatsapparat in der Sowjetischen Besatzungszone Deutschlands* (Cologne and Opladen, 1958), xi–xxxvi. For the centrality of this criterion, but with a different emphasis, see Karl-Dietrich Bracher, *Die totalitäre Erfahrung* (Munich, 1987), 24. For Carl J. Friedrich and a discussion of his not entirely unproblematic totalitarianism concept, see Lietzmann, *Von der konstitutionellen*, passim.

14. Sigrid Meuschel, *Legitimation und Parteiherrschaft in der DDR. Zum Paradox von Stabilität und Revolution in der DDR 1945–1989* (Frankfurt, 1992); Klaus Schroeder, *Der SED-Staat. Geschichte und Strukturen der DDR* (Munich 1998), esp. 634–48.

15. Based on the argument made somewhat differently in Linz and Stepan, *Problems of Democratic Transition*, 42–51; 295, fn. 4.

16. It is also possible to modify the use of the term "totalitarian," and to speak of more or less totalitarian modern dictatorships, thereby creating a theoretical framework that emphasizes change over time and allows scholars to look for the causes and effects of change.

17. See Ralph Jessen and Richard Bessel, eds, *Die Grenzen der Diktatur. Staat und Gesellschaft in der DDR* (Göttingen, 1996).

CHAPTER 2

MODERNIZATION AND MODERNIZATION BLOCKAGES IN GDR SOCIETY

Detlef Pollack

The question whether, and to what extent, the GDR can be described as a homogeneous society with a classless social structure is controversial in social scientific research. Sigrid Meuschel answers it basically in the affirmative, with some reservations.[1] She treats the GDR as a classless, uniform society, designed to be egalitarian, neither distinguished according to property nor according to performance and income.[2] To a large extent it lacked independent institutions and regulating mechanisms, even if this was not completely the case. In the GDR there was neither a free market nor a legal system, neither a general public nor a democracy.[3] That is why Meuschel also refers to the gradual death of society in the GDR and its absorption by the state.[4]

Such a concept, which starts from the top, has the advantage of stressing the unequal distribution of power and its precarious consequences for the political culture and an efficient dynamic economy. Its disadvantage is that it is prone to overlook tendencies that went against the clear conditions of power distribution, and to underestimate conflicts, forms of resistance, individual possibilities for action, cultural contradictions, communicative niches, forms of protest and pretended collaboration. The aspects of safeguarding the positions of power, of repression and leveling out predominate. This can explain the stability of GDR society that lasted for decades, but not the paradox of stability and collapse, as Sigrid

Meuschel claims. Where those people involved in the mass demonstrations in the GDR came from, where the willingness to opposition and protest derived from, remains unexplained.[5]

Meuschel's thesis has been strongly contradicted by Ralph Jessen, Karl-Ulrich Mayer, Johannes Huinink, Heike Solga, and others.[6] They pose the question whether the GDR was not much more shaped by social differences and structures of social inequality than Meuschel assumes. Ralph Jessen brings out the limits of the totalitarian transformation of GDR society, which he sees as having been set up by the importance of social structural and mental conditions, such as the persistence of structures that have been handed down, or the social autonomy of informal structures.[7] Heike Solga defines the GDR as a class society that is based on unequal access to the means of production and thus on unequal participation in social wealth.[8] Mayer and Huinink raise the question, whether it was not in fact due to the apparent omnipresence of control in the GDR that options of leading an independent life were sought and taken advantage of.[9] Naturally they know that citizens' lives in the GDR were regulated and controlled by state and party. They are, however, interested in the question which forms of structural scope of action were granted to individuals, or what those individuals claimed for themselves.[10]

This approach from below has the advantage of being able to point out in what way the access to the administrative mechanisms of ruling, control and suppression was limited, and to indicate deviations, differences, and cleavages within a society intended to be uniform.[11] The upheaval of 1989–90 is only comprehensible once society's inner cleavages have been recognized. Inquiring into the gaps in the political system of the GDR, the unintended after-effects of the political administration's social control, the individual strategies of refusal, and of deviant behavior as well as sharp social dissimilarities existing between different classes and between different generations in the GDR, can provide information on the conditions that made it possible to break radically with the system, the way it happened in 1989–90. This approach, however, runs the risk of misjudging the depth of the dictatorship's penetration and the enormous potential of political and social disciplining available to the SED.[12] An approach that primarily takes into account social dissimilarities, individual strategies of refusal or even the weakness of the repressive system may contribute to explaining the collapse of GDR society, but cannot account for its continued existence for decades. It is therefore necessary to probe the simultaneity of stability and instability, of steadfastness and collapse, of political rule and political impotence.

In order to explain this simultaneity, I will start from the assumption that every attempt to render society completely homogeneous politically must inevitably lead to its becoming fragmented, heterogeneous, and divided. Although it is correct that the leaders of the SED pursued the political homogenization of GDR society, the result of their efforts was anything but a homogeneous society with a classless social structure. The GDR was a politically constituted society. But rather than absorbing society in its political constitution,[13] the government's attempt to control and manipulate all social areas led instead to insoluble tensions within society. The GDR should neither be primarily defined as a society of work (which it also was),[14] nor as a community of values, e.g., as a socialist experiment or a culture with long-term ideological objectives,[15] but as a deeply divided and fissured society, essentially conflicted and contradictory. This term is meant to express the fact that the specific tensions running through GDR society were just as destructive as they were unavoidable and therefore need to be treated as contradictions or paradoxes. As long as these cleavages could be kept invisible – and this was possible as long as GDR society was closed and there was no independent public – the GDR created the impression of being a stable state. When the barriers of the system opened up in the late summer and autumn of 1989, first gradually and then completely, the cleavages came into the open together with the emergence of an independent general public. They had already been conspicuous when the GDR's barriers had been open towards the West, in other words until 1961.

Seven Cleavages

In general, I would like to mention seven of these cleavages or areas of conflict. Of course it would be possible to discover others, just as one might summarize some of them under another theoretical heading and to arrange them differently. The objective of the following observations is to correct and to differentiate the picture of the leveled-out society, homogenized politically and in its social structure.

Political Homogenization and Functional Differentiation

On the one hand the SED government attempted to control all subsystems of society centrally. State, economy, law, science and culture did not possess any functional independence, but were subject to its claim to leadership. With the aid of the hierarchical system of a party rule controlled from the center, and the construction of parallel state structures, the SED attempted to penetrate all of society politically and ideologically. No area free of politics would be permitted. Not only were the political organizations in the stricter sense meant to be monopolized politically, but also the formally nonpolitical institutions, associations, circles and initiatives. Even the individual was meant to be organized and influenced through different institutions under official control, although it must be added that the claim to regulating the private sphere politically clearly decreased during the course of GDR history, even though it was never given up completely. The political system of the GDR was firmly anchored in the structures of society through the vast numbers of members joining such organizations as the FDGB, the FDJ, the DSF or the SED.[16]

On the other hand, the individual subsystems of society were only able to function more or less, because tendencies to become autonomous, directed against the political system's claim to guidance, kept asserting themselves. The thorough organization of society reached its limits due to the complexity of social development, for instance, in the 1960s, when the economy developed symptoms of autonomy in conjunction with the New Economic System of Planning and Guidance (NÖSPL), or in the 1970s, when independent tendencies emerged in the field of art, literature and culture, or in the 1980s, when the churches insisted on organizational self-determination without state interference. In all cases powers of self-organization emerged from society in opposition to the SED's political claim to authority. Tendencies to political homogenization opposed tendencies to functional differentiation.[17]

While this conflict expresses the claim of the SED to control the whole of society, a claim that was never given up, it also demonstrates the fact that state control of society did not work out. Since it was impossible to suppress society's potential for self-organization, the SED was regularly confronted with the limits of its own influence. In order to assert its claim to political power, the SED had to fetter society, but at the same time it had to leave some scope for social autonomy, if society were to develop dynamically and be modernized. This contradiction showed itself clearly in the party's personnel policy. On the one hand, the selection of cadres made the possibility of occupational advancement highly dependent on membership in the SED or the bloc parties, and thus undermined the competitive orientation of the modern employment system. On the other hand, it also had to consider functional qualifications and honor these differences through distinctions in pay, and, in the course of time, the significance of a completed degree for the selection of cadre members even increased.[18] Modernizing society, especially the economy, was essential for the SED, since, due to its lack of democratic legitimation, economic success was meant to provide compensatory legitimation for political conditions. Despite its interest in the development of a competitive and effective economy, the SED considered safeguarding political power even more important, and as a consequence political regulation constantly dominated those tendencies to liberalization that were discernible. The complete political organization of society, based upon the fact that all social resources were at the party's disposal, shored up the political power of the SED, and simultaneously undermined it, since it tied society to political guidelines.

The issue of the degree of autonomy of the individual functional subsystems, such as economy, law, science, art or religion, coincides with the question to what degree GDR society was modernized, since the degree of a society's modernization is largely dependent on how much it is functionally differentiated into separate subsystems. By stressing the tension between political homogenization and functional differentiation, a connection has been established to a problem that has been dominant in GDR research since the 1970s. The aim of these studies was mainly to examine how far functional requirements of a modern, industrialized society were able to assert themselves in the authoritarian GDR, and against the claim of the political class to dispose of things as they wished.[19]

The Planned Economy and Individual Self-Interest

The socialist planned economy largely eliminated the given risk of the market, namely of an individual asserting himself, and achieved maximum social security.[20] Thus it not only reduced the economic autonomy of the acting subjects, but also, to a certain degree, it released them from the necessity of asserting themselves on the labor market. In order to bind the individual's self-interest, that had been released in this way to the planned economy, new coordination mechanisms had therefore to be established. A subtly graded sanctioning system took the place of the market that determined under what conditions the individual was to receive political and economic benefits administered by the central system. The basic rule was that only those who corresponded to the system's ideological expectations had an opportunity to be supplied its benefits, such as basic schooling, additional training, possibilities of professional advancement, social power or prestige. Whoever did not comply had to reckon with disadvantages. In other words, the individual was not rewarded for pursuing his economic or professional self-interest, but instead the bonus promised and the sanctions threatened by the state were separated from the individual's self-interest, and required merely fulfilling the political expectations of the state. In this respect the conformity of the majority of the people to the system was motivated rationally and purposefully.[21] This arrangement, however, also meant that much social potential for activity remained unused. One only became involved in society to the extent necessary to pursue one's private interests. Independent economic or even political activities of one's own were not at all in the individual's interest, but were more likely to be harmful.

When the economic output of the GDR decreased strongly from the second half of the 1970s onwards, the willingness to be loyal towards the system also declined. The close relationship between political acquiescence and economic reward disintegrated. What had kept the GDR stable for decades, the promise of relative prosperity and chances of promotion, eventually contributed to the erosion of GDR society, once this promise could no longer be kept. Expectations had been aroused which, in the 1980s, could no longer be fulfilled. Because self-interest asserted itself against social claims for commitment, socialist society was not capable of socially integrating individual self-interest.[22] It was precisely because the SED attempted to create ties by means of welfare state benefits, but failed to address personal initiative, that the economic dynamism not only receded, but the sense of loyalty towards the system inevitably diminished, in accordance with the decline of the system's economic efficiency.[23]

Right up to the end the SED leadership believed in and backed the expansion of the welfare state.[24] Due to the trauma of the 17 June 1953 uprising, the SED made great efforts to raise living standards and to avoid abrupt alterations in pricing as well as in laying down work norms and determining income.[25] It became an important aim of the SED's policy to satisfy material needs by freezing basic foodprices, rents and fares, by setting up kindergartens, by protecting against unemployment, and so on. The consequences of this welfare state policy were ruinous. In order to keep up this standard of living, hardly any investments were made in the 1980s. The GDR lived beyond its means, and, among other things, was destroyed by its claim of offering welfare state benefits, which it needed as a means of obtaining legitimization.

Isolation from and Orientation towards the West

Sealing its territory off from West Germany was another important prerequisite for the stabilization of the GDR.[26] Before 1961, one could not only leave the GDR, but also forms of resistance, protest and contradiction developed that were no longer possible afterwards.[27] The mobilization campaigns of the SED, the pressure of *Gleichschaltung* exerted by the political system and the attempt to completely remodel society triggered an enormous amount of social resistance. This was demonstrated by the conflicts between the state and the Church in the 1950s, the clashes over the collectivization of trade and agriculture as well as the fights about the subordination of bloc parties to SED leadership. During the 1950s GDR society was characterized by a sense of profound unrest. After 1961, when it was no longer possible to leave in case of negative repercussions of resistance, the majority of the population gradually started to adapt to the conditions. The construction of the Berlin Wall made it clear that the GDR would last for decades. It was pointless to oppose circumstances any longer. One had to come to terms with them, since one could no longer get out. Inevitably, individual energies flowed more and more into society. To a certain extent stability of social conditions was achieved, and the quieting of the social situation caused a certain amount of economic and cultural dynamism.

The ensuing calm was, of course, deceptive: since none of the citizens were able to express criticism towards the political conditions by migrating, the SED leadership no longer had to grapple with the economic, political and social problems of the country. It was able to deceive itself about the degree of dissatisfaction that was prevalent in society and thus largely lost touch with reality. The isolation from the Western world, however, not only permitted the head of the state and party to cherish pleasant illusions, but also promoted distance from the actual conditions that existed in society. As nobody who did not like it in the GDR had the freedom to leave, it was also not possible for anybody to make a positive decision to live in the GDR without a feeling of compulsion. The SED was not willing to permit citizens to feel neutral towards their state, but insisted on approval, involvement and enthusiasm right up to the end, even though the pressure to do so abated somewhat. Thus the SED itself contributed to a certain amount of distance which always interfered with the sense of loyalty among GDR citizens. Since one was forced to stay, even if one wanted to, saying "yes" to the GDR could only be half-hearted. The majority of the population outwardly adapted to GDR conditions while maintaining an inner distance.[28]

Many East Germans saw the West as their model for a successful and fully valid life. At the end of the 1960s and beginning of the 1970s forms of an independent GDR identity admittedly emerged, conveyed through art, culture and economic growth. But already in the middle of the 1970s this development was broken off and the Western model of a free society once again became attractive. Changing preferences in the style of clothing and popular music, in life style and values, demonstrated that a process of modernization according to the Western model was taking place beneath the political level, in the everyday sphere, during the second half of the 1970s.[29] The building of the Wall therefore had an ambivalent effect: It encouraged outward adaptation to the ruling system, but also contributed to mental emigration from a system that imprisoned the people.

Formality and Informality

In reaction to society being over-organized, informal networks increasingly developed in the economy, politics, and culture.[30] It was their task to compensate for the deficits caused in these areas through the central control of society. Parallel to the official economy a black market developed; apart from the official working relations there were informal working relations, and besides the standardized culture supported by the state there was an informal pluralistic subculture. The state partly fought these informal networks, but also partly tolerated them, since they largely fulfilled compensatory and thus socially stabilizing functions. They provided the individual with items that were scarce, such as services, consumer goods or information, therefore functioning as communities of expediency that helped the individual to overcome everyday problems. At the same time they were, of course, communities that were based on reciprocity and mutual trust.[31] Moreover, these informal networks represented places of retreat and distance, of denial, even partly of protest and criticism. The over-organization of socialist society inevitably produced such forms of contradiction and deviation. They were necessary in order to protect oneself against the system's impositions and to assert one's personal dignity against its demands. Such informal communicative contexts developed in all subsystems such as business, the universities, in artistic and literary circles, the technical intelligentsia, the Church, and even in the party. Since these individual communication contexts remained preoccupied with themselves, they were not able to strengthen each other's resolve interactively. The general degree of discontent could therefore not be recognized by the dissatisfied themselves. In the GDR, society was just as inaccessible to those living within it as to those attempting to take a look at it from the outside. Because the GDR lacked an uncontrolled public, it was standardized as a state and socially fragmented at the same time.[32]

Clearly, the informal networks that developed in society did not offer a real contrast to the political system. One cannot assume that they guaranteed freedom and were able to offer the flexibility and efficiency that the system was lacking at large. Werner Schmidt[33] is right in maintaining that informal communities, e.g., in the firms, were based on and supported through the system, and did not represent a form of connections independent of it. The significance and autonomy of the informal networks and practices are frequently overrated in literature. Thus Ilja Srubar's claim[34] that the official aims of formal organizations "were only pursued for the reason that the organization members saw the opportunity of reaching private goals by means of the organization" hardly applies to the GDR.[35] Even if the privatization of state and economy as well as the bureaucracy may have progressed considerably, it never went so far as to enable the network structures that were undermining the official structures to absorb them in turn. Just the opposite was true. The informal networks parasitically attached themselves to the official structures, took advantage of them and, precisely for that reason, were always dependent on them. The planners of state and economy arranged the balance sheets, allotted resources,[36] pursued their cadre policy, demanded compulsory reports and had the decisive word in all important issues.[37] In addition, they intervened in the network structures and combatted them. Though they were forced to rely on the achievements of the informal networks as a compensation for planning deficits, they partly denounced them as criminal and frequently excluded them. Hence the relationship of contractual and noncontractual contexts was by no means primarily characterized by constructive reciprocity, but also, and mainly, by conflict, contingency and asymmetry.[38] Rather than correcting the inequality caused through the labor market, the informal connections of exchange were more prone to strengthen the advantages caused by job hierarchy and political inclination.[39]

Nonetheless, the informal networks did not just become absorbed by the system either. Even if the system was constantly interfering with the connecting networks, they still developed a significance of their own that deviated from the system's expectations.[40] While the networks of relationships represented a reaction to the system and can be understood as emergency communities, that does not necessarily exclude the development of "really friendly relationships"[41] and activities in these instrumentally constituted communities that did not refer to the system. The networks were neither exclusively dependent on the system nor exclusively independent of it. Rather one must define the ambiguous relationship of independence and dependence, of individual significance and collectivity, of community and instrumentality more precisely.

Support for and Criticism of Progress

One important means of justification for the building of socialism was the prospect held out of modernizing society.[42] The SED always appeared in public with the claim of representing the more progressive social concepts and of being superior to all previous social systems. Belief in progress was an important source of legitimization for the system. At the end of the 1960s and the beginning of the 1970s, however, the concept of social modernization became the object of worldwide criticism – a critique that did not spare the design of a modern socialism either. In direct connection to Western modernization criticism, a critical attitude towards the problematic effects of industrialization, urbanization and rationalization also developed in the GDR, to a certain extent in the party's own ranks, but mostly outside of the SED. Moreover, belief in progress receded even in the socialist service class when the party's promises failed to materialize and socialism lost its utopian content. Party reformers such as Michael Brie, Rainer Land, Dieter Segert, Bernd Okun, and others,[43] criticized the concept of an industrial modernization of society semipublicly at the end of the 1980s. This combined the criticism of structures in the GDR that hampered modernization with a critique of the adverse effects of the Western path of modernization on the design of a modern democratic socialism.[44]

The dissident groups sheltered by the Lutheran Church were also critical of modernization. They not only criticized the authoritarian character of the GDR's regime, but also the GDR's integration into a modernization project that in their eyes represented a threat to peace, was ecologically costly, and anti-humane.[45] In addition, forms of a civilization criticism distinct from the SED's progress pathos can also be found in the works of some of the GDR literary figures such as Christa Wolf, Christoph Hein, Heiner Müller, Maxie Wander, Irmtraud Morgner, Werner Heiduczek or Hans Cibulka.[46] Not infrequently, they tried to justify their criticism of GDR conditions by an anti-capitalistic attitude. Apart from them, the critical discourse on modernization also played a large role in the sphere of the Lutheran Church.[47] This discourse found effective public expression in the ecumenical meetings that took place under the heading "justice, peace and preservation of creation" in Dresden and Magdeburg in 1988 and 1989.[48] Taking all these different forms of civilization criticism into account, one has to say that the political culture of the GDR was just as marked by the emergence of a new cleavage between criticism of growth and the promotion of industrial modernization of society as was the Federal Republic.

Breaking with or Preserving Tradition

The SED enforced its extensive claim to power and control by radically reshaping the social structure of East Germany, especially at the end of the 1940s and the beginning of the 1950s. Property rights were drastically altered; members of the old elite that had remained in their positions were driven out; the commercial and intellectual bourgeoisie were stripped of power; teachers, professors, judges and administrative officials were dismissed and replaced by new cadre members, mostly coming from the lower classes. In order to realize its political and ideological program, the SED replaced the entire elite, an unprecedented upheaval in modern German history. This process of restructuring destroyed traditionally developed milieus, basically changed the social climate and mobilized society to a considerable extent. This fundamental restructuring produced the unquestionable result that the working-class sphere as well as the milieus of the petite bourgeoisie and the employees were extended, social distinctions and mores correspondingly leveled and structural differences in society were evened out. Even if this transformation tended to weaken the efficiency of the entire system, it increased the legitimacy of the newly founded state in the population.[49]

In spite of these comprehensive restructuring efforts, the social structure of East Germany offered a certain amount of resistance, based especially on the private possession of means of production. Farmers resisted having their property turned into cooperatives. Collectivizing agriculture took more than ten years, since some private holdings persisted up to the 1970s. And even if the percentage of self-employed people declined over the decades, private commerce could never be stamped out completely in the GDR. The resistance of certain subsystems of society was not only the result of private ownership, but was also due to cultural and mental traditions. The members of the technical intelligentsia turned out to be relatively resistant over a longer period of time,[50] and so did the members of the medical profession[51] and especially the Protestant ministers.[52] By 1954, only 28.7 percent of college and university professors had joined the SED, and by 1965 their share had still only risen to 35.9 percent.[53] Of course, the relative resistance of certain professional groups was also due to the fact that the SED had to make political concessions to highly qualified experts. Apart from these privileges and the possibility of emigrating up to 1961, the main source of the resistance of these groups lay in their professional tradition, their sense of social standing and feeling of pride connected with it. In a society whose leading party's declared intention was to strip all aspects of society of tradition, pre-socialist attitudes such as class consciousness and professionalism could become advocates for Western modernization concepts and bourgeois values.

The System of Repression and Its Limits

The final example of securing the SED's rule was the party's disposal of the means of applying organized physical force. Police, army and a continuously expanding secret service were under the command of the SED leadership. Even so, these instruments of power could not be brought to bear without potentially adverse consequences. A repressive enforcement of SED policy not only contradicted the party's own ideological claims, but could also lead to considerable popular resentment and loss of face for GDR leadership abroad. No matter how necessary it might be for the SED's claim to leadership, the application of force always had counterproductive effects as well. For that reason the SED itself had to limit its exercise of power, even if it controlled all social instruments of leadership and resources. Especially in the 1970s and 1980s, when the government attempted to create the image of an economically growing, politically stable and widely respected state, when it sought to win the population by welfare state measures and increases in prosperity, and the GDR was included in the international process of détente, the party leaders were no longer able to rely on such harsh measures as they had previously.[54] They had to employ more sophisticated means to secure their power. Publicly visible force in securing their leadership was, at any rate, to be avoided as far as possible. That is the reason for the order to the secret service of "averting by preventative measures"[55] hostile actions against the GDR in advance. This task required a further extension of the security system and a greater tightening of the net of control than ever before.

In spite of the enlargement of the security system, the Stasi apparatus lost its effectiveness during the 1970s and 1980s. For its methods to have any silent effect, a certain measure of deterrence was unavoidable. But when methods of securing the leadership shifted from terror, repression and punishment to forms of political propaganda, ideological persuasion and personal interviews as well as material stimulation and privileges, they became ineffective, and occasional exemplary sanctions and harassment lost their force.[56] Even the possibilities supplied by the penal code of the GDR for the persecution of "political offenders" were no longer fully used. Although criminal law was tightened at the beginning of the 1980s, it was no longer rigorously applied. The SED leaders found themselves in an increasingly irresolvable dilemma: On the one hand they had at their disposal all means of power related to politics, police and the secret service, on the other hand any uncontrolled deployment of these means had negative consequences for their own rule. While they regularly had to apply force, they more and more harmed themselves by doing so. Thus their hands were tied to an increasing extent. Ironically, the security system failed precisely at the moment when its position of power was at stake.

From the point of view of self-preservation, it should have made up its mind to strike. But for so drastic an action the system was already lacking the courage to take risks, the will to power and the trust in its own ability to assert itself.

The Systematic Connection between the Cleavages

The above discussion of these contradictions should suffice to suggest that there are many further cleavages.[57] Therefore representing the GDR as a leveled-out and classless society does not do justice to its conflicting nature. It is true that certain differences, e.g., in salaries, in appearance and manner or between the functional areas were not as strongly accentuated as in Western Germany. In general, however, the GDR seems to have been socially much more fragmented and disintegrated than the old Federal Republic. The question of why it was still able to survive for so long can, it seems to me, only be answered if one approaches the length of its existence together with its problems in maintaining it. Hence, in conclusion, I would like to look into the problem of the systematic connection between these individually developed cleavages.

The basic linkage between these fissures seems to lie in the fact that the GDR was intended as a centrally planned reorganization project for the entire society, initiated from the outside,[58] that did not reckon with the power of persistence and the inherent dynamism of individual social subsystems and thus was constantly forced to deal with unintentional consequences. No matter what aspect one thinks of, whether it be the validity of functional requirements, the motivating power of individual self-interest, the attractiveness of the Western model, the development of informal network structures, the disillusionment with the belief in progress, the persistence of inherited structures or the counter-productive effects of governmental repressions, in each of these cases state actions produced different effects than were intended, which the state itself then had to adjust to.

The SED tried to cope with this situation by attempting to integrate these effects into the centralist system brought about by itself. (1) The validity of functional requirements was not only determined politically, but was also considered in regard to efficiency in the different social subsystems, in economy, law, education, medicine, science and art. (2) The motivating power of individual self-interest was not only brought to a standstill by the supply system of the welfare state, but also utilized by introducing performance incentives and widening differences in pay that were dependent on achievement.[59]

(3) The attraction of the Western social system was not only countered by ideological propaganda and political demarcation, but also taken advantage of by economic exchange, consideration of consumer needs, installation of Intershops, permission for visits from the West to the East, and, increasingly, also from the East to the West. (4) The informal networks were not only combated, but were also partly made use of, and there were attempts to incorporate them socially.[60] (5) The disillusionment of faith in progress was not only met by increased ideological propaganda, but also conceded by admitting that human processes were not free of conflicts, and that socialist ideology was just as exposed to problems of survival as capitalism.[61] (6) Traditions were not only treated as the relics of imperialism that had to be eradicated, but, in the course of the GDR's history, increasingly referred to positively as a means of integration for the construction of socialist society.[62] (7) Finally, reactions to the counterproductive effects of repressive rule were not only ignored by enforcing the security system, but also taken into account by making its deployment more flexible and limiting it. The extensive reduction of social reality, which was connected with the socialist construction of society, was, in other words, compensated for by a strange recognition of social complexity, which had been ignored initially. The aim of this acknowledgment was naturally not to find a balance with other interests and identities, giving the other side its due, but a matter of securing one's own power more and more. The modification of society was always intended to occur from the top. That meant, of course, that the system was unreformable, since any reform from the top did not change precisely that which made the reform necessary in the first place: the centralization of all authority of decision.

The main weakness of SED rule was that it was not able to let social power out of its hands. It could not share or limit it, since then it might lose it completely. Therefore, the lack of political legitimation was the central problem, causing the disease of the SED system and, eventually, its demise. Since the SED lacked political legitimacy, it had to borrow it by way of economics, science, culture or even sports, and was thus also compelled to control all social areas. The class enemy could be raising his ugly head anywhere. So everything had to be in the hands of the SED. In this way the whole of society was under rigid political control. The party was not able to grant any subsystem of society, institution, association or private person, any autonomy. According to an old insight from the field of differentiation theory, a higher degree of social homogeneity, however, does not necessarily also mean a higher degree of coherence. Instead it is the other way around, a higher degree of heterogeneity does not infrequently represent the prerequisite for the development of stronger social cohesion.[63] In this respect, the attempt at total political homogenization of society, as was practiced by the SED, at first sight contributed to stabilizing its rule, but in the long run made it fragile. This interpretation renders it possible to explain the decades-long stability of GDR society as well as its sudden demise.

Notes

1. Sigrid Meuschel, "Überlegungen zu einer Herrschafts- und Gesellschaftsgeschichte der DDR," *Geschichte und Gesellschaft* 19 (1993): 5–14; cf. idem, *Legitimation und Parteiherrschaft in der DDR. Zum Paradox von Stabilität und Revolution in der DDR 1945–1989* (Frankfurt, 1992).
2. Sigrid Meuschel, "Revolution in der DDR," in *Die DDR auf dem Weg zur deutschen Einheit. Probleme, Perspektiven, offene Fragen. 23. Tagung zum Stand der DDR-Forschung in der Bundesrepublik Deutschland*, ed. Ilse Spittmann and Gisela Helwig (Cologne, 1990), 3–14.
3. Sigrid Meuschel, "Revolution in der DDR. Versuch einer sozialwissenschaftlichen Interpretation," in *Die Modernisierung moderner Gesellschaften. Verhandlungen des 25. Deutschen Soziologentages 1990 in Frankfurt am Main*, ed. Wolfgang Zapf (Frankfurt, 1991), 558–571.
4. Ibid., 559.
5. Thus in her essay "Revolution in der DDR," Meuschel does not explain how the upheaval originated, but only its change of direction and which, strangely enough, she calls a revolution. Considering the social vacuum that allegedly prevailed in the GDR, the emergence of the change remains an unsettled issue, however. This is the starting point of political culture studies, such as Christiane Lemke, *Die Ursachen des Umbruchs 1989. Politische Sozialisation in der ehemaligen DDR* (Opladen, 1991) or Laurence H. McFalls, *Communism's Collapse, Democracy's Demise? The Cultural Context and Consequences of the East German Revolution* (New York, 1995).
6. Ralph Jessen, "Die Gesellschaft im Staatssozialismus. Probleme einer Sozialgeschichte der DDR," *Geschichte und Gesellschaft* 21 (1995): 96–110; Johannes Huinink and Karl-Ulrich Mayer, et al., *Kollektiv und Eigensinn. Lebensverläufe in der DDR und danach* (Berlin, 1995); Heike Solga, *Auf dem Weg in eine klassenlose Gesellschaft? Klassenlagen und Mobilität zwischen Generationen in der DDR* (Berlin, 1995).
7. Jessen, "Die Gesellschaft im Staatssozialismus," 98ff.
8. Solga, *Auf dem Weg*. Cf. Heike Solga, "Klassenlagen und soziale Ungleichheit in der DDR," *Aus Politik und Zeitgeschichte*, 1996, no. 46: 18–27.
9. Johannes Huinink and Karl-Ulrich Mayer, "Lebensverläufe im Wandel der DDR-Gesellschaft," in *Der Zusammenbruch der DDR. Soziologische Analysen*, ed. Hans Joas and Martin Kohli (Frankfurt, 1993), 151–71.
10. Johannes Huinink and Karl-Ulrich Mayer, et al., *Kollektiv und Eigensinn*, 9.
11. Jürgen Kocka, "Ein deutscher Sonderweg. Überlegungen zur Sozialgeschichte der DDR," *Aus Politik und Zeitgeschichte*, 1994, no. 40: 34–45, tries to bring out the traits of the ruling system as well as the limits to the "complete penetration of GDR society." See also Jürgen Kocka, "Eine durchherrschte Gesellschaft," in *Sozialgeschichte der DDR*, ed. Hartmut Kaelble, Jürgen Kocka and Hartmut Zwahr (Stuttgart, 1994), 547–53.

12. Jessen, "Die Gesellschaft im Staatssozialismus," 108. In a comparative village study by Winfried Gebhardt and Georg Kamphausen (*Zwei Dörfer in Deutschland. Mentalitätsunterschiede nach der Wiedervereinigung* [Opladen, 1994]), the approach of cultural and milieu sociology almost makes the differences between a church oriented village in West Germany and in East Germany disappear.

13. Detlef Pollack, "Das Ende einer Organisationsgesellschaft. Systemtheoretische Überlegungen zum gesellschaftlichen Umbruch in der DDR," *Zeitschrift für Soziologie* 19 (1990): 292–307; "Sozialstruktur und Mentalitätsstruktur in Ostdeutschland," in *Soziologen-Tag Leipzig 1991. Soziologie in Deutschland und die Transformation großer gesellschaftlicher Systeme,* ed. H. Meyer (Berlin, 1992), 272–85; and "Grundlinien der Gesellschaftskonstruktion der DDR," in *Kirche in der Organisationsgesellschaft. Zum Wandel der gesellschaftlichen Lage der evangelischen Kirchen in der DDR* (Stuttgart, 1994), 60–77.

14. Martin Kohli, "Die DDR als Arbeitsgesellschaft? Arbeit, Lebenslauf und soziale Differenzierung," in *Sozialgeschichte,* 31–61.

15. Winfried Thaa, et al., *Gesellschaftliche Differenzierung und Legitimationsverfall des DDR-Sozialismus. Das Ende des anderen Wegs in der Moderne* (Tübingen, 1992).

16. Mary Fulbrook, "Methodologische Überlegungen zu einer Gesellschaftsgeschichte der DDR," in *Die Grenzen der Diktatur. Staat und Gesellschaft in der DDR,* ed. Richard Bessel and Ralph Jessen (Göttingen, 1996), 275–97, argues that the stability of the GDR was based less on repression than on organization, integration and arrangement.

17. On the concept of functional differentiation, cf. Nikolas Luhmann, *The Differentiation of Society* (New York, 1982). The aim of the SED to bring society's political dynamism to a standstill was never completely successful, as evident in the emergence of tendencies in the block parties and the bureaucracy to become autonomous in the final stages of the GDR.

18. Karl-Ulrich Mayer and Martin Diewald, "Kollektiv und Eigensinn. Die Geschichte der DDR und die Lebensverläufe ihrer Bürger," *Aus Politik und Zeitgeschichte,* 1996, no. 46: 8–17.

19. GDR research, schooled on modernization theory, did recognize the conflict between the rationalization requirements of modern industrial societies and political centralism, as well as the fact that political and economic development was being blocked by it (Gert-Joachim Glaeßner, "Reformierbarkeit sozialistischer Systeme," in *Pipers Wörterbuch zur Politik,* vol. 4, ed. K. Ziemer [Zürich, 1986], 366–72; Walter Süss, "Gesellschaftliche Interessen und gesellschaftliche Organisationen in der DDR," in *Deutschland-Handbuch. Eine doppelte Bilanz 1949–1989,* ed. W. Weidenfeld and H. Zimmermann [Bonn, 1989], 152–64). But an evolutionary optimism inherent in modernization theory as well as political sympathies prevented a clearer recognition of the basic conflicting nature of GDR society. Cf. Konrad H. Jarausch, "Die DDR denken. Narrative Strukturen und analytische Strategien," *Berliner Debatte. Initial* 4–5 (1995): 9–15.

20. See Max Weber's distinction between a free-market and a planned economic system. Max Weber, *Wirtschaft und Gesellschaft. Grundriß der verstehenden Soziologie,* 4th edition (Tübingen, 1956), 14.

21. Therefore it is unnecessary to cite the authoritarian tradition in order to explain the willingness of the East Germans to conform. See Sigrid Meuschel, "Revolution," 564ff.

22. Individualization which, of course, also existed in the GDR (Wolfgang Engler, *Die ungewollte Moderne. Ost–West–Passagen* [Frankfurt, 1995], 31ff), always meant positioning oneself in contrast to society, isolating oneself from it, making it turn against one.

23. Michael Brie, "Staatssozialistische Länder Europas im Vergleich. Alternative Herrschaftsstrategien und divergente Typen," in *Einheit als Privileg. Vergleichende Perspektiven auf die Transformation Ostdeutschlands*, ed. Helmut Wiesenthal (Frankfurt, 1996), 39–104.

24. In the 1950s, compulsion and repression predominated as means of securing power. From the 1970s on, the social-political measures that were pushed by the SED state replaced force.

25. M. Rainer Lepsius, "Die Institutionenordnung als Rahmenbedingung der Sozialgeschichte der DDR," in *Sozialgeschichte*, 24.

26. In contrast to Albert O. Hirschman, *Abwanderung und Widerspruch. Reaktionen auf Leistungsabfall bei Unternehmungen, Organisationen und Staaten* (Tübingen, 1974), I believe that the opportunity to exit is almost a prerequisite for the possibility of contradiction. Cf. Detlef Pollack, "Das Ende einer Organisationsgesellschaft," passim; John Torpey, "Two Movements, Not a Revolution. Exodus and Opposition in the East German Transformation, 1989–1990," *German Politics and Society* 26 (1992): 21–42.

27. A survey of escaped members of the GDR intelligentsia stated: "The possibility of escaping lends the old itelligentsia some backbone. The proximity to the West prevents incorporation." Infratest, *Die Intelligenzschicht in der Sowjetzone Deutschlands*, vol. 3: *Ideologische Haltungen und politische Verhaltensweisen* (Munich, 1960), 196.

28. Since one wanted to obey with a clear conscience, to a certain extent one even adapted inwardly to the system's expectations. Terms such as socialism, antifascism or peace described values that rulers and ruled alike mostly adhered to, but their obvervance often had a twisted, and artificial quality about it.

29. The increasing permission to make family visits to the West – meant as an outlet for discontent – actually had the reverse effect. Cf. Eckard Jesse, "War die DDR totalitär?" *Aus Politik und Zeitgeschichte*, 1994, no. 40: 12–23.

30. The development of informal structures is complementary to the thorough organization of society. Precisely because accumulated organizational problems were not dealt with, they had to be treated informally on a lower level of society. Cf. Elmer Hankiss, "The 'Second Society.' Is there an Alternative Social Model Emerging in Contemporary Hungary?" *Social Research* 55 (1988): 13–42; H. Ganßmann, "Die nichtbeabsichtigten Folgen einer Wirtschaftsplanung. DDR-Zusammenbruch, Planungsparadox und Demokratie," in *Der Zusammenbruch der DDR*, 172–93.

31. Martin Diewald, "'Kollektiv', 'Vitamin B' oder 'Nische'? Persönliche Netzwerke in der DDR," in *Kollektiv und Eigensinn*, 223–60.

32. For forms of an institutionally protected semi-publics see Detlef Pollack, *Kirche in der Organisationsgesellschaft*, 297–318.

33. Werner Schmidt, "Metamorphosen des Betriebskollektivs. Zur Transformation der Sozialordnung in ostdeutschen Betrieben," *Soziale Welt* 46 (1995): 305–25.

34. Ilija Srubar, "War der reale Sozialismus modern? Versuch einer strukturellen Bestimmung," *Kölner Zeitschrift für Soziologie und Sozialpsychologie* 43 (1991): 415–32.

35. In contrast to Jessen, *Die Gesellschaft im Staatssozialismus*, 109, Brie, *Staatssozialistische Länder*, 92, stresses that patrimonial or clientelistic forms of leadership remained secondary in the GDR. Cf. also Engler, *Die ungewollte Moderne*, 49.

36. Richard Rottenburg, "'Der Sozialismus braucht den ganzen Menschen.' Zum Verhältnis vertraglicher und nichtvertraglicher Beziehungen in einem VEB," *Zeitschrift für Soziologie* 20 (1991): 305–22.

44   Detlef Pollack

37. Michael Thomas, "Private Selbständigkeit in Ostdeutschland. Erste Schritte in einem neuen Forschungsfeld," *Soziale Welt* 44 (1993): 223–42.
38. Rottenburg, "Der Sozialismus," 315.
39. Mayer and Diewald, "Kollektivität und Eigensinn," 15.
40. Rudolf Woderich, "Mentalitäten zwischen Anpassung und Eigensinn," *Deutschland Archiv* 25 (1992): 21–32.
41. Srubar, "War der Sozialismus modern?," 422.
42. One should, however, not overestimate the significance of ideology as a means of integrating society. In contrast to Winfried Thaa, et al., *Gesellschaftliche Differenzierung*, I agree with M. R. Lepsius, "Die Institutionenordnung", 28f., who argues that the conformity of the GDR population was institutionally motivated.
43. Michael Brie, "Die Erarbeitung einer Konzeption des modernen Sozialismus. Thesen in der Diskussion," *Deutsche Zeitschrift für Philosophie* 38 (1990): 218–29; Michael Brie and Rainer Land, *Studie zur Gesellschaftsstrategie* (Berlin 1989); Dieter Segert, "Einige Probleme einer politischen Theorie des modernen Sozialismus," *Deutsche Zeitschrift für Philosophie* 38 (1990): 230–44; H.-P. Krüger, "Moderne Gesellschaft und 'Marxismus–Leninismus' schließen einander aus," *Berliner Debatte. Initial* 2 (1990): 149–54.
44. Rainer Land and Ralf Possekel, *Namenlose Stimmen waren uns voraus. Politische Diskurse von Intellektuellen aus der DDR* (Bochum 1994).
45. Peter Wensierski and Wolfgang Büscher, ed., *Beton ist Beton. Zivilisationskritik aus der DDR* (Hattingen 1981), 71f.
46. Christa Wolf, *Kassandra. Erzählung und Voraussetzungen einer Erzählung* (Darmstadt 1984); Maxie Wander, *Leben wär' eine prima Alternative. Tagebuchaufzeichnungen und Briefe* (Darmstadt 1983); Werner Heiduczek, *Tod am Meer* (Stuttgart 1981); Helga Königsdorf, *Respektloser Umgang. Erzählung* (Berlin 1980); Irmgard Morgner, *Leben und Abenteuer der Trobadora Beatriz nach Zeugnissen ihrer Spielfrau Laura. Roman in 13 Büchern und 7 Intermezzos* (Berlin 1974); Hanns Cibulka, *Swantow. Die Aufzeichnungen des Andreas Fleming* (Halle 1982). See also Michael Schenkel, "Die Öffentlichkeit der künstlerischen Literatur. Fortschritt- und Modernitätskritik in der DDR-Literatur," in *Gesellschaftliche Differenzierung*, 303–89.
47. Friedrich Wilhelm Graf, "Traditionsbewahrung in der sozialistischen Provinz. Zur Kontinuität antikapitalistischer Leitvorstellungen im neueren deutschen Protestantismus," *Zeitschrift für Evangelische Ethik* 26 (1992): 175–91.
48. Aktion Sühnezeichen, ed., *Ökumenische Versammlung für Gerechtigkeit, Frieden und Bewahrung der Schöpfung. Dresden-Magdeburg-Dresden. Eine Dokumentation* (Berlin, 1990).
49. Jürgen Kocka, "Ein deutscher Sonderweg," 37.
50. G. Wagner on "Elites in the chemical industry of central Germany in the Fifties" at the elite workshop of the Zentrum für Zeithistorische Forschung in Potsdam on 7 June 1996.
51. Christoph Kleßmann, "Relikte des Bildungsbürgertums in der DDR," in *Sozialgeschichte*, 254–70.
52. Christoph Kleßmann, "Zur Sozialgeschichte des protestantischen Milieus in der DDR," *Geschichte und Gesellschaft* 19 (1993): 29–53.
53. Ralph Jessen, "Professoren im Sozialismus. Aspekte des Strukturwandels der Hochschullehrerschaft in der Ulbricht-Ära," in *Sozialgeschichte*, 217–53.
54. The GDR's self-representation as a democratic and modern state thus had counter-productive effects, since it increased expectations which citizens used as a standard to judge the system.
55. *Die Inoffiziellen Mitarbeiter. Richtlinien, Befehle, Direktiven*, ed. by the BStU, Series A, no. 1/92 (Berlin, 1992), 659–93.

56. It is strange that the GDR state was just as hybrid as it was ineffective, while power under Western conditions is both limited and controlled, but also appears to be quite effective.

57. Other differences might be the distinctions between the socialist service class and the majority of employees (cf. Artur Meier, "Abschied von der sozialistischen Ständegesellschaft," *Aus Politik und Zeitgeschichte*, 1990, no. 16: 2–14; Heike Solga, *Auf dem Weg in eine klassenlose Gesellschaft?*), or the tensions between the generations (Karl-Ulrich Mayer and Heike Solga, *Mobilität und Legitimität*; Hans-Günter Hockerts, "Grundlinien und soziale Folgen der Sozialpolitik in der DDR," in *Sozialgeschichte*, 519–44; and Thomas Gensicke, "Vom Pessimismus zum Optimismus und vom 'konservativen' Protest zur Selbständigkeit?" *BISS-public* 4 [1991]: 98–115).

58. The military, political and economic influence of the Soviet Union undoubtedly represents the most important basis of stability but it also caused conflicts, since it looked like a regime imposed from the outside.

59. See also the discussion about the increase in income differences as motivating device in Manfred Lötsch, "Sozialstruktur und Wirtschaftswachstum. Überlegungen zum Problem sozialer Triebkräfte des wissenschaftlich-technischen Fortschritts," *Wirtschaftswissenschaft* 29 (1981): 56–69.

60. The only new institutional creation in the 1980s was the installation of the *Gesellschaft für Natur und Umwelt*. Walter Süß, "Gesellschaftliche Interessen und gesellschaftliche Organisationen in der DDR," in *Deutschland-Handbuch. Eine doppelte Bilanz 1949–1989*, ed. Werner Weidenfeld and Hartmut Zimmermann (Bonn, 1989), 152–64.

61. Max Schmidt, ed., *Sicherheit und friedliche Koexistenz. Umfassende internationale Sicherheit – Umsetzung friedlicher Koexistenzbedingungen heute* (Berlin, 1989); Uwe Ziegler, "Die neue Sicht der DDR zur 'Systemauseinandersetzung,'" *Aus Politik und Zeitgeschichte*, 1989, no. 34: 28–38.

62. An example of this trend was the Luther-Jubilee of 1983, as well as the reactivation of Prussian traditions, or the resurgence of regional identities in the 1980s.

63. The question of social differentiation is already addressed by the sociological classics of Durkheim or Spencer. See Uwe Schimank, *Theorien gesellschaftlicher Differenzierung* (Opladen, 1996), 29.

CHAPTER 3

CARE AND COERCION

THE GDR AS WELFARE DICTATORSHIP

Konrad H. Jarausch

Public and scholarly debate about the nature of the GDR regime has revolved around a few, often contradictory terms. The SED regime has been called many things, depending on one's interests or point of view. Most frequently the regime's critics have considered it an *Unrechtsstaat*, or a fundamentally illegitimate regime. Its apologists like to see it as an experiment, that – despite the good intentions of its founders – somehow went awry. Those commentators desiring to inject more objectivity into the discussion have relied on more neutral terms, such as "modern dictatorship," in their analyses.[1] The emotional charge associated with different approaches has often served as a catalyst in the creation of public opinion, and characterizations of the regime have functioned as visible symbols of ideological self-perceptions and as rallying cries for potential supporters. Rooted as they are in different social theories, these terms suggest various and often conflicting frames of analysis, thereby shaping and structuring both public and academic debates. Because these different approaches combine various levels of abstraction, methodologies, and contrasting personal experiences, in the almost ten years since the fall of communism no agreement has emerged on what to call the GDR.

This confusion does not mean that there have been no attempts to reach a consensus or to find a fitting epithet for the regime. During the democratic awakening in the fall of 1989, a number of East German jokes played on the regime's abbreviation, DDR. One, referring to the vast numbers choosing to leave the country, called the GDR the place where the "Dumb Dudes Remain" (*Der Dumme Rest*).[2] The ironic use of the term "real existing socialism" could signal a sense of disappointment with what had actually been realized or serve to shore up belief that "real" socialism was just around the corner.[3] In conservative circles in the West, scholars refashioned Reagan's condemnation of the USSR as an "Evil Empire" into theories about communism's "ideological party rule" in the Soviet Union and its satellite states.[4] Other commentators with more sympathy for egalitarian experiments – such as the head of the FRG's diplomatic office in East Berlin, Günter Gaus – discovered in the GDR the small freedoms of a "niche society," in which citizens could avoid the party's claims to rule by retreating into the private sphere.[5]

Although sociologists have led the way in formulating approaches to the GDR, their new terms have often proved so ephemeral that a certain conceptual weariness has been the result.[6] Moving beyond the debates that ensued immediately after the fall of the Wall, which were often more ideological than substantial, most historians have by now, almost a decade after the regime's fall, turned towards detailed empirical studies based on primary sources. Unlike earlier works, which drew almost exclusively on published sources, these new studies, based on internal documentation, focus on individual aspects of the GDR and provide a more nuanced view of the regime. At the same time, however, by concentrating on single issues or topics they tend to lose sight of larger structural developments.[7] In order to achieve a more comprehensive understanding of the SED regime, it therefore seems necessary to reformulate basic theoretical and interpretive approaches. "We need, more than ever, a new language," the sociologist Ulrich Beck has argued in his attempt to find some bearings in the aftermath of postmodernism, "that will allow new ways of conceptualizing the flood of novelties that threaten to overwhelm us, and enable us to live with and control them."[8]

One possible way out of the impasse of ideological determinism associated with previous interpretations would be to historicize the terms themselves. Rather than assuming that one interpretation is the only possible or correct one, the method of investigating changes in "the main concepts of historical development," as practiced by Reinhart Koselleck, traces the temporal and ideological transformations of meaning. This critical, historical approach also identifies those individuals and groups with an investment in certain definitions of terms, placing the development of ideas within a social context.[9] But although it underscores the importance of analyzing the regime's own self-representations or characterizations of it made by others, this approach can do little to explain which of the various alternatives best captures it in its historical complexity.

Evaluating the strengths and weaknesses of any given term requires a serious sociolinguistic reflection on the interpretative implications of some of the most important terms in the debate. Such reflection would be able to judge various concepts according to their relative validity or usefulness.[10] For instance, the surprising renaissance of totalitarianism theory after the collapse of communism must be examined. This seems particularly pressing in view of the role totalitarianism theory has played in shaping public perceptions, as the debates within the German parliament's commission of inquiry attest. It would also be useful to consider why so many of the sociological terms coined after 1990 to describe the GDR system of rule, could, in the face of changes in research interests that have focused on post-communist transformations, so quickly vanish from view. And finally, more complex approaches emphasizing modernization processes should be analyzed in order to determine whether their characterizations of the basic nature of the GDR might form the basis of a more adequate conceptual framework.[11] Such considerations could lead to a leap forward in conceptualization, resulting in a more differentiated picture of the East German past.

Contemporary Definitions

Past debate about the existence of two separate German states has left behind a score of epithets with which various commentators have attempted to either legitimate or defame the GDR. These classifications did have some basis in reality, but were greatly exaggerated in the name of different political causes. Changes within the political and international scene have made these terms often more fitting for some phases of development than others. Additionally, most of the concepts were conceived not in isolation, but as a response to, or the other side of the coin of, other terms. As one side of a pair of opposites, they could therefore only be understood in relationship to the whole. Because these contemporary terms have become so much a part of political rhetoric, historical research has only considered them marginally, if at all.[12]

The self-definition of the GDR and the SED regime, as it is presented in the sixth edition of the *Abridged Political Dictionary* of the East Berlin publishing house Dietz in 1986, was a markedly positive one. Based on the constitution of 1974, the entry defined the GDR as "a socialist German state, in which the working class, led by the Marxist–Leninist party of the SED, exercises power in conjunction with the class of cooperative farmers, intellectuals, and other workers."[13] While this definition underscored the ideological nature of the regime, it also emphasized the national origins of the state, the role of the ruling party, and its social basis in a union between workers, peasants, and other working members of society. The GDR was legitimated historically as "the realization of the heritage of the German labor movement and the anti-fascist struggle" against National Socialism, and as the first German state "whose path is determined exclusively by the laws of social progress." Since it grew out of the "antifascist-democratic transformation," the "development towards a sovereign socialist German state" was interpreted as "a heavy blow to imperialism" demonstrating the creation of an independent "socialist nation" as the better alternative to the Federal Republic.

This pronounced self-perception of the GDR as a "socialist state" was meant to cover up a score of fundamental structural problems.[14] By defining the GDR regime as "a dictatorship of the proletariat that represents the interests of all people in the GDR," the article conceded that the state was a form of forced rule not by, but rather for the people. But by claiming to be socialist in nature, the state continued to posit a belief in the "indissoluble unity" with "socialist democracy," defined as a collection of broad social organizations that would represent the realization of workers' interests.[15] After "creating the basis of socialism" with the help of the Soviets, the GDR had supposedly entered a new, more mature phase of development during the 1960s: "The period of reconstruction of the developing socialist society is best defined by the fact that socialist society will now develop according to its own socioeconomic basis." This independent economic development would not only result in a higher standard of living, but give the state "a higher quality" as well. The basic tenor of this self-perception in the GDR's later history was an optimistic outlook on the future that played down internal conflicts and looked forward to the worldwide victory of socialism.

West German descriptions of East Germany, on the other hand, have until most recently focused on the GDR's lack of legitimization and only slowly adjusted to changes in postwar realities. The term "SBZ" or "Soviet Occupied Zone," favored by Chancellor Konrad Adenauer, denied the East German state any form of independence, reducing the rival to a mere occupation zone in the hands of Red troops.[16] It was customary to refer to East Germany as "the so-called GDR," and the use of quotation marks whenever the regime was mentioned (a practice carried out by the *Bildzeitung* until

1989) was a result of the Hallstein doctrine, which attempted to deny the establishment of an independent state in East Berlin by simply refusing to acknowledge its existence. In the sixth edition of the *State Encyclopedia: Law, Economy, Society,* published by the Herder Press in 1958, there was still no entry for the GDR, and the otherwise straightforward article about "Deutschland," adorned the term "German Democratic Republic" and the regime's claims to be a "People's Democracy" with quotation marks in order to underscore the editors' skeptical stance towards a rather dubious terminology. Further, the SBZ was treated as a product of the "division of the German Reich into occupied zones," while the KPD line was interpreted as a diversionary tactic, since the party "pretends it wants to be just one democratic party among others."[17]

It took the *Ostpolitik* of the social-liberal coalition to break through this wall of silence, since Willy Brandt's policy of "two states, one nation" made a more realistic reckoning with the GDR necessary.[18] Negotiations surrounding the Berlin Agreement and the Basic Treaty between the FRG and the GDR forced West Germans to agree to official East German pronouncements in order to facilitate the guarantee of human rights, even if the West German government still refused to grant the GDR official recognition. In the seventh edition of the Herder encyclopedia of 1985, there was still no separate entry for the GDR, but in the section entitled "The German Question," the GDR was referred to without quotation marks and in a more matter-of-fact and detailed manner. Although the authors described the Federal Republic's continued claims to speak for all Germans in positive terms, they discussed constitutional changes in the GDR, the party policies of the SED and its return to older German traditions.[19] *Ostpolitik* therefore resulted in a greater variety in West German approaches to the GDR that emphasized different aspects of the Eastern neighbor, sometimes in a more positive and at other times in a more critical light.

Since these self-perceptions and definitions were associated with the political confrontation between East and West, they could hardly serve as lasting analytical tools. Official representations made by the GDR regime possessed a programmatic nature, but were nevertheless slowly adopted by the East German populace, albeit in shortened form (such as public references to the regime as "the republic").[20] West German appellations were also too much products of the Cold War to be used without a consideration of the circumstances in which they were coined (which nonetheless continues to occur). Because these designations were so instrumental in shaping consciousness in both German states, they provide important indications of ruling self-perceptions and representations, while offering insights into postwar experiences that were separate, yet often shared. Ironically, it took the fall of the "second German state" to provide the basis for partial consensus, since both parties could now agree to call the SED system "the former GDR."

Analytical Alternatives

The unexpected collapse of the SED system in 1989–90 led to a search for new terms, inspired by the more general question of why socialism had failed. A few early commentators revived the term "Stalinism," which had originally been coined by Trotsky, so as to describe a system of organized violence that had been imposed upon the GDR from the outside. Putting a personal name on the distortions allowed them to redeem the ideals of equality and fraternity they still associated with socialism.[21] More thorough critics of this ideology made – depending on the degree of their rejection – either Leninism or Marxism responsible for what had transpired within the Soviet system, often linking their critique with ruminations about the corruptibility of intellectuals.[22] Understandably influenced by the end of the Soviet Union, this discussion could hardly offer compelling explanations for Bolshevism's long-term stability as a system of rule.

Totalitarianism theory experienced a surprising revival after the collapse of communism because it offered a clear conceptualization of both the socialist and National Socialist dictatorships. Developed by democratic intellectuals like Hannah Arendt during the Second World War, it was originally conceived as a way to explain the claims to total power by both the Italian fascists and German National Socialists and to distinguish these systems from older forms of oppression. Motivated by an Orwellian-like shock caused by the atrocities of Stalinism, these intellectuals' views sometimes also reflected the bitter disappointment of former sympathizers who had been repelled by the degree of violence in the USSR and its satellite states, where anti-fascist rhetoric masked the absolute repression of the Left. In the West, totalitarianism theory made it easier in the late 1940s to replace one enemy with another – instead of the defeated Nazis, it was now the dangerous Communists in the East who threatened the peace and against whom democrats had to stay on guard. In the wake of coexistence and détente, such characterizations faded, but they continued to exist in the form of a decided anti-communism.[23]

Unlike the two competing definitions sketched out above, totalitarianism theory offers significant theoretical advantages that help to explain its broad acceptance as an analytical concept after the collapse of the GDR. Although there are some variations within different authors, Carl J. Friedrich's six point catalog of totalitarian rule (dominant ideology, ruling party, secret police terror, control of the media, weapons monopoly, and planned economy) provides clear criteria for classifying political regimes and distinguishing between authoritarian and totalitarian systems. At the same time, this description suggests a functional relationship that sees oppression as a complex, interrelated system of repressive measures. Western democracy is the implicit standard of this definition, since by reversing the above criteria it serves as a perfect foil for comparisons with totalitarian regimes. This typological polarization allows scholars to use a moral perspective that not only describes any given regime, but judges it politically, sometimes even condemning it. Especially for those who suffered under such repression, or for the ideological opponents of such systems, this model offers not only important insights into mechanisms of rule, but also provides arguments unmasking the justifications of sympathetic leftist intellectuals.[24]

Yet totalitarianism theory also continues to evoke criticism, which points out some of the limits of its analytical usefulness. By focusing on the rhetoric of dictatorial rule, the model merely tends to reproduce the intentions of the ruling party while overlooking what is often quite chaotic in practice. Since it identifies those characteristics that make a regime totalitarian, the model is rather static, and can do little to explain the complex dynamics of dictatorial rule and its changing methods. Because totalitarianism theory concentrates on the application of state power, it underestimates the importance of the collaboration of the masses and proceeds from a simplistic model of action and reaction that leaves social processes largely unexplained. Further, this approach draws on the written records of the state's own repressive agencies, which cannot recreate the complexities of life under a dictatorship.[25] Overall, totalitarianism theory often argues in a circular fashion, since it leaves unexamined the standards of Western democracies it applies to totalitarian regimes.

The application of totalitarianism theory to the history of the GDR has met with limited success, mainly because it relies on a Stalinist understanding of communism. Hannah Arendt, for instance, was fascinated by the possibility of further development in this ideology, but her lasting impressions of the Soviet system were drawn from the heyday of Stalinism. Formulated in the 1940s and 1950s, classical totalitarianism theory could not adequately reflect subsequent changes in the methods of rule.[26] Those who use it therefore have attempted to extend the term further for the later decades of communist rule. Eckhard Jesse has coined the phrase "autolitarian," and Juan Linz has suggested using the term "post-totalitarian."[27] While totalitarianism theory emphasizes the unique nature of totalitarian rule in fascism and communism, in detailed research it runs the danger of glossing over complex realities and of simplifying difficult ethical situations. Although totalitarianism theory is an important tool of analysis, it can only serve as the first and as yet incomplete step on the path to understanding the complicated and contradictory GDR past.[28]

Commentators from sociology and history have suggested a number of more modest alternatives to capture the uniqueness of a real socialist society under total state rule. Drawing on Max Weber, Artur Meier has developed the term "socialist *Ständegesellschaft*" to describe the precapitalist nature of an "omnipotent militaristic–bureaucratic dictatorship."[29] While Meier's approach correctly identifies central elements of hierarchy and privilege specific to the GDR, it ignores the modernity of East German industrial society and underestimates the complexity of its social realities. Sigrid Meuschel's theory of social "de-differentiation" suffers from similar weaknesses. While her description of the GDR as a "classless, egalitarian and level society"[30] addresses the question of the party's success at achieving legitimation, it does little to explain the causes for the social upheaval that led to the regime's collapse. Finally, Michael Thomas' thesis regarding the "de-subjectification" of East Germans highlights interesting aspects of disempowerment and structural stagnation. Yet because such works concentrate on the application of power, they can do little to consider developments that contradict or go against methods of control.[31]

More complex terms that include processes of differentiation and atomization have also failed to win general support, largely because by pointing to shades of gray they cannot overcome basic black and white dichotomies. In her study of socialization in the GDR, Christiane Lemke has spoken of a "dual political culture," in which official goals and personal behavior diverged, thereby discovering the existence of oppositional tendencies under the surface of the dominant political culture.[32] Although Ralf Rytlewski's study of the development of an alternative political culture sees a re-differentiation of East German society along generational, educational, and confessional lines, it also proceeds from an understanding of the predominance of state and party culture.[33] Wolfgang Engler's attempt to understand the GDR in terms of a "negotiating society" points to elements of daily compromise between rulers and the ruled, but fails to consider the asymmetric distribution of power in East Germany, where "ordinary" citizens were at the mercy of the party's every whim.[34] While such approaches refine totalitarian interpretations of the second German dictatorship, they can offer no all-encompassing theoretical explanation for the regime because of the limited nature of their focus.

The main alternative to totalitarianism theory has been modernization theory, which examines the GDR more generally in terms of one modern industrial society among many others. This perspective draws on a comparison of systems that developed in the wake of détente, which allowed a more balanced consideration of the real achievements and deficits of the East German regime, without moralizing tones. Rather than condemning the SED rule out of hand, this approach takes seriously East German political goals of a socialist society. Inspired by the work of Peter Christian Ludz, numerous studies have compiled important data about the GDR's political and economic systems.[35] Unfortunately, much of this data is fundamentally flawed, since it is often based more on official SED rhetoric than actual empirical evidence. Advocates of totalitarianism theory could therefore criticize this approach, particularly after 1989–90, and accuse those who sought to compare the FRG and GDR systems of overlooking the fundamental differences between democracy and dictatorship, and abandoning the cause of reunification.[36]

With his term "modern dictatorship," Jürgen Kocka has made a remarkable contribution to the debate by attempting to apply modernization theory to the GDR. While Kocka sees GDR society as one "thoroughly ruled" from above, he is interested in understanding social change as well. By using a comparative approach, he comes to interesting conclusions about the central contradictions of the GDR regime which vary with the point of reference. When compared to the Third Reich or other Soviet satellite states, the GDR reveals characteristics of relative modernity, such as methods of rule through propaganda and control, a high level of gender equality, a significant degree of industrialization, etc. But when considered in the same light as the Federal Republic, the GDR seems less modern, since one can find numerous indices signifying serious modernization deficits. The weak tertiary sector in employment, the lack of development in consumer goods, and the undifferentiated nature of political, social, and economic subsystems, as well as an underdeveloped intermediary sector of "civil society" can even be considered a form of "de-modernization." Overall, Kocka has come to the plausible, but somewhat unsatisfactory conclusion: "A comparison of historical modernity seldom leads to simple results, but rather more often to conclusions that are qualified with such statements as 'on the one hand...but on the other hand'."[37]

Detlef Pollack, an East German sociologist, has also made a significant contribution to the debate on the modernity of the GDR with his term "organization society." In his analysis of the role of the churches in the GDR, he sees the transformation of East German society as a "form of functional differentiation," as an increasing distinction between "individual system levels" that leads to an "enormous increase in the level of complexity" and the creation of "self-regulative media such as currency, law, the market, the public sphere, bureaucracy," etc. Using these four criteria, he comes to the conclusion that "the GDR possessed characteristics typical of modern societies, but that these could not be fully operative, since the further modernization of society was blocked by the SED leadership's policies of centralized control of all social processes." Pollack sees the system therefore as a "semi-modern mixed society," in which processes of differentiation and homogenization, the minimization and maximization of system levels, development and stagnation, and self-regulation and instrumentalization were strangely intertwined, therefore ultimately canceling each other out.[38]

The discussion about modernization theory and the GDR, encapsulated in the term "modern dictatorship," reveals that the use of this approach raises more interesting questions than it provides definitive answers. One positive result of the debate has been a shift in focus away from the political system of rule towards the realities of social life, as well as more sophisticated analyses based on a recognition of the regime's complexities and contradictions, social change over time, and a clear sense of the limits to the dictatorship's own claims to power.[39] However, the manner in which concepts originally developed for an analysis of Western societies have been applied to Eastern phenomena remains somewhat troubling. Additionally, it has proven hard to determine the degree of "modernity" of any given subject, and difficult to distance oneself from the implied normative nature of modernization theory in general. Terms such as "thoroughly ruled society" have served as valuable correctives for black-and-white portrayals of GDR society based on totalitarianism theory. Yet without further modification, the term "modern dictatorship" suggests merely a generic category, able only to distinguish more recent forms of rule from ancient ones, without doing justice to the contradictory nature of modernization itself.[40]

Perhaps some problems associated with modernization theory could be avoided if studies paid more attention to the specifics of GDR development. One important prerequisite would be to examine the ways in which previous scholarship has conflated democracy with modernity and to take more seriously the communist vision of social progress as an "alternative modernity" that was pursued with much pathos.[41] Scholars should also perhaps consider using a periodized approach to modernization in the GDR in order to distinguish different stages of development from each other. The first phase might be characterized by a bold attempt at a rapid modernization via anti-fascist measures and democratic reforms (with simultaneous re-differentiation), which was then followed by a scientific–technological revolution that eventually stalled, only to be replaced by social spending that placed increasing stumbling blocks in the path of innovation and was accompanied by growing criticism of modernization in general.[42] Or might it perhaps be useful to analyze the continual conflict between economic rationalization as well as scientific autonomy and the party's claims to leadership as well as the nomenclature's attempts to maintain its social privileges?[43] Despite the difficulties associated with social and cultural approaches, these perspectives promise, in comparison to a purely political focus, to provide a more fruitful frame of analysis and a more nuanced understanding of the realities of the GDR.

Conceptualizing Complexity

As the above considerations have made clear, any political or analytical term must fulfill a wide range of requirements in order to capture the contradictory nature of real existing socialism in East Germany. First, concepts should attempt to capture at least in some manner the various personal experiences of GDR citizens and to address their often ambivalent memories. Second, terms ought to avoid emphasizing one single aspect of the system, but be comprehensive enough to reflect the regime's agenda of totally transforming society. Third, any concept must do justice to the system's dictatorial nature – articulated in its self-description as "dictatorship of the proletariat" – and allow an analysis of the party's various methods of rule. And finally, any definition should point to the unfinished nature of such claims and the remaining spaces as well as forms of resistance that allowed a degree of normality within the abnormal confines of SED rule. A more adequate description of the GDR than defining it as "fundamentally illegitimate" should permit a general categorization of the regime while also encouraging an analysis of its uniqueness and specificity.[44]

Decisive for the choice of a concept are the basic characteristics of the second German state which are to be emphasized by it. While Cold War analyses pronounced either positive or negative judgments on the GDR, research of the past few years has started to provide a more nuanced picture. More recent works emphasize the many contradictions between party ideology and actual practice, government claims and social realities, surface appearances and hidden countertrends, while pointing to a "dual consciousness" or "double speak" as characteristic of daily life.[45] The ambivalent results of modernization theory as applied to the GDR reinforce a picture of an East German society marked by complexities and contradictions. In commenting on the controversy about the level of egalitarianism and the degree of citizen influence, Detlef Pollack has identified numerous tensions and conflicts which suggest that one should consider "the nature of the GDR as fundamentally contradictory." Stefan Wolle, who has been more prone to criticize than to condone the SED regime, similarly draws from the obvious failure of the "one-sided orientation of GDR research on repression and resistance" the following conclusion: "The problem rather lies in perceiving the phenomenon GDR as contradictory, or at least ambivalent, in and of itself."[46]

Unfortunately, attempts to capture this paradox by dual terms such as "educational dictatorship," or "commodious dictatorship" have not yet been entirely convincing.[47] However, Rolf Henrich's internal criticism of late GDR society is more suggestive. His critique, which appeared under the title "The Tutelary State," pointed to the contradictions between the regime's proclaimed emancipatory goals and the repressive practice of its policies. This surprisingly open criticism, written by a lawyer and founding member of the *Neues Forum*, sought to renew "the enterprise of enlightenment that has been silenced here at home" in order to assist his fellow citizens in achieving "the principle of self-realization through our own actions." Essentially, Henrich's argument rejected Honecker's formula of the "unity of economic and social policies," and renounced the social contract between the regime and the populace that had been based on a *quid pro quo* of satisfying consumer demands in return for political acquiescence. Henrich's "tutelary state" not only referred to the lack of individual rights for GDR citizens, but to Soviet tutelage of the GDR which contradicted the ideological claims to freedom inherent in Marxism.[48] Because it was composed before the fall of the regime, this spirited attack could not call the "despotism of the Politburo" by its real name of "dictatorship," and could say little about the actual goals of "bureaucratic socialism."

This dissident criticism of "state socialism" calls to mind the term "authoritarian welfare state" that suggests a conceptual link between state support and civic impotence characteristic of Prussian social politics.[49] The more democratic Weimar Republic reformed this paternalist tradition by somewhat loosening the bonds of dependence on poor relief and introducing measures that allowed individual participation. To denote this change of spirit, the older word welfare (*Wohlfahrt*) was replaced by the newer term social service

(Fürsorge). The latter appears in the *Reichsfürsorgepflichtverordnung* of 13 February 1924, and in the "Reich guidelines related to the conditions, nature, and degree of social services" of December of the same year. Both regulated state assistance for the "new poor" of war veterans, widows, and orphans, as well as pensioners and retirees.[50] Unlike religious or private charity from religious volunteers or charitable organizations, the term *soziale Fürsorge*, or "social service," as propagated by middle class and social democratic circles, suggested secular, public assistance, delivered generally by professionals who were predominately women. Repeated calls for a "social service state" that appeared in numerous articles and pamphlets expressed the desire to "free humanity from risk" and protect everyone from any form of potential misfortune.[51]

Although this utopian vision was distorted under the National Socialists into a eugenic nightmare of "preventive care" or *Vorsorge*, utterly callous of human life, the SED regime made another effort to attain the original goal in the dire circumstances after 1945. As a direct response to the crisis of world capitalism and the political oppression of the Third Reich, the Communists strenuously sought to insure that economic security and social equality which, according to Peter Flora, are the basic features of the modern welfare state. So as to create a better Germany by force, if need be, the SED regime refashioned traditions of authoritarianism inherited from Wilhelmine Germany and aspects of social reform from Weimar into an open dictatorship of the proletariat that would achieve a revolutionary transformation of society. By radicalizing both its methods of rule and its social goals, the GDR also consciously distanced itself from its FRG rival to the West, which had, after much internal struggle, chosen to develop a social market economy and welfare oriented democracy.[52]

From this perspective the GDR appears as a radicalized welfare state that might be characterized by the two somewhat contradictory epithets of "welfare" and "dictatorship." In German, the idea of *Fürsorge* suggests "care and assistance granted someone" as well as "efforts on behalf of someone in need of the same." More broadly defined, the notion encompasses "politically organized assistance for support in need or special circumstances."[53] The connotations of individual care and collective assistance underscore the ethical aspirations of socialism not only to help the needy, but to effect a broad transformation of society along egalitarian lines. At the same time, when paired with such words as "institution" in a "poor-house" or "education" in a "reformatory" the word *Fürsorge* takes on undertones of severity and supervision that Günter Grass satirized in his novel *Ein weites Feld*, when he noted, "Your solicitude means surveillance."[54] Combining a reference to welfare with the term dicta-

torship heightens this sense of ambiguity by adding the dimension
of political repression. The neologism _Fürsorgediktatur_, or welfare
dictatorship, could thus attempt to capture the central contradiction
between socialism's emancipatory rhetoric and the corrupt practice
of Stalinism within a single analytical category.[55]

Which aspects of GDR history can be explained with this new
term of "welfare dictatorship"? First, the two-part designation
emphasizes the basic contradiction between care and coercion of
the SED system that color the seemingly paradoxical memories of
former GDR citizens. Second, the term welfare dictatorship recalls
the ideological goals of socialism, and the vision of an egalitarian
social reform that it hoped to achieve for the benefit of the lower
classes such as workers and peasants. It sees the GDR as part of a
worldwide movement of emancipation that was motivated by social
goals of solidarity and humanitarianism. And yet third, this neologism also entails an unambiguous critique of communist repression,
since the second part of the term, "dictatorship," underscores the
forced nature of the GDR's socialist utopia and the coercive methods
used to achieve its goals. By encompassing both the progressive
claims _and_ the repressive realities of the SED system, this new term
attempts to elucidate the specific nature of the GDR in the context
of other modern dictatorships of the twentieth century.[56]

Through the tension created by its two separate components,
the neologism _Fürsorgediktatur_ places almost all areas of social life
in the GDR in a new light.[57] How precisely did the methods of rule
function in this dictatorial system that wanted to force its citizens
to achieve happiness defined on its own terms? Because the GDR
began as an occupation regime that had to rely on Soviet tanks to
stay in power and wanted to achieve socialist goals that were supported only by a few, the realization of a socialist democracy of
workers and peasants demanded the monopoly rule by one party,
the SED, supported by Stasi methods of surveillance as well as
bureaucratic controls. The Politburo attempted to overcome this
inherent contradiction with a patriarchal political style that
demonstrated its concern for the powerless populace with a unique
combination of social services, material security, artistic cultiva-
tion, etc. The institution of the security service was characteristic
for this combination of coercive care, and during the last years of
the regime, its surveillance of suspected deviants took on almost
pathological features. The increasing bureaucratization of the decision-making processes led to a rule for, but not by the people, and
relegated the populace to obedience and mere acclamation.[58]

What contradictions did these patriarchal policies and attempts
to realize socialist dreams produce in daily social practice? The

caretaker component of the term welfare dictatorship points to the central role of Honecker's slogan of the "unity of economic and social policies," for the SED dictatorship increasingly relied on social achievements to win the support of the populace.[59] While the planned economy succeeded in overcoming its initial shortages, after the scientific-technological revolution stalled Günther Mittag directed its efforts mainly toward satisfying consumer demands by increasing foreign debt, which led to a decline in investments and innovation. The state's social policy found expression in costly subventions for food, housing, public transport, public services for women such as nurseries, or FDGB vacation spots. While these services met many popular demands, the populace had to demonstrate absolute political acquiescence in return for a feeling of belonging and security.[60] The ironic result of such over-extended social services was a lack of economic resources, the complete subordination of social organizations and the disappearance of individual initiative in the private sphere – in effect the shutting down of that civil society they had hoped to create.

What were the cultural consequences of an ideology that wanted to create a new, socialist society based on equality and security? On the one hand, GDR propaganda could build on the traditions of antifascism, bourgeois humanism, and working class culture to cast SED rule as a protector of the cultural interests of the general population. One consequence of this pose was the project of introducing the masses to a democratic form of high culture – an intellectually fascinating hope that was doomed to continual failure. On the other hand, the party's reliance on producers of ideology and creators of culture led to the development of a strict, if somewhat erratic system of censorship that at least initially attempted to establish a petit bourgeois style of socialist realism, defamed modern art as decadent and fanned rabid anti-Americanism in popular culture. By repressing public opinion, claims for emancipatory freedom and social services for ordinary citizens were transformed into patriarchal tutelage and the stifling of creativity, which reduced culture to yet another instrument of control. And so in the area of culture – as in others – the effect of the repressive solicitude of the SED regime was quite ambivalent.[61]

The term welfare dictatorship might also help to explain the surprising stability of the GDR that allowed an unpopular system to maintain power over four decades with increasingly sophisticated methods that extended beyond the threat of Soviet intervention. After a mixture of expulsion, repression and the building of the Wall had broken older forms of anti-Communist resistance, the SED's strategy slowly shifted in the 1960s from intimidation through a

show of force to more subtle forms, such as the creation of a socialist mentality, or the satisfaction of material needs. Because the population had no other alternatives and Western policies of *Ostpolitik*
assumed the long-term existence of the GDR, East Germans had to
learn to live with the system, and to curb critical impulses themselves, without entirely abandoning their own beliefs.[62] Yet this
"reluctant loyalty" remained conditional and was based on fulfilling
material needs. This meant that the regime was always potentially
unstable since the population's acquiescence hinged on the SED
regime's performance in providing it with consumer goods. Compared to the parliamentary democracy and social market economy
of the West, where such institutions were valued in and of themselves, "socialist democracy" in the East could perhaps win temporary loyalty, but could achieve no long-term legitimation.[63]

Finally, the concept of *Fürsorgediktatur* could assist in explaining
certain self-destructive tendencies of real existing socialism that
eventually led to the collapse of the regime.[64] Conceived as a radical answer to the problems of classic industrial society, the GDR
was not prepared to meet the challenges of a postindustrial risk
society.[65] Since social attempts to reform capitalism had failed to
stop the Great Depression, racial genocide and two world wars, the
communist transformation of society intended to remove the roots
of such suffering by ensuring that nationalism would never again
lead to such destruction. Ironically, the methods employed to reach
this goal – the creation of a classical, labor-intensive industrial
structure and a bureaucratic party dictatorship – blocked the creativity needed for the transition to an information age and consumer society while also hindering the development of civil society.
Ultimately the inefficiency of the East German planned economy
made extensive social and cultural services too costly to continue.
Because the SED dictatorship failed to meet the challenge of *perestroika* abroad and of oppositional movements at home, the combination of the two contradictory elements, care and coercion,
proved to be a dead end. Ultimately the failure of a welfare dictatorship even became obvious in the eyes of its own citizens.[66]

The GDR in Perspective

Controversies about which terms best describe historical events
belong themselves to history, and are thus another aspect of coming to terms with the past. Although it often seems pointless to
argue about usages or definitions, such discussion is necessary
because words influence contemporary perception and later reflec-

tion due to their value references and emotional charge. This predicament is obvious in the way that scholars have discussed the genocide of the Jews, where terms as diverse as "destruction of the Jews," "Shoah," or "Holocaust" serve as markers in different stages of the debate and as signals of diverse interpretative positions.[67] Koselleck's and Conze's research on historical key words has shown how categories are loaded with multiple emotions and meanings, advancing through developmental stages that make their use anything but fixed. The popularity of the phrase *Wende* or "turn," to describe the fall of communism in 1989-90, rather than "collapse" or even "revolution" reveals that one cannot decree the use of any one epithet. Rather, scholars must also position their concepts within larger public debates. A socio-linguistic perspective should go beyond deconstructing terms and ask the crucial question: what can and what should any analytical category explain and achieve?

Historical debates about the nature of the GDR have revolved around constructs that emphasize either care or coercion as the defining characteristic of the regime. The former classification, drawing on the regime's own self-image, has generally been used by sympathizers or former representatives of the regime to describe socialism "in the colors of the GDR." By using the term "real existing socialism," scholars can discuss the "crisis symptoms" of the regime and engage in an intellectual critique of the causes of the decline of the "state socialist" system.[68] More specific hybrids such as "party bureaucratic socialism" or "administrative-centralized socialism" point to particular forms of SED practice and aim at separating the developmental teleology of Marxism from its failed realization in the GDR so as to save its emancipatory goals for another attempt in the future. However, many neologisms that end with "socialism" tend to minimize the crimes of the regime and employ the rhetorical strategy of making its negative aspects a result of Soviet occupation or of Ulbricht's and Honecker's mistakes, rescuing socialist ideology as such from any responsibility or blame.[69]

Located on the other side of the analytical spectrum are those concepts that emphasize the dictatorial nature of the GDR regime as an illegitimate state, or *Unrechtsstaat*. It should come as no surprise that such characterizations as "SED dictatorship" are primarily supported by the victims and one-time opponents of the regime. These observers question the humanistic rhetoric of the system, and do not only make its practice, but also its basic ideology responsible for the repression of the East German populace.[70] Emphasizing the system's despotic nature has the advantage of unequivocal moral condemnation of and clear analytical distance from the Honecker/Mielke regime. But such appellations as "the second German dictatorship," frequently used by advocates of totalitarianism theory who wish to suggest similarities with the first Nazi dictatorship, say too little about the different ideological direction of the SED regime.[71] Although the term "modern dictatorship" asks more differentiated questions about the social limits of SED rule, without further qualification it remains too unspecific to characterize the paradoxes of the GDR.

In contrast, the neologism "welfare dictatorship," presented here, is intended as an attempt to overcome the polarization of the dominant approaches by combining essential elements of both. Instead of overlooking or playing down the multiple contradictions of the GDR, this term uses them as a starting point by refashioning them into two parts of one analytical whole.[72] On the one hand it seeks to express some empathy with the ambivalent experiences of those people who lived within the system, while on the other it insists on the necessity of a certain analytical distance to the regime which allows placing it within a larger historical context. A perspective that examines the unique relationship between social provision and political repression understands the GDR as a problematic combination of welfare state aspirations with illiberal paternalist practices, and thereby links the development of the system to older German traditions. This new term therefore asks historians to consider the dictatorship diachronically in comparison with the Weimar Republic or the Nazi regime, and synchronously in comparison with the social market economy of the Federal Republic and the post-Stalinist regimes of the Eastern Block.[73]

Can a single term, no matter how thoroughly justified, encompass the entire range of the contradictory East German past? It seems unlikely that one concept can capture the full complexity of historical realities, but by emphasizing the essentially contradictory nature of the GDR the notion of "welfare dictatorship" seeks to open a fresh perspective that could pave the way for new interpretations and analyses. Of course, a single term will not be able to cover all different developments of four decades, but an emphasis on certain aspects of dictatorial rule, such as its fundamentally paternalistic nature, can highlight elements of social and cultural policies that began to emerge under Ulbricht and became characteristic of the Honecker era. Finally, as no concept is entirely free from ideological and emotional overtones, scholars must take care to control such associations – for instance by combining terms of more positive connotations with those that have more negative resonances.[74] Since every concept possesses definite limits, various terms will be likely to compete as definitions of the GDR in the future.

For this reason, the term "welfare dictatorship" does not claim to put an end to debate about the SED regime, but rather it seeks to serve as a way of refocusing the discussion. The neologism *Fürsorgediktatur* attempts to address some of the main weaknesses of totalitarianism and modernization theory by placing the emancipatory goals of the regime in direct relationship to its repressive practices and describing the GDR explicitly as a system in conflict. Instead of providing ready answers, its emphasis on paradox asks more pointed questions about the ambivalent agenda and practice of the SED system. The term's open-endedness tries to advance a more differentiated, but not uncritical, reading of the complexity of the GDR, and thereby to promote a deeper understanding of the various reactions and behaviors of its citizens. Without a doubt, the term "welfare dictatorship" will itself provoke criticism, but if it succeeds in stimulating the development of more complex perspectives, it will have fulfilled its analytical purpose.

Notes

1. Deutscher Bundestag, *Enquete-Kommission "Aufarbeitung von Geschichte und Folgen der SED-Diktatur in Deutschland"* (Frankfurt, 1995); Lothar Bisky, Jens-Uwe Heuer, Michael Schumann, *Unrechtsstaat? Politische Justiz und die Aufarbeitung der DDR-Vergangenheit* (Hamburg 1994).
2. Wolfgang Schneider, ed., *Leipziger Demontagebuch. Demo Montag Tagebuch Demontage* (Leipzig, 1991); Ewald Lang, ed., *Wendehals und Stasi-Laus. Demo-Sprüche aus der DDR* (Munich, 1990).
3. Rainer Eckert and Bernd Faulenbach, eds, *Halbherziger Revisionismus. Zum postkommunistischen Geschichtsbild* (Munich, 1996).
4. Martin Malia, *Vollstreckter Wahn. Rußland 1917–1991* (Stuttgart, 1994).
5. Günter Gaus, *Wo Deutschland liegt. Eine Ortsbestimmung* (Hamburg, 1983).
6. Hans Joas and Martin Kohli, eds, *Der Zusammenbruch der DDR* (Frankfurt, 1993). Christoph Kleßmann and Martin Sabrow, "Zeitgeschichte in Deutschland nach 1989," *Aus Politik und Zeitgeschichte,* 1996, no. 39: 3–14.
7. See the papers presented at the Otzenhausener Jahrestagung zur DDR-Geschichte, in Heiner Timmermann, ed., *Diktaturen in Europa im 20. Jahrhundert – der Fall DDR* (Berlin,1996).
8. Ulrich Beck, *Risikogesellschaft. Auf dem Weg in eine andere Moderne* (Frankfurt, 1986), 16.
9. Otto Brunner, Werner Conze, and Reinhart Koselleck, eds, *Geschichtliche Grundbegriffe: Historisches Lexikon zur politisch-sozialen Sprache in Deutschland* (Stuttgart, 1972), vol. 1: xiiiff.
10. Ralph Jessen, "Die Gesellschaft im Staatssozialismus. Probleme einer Sozialgeschichte der DDR," *Geschichte und Gesellschaft* 21 (1995): 96–110. For linguistic approaches, see Ute Daniel, "Clio unter Kulturschock," *Geschichte in Wissenschaft und Unterricht* 48 (1997): 259–78; Wolfgang Hardtwig and Hans-Ulrich Wehler, eds, *Kulturgeschichte heute* (Göttingen, 1996).

11. Clemens Burrichter and Gerd-Rüdiger Stephan, "Die DDR als Untersuchungs-
    gegenstand einer historischen Sozialforschung. Ergebnisse, Defizite und Per-
    spektiven," *Deutschland Archiv* 29 (1996), 444–54.
12. Klaus von Beyme, "Stalinismus und Poststalinismus im Osteuropäischen Ver-
    gleich," *Potsdamer Bulletin für Zeithistorische Studien*, 13 (1998): 8–22; Her-
    mann Weber, *DDR. Grundriß der Geschichte 1945–1990* (Hannover, 1993),
    13–15.
13. *Kleines Politisches Wörterbuch* (Berlin, 1996), 176–79; see also the evolution in
    the second edition in 1973: 152–155; and in the *Sachwörterbuch der Geschichte
    Deutschlands und der deutschen Arbeiterbewegung* (Berlin, 1969), 394–407.
14. Ibid., "Sozialistischer Staat," 880–83; "Diktatur des Proletariats," 194–97;
    "Nation," 632–37; "Volksdemokratie," 1020.
15. Joachim Petzold, "Die DDR und das Problem der Diktatur des Proletariats," in
    *Das Scheitern didaktischer Legitimationsmuster und die Zukunftsfähigkeit der
    Demokratie*, ed. Richard Saage (Berlin, 1995), 59–78.
16. Technically, this term was only valid for the occupation period. Martin Broszat
    and Hermann Weber, eds, *SBZ-Handbuch. Staatliche Verwaltungen, Parteien,
    gesellschaftliche Organisationen und ihre Führungskräfte in der Sowjetischen
    Besatzungszone Deutschlands 1945–1949* (Munich, 1993).
17. Görres-Gesellschaft, ed., *Staatslexikon. Recht, Wirtschaft, Gesellschaft* (Freiburg,
    1958), 745–52.
18. The term was used in Christoph Kleßmann, *Zwei Staaten, eine Nation. Deutsche
    Geschichte 1955–1970* (Bonn, 1997). Cf. Christian Hacke, "Die Deutschland-
    politik der Bundesrepublik Deutschland," in *Deutschland-Handbuch. Eine dop-
    pelte Bilanz 1949–1989*, ed. Werner Weidenfeld and Hartmut Zimmermann
    (Bonn, 1989), 535–50.
19. Görres-Gesellschaft, ed., *Staatslexikon. Recht, Wirtschaft, Gesellschaft* (Freiburg,
    1985[7]): 1263–77.
20. Barbara Marzahn, *Der Deutschlandbegriff der DDR* (Düsseldorf, 1979), 156ff.
21. Gerd Lozek, *Stalinismus – Ideologie, Gesellschaftskonzept oder was? Klartext Nr.
    4 des Vereins Helle Panke* (Berlin, 1993); Theodor Bergmann and Mario Keßler,
    eds, *Ketzer im Kommunismus. Alternativen zum Stalinismus.* (Mainz, 1993).
22. François Furet, *Le passé d'une illusion. Essai sur l'idée communiste au XXe siècle*
    (Paris, 1995).
23. *Totalitarismus im 20. Jahrhundert. Eine Bilanz der internationalen Forschung*,
    ed. Eckhard Jesse (Baden-Baden, 1996): 70–94; Alfons Söllner, Ralf Walken-
    haus, and Karin Wieland, eds, *Totalitarismus. Eine Ideengeschichte des 20.
    Jahrhunderts* (Berlin, 1997).
24. Eckhard Jesse, "Die Totalitarismusforschung im Streit der Meinungen," in
    ibid.: 9–40.
25. Ralph Jessen, "DDR-Geschichte und Totalitarismustheorie," *Berline Debatte Ini-
    tial* 4/5 (1995): 24–27; Martin Sabrow, "Herrschaftsstrukturen und Erfahrungs-
    dimensionen. Das Potsdamer ZZF und sein Beitrag zu einer reflecktierten
    Historisierung der DDR," in *Die DDR – Ideologie und Politik als politisches Instru-
    ment*, ed. Heiner Timmermann (Berlin, 1998).
26. Hannah Arendt, *Elemente und Ursprünge totalitärer Herrschaft* (Munich, 1991).
    Cf. Gert-Joachim Glaeßner, "Das Ende des Kommunismus und die Sozialwis-
    senschaften. Anmerkungen zum Totalitarismusproblem," *Deutschland Archiv*
    28 (1995): 920ff.
27. Eckhard Jesse, "War die DDR totalitär?" *Aus Politik und Zeitgeschichte*, 1994,
    no. 40: 12–23; Juan Linz and Alfred Stepan, *Problems of Democratic Transition
    and Consolidation: Southern Europe, South America, and Post-Communist
    Europe* (Baltimore, 1997); Heinrich A. Winkler, "Deutschlands gespaltene

Geschichtskultur. Steoreotype und Herrschaftsformen: War die DDR eine 'totalitäe' Diktatur?" *Berliner Zeitung*, June 25, 1997.

28. For the limits of this approach see Günther Heydemann and Eckhard Jesse, eds, *Diktaturvergleich als Herausforderung* (Berlin, 1998).

29. Artur Meier, "Abschied von der sozialistischen Ständegesellschaft," *Aus Politik und Zeitgeschichte*, 1990, no. 16: 3–14.

30. Sigrid Meuschel, *Legitimation und Parteiherrschaft. Zum Paradox von Stabilität und Revolution in der DDR* (Frankfurt, 1992), 10ff.

31. Michael Thomas, "Vernachlässigte Dimensionen soziologischer Analyse. Transformationsprozeß als soziologische Herausforderung," in *Abbruch und Aufbruch. Sozialwissenschaften im Transformationsprozeß*, ed. Michael Thomas (Berlin, 1992); Frank Adler, "Zur Rekonstruktion des DDR-Realsozialismus," in ibid., 36–59, calls the GDR a "side path of modern social development."

32. Christiane Lemke, *Die Ursachen des Umbruchs 1989. Politische Sozialisation in der ehemaligen DDR* (Opladen, 1991).

33. Ralf Rytlewksi, ed., *Politische Kultur in der DDR* (Stuttgart, 1989).

34. Wolfgang Engler, *Die zivilisatorische Lücke. Versuch über den Staatssozialismus* (Frankfurt, 1992).

35. Peter Christian Ludz, *Parteielite im Wandel. Funktionsaufbau, Sozialstruktur und Ideologie der SED-Führung* (Cologne, 1968); idem, *Ideologiebegriff und marxistische Theorie. Ansätze zu einem immanenten Vergleich* (Opladen, 1977²); and Dietrich Staritz, *Geschichte der DDR* (Frankfurt, 1996).

36. Jens Hacker, *Deutsche Irrtümer. Schönfärber und Helfershelfer der SED-Diktatur im Westen* (Berlin, 1992²); Gerhard Meyer, "Die westdeutsche DDR- und Deutschlandforschung im Umbruch," *Deutschland Archiv* 25 (1992): 273ff.

37. Jürgen Kocka, ed., *Historische DDR-Forschung* (Berlin, 1992), 25f; see also idem, "Ein deutscher Sonderweg. Überlegungen zur Sozialgeschichte der DDR," *Aus Politik und Zeitgeschichte*, 1994, no. 40: 34–45.

38. Detlef Pollack, *Kirche in der Organisationsgesellschaft. Zum Wandel der gesellschaftlichen Lage der evangelischen Kirche in der DDR* (Stuttgart, 1994), 57–60, 76.

39. Richard Bessel and Ralph Jessen, eds, *Grenzen der Diktatur. Staat und Gesellschaft in der DDR* (Göttingen, 1996).

40. Hartmut Kaelble, Jürgen Kocka, and Harmut Zwahr, eds, *Sozialgeschichte der DDR* (Stuttgart, 1994).

41. Dieter Langewiesche, "Fortschritt als sozialistische Hoffnung," in *Sozialismus und Kommunismus im Wandel*, ed. Klaus Schönhoven and Dietrich Staritz (Cologne, 1993), 39–55.

42. Mitchell Ash, "Wissenschaft, Politik und Modernität der DDR – Ansätze zu einer Neubetrachtung," in *Wissenschaft und Politik – Genetik und Humangenetik in der DDR 1949–1989*, ed. Karin Weisemann, Peter Kröner, and Richard Toellner (Münster, 1997), 1–25.

43. Rolf Reißig, ed., *Rückweg in die Zukunft. Über den schwierigen Transformationsprozeß in Ostdeutschland* (Frankfurt, 1993).

44. Richard Schröder, "Diktatoren wollen geliebt werden," *Der Tagesspiegel* (10 July 1997).

45. Konrad H. Jarausch, "Historische Texte der DDR aus der Perspektive des linguistic turn," in *Die DDR-Geschichtswissenschaft als Forschungsproblem* (special issue no. 27 of *Historische Zeitschrift*) ed. George Iggers, Konrad H. Jarausch, Matthias Middell, and Martin Sabrow (Munich, 1998).

46. Detlef Pollack, "Die konstitutive Widersprüchlichkeit der DDR. Oder: War die DDR-Gesellschaft homogen? Eine Fortsetzung der Diskussion zwischen Sigrid Meuschel und Ralph Jessen," *Geschichte und Gesellschaft* 24 (1998): 110–31;

Stefan Wolle, "Herrschaft und Alltag. Die Zeitgeschichtsforschung auf der Suche nach der wahren DDR," *Aus Politik und Zeitgeschichte,* 1997, no. 26: 30–38.

47. See Dorothee Wierling, in this volume, and Günter Grass, *Ein weites Feld* (Göttingen, 1995): esp. 16f; 324f.

48. Rolf Henrich, *Der vormundschaftliche Staat. Vom Versagen des real existierenden Sozialismus* (Frankfurt, 1989), 9–22.

49. Hermann Beck, *The Origins of the Authoritarian Welfare State in Prussia* (Ann Arbor, 1995).

50. Hans Maier, *Die rechtlichen Grundlagen und die Organisation der Fürsorge einschließlich des Armenrechts und des Rechtes des Kindes* (Berlin, 1926); Else Wex, *Vom Wesen der sozialen Fürsorge* (Berlin, 1929).

51. Jürgen Kocka et al., eds, *Von der Arbeiterbewegung zum modernen Sozialstaat. Festschrift für Gerhard A. Ritter* (Munich, 1994); Young-Sun Hong, *Welfare, Modernity, and the Weimar Republic, 1919–1933* (Princeton, 1997), 35, 114, 204, 217.

52. See "sozialistischer Staat" in *Kleines Wörterbuch,* 881ff. Cf. Jens Alber, *Der Sozialstaat in der Bundesrepublik 1950–1983* (Frankfurt, 1989), 22–33; Hans-Günter Hockerts, "Einführung," in *Drei Wege deutscher Sozialstaatlichkeit. NS-Diktatur, Bundesrepublik und DDR im Vergleich,* ed. Hans-Günter Hockerts (Munich, 1998).

53. For the orginal meaning in middle high German: *Vürsorge,* or "preparing for things to come," see *Duden. Etymologie. Herkunftswörterbuch der deutschen Sprache* (Mannheim, 1989), 682. For present connotations see *Duden. Bedeutungswörterbuch* (Mannheim, 1985), 274 and 592f, as well as *Duden. Deutsches Universalwörterbuch* (Mannheim, 1989), 550f.

54. Grass, *Ein weites Feld*: 598f.

55. Since the German notion *Fürsorgediktatur* does not translate exactly into English, the somewhat vaguer term "welfare dictatorship" is used synonymously with it in this text.

56. M. Rainer Lepsius, *Demokratie in Deutschland. Soziologisch-historische Konstellationsanalysen* (Göttingen, 1993). See also Günter Heydemann and Christopher Beckmann, "Zwei Diktaturen im Deutschland. Möglichkeiten und Grenzen des historischen Diktaturenvergleichs," *Deutschland Archiv* 30 (1997): 12ff.

57. The following discussion is based on the lines of conflict mapped out by Detlef Pollack, "Die konstitutive Widersprüchlichkeit der DDR," 5ff.

58. See ibid.: 11, 20; and Mary Fullbrook, *Anatomy of a Dictatorship: Inside the GDR 1949–1989* (New York, 1995) as well as Deutscher Bundestag, ed., *Materialien der Enquete-Kommission "Aufarbeitung von Geschichte und Folgen der SED-Diktatur in Deutschland,* vol. 5 (Frankfurt, 1995), 680–733.

59. Peter Hübner, *Konsens, Konflikt und Kompromiß. Soziale Arbeiterinteressen und Sozialpolitik in der SBZ/DDR 1945–1970* (Berlin, 1995); Franz Joseph Hutter, "Sozialer Wandel in der DDR im Lichte neuer Publikationen," *Zeitgeschichte* 24 (1997): 213–21.

60. Charles S. Maier, *Dissolution. The Crisis of Communism and the End of East Germany* (Princeton, 1997),59–107; Hans Günter Hockerts, "Soziale Errungenschaften? Zum sozialpolitischen Legitimitätsanspruch der zweiten deutschen Diktatur," in *Von der Arbeiterbewegung,* 790–804.

61. Simone Barck, Martina Langermann, and Siegfried Lokatis, *"Jedes Buch ein Abenteuer." Zensursystem und literarische Öffentlichkeit in der DDR bis Ende der sechziger Jahre* (Berlin, 1997).

62. See Thomas Lindenberger, ed., *Herrschaft und Eigen-Sinn in der Diktatur, Studien zur Gesellschaftsgeschichte der DDR* (Cologne, 1999) and Martin Sabrow, ed., *Geschichte als Herrschaftsdiskurs. Fallstudien zum Umgang mit der Vergangenheit in der frühen DDR* (Cologne, 1999).

63. Meuschel, *Legitimation*, 22ff.
64. Harmut Zwahr, *Ende einer Selbstzerstörung. Leipzig und die Revolution in der DDR* (Göttingen, 1993).
65. Ulrich Beck, and Peter Sopp, eds, *Individualisierung und Integration. Neue Konfliktlinien und neuer Integrationsmodus?* (Opladen, 1997); Johannes Saltzwedel, "Ratlos unterm Regenbogen," *Der Spiegel* 28 (1997): 160–63.
66. Konrad H. Jarausch, *Die unverhoffte Einheit 1989–1990* (Frankfurt, 1995), 15.
67. See the arguments in Omer Bartov, *Murder in our Midst. The Holocaust, Industrial Killing, and Representation* (New York, 1996).
68. Rolf Reißig and Gert-Joachim Glaeßner, *Das Ende eines Experiments* (Berlin, 1991), 44ff. Cf. Rainer Eppelmann, Horst Möller, Günter Nooke, and Dorothee Wilms, eds, *Lexikon des DDR-Sozialismus. Das Staats- und Gesellschaftssystem der Deutschen Demokratischen Republik* (Paderborn, 1996).
69. Konrad H. Jarausch, "'Sich der Katastrophe stellen': (Post-)kommunistische Erklärungen für den Zusammenbruch der DDR," in *Halbherziger Revisionismus*, ed. Eckert and Faulenbach, 141–50.
70. Karlheinz Blaschke, "Als bürgerlicher Historiker am Rande der DDR. Erlebnisse, Beobachtungen und Überlegungen eines Nonkonformisten," in *Historiker in der DDR*, ed. Karl H. Pohl (Göttingen, 1997), 45–93; Ilko-Sascha Kowalczuk, *Legitimation eines neuen Staates. Parteiarbeiter an der historischen Front. Geschichtswissenschaft in der SBZ/DDR 1945 bis 1961* (Berlin, 1997), esp. 24ff.
71. Horst Möller, "Der SED–Staat – die zweite Diktatur in Deutschland," in *Lexikon des DDR-Sozialismus*, 5–12.
72. Klaus Schroeder, *Der SED–Staat. Partei, Staat und Gesellschaft 1949–1980* (Munich, 1998), 632–48, calls the GDR a "late totalitarian caretaker and surveillance state."
73. Stefan Wolle, *Die heile Welt der Diktatur. Alltag und Herrschaft in der DDR 1971–1989* (Berlin, 1998), 83, 124ff, 227ff. "The dictatorship was draped in the cloak of fatherly love."
74. For the early period see Harold Hurwitz, *Die Stalinisierung der SED. Zum Verlust von Freiräumen und sozialdemokratischer Identität in den Vorständen 1946–1949* (Opladen, 1997).

MECHANISMS OF
POLITICAL REPRESSION

FROM DISMANTLING TO CURRENCY REFORM

EXTERNAL ORIGINS OF THE DICTATORSHIP, 1943–1948

Jochen Laufer

"As far as one can tell from current developments, it is becoming increasingly clear that economics and politics, and indeed the very way of life in the Russian zone are quickly approaching the Soviet model." Offered by a pessimistic commentator of the East German scene as early as a few weeks after the end of the Second World War,[1] this assessment of trends in the Eastern zone reflects the dramatic transformations experienced by East German society in the postwar period. What was the role of the Soviet Union in this development? In the past few years scholars such as Wilfried Loth,[2] Norman Naimark,[3] Michail Semirjaga,[4] and Stefan Creuzberger[5] have addressed this question. Despite their different approaches, all of these authors assign a great degree of agency to individual actors within the Soviet military administration. But what were the consequences of the political and economic reforms carried out by the military government? This essay will attempt to answer that question.

Documentary material now available in Moscow's archives has made it possible for historians to analyze the Soviet military administration and its dealings with the Kremlin. While little is known about the processes involved in decisions made at the highest levels, scholars have been able draw on these sources to reconstruct how policy was determined on an individual, day to day basis. They have discovered that only rarely did decisions originate with Stalin, the Politburo, or the Council of People's Commissars/ Council of Ministers.[6] Instead, proposals about German policies were generally forwarded at the ministerial level by SVAG officials or by the "representatives" of the Council of People's Commissars/Council of Ministers in Germany. Because they had to be approved at the "highest level" (the Politburo), decisions were often delayed, and sometimes never even reached at all.

These delays made planning extremely difficult, and also severely hindered the actual implementation of Soviet policies. Soviet officials in the occupied zone felt that their hands were tied and they were unable to solve the problems they faced on a daily basis. They demanded that the SVAG either be given the powers to act independently, or that special "representatives" be appointed with the ability to make "operative decisions," especially regarding economic policies. To solve their dilemma, many Soviet officials in Germany did not even wait for orders from Moscow, but acted on their own initiative. Naturally these "individual initiatives" in the Soviet system cannot be confused with independent, rational actions, as they still occurred within the context of the ideological norms established by Stalin.[7] On the basis of the "lessons" of the Russian revolution, as well as experiences made during the Soviet occupation of Poland, the Baltic states, and the Bukovina during the Second World War, the Soviet leadership and troop commanders of the Red Army, political officers and economic experts had formulated concrete plans about the measures to be implemented in occupied Germany.

The economic organization of the Soviet Military Administration was part of the larger administrative system of Soviet economic planning. From the outset SVAG had three main goals: first, to equip the occupying forces with the necessary supplies; second to secure the payment of reparations; and finally to insure the basic needs of the German population. In order to fulfill all of these objectives, SVAG adopted the command practices of the German war economy, and all economic activities in agriculture, industry and trade were placed in the hands of the military authorities or those local governments directly subservient to them.

Soviet Dismantling Policies

The USSR's reparation policies had been formulated even before the Soviet decision to participate in the Allied occupation of Germany in 1943.[8] Eugen Varga, Stalin's "economic advisor,"[9] was the chief architect. In an attempt to avoid the mistakes made in reparation struggles after the First World War, the Soviets intended to remove equipment rather than currency from defeated Germany. The removal of German machinery and industrial equipment was also linked to the "industrial disarmament" of the Germans on a long-term basis. This was not an idea unique to the Soviets, since the Western powers also considered similar plans.[10] The possibility of a unified, binding policy of reparations was therefore not doomed from the outset. In fact, at the end of 1943 the People's Commissar for Foreign Affairs called for the formulation of joint reparation plans in conjunction with the West.[11] But Stalin avoided reaching a final decision. Unwilling to allow the West any influence in determining Soviet damage during the war, he was even more unlikely to consider joint reparation measures within the Soviet sphere of influence after its end. Instead, the Soviets carried out their dismantling policies unilaterally, removing their "trophies" with little concern for Allied reactions. As early as December 1941, Soviet troops had begun to collect materiel left on the battlefields by the retreating Germans. In a direct line of continuity with these measures, they continued dismantling in the Eastern zone in 1945.[12]

At the close of hostilities the USSR had already established an independent reparations policy, rather than a course of cooperation with the Allies. As early as the end of 1944, conflicts arose between the Soviets and the Western powers in the formulation of armistice agreements with Rumania, Finland, Bulgaria, and Hungary.[13] Available sources support the interpretation that the Soviets were interested in settling these conflicts. At the Yalta and Potsdam conferences they sought to negotiate with the West, while avoiding any promise of direct cooperation.

Soviet reparation policy was therefore composed of two distinct, and opposing elements. On the one hand the Soviets had created a "Special Committee for Germany" – a top-secret organization with extensive powers and a large staff under the direction of the Politburo member Georgij Malenkov. On the other hand, the Reparations Committee of the Foreign Commissariat was restructured as the Soviet section of the Allied Reparations Committee, itself founded at the Yalta Conference. While the "Special Committee" formulated and carried out plans to dismantle German manufacturing facilities – making East German resources an essential part of Soviet economic development – the short-lived Reparations Commission remained relatively insignificant. Unable to formulate a joint Allied reparations plan, it exercised no decisive influence on Soviet dismantling policies. Even Soviet officials serving on the Commission were only partially informed about the removal of materials within their zone.

The most likely motivation for the establishment of the Special Committee was not the Allies' inability to reach a settlement on the reparations question at Yalta, but the surprising capture of intact German manufacturing sites in Upper Silesia.[14] Even before the Red Army marched into what was to become the Soviet occupation zone, the German Eastern provinces had become a proving ground for Soviet dismantling procedures. Dismantling occurred not erratically or spontaneously, but in a highly systematic manner. The Russian historian Pavel Knyshevskij has described the process as a "symbiosis between the well-oiled mechanisms of state normative rule and operational planning." After personally inspecting the "objects" in question, representatives of the Special Committee sent descriptions of production facilities to the State Committee for Defense. All dismantling took place formally on central orders – issued at first by the State Committee for Defense, followed by the Council of People's Commissars (after September 1945) and then the Council of Ministers (after March 1946). All the orders were signed by Stalin, who was the head of each of these organizations.[15] Decisions were made strictly on the basis of the USSR's strategic or economic needs, and foreign policy considerations played no role in their formulation.

The zonal solution to the reparation question reached at Potsdam that hastened the economic and political division of Germany was not a direct result of the conference.[16] Rather, the solution (which saw the Soviets and Poles drawing reparations from the East and the Western powers from the West)[17] stemmed from dismantling policies that the Soviets had already implemented in their own zone. Still during the fighting, the Soviets had dismantled manufacturing facilities in the Eastern sections of Germany in March of 1945. The scope of the activities in these areas (later part of the Polish state) has often been overlooked and underestimated by historians. On 20 April 1945, two weeks before the German capitulation, the Soviet State Defense Committee approved the removal of 61,828 railroad cars of industrial materials taken from areas east of the Oder.[18] On 10 May half of the materials (26,870 box cars) had already been dismantled and loaded.[19] The dismantling of manufacturing facilities in the SBZ and West Berlin (occupied by Soviet troops until June 1945) soon followed. On the evening before the beginning of the Potsdam Conference – 1 July 1945 – the State Defense Committee had approved the *Demontage* of some 2,000 German plants.[20] That was 43 percent of all total properties dismantled by the Soviets after the Second World War.[21] At the end of June 1945, when the zonal reparation solution was reached at Potsdam, the Soviets had already removed 1,575 factories from their zone.[22]

Yet these figures give an incomplete picture of events and the damage done to the area's entire industrial infrastructure. In the immediate aftermath of occupation, special reconnaissance divisions catalogued over 6,000 potential industrial targets. The approximately 3,000 large industrial sites located in the SBZ were undoubtedly among these objects.[23] Most of these facilities were immediately put under the directorship of Soviet plant managers, which meant their factual appropriation. Those plants with more than 100 employees were particularly hard-hit by dismantling policies. In a report of the Special Committee's representative from the fall of 1946, 1,553 such factories are listed by name. Before their dismantling they employed 1,699,288 workers.[24] In their dismantling policies the Soviets saw themselves above property rights and regulations, and at no point did they consider formally expropriating materials or compensating previous owners.

In June 1945, when the Soviet Military Administration was formed, a special division for reparation questions was established, but it did not assume responsibility for dismantling policies. Instead, these remained in the hands of the representative of the Special Committee for Germany until September 1946. With his powers largely beyond SVAG's sphere of influence, this representative also controlled an extensive administration to carry out dismantling policies. In the spring of 1946 the number of Soviet personnel working outside the SVAG administration on reparations questions surpassed 12,000.[25] The fact that dismantling policies remained separate from any economic considerations within the SBZ led to conflicts between the Special Committee and the Economic Division of the SVAG. The main goal of the Special Committee was a policy of "industrial disarmament." In practice, this policy aimed at reducing Germany to an agrarian economy.[26] Yet while the Special Committee carried out its dismantling with this goal in mind, SVAG authorities were attempting to resuscitate the economy in the SBZ. Within SVAG, many were aware of the problems associated with a policy aimed at weakening Germany to the fullest extent. Not only would such policies endanger the Soviet position within the SBZ, but they also threatened Soviet influence in Germany and Central Europe as a whole.

Konstantin Koval', named as the representative of the Chief of SVAG and responsible for the direction and control of the entire economy in the SBZ until 1950,[27] recognized the dangers of a policy aimed at creating an "economic vacuum" in the occupied zone. Koval' was not willing to wait for orders handed down from above, choosing instead to formulate his own plans. He called for a modification of Soviet dismantling policies and advised the creation of

Soviet stock companies (SAGs) in the SBZ.[28] Such corporations (companies with limited liability) would take over former German property located within the Soviet sphere of influence. This change of direction in reparation policies was supported by the head of SVAG, Marshal Zhukov, who announced the formation of the SAGs to the presidents of the German federal and provincial administrations in November 1945.[29] In January 1946 four different proposals regarding Soviet economic policies in the SBZ, formulated under Koval's direction, were presented to the Soviet government. On this basis, the Council of People's Commissars passed several rulings on 25 January 1946. Among them was the order "Regarding the transition of German factories to Soviet property and their organization into (Soviet) corporations."[30] As a result, 200 of the largest industrial sites in the Soviet zone – originally targeted for dismantling – passed into Soviet hands. They remained in their original locations and in the following years were slowly handed back to the Germans, but not to their original owners. The orders of January 1946 were crucial for shifting priorities towards economic and political independence for the SBZ. They granted the SVAG new responsibilities and powers, allowing it a degree of independence from Moscow, and forging a special tie between the interests of SVAG and the SBZ.

In October 1945, at about the same time that plans were underway to establish the SAGs, the head of SVAG, Marshal Zhukov, issued Order No. 124 (subsequently supplemented by Order 126). It envisaged the expropriation or seizure (not formally the dispossession) of property belonging to Nazis and other war criminals. Affecting factories, real estate, and other properties, Zhukov's order targeted not only active Nazis, but also other "persons who ... have been identified by the Soviet Military Command."[31] No directive from Moscow can be found predating this initiative. The criterion of *individual guilt* had previously not been a determining factor in dismantling policies. Since the Germans had before tried to determine guilt and carry out expropriation on that basis, legal historians have recently concluded that the Soviet occupation forces "did not previously carry out expropriation as a punishment, but only coordinated existent efforts made by native forces."[32] At first, the factories were transferred to a trust company. But already in early 1946 the KPD demanded that the expropriated firms be formally dispossessed. The party organized a plebiscite regarding the issue, which was held on 30 June 1946. Although SVAG hesitated to approve the German Communists' initiative, and SVAG's political advisors expressed concern,[33] the KPD managed to overcome these objections. The plebiscite, promoted by vehement propaganda and demagogic rhetoric, was a success for the

SED and a decisive step on the path towards creating the foundations of "people's property" in the SBZ.[34]

The creation of SAGs and *"Volkseigene Betriebe"* (VEB) marked a modification of Soviet reparation policies, and was one of the reasons for the transformation of the USSR's general policies towards Germany's future. Molotov announced the change of course at the Paris meeting of the Foreign Ministers, particularly in his declaration of 10 July 1946 entitled "Regarding the future of Germany and a peace treaty with Germany."[35] As with previous efforts to safeguard the results of land reform, the development and long-term security of "people's property" needed the backing of appropriate political measures. SVAG could formulate such measures only in cooperation with the newly founded Socialist Unity Party (SED), which further reduced the chance of a settlement with the Western powers regarding Germany's future. Just how little room for maneuver was left is evidenced in the controversies surrounding currency reform.

Soviet Policies towards Currency Reform

By August 1945, Soviet troop commanders and regional army commanders had ordered the closing of all banks and had confiscated existing *Reichsmark* (RM) reserves.[36] Deposits made prior to 8 May 1945 were frozen and the majority of accounts expropriated.[37] In the spring of 1946 only savings accounts with amounts up to 3,000 RM were gradually returned to their original owners. The closing of banks and freezing of accounts, which the USSR had practiced in the occupation of Eastern Poland and the Baltic states,[38] were aimed at curbing inflation, but also had transformatory goals as well.[39] Not only would all bondholders be punished for their financial support of the war by a de facto dispossession, but "the demise of business stripped of capital was planned, as was a liquidity crisis for industry and agriculture."[40] The opening of a new banking system based on a SVAG order [41] completely destroyed the previous German system.

Like the Western powers, the Soviet Union introduced an allied military Mark, the so-called "M-Mark" as legal tender at a 1:1 parity with the Reichsmark. In the SBZ M-Marks were not only used for supplying Soviet troops, but also paid for goods sent to the USSR. Without ever publicly justifying its actions, the Soviet Union issued large amounts of such occupation currency between 1944 and June 1946. The Council of People's Commissars and the Soviet Council of Ministers approved the "allotment" (in actuality the issuing) of 17.5 billion M-Marks between 7 February 1945 and 20 April 1945.[42] The printing of such a large amount of currency, which had to be accepted in all four zones as legal tender, further worsened the relationship between money and goods in the SBZ, which was already weakened by the war economy. Nevertheless, here as in the other zones, hyperinflation was avoided, while prices and salaries remained relatively stable. The East compensated for the resultant lack of private initiative by command economy measures such as production plans, reparation commissions, required cash payments for public and private enterprises, etc.

The need for currency reform was seen differently by various groups in the SBZ. On 7 January 1946 the KPD released its economic policy guidelines, which demanded a reduction in circulation.[43] In May 1946 the head of the SVAG also remarked upon the necessity of reform.[44] But SVAG's political advisor emerged as an adamant opponent of any measures. Drawing on a detailed analysis prepared by one of his administrative aides,[45] he painted a rosy picture of the financial situation in the SBZ without once mentioning currency reform.[46] The Allies had begun discussing steps leading to a reform after the Americans proposed measures aimed at fighting inflation on 15 November 1945.[47] Marshal Zhukov, head of SVAG, called internally for a unified reform in all of Germany as early as 23 March 1946.[48] Although there was never any risk of the proposal being approved by the Control Council, Moscow's Foreign Ministry refused to approve Zhukov's proposal.[49] He was allowed, however, to meet unofficially with the Allies and hold secret talks about the basic principles of any currency reform.

In mid-May 1946 Vaslilij Sokolovskij, who had taken over as Zhukov's successor, initiated a second currency reform program for all of Germany.[50] Sokolovskij attempted to bring the American proposals, which the Americans had laid out in "private talks" with their Soviet colleagues in the first months of 1946,[51] in line with Soviet interests. SVAG's currency reform proposals were the source of intense debate between the appropriate ministries in Moscow and SVAG representatives. Following a conference in June 1946 held in Moscow, attended by members of the Finance Ministry, the Soviet state bank (Gosbank), the Foreign Ministry, and the financial section of SVAG, officials decided against an outright rejection of any joint projects. Instead, reform was to be linked to zonal issuance rights.[52] At the same time Sokolovskij was instructed to prepare for an independent reform within the SBZ, since an independent Allied reform within their own zones could not be ruled out entirely.[53]

Still, the Soviets continued to search for a common solution to the currency question with the other occupying forces. The head of SVAG's financial section, Pavel Maletin, together with the Soviet Finance Minister, prepared a memorandum for Molotov on 21 January 1947. Soviet financial experts recognized that a rejection of the Allied currency reform proposals would not make such plans disappear. Indeed, they feared a rejection could be used as an excuse by the Allies to carry out unilateral currency reform in the West, which would result in further "*economic isolation*" of the Soviet zone. Maletin and Zverev proposed that a joint reform should be approved under the condition that the Allies would guarantee all Soviet occupation and reparation expenses.[54] Their proposal was not sent on to Stalin. Even the supporters of a joint currency reform were not wedded to the idea of compromise with the Western powers and asked expressly that "preparations be made for separate reform as a reaction to potential unilateral action by the West." Thus officials were ordered to begin with the printing of special coupons, independent of preparations for the issuance of new currency.[55]

While SVAG continued to wait for instructions from Moscow, Soviet representatives in Berlin decided on 19 February 1947 to commence with the formation of issuing and transfer banks within the SBZ.[56] The central banks opened in the American and French zones served as models. This decision should not be interpreted as a demonstrative manifestation of Soviet interest "in currency reform and the creation of a German central bank,"[57] since Soviet representatives in the Allied Control Council gave no sign of any change of course. At the Moscow meeting of the Council of Foreign Ministers (10 March to 24 April 1947), Molotov did not introduce any new proposals for currency reform. During the early months of 1947 Cold War divisions were becoming even more pronounced and expanded beyond debates about currency reform. This found expression in SVAG's attempt (made with the knowledge of the Soviet Foreign Ministry) to prohibit the premiers of the East German states to attend the planned conference of prime ministers in Munich.[58] Shortly afterwards the Soviet Union (after initial indecision) refused to participate in the European Recovery Program proposed by U.S. Secretary of State George Marshall.[59] The Communist Information Office (COMINFORM) was founded in September 1947, with the aim of assisting those forces in the "peace camp" in their battle against "imperialist" forces under U.S. leadership.[60] All of these steps further narrowed the chances of achieving a common currency reform under joint Allied leadership.

In the fall of 1947, the indications were becoming more obvious that the Allies were planning a separate currency reform in the Western zones.[61] SVAG took these portents as an impetus to take independent action. Sokolovskij renewed his calls for the issuing of new bills. Due to security reasons printing was to take place in the state mint at Goznak in the USSR.[62] But Moscow refused to heed

such calls, and a week before the beginning of the London Conference (25 November 1947 to 15 December 1947), Sokolovskij
repeated his proposal, this time together with his political consul-
tant, Vladimir Semenov. His plan envisaged the printing of 400,000
new bills with a value of five billion marks.[63] Moscow still refused
to approve issue, but before the London Conference ended, on 10
December 1947 a decision was reached regarding preparations for
currency reform in the SBZ,[64] which included the creation of a central German issuing bank.[65] After the failure of the Conference, the
Politburo of the Bolshevik Party moved to transform the German
Economic Commission, founded in June 1947, into a zonal coordi-
nating agency with binding powers.[66]

Sokolovskij therefore viewed the American proposal to initiate a
currency reform in all of Germany, which included a plan to print
currency in Berlin and circulate it under the authority of a Four
Power Commission,[67] with suspicion. Once the Soviets had rejected
the plan, he feared that the Americans would claim to be justified
in carrying out independent reforms in the West. To undermine
these plans, on 30 January 1948 Sokolovskij approved the centralized printing of new money under the condition that a financial
administration for all of Germany be established. Based on previous negotiations within the Control Council he could be sure that
the French would reject such a proposal. To make sure of their dis-
approval, he included a ban on independent currency reforms
within the different zones. During the following weeks, in which no
definite decision regarding reform had yet been reached, SVAG
authorities played a double game. Hoping to achieve the best possible provisions for a reform in their own zone, they also (as did
their Western colleagues) tried to pin the failure of the negotiations
within the Control Council on their political opponents. While the
Soviet representatives in the Control Council appeared to be willing
to compromise, the head of SVAG's financial section in Berlin continued to prepare for reform in the SBZ and continued to push
Moscow for the necessary directives.

Immediately after the unsuccessful conclusion of the London Conference of the Council of Foreign Ministers, the immediate political
preparations for the proposed currency reform began.[68] It was the
SVAG authorities who, in anticipation of actions carried out in the
West, took the initiative – and not Moscow, or any German agencies.
SED leaders were kept in the dark about SVAG's preparations until
28 January 1948. Only then did Maletin inform Pieck, the head of
the SED, about the SVAG's plans for a currency reform aimed at all
of Germany. He announced that instead of the previous stabilization
policies, the old currency was to be turned in and exchanged for new

money. He also confided in Pieck that the creation of four-zonal financial administration and a central issuing bank would be necessary before a currency reform could be achieved for all of Germany. Rather than informing the SED leaders about the SVAG's real assessment of the situation, Maletin dwelt on recounting the details of a reform, long since abandoned by the SVAG.[69]

Sokolovskij had already relayed the plans to the Soviet foreign ministry for both the directive issued by the Soviet Council of Ministers on currency reform in the SBZ as well as the necessary implementation decree. The former provided the basis for Order No. 111 of the head of SVAG,[70] issued on 23 June 1948, while the latter was released in revised form as the decree of the German Economic Commission (DWK).[71] In making the decision, authorities in Moscow did not choose between a reform affecting all of Germany or merely the SBZ, but only decided the particulars of the reform for the SBZ. They were *no longer* considering the alternative plan to make concessions to the Allies in order to hinder a separate reform in the West, which would allow the possibility for a reform in all of Germany. On 14 May 1948, Sokolovskij's proposal – which had been first introduced in December 1947 and had seen numerous revisions since then – regarding a decree of the Soviet Council of Ministers affecting currency reform in the SBZ was sent to the Politburo of the Central Committee of the Bolshevik Party for approval.[72] Since no formal decision of the Soviet Council of Ministers can be found, it can be assumed that Stalin personally approved the decree. The coupons, which were to be pasted onto the old *Reichsmark* banknotes, had been ready since December 1947.[73]

The political decision regarding the issuing of a new currency in the SBZ was not only prepared by the SVAG and made in Moscow, but the details of the plan's implementation were also discussed by the SVAG's financial administration and the Soviet Finance Ministry. The plan further shifted the cost of transfer to currency holders, while benefiting those Germans with little savings or hardly any reserves at all. When the Western powers announced the date of their currency reform as 17 June 1948, SVAG had a prepared response, but no new currency for the SBZ.[74] This circumstance seems to have been premeditated.[75] In order to convince their own population and the public outside of their zone of their unpreparedness, authorities announced that the exchange planned for 23 June 1948[76] would consist of initially pasting "special coupons" onto old mark notes.[77] The currency reform therefore became an instrument of propaganda: while the SVAG and the SED could pretend they were standing up for German national interests, large sections of the populace in the Eastern zone could believe that the Western powers and their West German "helpers" had finalized the "division" of Germany with their separate currency reform in the Western zones.[78]

The first stage of the currency exchange had been completed on 28th June, and the exchange of couponed marks for new banknotes not yet announced, when the party leadership of the SED published a proposed two year plan (1949–50) "for the restoration and development of the peacetime economy in the Soviet occupied area of Germany."[79] This shift to long-term economic planning had been decided at the SED's Second Party Congress (September 20–24 1947). The actual goal of the currency exchange in the SBZ was to create a basis for achieving these goals, independent of all the activities of the Western powers and the West Germans.[80] The publication of the two year plan according to the principles of planned economies in the USSR and other Eastern block nations was symptomatic of the political and economic transformation of the SBZ. "The relationship between the party and the state had obviously changed. The SED considered the state itself and public revenue as instruments of power that had been removed from the public and placed within its own hands."[81]

The Founding of the GDR

It was not the dismantling policies and currency reform in and of themselves, but the manner in which they were carried out by the USSR that had a decisive influence on economic and political conditions in the SBZ. As a way of redressing damage caused by the Germans during the Second World War, the process of dismantling was necessary and possible. Dismantling was not only used as a means of reviving the Soviet economy, but became an instrument aimed at weakening the German grande bourgeoisie. Dismantling was carried out against the will of the majority of the populace in the SBZ, who saw their own existence threatened by the drastic measures employed. Nevertheless the KPD and SED could mobilize large sections of the population to support other occupation reforms (such as land reform, confiscation of the property of Nazi and other war criminals, and economic planning) in order to stabilize Soviet rule. This was in turn possible only because there were political forces which desired revolutionary change within the SBZ. These anticapitalist forces had more chances than ever before in German history to realize their goals, but they were constantly hemmed in by the interests of the victorious Soviet power.

Neither the SVAG nor the SED was prepared to stop the transformation of the SBZ set in motion by the dismantling policies in order to achieve a more congenial relationship with the Western powers, or for the sake of German unity. This became particularly clear in the currency question. The "antifascist democratic transformation" of society promoted by the SVAG and the SED led to conditions in the SBZ that were increasingly similar to those of other states within the Soviet sphere of influence. Opponents of this transformation were quick to characterize them as Sovietization. Securing the revolutionary accomplishments[82] achieved in the SBZ in the face of German fascism and "world imperialism" demanded a centralization of politics and the economy under single-party rule (namely the SED) – independent of developments in the Western zone. With the creation of state governments, central administration, the German economic commission and its transformation to a "central state ruling organ" in February of 1948, this condition was fulfilled long before the creation of the GDR.[83] And thus the lengthy path from dismantling to currency reform is an important part of the story of the founding of the East German state.

Notes

1. *Gruppe Ulbricht in Berlin April 1945 bis Juni 1945*, ed. Gerhard Keiderling (Berlin 1993), document 146: 616; Unknown, "Die Lage im russischen Raum nach dem Stand von Ende Juni 1945." Keiderling believes Andreas Hermes (CDU) is the author of this document.
2. Wilfried Loth, *Stalins ungeliebtes Kind. Warum Moskau die DDR nicht wollte* (Berlin, 1994).
3. Norman M. Naimark, *The Russians in Germany: The History of the Soviet Zone of Occupation, 1945–1949* (Cambridge, 1995).
4. Michail I. Semirjaga, *Kak my upravljali Germaniej* (Moscow, 1995).
5. Stefan Creuzberger, *Die sowjetische Besatzungsmacht und das politische System der SBZ* (Weimar, 1996).
6. Jochen Laufer, "Die UdSSR und die Einleitung der Bodenreform in der Sowjetischen Besatzungszone," in *"Junkerland in Bauernhand?" Durchführung, Auswirkungen und Stellenwert der Bodenreform in der Sowjetischen Besatzungszone*, ed. Arnd Bauerkämper (Stuttgart, 1996), 21–35.
7. On "aviation day" (no date, August 1945) Konstantin Ovchinikov, head of the Political Division of SVAG, intoned: "In order to create security for our homeland it is not enough that we have run the Germans from our homes and destroyed their war machine. It remains the task of the Red Army to destroy once and for all Hitler's state apparatus and his social order. Only through their destruction can we ban the danger of German aggression and hinder the rebirth of German imperialism.... We cannot secure such a peace without complete destruction of the German war capacity, the destruction of its industrial capacity and the complete removal of fascist ideology...." State Archive of the Russian Federation (in the following GA RF) R-7317/8/23: 24–39.
8. *SSSR i germanskij vopros 1941–1945: Dokumenty is Archiva vnesnej politiki Rossijskoj Federacii*, ed. Georgij Pavlovich Kynin and Jochen Laufer, Vol 1 (Moscow, 1996).

9. Gerhard Duda, *Jenö Varga und die Geschichte des Institutes für Weltwirtschaft und Weltpolitik in Moskau 1921–1970* (Berlin, 1994).

10. Alec Cairncross, *The Price of War. British Policy on German Reparations, 1941–1949* (New York, 1986), and O. Nübel, *Die amerikanische Reparationspolitik gegenüber Deutschland 1941–1945* (Frankfurt am Main, 1980).

11. Jochen Laufer, "Die Reparationsplanungen im sowjetischen Außenministerium während des Zweiten Weltkrieges," *Wirtschaftliche Folgelasten des Krieges in der SBZ/DDR*, ed. Christoph Buchheim (Baden-Baden 1995), 21–45.

12. Pavel Knyschewskij, *Moskaus Beute. Wie Vermögen, Kulturgüter und Intelligenz nach 1945 aus Deutschland geraubt wurden* (Munich 1995), 35ff.

13. Hannu Heikkilä, *The Question of European Reparations in Allied Policy 1943–1947* (Helsinki 1988), 29ff.

14. Report "Über die Industrie im von der Roten Armee besetzten Teil Deutschlands," 14 February 1945 in Russian Center for the Preservation and Research on Documents of Contemporary History (in the following RTsKhIDNI) 17/125/320: 26–29. The titles of the Russian documents cited in notes 14, 18–22, 24 and 29 have been translated into German.

15. Knyschewskij, *Moskaus Beute*, 44–45.

16. Jörg Fisch, *Reparationen nach dem 2. Weltkrieg* (Munich, 1992), 69ff.

17. *Dokumente zur Deutschlandpolitik*, 2nd ed., Vol. 1/3 (Kriftel, 1992), 2112f.

18. "Bericht über die Ausfuhr von Ausrüstungen und Material aus deutschen Betrieben," 20 April 1945, in Russian State Archive for Economics (in the following RGAE), 1562/329/1771: 203–4.

19. "Bericht über Demontage und Ausfuhr von Beutebetrieben," 10 May 1945, in RGAE, 1562/329/1771: 161–162.

20. "Bericht über die Ausfuhr von Ausrüstungen und Material aus deutschen Betrieben," 1 July 1945, in RGAE, 1562/329/1771: 11–17.

21. "Bericht über die Ausfuhr von Ausrüstungen und Material aus deutschen und japanischen Betrieben," 1 January 1948, in RGAE, 1562/329/2579: 209–211. Of the total 4,647 enterprises removed to the USSR, 3,147 were located in the SBZ, 1,118 in Poland (formerly German territories), 219 in Austria, 16 in Hungary, 36 in Czechoslovakia, and 111 Japanese enterprises in Manchuria.

22. "Bericht des Bevollmächtigten des Sonderkommitees für Deutschland, Teil 1," 10 May 1947, in RGAE 1562/329/2155: 1–141.

23. Ibid., 10.

24. "Liste der im der SBZ in Deutschland demontierten und in die UdSSR ausgeführten Betriebe" (no date, fall 1946), in RGAE 1562/329/2150: 1–461.

25. Mikojan to Berija, 6 June 1946, in GA RF, R-5446/48a/298: 65–61.

26. Jochen Laufer, "Das Problem der deutschen Reparationen in den Beziehungen der vier Besatzungsmächte," *Die Welt nach dem Ost-West Konflikt*, ed. M. Robbe and Dieter Senghaas (Berlin, 1990), 59–73.

27. See General Konstantin I. Koval', *Poslednij Svidetel. "Germanskaja Karta" v cholodnoj vojne* (Moscow, 1997).

28. Interview with K. I. Koval' from 18 June 1992 by the author.

29. "Bericht über die Beratung der Präsidenten und Vizepräsidenten der Länder und Provinzen sowie der Leiter der Zentralverwaltungen der SBZ, " 14 November 1945, in Archive for Foreign Affairs of the Russian Federation (in the following: AVP RF), 0457/1/2/7: 5–29.

30. Only the drafts are available in AVP RF, 6/8/32/500: 30–59. The date of the order is noted in a report from Semenov to Molotov on 5 March 1946 (see AVP RF, 06/8/32/501: 22).

31. The orders 124 and 126 are published in Minsterium für Auswärtige Angelegenheiten der DDR, ed., *Um ein antifaschistisch-demokratisches Deutschland. Dokumente aus den Jahren 1945–1949* (Berlin, 1968), 189–92 and 194–96.

32. Tillmann Bezzenberger, "Wie das Volkseigentum geschaffen wurde. Die Unternehmensenteignungen in der Sowjetischen Besatzungszone 1945–1948," *Zeitschrift für neuere Rechtsgeschichte* 19/3 (1997): 177–92.

33. Vladimir S. Semenov to V. D. Sokolvskii and F. E. Bokov, 21 May 1946, in AVP RF 0457/a/2/3/3: 3–5.

34. Winfried Halder, "Der Volksentscheid in Sachsen 1946," *Wirtschaftspolitik und Wirtschaftsplanung in Deutschland 1933–1993*, ed. Jürgen Schneider and Wolfgang Harbrecht (Stuttgart, 1996), 105–38.

35. Viacheslav M. Molotow, *Fragen der Außenpolitik. Reden und Erklärungen, April 1945–Juni 1948* (Moscow, 1949).

36. Bank closures in Berlin resulted from Order No. 1 of the Head of the Occupation of Berlin from 28 April 1945 in: G. Kohlmey and Ch. Dewey, *Bankensystem und Geldumlauf in der DDR 1945–1955. Gesetzessammlung und Einführung* (Berlin, 1956), 115.

37. Kurt Schmalfuß, *Die Entwicklung des Bankwesens in der Deutschen Demokratischen Republik (1945–1961)* (Diss. Berlin East, 1984), 101–3.

38. Vladimir Petrov, *Money and Conquest. Allied Occupation Currencies in World War II* (Baltimore, 1967), 172ff.

39. Schmalfuß, *Entwicklung des Bankwesens*, 21.

40. Günther Mai, *Der Alliierte Kontrollrat in Deutschland 1945–1948. Alliierte Einheit – deutsche Teilung?* (Munich, 1995), 258.

41. Order No. 01 of the Commander in Chief of SVAG from 23 July 1945, published in Kohlmey and Dewey, *Bankensystem und Geldumlauf*, 115–18.

42. See Jochen Laufer, "Zur Politik der UdSSR in der deutschen Währungsfrage 1944 bis 1948," *Vierteljahrshefte für Zeitgeschichte* 46 (1998): 455–85.

43. *Dokumente und Materialien zur Geschichte der deutschen Arbeiterbewegung, Reihe III* (Berlin,1959), 399.

44. Sokolovskij to Molotov, 17 May 1946, in AVP RF 082/30/130/32: 46–50.

45. Tarchov, "Zur finanziellen Lage in der SBZ" (no date, before 8 June 1946), AVP RF 07/11/13/177: 18–30.

46. Semenov to Vyshinskij, 8 June 1946, AVP RF 07/11/13/177: 15–17.

47. For the proposal from 15 November 1945 see OMGUS-ACA, 2/121–2/10–17, DFIN/P (45)42.

48. Zverev to Motolov, 21 March 1946, AVP RF 082/30/130/32: 20.

49. Draft of a decree from Zverev to Sokolovskij, 21 March 1946, AVP RF 082/30/130/32: 21. Behind this proposal were Soviet-American contacts which intensified when US specialists charged with preparing a currency reform arrived in Germany on 6 March 1946. Cf. Wolfram Hoppenstedt, *Gerhard Colm. Leben und Werk* (Stuttgart, 1997), 194–205.

50. Sokolovskij to Molotov, 17 May 1946, AVP RF 082/30/130/32: 46–50.

51. Ibid. Sokolovskij was sent a version of the American proposals as well.

52. Zverev to Molotov, 3 June 1946, AVP RF 07/11/13/177: 13–14.

53. Martynov, "Bericht zur Frage der Durchführung einer Finanzreform in Deutschland," 1 January 1947, AVP RF 082/30/131/33: 117–20.

54. Zverev and Maletin to Molotov, 1 January 1947, AVP RF 06/9/48/704: 7–13.

55. Ibid.

56. Order of the Head of SVAG No. 37 from 19 February 1947, printed in Kohlmey and Dewey, *Bankensystem*, 128–29.

57. Josef Deckers, *Die Transformation des Bankensystems in der sowjetischen Besatzungszone/DDR von 1945 bis 1952* (Berlin, 1974), 72.

58. Jochen Laufer, "Auf dem Wege zur staatlichen Verselbständigung der SBZ. Neue Quellen zur Geschichte der Münchener Konferenz der Ministerpräsidenten," *Historische DDR-Forschungen, Aufsätze und Studien*, ed. Jürgen Kocka (Berlin, 1993): 27–56.

59. Geoffrey K. Roberts, "Moscow and the Marshall Plan: Politics, Ideology and the Onset of the Cold War, 1947" *Europe-Asia Studies* 46 (1994), No. 8: 1371–86.

60. Giuliano Procacci, ed. *The Cominform. Minutes of the Three Conferences 1947–1949* (Milan 1994).

61. Gribanov to Orlov, 13 September 1947, AVP RF 082/34/150/40: 29–30.

62. Zverev to Molotov, 20 September 1947, AVP RF 06/9/48/704: 34–35.

63. Semenov and Sokolovskij to Molotov, 16 November 1947, AVP RF 082/34/150/40: 31–33.

64. Decree of the Soviet Council of Ministers, No. 3983–1357ss, 10 December 1947 regarding the creation of a German Issuing Bank.

65. The creation of the "German Issuing and Savings Bank" in the SBZ followed SVAG's Order No. 94 from 21 May 1948. See Frank Zschaler, "Von der Emissions- und Girobank zur deutschen Notenbank – Zu den Umständen der Gründung einer Staatsbank für Ostdeutschland," *Bankhistorisches Archiv. Zeitschrift für Bankgeschichte* 2 (1992): 59ff.

66. Meeting of the Politburo on 6 January 1948, Point 53: "Regarding the Reorganization of the Economic Commission in the SBZ." RTsKhIDNI, f. 17, op. 3, d. 1068. This decision formed the basis of SVAG Order No. 32 issued on 12 February 1948.

67. Christoph Buchheim, "Die Währungsreform 1948 in Westdeutschland," *Vierteljahrshefte für Zeitgeschichte* 36 (1988): 208.

68. OMGUS–ACA 2/108–3/5, CONL/M (48): 2.

69. Frank Zschaler, "Die vergessene Währungsreform. Vorgeschichte, Durchführung und Ergebnisse der Geldumstellung in der SBZ 1948," *Vierteljahrshefte für Zeitgeschichte* 45 (1997): 204. Refers to an undated note from Pieck (early 1948); see German Federal Archives, SAPMO NY 4036/690: 35–41.

70. Printed in *Um ein antifaschistisch-demokratisches Deutschland*, 659–66.

71. Printed in Kohlmey and Dewey, *Bankensystem*, 201–9.

72. Molotov to Stalin, 14 May 1948, AVP RF 06/10/42/560: 2.

73. Sokolovskij to Molotov, 23 December 1947. AVP RF 07/21z/44/8: 1–7. Refers to a directive from Molotov not yet found.

74. The preparations for the new currency were introduced on the basis of a decision made by the Soviet Council of Ministers on 7 May 1948. Only one-third of the new notes were ready by mid-June. Kosygin to Molotov 25 June 1948, AVP RF 06/10/41/559: 2.

75. On 22 June 1948 the newspaper *Neues Deutschland* headlined "Im Osten keine neuen Banknoten" to declare: "The Eastern zone has not prepared a currency reform. The zone's sound financial and economic policies have defused the urgency of such an issue. Therefore the East does not have any prepared notes, while new notes were delivered to the West from America months ago."

76. First clues could be found in *Neues Deutschland* on 20th June under the headline "Jetzt in der Ostzone und Berlin".

77. The coupons were differently shaped and colored for the different banknotes from 1 to 100 Mk. 1,000 mark notes were not pasted with coupons.

78. "Westmächte vollenden Spaltung Deutschlands," *Neues Deutschland*, 19 June 1948, 1.

79. Ibid, 30 June 1948.

80. Schmalfuß, "Entwicklung des Bankwesens," 86.

81. Zschaler, "Vergessene Währungsreform," 220.

82. Molotov remembered: "They [the Western powers] were naturally bitter towards us, but we had to hold on to and strengthen what we had gained. We had to make a part of Germany our socialist Germany, and as to Czechoslovakia, Poland, Hungary, and Yugoslavia, these countries were in a chaotic state. We had to create order and get rid of the capitalist order. That was the 'Cold War.'" Feliks Chuev, *Sto sorok besed s Molotovym* (Moscow, 1991), 86.

83. Wolfgang Weißleder, "Die Gründung der Deutschen Wirtschaftskommission: Zentrale Staatsorgane der antifaschistisch-demokratischen Ordnung auf dem Wege zum Zweijahrplan," *Jahrbuch für Wirtschaftsgeschichte* 4 (1977): 62.

CHAPTER 5

FOREIGN INFLUENCES ON THE DICTATORIAL DEVELOPMENT OF THE GDR, 1949–1955

Michael Lemke

GDR scholars have not yet adequately examined the extent to which the East German dictatorship was influenced by external factors, nor have they fully explored the role which such factors played in the formation of the regime, or their influence on society and the state in general. Instead, in both more general works describing conditions in the GDR, and more specific studies focusing on the definition and particular nature of East German rule, scholarship has addressed endogenous, rather than exogenous factors. While some authors have raised the question of the *implanted* nature of the GDR dictatorship, the issue has not yet been sufficiently examined or theorized.[1] This deficit may be related to the fact that "classical" definitions of dictatorship and totalitarianism largely exclude external factors.[2] But theories about societies, not necessarily dictatorial by nature and yet influenced by external forces, could provide new insights.[3]

Any consideration of how foreign factors influenced dictatorial rule raises a methodological problem, since scholars must first unravel theoretically what in practice is a complex web of both internal and external factors. Generally, external factors only gain political relevance when they find internal expression within any given system. Foreign policy functions as a mediator in this process, allowing internal and external factors to meet and interact. It serves as "the ensemble of all activities reaching beyond sovereign

borders by which the state – or other organizations operating at an
international level – protects its interests or follows certain
goals...."[4] Obviously the term "foreign policy" presupposes some
degree of independent agency, and can only conditionally reflect
the influence of foreign factors. These are defined as those external
conditions facing any given state. Sovereign and internally strong
states are usually less susceptible to foreign influences than weak
states that in comparison have little influence on international
events. Helga Haftendorn has distinguished between dependent
and autonomous systems. "An autonomous system masters international challenges by asserting its own goals and values; it influences other systems so that these respect its goals and values or
come to terms with them; a dependent system is forced to follow a
strategy of constant accommodation." The autonomy of any system
indicates the amount of freedom it enjoys in the sphere of foreign
relations – the degree of dependence is determined by the interplay
between international and domestic demands.[5]

After 1949 the GDR was – similar to the Federal Republic – technically an independent state, but it was neither externally sovereign,
nor did it enjoy internal independence. In comparison to the FRG –
which due to economic and social developments began to achieve
domestic stability after 1951 and gradually gained autonomy on the
international scene – the GDR remained a weak state, subjected to
the external influences that such weakness implied. Yet the GDR –
and the SED – did possess some "basic interests" like other states,
concerning political independence, economic protection and "freedom from outside intervention" that must be contrasted with the
limited means which the state possessed to achieve them.[6] At stake
was not only the question of whether such basic interests were compatible with the foreign policy goals of the Soviet Union, but whether
they stood in conflict with the interests of other international forces,
particularly those opposed to the GDR's existence.

In order to secure that existence, after 1949 the SED was forced
to counter such oppositional forces, either alone or with outside
assistance. Because the only available support could be obtained
from the USSR, the SED became highly dependent on the Soviets,
and had to accept Russian definitions of East German interests as
well as Moscow's interpretation of the degree of its autonomy. But
the party was willing to make these concessions, not only because
it saw the USSR as a guarantor of the GDR's precarious existence
and of its own power but also because there were very few alternatives open to it on the international scene. Particularly in the
period from 1949 to about the mid-1950s, SED strategy can best be
described as what James Rosenau has termed "acquiescent adap-

tion,"[7] in which the GDR largely conformed to the demands placed on it by the Soviet Union. In the final analysis the state replaced external with internal dependence.

The following essay will attempt to describe briefly the role of Sovietization and illuminate the effect of Soviet and Western influences on the development of the GDR dictatorship through specific examples from the period 1950-53. Because Jochen Laufer has analyzed this topic in the previous chapter, the extent of Soviet influence during military occupation and possible continuities with later periods will not be discussed here.[8] In general, two hypotheses apply to the period in question and will be discussed in detail below.

1. The development of the GDR and the SED occurred within an international system that owed its existence to the Second World War and was determined by such elements as the East-West conflict, the Cold War, bipolarism, block-building, and open confrontation. The "special German confrontation" reflected the general characteristics of the Cold War as a particular phase in the East-West antagonism, while containing specific German elements that were introduced into the global conflict. These in turn had a decisive influence on developments in post-war Europe.

2. The SED's politics during the period in question were largely dominated on the one hand by the Soviet Union's role as occupying, hegemonial, and leading power and on the other hand by the Federal Republic's role as a strong, democratically legitimized German state. Together both states were the main determinants of the GDR's inner development which attempted to follow its own interests and goals in the contested field of Soviet and West German politics. East German interests generally coincided with the power and hegemonial goals of the Soviet Union, while the interests of the "ruling classes" in both German states conflicted in principle. Although Soviet influence tended to have a stabilizing effect, the existence of West Germany threatened the SED's system of rule. Soviet factors were on the whole fundamental, definitive and defining, whereas West Germany exerted only a corrective and modifying influence. The extent and intensity of foreign influence depended on international relations in general as well as various bilateral and multilateral interactions.

The Pattern of Sovietization

The most important means which the USSR had at its disposal to influence post-war East Germany was the Sovietization of the entire society – the application of Soviet political and social models to practically all areas of life. Although the process of Sovietization lacked uniformity and developed at an uneven pace, it included both external and internal factors. These could work in tandem or in opposition, as aids or hindrances, and with planned and unexpected consequences.[9] Some of the measures carried out by the Soviets included land reform, the dismantling and dispossession of manufacturing facilities, the imposition of a planned economy, the transformation of the state apparatus along Soviet lines (including the state security system), the abolition of bourgeois forms of justice, the installation of an "antifascist–democratic" school system, the creation of a party cadre system, and other control mechanisms.

But not all developments were merely Sovietization. The USSR also influenced East German society in its role as an occupying power. The Soviet Control Commission in Germany (SCC) and other Soviet administrative organs formed a kind of "supra-government" in control of developments in the GDR. Together they oversaw the Sovietization process and managed the application of "pure" administrative directives. Nonetheless, any analysis of Soviet influence has to proceed from the fact that both the USSR and the GDR (to a lesser degree) were dependent on each other. The Soviets were in need of East German services, particularly in matters relating to the fate of Germany.

Generally, Sovietization after 1949 had an ambivalent relationship to the "German question," both as a symbol for and against a united Germany. On the one side a sovietized East Germany could serve as the core of a reunited Germany – reunited around the concept of an "antifascist-democratic" state. Soviet rulers still considered such a unification possible, particularly with the help of a "popular front" in the West. On the other side, increased Sovietization also translated into increased independence for the East, especially when unification seemed an increasingly unrealistic goal.

The "German question" was an existential issue for the SED. The seeming inability to "solve" it within the context of the Cold War was also a general pre-condition for the existence of the GDR, and in the years immediately following 1949 perhaps even its most important means of survival. Its unsolved nature also possessed an instrumental function for both the SED and the USSR. As a very important domestic issue that at the same time affected all Germans, the "German question" could have been a stabilizing factor in the GDR due to its patriotic appeal, if the SED had been able to realize its claims to speak for the entire German nation. Particularly during the German "year of destiny," 1952, Communist leaders in the East were acutely aware of the fact that whoever succeeded in the inner-German conflict would set the agenda for the entire nation. Conscious of the repercussions of their decisions on West Germany, the SED and CPSU leaders were therefore aware that Soviet influences on the GDR would have indirect consequences on questions related to Germany's fate. Hence questions about the undesired effects of Sovietization not only affected GDR politics, but the future of the "German question" as well.

Although Sovietization also occurred in other Eastern block countries, it took a particular form in the GDR, especially in the face of the "Americanization" or "Westernization" of the Federal Republic.[10] Information about changes and events in the West was only available through GDR media and informal communication channels. The West's transformation also deeply affected East German society, albeit through the prism of the inner-German conflict and through the lens of specific interests. The most direct consequence of this development in the GDR was an increased desire for cultural entertainment and consumer goods. The fact that these needs could not be met resulted in a great degree of unhappiness in many social groups in East Germany. The SED attempted to curb these influences and to strengthen and popularize its own image in the Federal Republic. This "exchange" at the ideological level was not dialogic, but confrontational. It was carried out by ruling groups in both states who wished to maximize their respective influence within the opposing state, while minimizing the effects of the other side's propaganda within their own system. The result was a confrontation between the processes of "Sovietization" and "Americanization" as two competing strands of German identity in the post-war period.[11] Both influenced the two German states to varying degrees, and both were "translated" by different segments of society and various political forces in widely disparate ways, all of which were marked by a combination of the foreign and the familiar. The SED used this symbiosis particularly in the political arena, which could be easily influenced at an administrative level. It was there that Soviet directives could mesh with the bureaucratic methods of East German interests to stabilize and further SED rule. By modifying the Soviet model and combining it with more national elements, the SED state hoped to win the support of its own populace.

The transfer and adaptation of Soviet ideology, from Marxist–Leninist teachings to Stalinist dogma, played an important role in the process of Sovietization. Particularly in the years of 1953 to 1954, the personality cult around Stalin determined the nature and course of dictatorial processes in the GDR. Stalin did not just represent the Soviet Union, he embodied it – he *was* the Soviet Union. His cult, originally formulated as a means of ruling the masses, became over time a goal in and of itself. Stalin's word was law; it confirmed and contradicted, damned, punished, and rewarded – *ex cathedra*. Stalin was all-powerful and all-knowing.

Ideological Determination from the Outside

The Soviet "doctrine" of the two "opposing camps" (1947) helped to create a sort of "theory" to explain the Cold War. Although carried out and escalated by both sides, the Cold War was mainly instigated by the Stalinist system in the USSR, since its inner turmoil provided one of the conflict's most important causes. This raises the question of whether the transfer of Stalinist ideology necessarily "infected" East German society with the "virus" of Soviet social and political confrontation, defined by unceasing "class warfare" and the inability to settle differences in a peaceful manner. But what sort of reception did Soviet proclivities – the rejection of democratic majority rule, consensus, and compromise – receive within the specific context of the East German state? Various principles could be derived from the Stalinist theory of opposing camps.

Stalin's prediction that the further development of socialism would lead to increased class warfare became one of the guiding principles of the GDR during the 1950s. To justify repressive measures against oppositional Social Democrats, non-conformist politicians in the "block parties," critical intellectuals, the Church, and private, independent farmers, the Politburo could brand them as extremely dangerous "class enemies."[12] For instance, Fred Oelßner used Stalin's "doctrine" to defend calls for a repressive course aimed at East German large landowners. "We are now living in a stage of development in which we can almost feel the increased tension in the countryside with our hands," he declared at a Central Committee meeting in October 1951. Farmers with large holdings had, in his words, "already declared war against us"; they were sabotaging democracy and needed to be isolated from the rest of society. According to Oelßner, the state had applied insufficient "methods of political force" in trying to achieve this aim.[13]

In the following years the SED leadership believed that "it is an indisputable fact that class warfare and enemy methods of terror in the countryside are continually on the rise."[14] Indeed, independent farmers were resisting the interventions of a state which accused them of working hand in glove with Western organizations to ruin East German agriculture. Time and again the state discovered "warning signs and indications" of increased subversive activities of "enemy groups" and repeated its calls to arm against supposed "economic saboteurs."[15] On the one hand, this psychosis, fueled by Soviet "doctrine," was a special expression of that Cold War climate in which the SED thought and acted and which developed a singular momentum and inner dynamic over time. On the other hand, Soviet dogma released repressive mechanisms which were less a result of international conflict than of the needs of the GDR dictatorship. Imported sentiments about the inevitability of intensified class warfare provided a political and moral basis for the system's repressive policies – counterrevolutionary forces "compelled" the state to take ever stricter measures.

Ideological dogmatism created a new political reality, since it meant that the state had to underscore the importance of an effective security system which saw a tremendous expansion after 1950.[16] It also found expression in the tightening of East German criminal codes, such as the draconian "Law regarding the protecting of inner German trade,"[17] and influenced the GDR judicial system, in the establishment of which Stalin was supposed to have exercised "decisive assistance."[18] The doctrine of opposing camps also formed the basis of SED policies aimed at intimidating oppositional and non-conformist forces within society. Terror and the threat of repressive measures had great preventative effects, but the dogma of opposing camps was also instrumentalized to legitimate "punitive actions" carried out between 1949 and 1954, especially against "the bourgeoisie."[19]

The supporters and apologists of the opposing camps theory associated the term "class warfare" with confrontations between internal and external enemies. While internal and external counter-revolutionary forces might differ, in Communist thought and practice they were one and the same thing. Communist conspiracy theory played an essential role in the construction of various associations or plots.

The opposing camps theory gained an additional element of danger through its connection with the "purges" in the Soviet satellite states between 1949 and 1953. With the "show trials," directed mainly at leading party functionaries in Czechoslovakia, Hungary, Bulgaria, and Rumania, Stalin enforced the "coordination" of the Communist party and its leaders in the different states, and the establishment of political control from afar. Party discipline and the practice of terror also hit the SED, which saw a "cleansing" war waged against such enemies as "Titoism," "Social Democracy," or suspected "appeasers." But in the GDR these purges were less bloody and terrorist than in the other Eastern block countries, if also less thorough.[20]

The SED leadership, forced always to consider reactions in the Federal Republic, carried out its "class war" more on an ideological level, which also included some repression. Especially active in the areas of art and culture, the party led a campaign against the threatening influence of "cosmopolitanism," "formalism," and "Americanism." Although some impulses in this matter still originated with Stalin, little assistance from Moscow was needed, once the purges were underway. The SED seemed more than willing to out-trump its "master." Thus Ulbricht sharply criticized "American forms of architecture, which are foreign to our national culture," and "formalistic set design [in the theater] created under the reactionary influence of America."[21] The elimination of "Western, decadent" influences was intended to be constructive in a certain way – art and culture of the Soviet Union were a better alternative, while Soviet science "had long since surpassed the science of the capitalist countries."[22]

The doctrine of opposing camps thus provided an enemy image and a positive role model. And practice seemed to bear out Stalinist principles. Repressive measures called forth reactions directed against the state – flight to the West, passive resistance, desperate acts, among many others. Resistance in turn resulted in new repression and a fatal vicious cycle, which was additionally charged by external factors. Finally, the SED leadership viewed any attempt to promote integration with the West as another step in class warfare.[23] In general this form of foreign influence (in the shape of ideological premises) in combination with other factors had a profound impact on the internal development of dictatorial rule in East Germany, especially in regards to the increased weight of ideology and brutality within the state security system.

The Soviet Directives of 1952

The Soviet political directives of 1952 are a prominent example of how foreign factors influenced the internal development of the GDR. The context in which they were issued was marked by international, inter-German, but also internal factors. On 25 March 1952, the Western powers rejected the Soviet offer of 10 March, which had promised the re-unification of Germany at the price of political neutrality. In response, they demanded that free elections be held in all of Germany. The USSR reacted with a new note delivered to the Western powers on 9 April. In the interim, Wilhelm Pieck, Otto Grotewohl and Walter Ulbricht carried out talks with the Politburo in Moscow. Perhaps they already had similar plans, but Stalin made the announcement that the GDR would have to create its own army and establish agricultural cooperatives.[24] This Moscow directive was certainly also a reaction to the rejection of the Soviet note from 10

March. The failure of the plan to neutralize Germany and hinder the Western integration of the FRG – which would ultimately mean the reduction of American influence in Central Europe – increased Soviet security concerns. At the same time, the directive set the stage for the development of socialism in the GDR, which was proclaimed in July of the same year at the SED's Second Party Congress.

The Moscow decisions resulted in a further wave of Sovietization. They not only led to the creation of a "people's army" and of agriculture collectives, but also to the abolition of the previous states of the GDR, the creation of a centralized administration along Soviet lines, and the tightening of border controls towards West Germany.[25] On 11 April 1952 the Politburo released "Measures against profiteering" and announced "some public trials directed at groups of bandits from West Berlin and West Germany."[26] The meshing of ideological doctrine with political directives was obvious. Following Stalin, Grotewohl announced his belief that "in the future there will be a sharp increase in class warfare," from outside, rather than from within. He announced internally the goals of the repressive measures and show trials on 1 August 1952: "We have not organized these show trials just for sheer pleasure, but because we want to show the public just exactly what is happening. This is a learning process to illuminate the increasing dangers of class warfare and our need for further vigilance."[27] By punishing certain individuals, the SED leaders attempted to warn the public and by creating a public enemy they also hoped to mobilize elements within their own party.

Initiated, ordered, or approved by Soviet *ukas*, these reforms fundamentally altered the structures of East German society. Two of the most important measures were the abolition of the private sector in industrial production – "people owned factories" were to make up 81 percent of all facilities by the end of 1952 (in 1950 it was 73.1 percent) – and the collectivization of agricultural production.[28] Also significant was the systematic elimination of private retail trade.[29] The state supplemented these transformations with new repressive measures against large landowners, who were accused of sabotaging attempts to feed the populace, resulting in calls from the SCC to punish them.[30] In addition, those GDR companies whose owners lived in the West were systematically taken over.[31] All of these measures – and particularly those dealing with security – were strictly controlled by the SCC.[32]

The creation of an East German army was another "problem area" for GDR socialism. Although there had been secret plans as early as 1950 to begin to arm certain sections of the police and the Ministry for State Security (the SCC armed them with captured

German weapons),[33] Ulbricht had repeatedly declared that there
would never be "any sort of remilitarization."[34] But faced with the
threat of West German rearmament, the SED felt that the East German populace, and particularly pacifist youth in the East, had to be
convinced that rearming was necessary to "protect the accomplishments" of the GDR. East German youths were to be prepared for
their new tasks through participation in a paramilitary "Service for
Germany." In order to make rearmament more palatable, the Politburo cloaked its demands for the creation of "national troops" in
nationalist rhetoric, deeming them "the foundation of the sovereignty and independence of every state."[35]

Another difficulty with the rapid creation of the armed forces
was the need for barracks and housing.[36] In a secret document from
1952, party leadership pointed out that the arming of troops
demanded "particularly valuable raw materials such as alloyed
steel, steel refiners, light metals and alloys, rubber and other chemical raw materials, fuel, textiles," and much more. "Cadres" with the
necessary skills were also needed for weapons production. The
Party leaders anticipated yet a further problem: the creation of the
army would entail using resources valued at 500 million DM (not
including foodstuffs) that would "need to be taken away from other
consumers."[37] The Moscow directive therefore had a high price for
the GDR. It resulted in an enormous burden on the state's finances,
because the systematic creation of armed forces for 1952–53 had
not been planned in the budget, which meant that funds had to be
taken away from other projects. It also required removing of qualified specialists from the civilian sector and using them in military
service or the armaments industry. The transfer of graduates to military units also sorely hindered the creation of social elites.

On 1 July 1952 the party leadership ordered all offices not to
place young men between 18 and 24 years of age in industrial
positions, but rather to "release" them for service as barracked
police troops (an early form of the planned people's army). They
were also instructed to instigate a "broad campaign" directed at the
nation's young women, "to learn an industrial career, so that they
can replace the young male workers in the factories."[38] This directive greatly strengthened the trend towards employing women in
the economy, particularly in industrial jobs. Since the weak and
underdeveloped GDR economy was also burdened by the demands
of continued reparation payments to the Soviets, which had a negative effect on the trade balance, GDR society was headed towards
an acute crisis situation.[39] Although the difficulties were largely
social and economic in nature, they quickly involved Sovietization
as well. The Korean War contributed to the prevailing sense of

urgency, resulting in renewed fears of war in both the East and the West, which were only intensified by East German rearmament.

Stalin apparently reckoned with an unavoidable military confrontation with the West. He informed the writer Konstantin Simonow, a Central Committee representative at the 19th Party Congress of the CPSU, that a "difficult battle with the capitalist camp" loomed on the horizon. "Fear and hesitancy, weakness and capitulation [are] the most dangerous things in this battle."[40] The aging dictator ordered an increase in armaments production for the entire area of Soviet influence, at the expense of consumer goods.[41] This increased the disparities in GDR production and created a new, unfulfillable demand for energy and raw materials, especially steel. Meeting this need required speeding up the erection of blast furnaces on the Oder (Stalinstadt), and siphoning off already limited investment funds from other projects. The dictatorial nature of Soviet politics was instrumental in aggravating a basic deficit in the GDR's economy – the lack of investments.[42] Overall, the second half of 1952 was marked by a "war communism" that had a negative effect on the living standards of wide segments of GDR society. The SED seemed unable to recognize the growing sense of dissatisfaction in the populace, or incapable of understanding the reasons for such discontent. That is the sole explanation for measures that only served to further worsen conditions. For instance, the party attempted to relieve foodstuff shortages by suspending rationing for certain groups, which did not relieve the situation and only created new frustrations.[43]

The West as Catalyst

At the same time as the GDR slid towards a state of crisis, West Germany began to increase its influence on the development of East Germany's party, state and populace. Whereas 166,000 people had fled from the East in 1951, in 1952 the number rose to 182,000.[44] Since the beginning of the so-called "Korea boom," the FRG's economy developed at a rapid pace during the second half of 1952, and increases in salaries led to an improved standard of living for many people.[45] In addition to these positive developments, social and political reforms, such as the recognition of workers' codetermination in the coal industry (1951) supported such trends. At the same time the parliamentary system of the FRG was beginning to prove itself, even if it did not yet function as smoothly as possible. In any case it was accepted by the majority of the population. In short, the West was increasingly stabilizing itself, while the East was becoming rapidly destabilized.

During this internal radicalization and dissolution, prompted by
Soviet directives, large sections of the GDR populace turned to the
alternative offered by West Germany as they had not done before
1952. Now the FRG became the yardstick not only for the masses
in the East, but also for the SED and its leaders as well. Thereafter,
West Germany sat at the conference table of the Politburo in East
Berlin as a "silent guest." No decision was made that did not consider how the West would react, or rather, what domestic consequences such a reaction would have for the SED. Particularly in
daily life, Western patterns of behavior determined consumption,
culture, art, and fashion for many East Germans.[46] Sovietization
"from above" now had to compete with Western influence "from
below."[47] The propagation of Soviet values, culture and ideals, as
well as an increased use of force could not effectively halt such
Westernization. After 1952 the repressive elements of Sovietization and SED rule took center stage, reinforcing the sense of help-
lessness among those ruled.

In this process the open border to West Berlin and its role as a
"showcase" of Western culture functioned as a catalyst. In 1952–53
the Western portion of the city offered not just a doorway for flight
but also a chance to enjoy something new, and to leave GDR existence behind at least for a few hours. Especially threatening for the
SED was the combination of the Western portion of the city and
East German youth, who crossed the border in hordes. To stop such
movement, sanctions were the only possibility. Ulbricht declared in
June 1952, "Every young person at a university or any other kind
of school will be immediately expelled if he has connections with
West Berlin. Whoever is a member of the state youth organization
will be kicked out of the FDJ....There is no other way."[48]

But the influence of the Federal Republic in the East cannot be
reduced to mere "magnetic attraction" or Westernization of the
GDR "from below." The government of the FRG maintained its
right to speak for all Germans – and to speak for the rights of East
German citizens – in Germany and internationally. Western politicians worked hard against any and all attempts to support or
strengthen the GDR that would lead to recognition of the regime in
the "Soviet zone," as they called the GDR.

Although the Federal Republic did not systematically or mili-
tantly plan the fall of the SED dictatorship, which they viewed as a
Soviet protectorate, the Bonn government did support or tolerate
Western organizations, groups and individuals who sought to
oppose or overthrow the regime. Adenauer's government made no
secret of its goal to remove the GDR dictatorship by holding free
elections. The SED viewed such actions as a form of annexation. In

addition, the American ban on the export of strategically important West German goods that might travel through the East to the Soviet Union strained German trade relationships. In the eyes of the SED such a prohibition was discriminatory and would only harm the German economy.[49] New GDR sanctions against "profiteers and speculators" only escalated what had become a kind of economic warfare. Targeted were those individuals who exchanged East German marks for Western currency or those who transported Eastern products and materials to West Berlin in order to trade them for "hard" currency.[50] To defend the East against Western ideology, the Politburo initiated more stringent controls on receiving Western radio stations. "Those who listen to RIAS or NWDR are lending their ears to war-mongers and opening their homes to the worst enemies of our people."[51]

Even when they were not directly ordered, these and other activities were recommended and controlled by the SCC. This observation especially applies to the Western policies of the SED and their East German partners. Despite the fact that such propaganda and infiltration were very complicated and expensive, which only further strapped the state's finances, they were stepped up in the wake of the Soviet directives. These demanded new steps aimed at "Adenauer's fall," which were less effective and therefore more aggressive than ever before.[52]

Thus West German and Soviet influences were the main external factors that determined developments in the GDR. Together they formed two sides of a dialectic relationship that was accompanied by yet other foreign factors, such as international and bilateral relationships. In June 1953, the acute system problems of the GDR culminated in a popular revolt which had developed as a crisis of Sovietization or Stalinization in the previous year. The crisis led to an explosion, but it was in no manner resolved, since all the causes for its occurrence still remained thoroughly entrenched.

Implications of Outside Influence

The period from 1949 to 1954 – the phase of intensive Stalinization in the GDR – is prototypical for the way in which foreign factors interacted with internal conditions within the SED dictatorship. The examination of a period of Sovietization and the analysis of certain examples from ideology and politics, shows the influence of foreign factors on the formation of the GDR dictatorship in this its perhaps "purest" form. Key questions asked in what manner Soviet factors were capable of influencing the nature of dictatorship in East Germany, helped form its basic features or were relevant to its definition. This analysis of important elements of Sovietization, the USSR's ideological influence on the GDR in the years following 1950 and of Moscow's directives in 1952 has underscored the significant weight that external factors possessed in the dictatorial penetration of state and society in the GDR.

Eastern, but also Western, influences in the wake and atmosphere of the Cold War had their greatest impact on the formation of repressive measures that took on terrorist features during the Stalinist phase of the development of GDR dictatorship. It can be considered proven that Soviet developments had a significant influence on the GDR, particularly in the shaping of administrative structures, the expansion of the state security system, and the methods and perpetuation of party rule. Affected were not only those images of scapegoats and the dogmas of class warfare that dominated public discourse, but also the disproportionalities in economic investments and the subordination of economics to politics. In this regard, attempts to close society to the West were as important as the militarization of society, which also had its origins in Soviet directives.

But in the end such results still leave us with the question of whether or not these significant foreign influences actually had long-term consequences for the GDR, and if so, what these entailed. It is not clear if these factors only determined initial variables or whether they created patterns that had a lasting influence on methods of rule. The question of how much and how long such repression, forced or provoked from the outside, determined the nature of rule in the GDR and in which way it contributed to its becoming accepted as normal needs to be further addressed. We also need to consider if such factors were systematized, codified, or removed altogether. Such a definition of a dictatorship of limited autonomy, subordinated to foreign factors, can also be helpful for research that concentrates on later periods of GDR history. A characterization of the GDR in this period as a communist dictatorship along Soviet lines remains, therefore, open to discussion.

Notes

1. See Detlev Pollack's contribution in this volume for theoretical insights into this problem.
2. Works by Hannah Arendt and Carl Joachim Friedrich, for instance, do not consider this aspect.
3. Wolfram Hanrieder defines a system as "penetrated" when foreign events are the determining factor of the political order as well as the mobilizing factors in

support of this order. See Wolfram Hanrieder, *West German Foreign Policy* (Stanford, 1967), 230. James N. Rosenau argues that external penetration of a state presupposes the cooperation of its elites and acquiescence of the ruled. See James N. Rosenau, *The Scientific Study of Foreign Policy*, 2nd ed. (London, 1980), 137–69.

4. Wilhelm G. Grewe, *Machtprojektionen und Rechtsschranken. Essays aus vier Jahrzehnten über Verfassungen, politische Systeme und internationale Strukturen* (Baden-Baden, 1991), 415; and Helga Haftendorn, "Außenpolitische Prioritäten und Handlungsspielraum. Ein Paradigma zur Analyse der Außenpolitik der Bundesrepublik Deutschland," *Politische Vierteljahresschrift* 30 (1989): 32–49.

5. Helga Haftendorn, "Die Alliierten Vorbehaltsrechte und die Außenpolitik der Bundesrepublik Deutschland. Eine Einführung," in *"...die volle Macht eines souveränen Staates..." Die Alliierten Vorbehaltsrechte als Rahmenbedingung westdeutscher Außenpolitik 1949–1990* (Baden-Baden, 1996), 12f.

6. Gottfried H. Kindermann, "Außenpolitik im Widerstreit," *Internationale Politik* 9 (1997): 1.

7. James N. Rosenau, *The Study of Political Adaption* (New York, 1981), 56ff.

8. See Jochen Laufer's article in the present volume.

9. Michael Lemke, "Die Sowjetisierung der SBZ/DDR im ost-westlichen Spannungsfeld," *Aus Politik und Zeitgeschichte*, 1997, no. 6: 41–53.

10. Konrad H. Jarausch and Hannes Siegrist, eds, *Amerikanisierung und Sowjetisierung in Deutschland 1945–1970* (Frankfurt am Main, 1997).

11. Jarausch and Siegrist, "Amerikanisierung und Sowjetisierung. Eine vergleichende Fragestellung zur deutsch-deutschen Nachkriegsgeschichte," in ibid., 11–34.

12. Erhardt Neubert, *Geschichte der Opposition in der DDR 1949–1989* (Bonn, 1997), 55–59.

13. Conclusion at the 7th Congress of the SED's Central Committee, 18–20 October 1951, in Federal Archives, SAPMO, Zentrales Parteiarchiv DY 30, IV 2/1/49: 165f.

14. Minister of the Interior Maron to Ulbricht, 5 January 1954, in ibid., J IV 2/202/63.

15. Speech of the State Secretary for State Security Wollweber at the 21st Congress of the SED's Central Committee, 12–14 November 1954, in ibid., IV 2/1/67: 140.

16. Maron to Ulbricht, above. Maron demanded the creation of an "absolute system" of police "ready to strike" and therefore in need of 13,000 new recruits.

17. See proposal for a "Law for the protection of inner German trade," Supplement 1 to Protocol 101, 17 April 1950 in ibid., J IV 2/3/101: 7.

18. Report of an aide to the vice president of the highest court of the GDR, Benjamin 10 December 1951 in ibid, NY 4090/301: 138.

19. Neubert, *Geschichte*, 58.

20. Ulrich Mählert, "Schauprozesse und Parteisäuberungen in Osteuropa nach 1945," *Aus Politik und Zeitgeschichte*, 1996, no. 37: 44–46.

21. Manuscript of Ulbricht's speech for the First FDJ Functionary Conference, 26 November 1950, SAPMO, NY 4182/377.

22. Report from Ulbricht at the 10th Congress of the SED's Central Committee 20–22 November 1952, in ibid., DY 30, IV 2/1/56: 15.

23. See ibid., 45.

24. Copy of Pieck's handwritten note, plan of the meeting in Moscow, 7 April 1952, in ibid., NY 4036/696: 27. Cf. Michael Lemke, "Wer demontierte das zweite Gleis? Zum Realitätsgehalt der Wiedervereinigungskonzeptionen von

Bundesregierung und Führung der DDR," *asien, afrika, lateinamerika* 4 (1991): 630f.

25. "In the meeting of the Politburo from April 11, 1952 the following directive was taken as a basis," in SAPMO, NY 4036/657: 128.

26. See ibid.

27. Remarks from Grotewohl at the "Konferenz mit den Vorsitzenden und Sekretären der Räte der Bezirke," in ibid., NY 3090/401: 40.

28. Letter of the SED Politburo to Stalin, 1 June 1952, supplement 2 to protocol 118/52, meeting of the Politburo of 1 June 1952, in ibid., DY 30, J IV 2/2/218: 38.

29. From 44.2 percent (1951) to 32.5 percent (plan 1953). See the secret plan, "Die Sicherung der Durchführung des Fünfjahrplanes und der Aufbau der nationalen Streitkräfte der DDR," undated, likely Fall 1952, in ibid., NY 4090/473: 39.

30. SCC to the government of the GDR, 21 October 1952 in ibid., NY 4090/303: 161.

31. Politburo decision, protocol 129/52, meeting of 2 September 1952, in ibid., DY 30, J IV 2/2/129: 3.

32. SCC Materials, 22 December 1952, in ibid., J IV 2/202/62.

33. Semitschastnow, first representative of the head of SCC to the Minister for State Security Zaisser, 28 July 1950, in ibid., NY 4182/1194: 143, and Ulbricht to Tschuikow, head of the SCC, 9 August 1950, in ibid., 153.

34. Ulbricht's speech at the 6th Meeting of the Central Committee of the SED, 13–15 June 1951, in ibid., DY 30, IV 2/1/48: 9.

35. "Argumentation zu den hauptsächlichen Angriffen der Westpresse gegen die DDR," September 1952, in ibid., NY 4036/754: 8.

36. Situationsbericht of 8 November 1952, in ibid., NY 4090/449: 25.

37. "Die Sicherung," 44, 59.

38. Secret "Bericht der zentralen Kommission zur Werbung für die Volkspolizei," Appendix 4 to Protocol 188/52, Meeting of the Politburo on 1 July 1952, in ibid., DY 30, J IV 2/2/218: 24f.

39. Foreign trade was in a critical state in 1952, since the deficit reached 740 million rubles, and conditions were expected to worsen. See, *Die Sicherung*: 53f.

40. Konstantin Simonow, "Mit den Augen eines Menschen meiner Generation. Nachdenken über Stalin," *Sowjetliteratur* 6 (1989): 56.

41. See Peter Hübner, "Löhne und Normen. Soziale Spannungen im Vorfeld des 17. Juni 1953," in: *Brüche, Krisen, Wendepunkte. Neubefragung von DDR-Geschichte*, ed. Jochen Cerny (Berlin 1990), 123.

42. *Die Sicherung*, 43, 45.

43. Horst Barthel, "Die Versorgungskrise. Bevölkerungsversorgung und Systemstabilisierung im Umfeld des 17. Juni 1953," *Brüche*, 113.

44. Hübner, "Löhne," 120.

45. The Korean War triggered a demand for investment goods which gave West German industry an opportunity to resume higher production levels without restrictions.

46. See Stefan Merl, Gunilla-Friederike Budde, Uta G. Poiger and Siegried Lokatis, in Jarausch and Siegrist, *Amerikanisierung*.

47. Michael Lemke, "Deutschlandpolitik zwischen Sowjetisierung und Verwestlichung 1949–1963," in ibid., 94–99.

48. Ulbricht's final comments at a Conference of Regional Secretaries of the SED, 4 June 1952, in SAPMO, NY 4182/409.

49. "Thesen der SED zur Internationalen Wirtschaftskonferenz in Moskau," 3–12 April 1952, undated, in ibid., NY 4062/115: 38.

50. "Beschluß des Politbüros," protocol 79/53, meeting of 20 November 1953, in ibid., DY 30 J IV 2/2/333: 2.
51. "Kampagne und Maßnahmen gegen das Abhören des feindlichen Rundfunks und gegen die feindlichen Lügen- und Verleumdungskampagnen," Appendix 4 to Protocol 87/52, meeting of the Politburo on 15 January 1952, in ibid., J IV 2/2/187: 18.
52. See Pieck's notes regarding his meetings with unnamed members of the SCC, 20 October 1952, in ibid., NY 4036/736: 327.

CHAPTER 6

REPRESSION AND TOLERANCE AS METHODS OF RULE IN COMMUNIST SOCIETIES

Mario Keßler and Thomas Klein

Can one draw conclusions about the logic of communist societies by considering changes in such systems' methods of rule, particularly their specific blend of repression and tolerance? Both authors of the following article do not wish to underestimate the significance of such analyses. Yet we believe that they cannot suffice to explain how communist societies actually function. Neither totalitarian theories nor theories that distinguish different types of government can do such systems justice. And yet it is important to differentiate carefully between the various methods of rule which they employ. In this short essay we analyze two such methods, and consider what an examination of the changing forms of repression and tolerance can offer to theories of communist societies.

Repression in Stalinist and post-Stalinist Systems

A central question in analyses of nominally socialist societies is the function of repression in such systems, and its changes over time. Totalitarianism theory places particular emphasis on repression as a central characteristic of totalitarian rule, but other approaches also consider this attribute important.[1] Totalitarianism emphasizes the role of the party as organizer of repression and sole possessor of all mechanisms of control. But what remains unclear is what exactly the "party" was, and what its forms of repression consisted of. These questions can only be answered if we consider the origins, organization, and internal logic of one-party rule.

An examination of repression in the Stalinist era raises the question of whether terror is not only the key to understanding one particular developmental phase of Soviet society, but if it can also explain the pre-Stalinist period in the Soviet Union as well as post-Stalinist systems with their modified methods of rule. Repression and totalitarian claims are therefore central categories in the discussion. But how effectively do these terms help us to grasp the specific nature of communist societies?

At first glance, an exclusive focus on repression appears to be rather implausible. Undoubtedly, nominally socialist societies of the Stalinist or post-Stalinist type could not have existed without state control (whether via the military, the police, or secret service) any more than could nominally democratic systems (such as Turkey) or modern bourgeois civil societies (such as the Federal Republic). It is *how* such measures functioned and what form they took that is of central import for any comparative analysis.

Stalinist societies, such as the Soviet Union from 1935 to about 1955, or post-war Eastern Europe up until 1956–57, were based generally on state surveillance systems created and used by the party to maintain social order. In the USSR, this development was preceded by the collapse of the party's social basis (peasants and the developing working class) that it had won at the beginning of the 1930s. The gradual switch to terror was made possible only by previous changes in party rule. From its very beginnings, the Bolshevik party had focused on creating a party apparatus, and after the revolution it established a nomenclature system for party and state positions.[2] The highest members of the party hierarchy began to build a special party bureaucracy. The defining characteristic of emerging Stalinism was a concentration of power in the hands of a few privileged members of this bureaucracy, which became increasingly independent over time. This development was accompanied by the expansion of the state security service that sought to replace voluntary submission with absolute obedience.

The defeat of alternative platforms within the Soviet party was not a result of this concentration of power, but rather, preceded it. Controversies within the party's upper ranks were increasingly seen as a danger to party rule rather than as an important element of party development. The Stalinist faction won battles against other party wings with the help of not only an objective, but subjective campaign of abuse against these factions. Their demise marked the beginning of a complete reorganization of the party carried out with terrorist measures, justified by claims that such "vermin" had to be identified and destroyed.[3] This terror was directed largely at the party itself, as well as the party bureaucracy, which had to adjust to a new social structure as well as a novel organization centered on party leadership. Both actions were based on a complete re-ordering of the party by terrorist means to become an instrument aimed at achieving those very ends.

The terrorist transformation of the party could therefore only be completed after every possible avenue of resistance to or opposition within it had been extinguished. As soon as the party became the sole source of social synthesis, its public support, which it had lost in the wake of industrialization, could only be regained with violent measures. The real "achievement" of Stalinist social measures was the terrorist manner in which the masses were mobilized for the state and the means by which functional elites were co-opted into the state and party.

Revisionist approaches to Stalinist rule developed in the wake of functional deficits in the party's claims to absolute control and the inability of the system to come to terms with increasingly complex social and economic developments. This process was characterized by a reinstatement of a collective bureaucratic leadership (the power elite), the suspension of terror in favor of more differentiated methods of repression, party control over security organs, the increased significance of functional party elites, and the reintroduction of forced measures of work. As the system continued to resort to methods of Stalinist rule, its backwardness became ever more obvious. In post-Stalinist, bureaucratic systems, repression was no longer total, and every failure had consequences for the entire system.

Post-Stalinist dictatorships were only totalitarian insofar as they made ideological claims to the total control of society; they were not totalitarian in the actual forms of rule practiced within them. As in nominally socialist societies, the party's ideological claims became the measure of reality, rather than information resulting from an analysis of the actual social conditions of rule. By basing its analytical tools on the very constructs it proposes to examine, totalitarian theory merely reproduces totalitarian ideology instead of analyzing it. Just as repression is not synonymous with rule, totalitarian claims to total control cannot be taken as proof of "total rule." Theoreticians who point to the "potential" of terror in post-Stalinist bureaucracies not only contribute to the relativization of Stalinist repression, but reveal their inability to understand the real sources of rule within such systems. It seems that many supporters of totalitarian theory view the possibility of the existence of non-totalitarian dictatorships as absurd.[4]

Internal Repression and Social Control in the SED

The history of the SED reflects the larger evolution of GDR society as an example of how Soviet systems, developed under strict party control, were transformed into regimes geared at gratifying internal needs and allowing some competition.[5] What remained constant during this transformation was the main characteristic of the system – its compulsive nature. But the aims of post-Stalinist party leaders were fueled by different motives, such as the move to a "patriarchal dictatorship," directed toward social gratification: in other words, these goals were not just a continuation of totalitarian differentiation and subjugation, typical of the terrorist phase of social formation. The following example of changes in internal party disciplinary techniques from the 1940s to the early 1960s will serve to illustrate the nature of this transformation.

The KPD, re-organized after the war within the context of Soviet occupation, was established as a Stalinist-ruled, cadre-oriented political party as early as 1945. The "Bolshevized" party of the 1920s had already rid itself of dissidents, and the party's exiled members who had survived the Soviet purges of the 1930s were ardent supporters of the Soviet line. But unlike in the Soviet Union, the Communist party in the SBZ had not yet experienced the "liquidation" of alternative political directions. The situation in occupied Germany presented the KPD with a host of novel challenges. In deference to the interests of their Western allies, the Soviets dispensed with an open imposition of their system within their zone after the end of the war. But according to Stalin's wishes, as they were expressed in June 1945, "the hegemony of the working classes and its revolutionary party" were to be guaranteed in a "parliamentary-democratic republic."[6] The KPD was forced to show a large degree of tolerance for the re-instated bourgeois parties, and particularly for its main opponent, the SPD. In the face of the complicated post-war situation, it was clear from the outset that everything depended on whether the KPD would be able to create the conditions necessary for central control of the party to effectively limit any political change of course. This was a well-known and often proclaimed demand. It had much to do with the Stalinization of a new type of party, the "unity and purity" of which was to be protected at all costs. Such a party was not only to address German interests, but had to help serve the purposes of East Germany's Soviet occupiers as well.

The party's path toward a unified system of rule began even before the Stalinization of the newly formed KPD. The unexpected pace of political development in the first months after the end of the war, particularly the surprising strength of the SPD, complicated the situation. The KPD leadership drew on Soviet examples to develop a "special German path" that would neutralize the SPD and the bourgeois parties politically, while preserving its own claims to leadership and control. The KPD tactic of neutralization toward its political opponents was the only alternative to open terror, carried out by the occupying Soviet troops. But without overt repression by the SMAD, this neutralization was almost impossible to achieve. From this situation arose the practice of concealed terror as the most effective method which the Soviets could exercise in East Germany. Often employed against opponents within the SPD, these measures allowed the SVAG and the KPD to base their power on the willingness of many, if not all, East German Social Democrats to consent to a fusion with the Communist Party.

The goal of a unified party forced Stalinists within the KPD to accept a strategy of tolerance toward the SPD. Within the newly founded SED, this practice continued in the guise of consideration for the former Social Democrats. After the zonal unification of the KPD and SPD in April 1946, the SED was seen by the leading "Moscow" trained party elites as "mixed." It was permeated by "foreign bodies" that needed to be brought under control. In addition, in both parties most of the members were newcomers – KPD members had not been trained according to Stalinist disciplinary tactics, while the majority of SPD members had not yet been schooled in the concepts of democratic centralism. This trend was continued with new membership to the SED. The pressure to cleanse the party of dissidents in no way matched the potential threat posed by former Social Democrats.

Research on leftist socialist and communist dissidence remains rudimentary, but current work provides surprising insights into the readiness of a small number of individuals within certain circles and groups to resist the Stalinization of the SED. The Soviets and their German allies were well aware of this potential for resistance. In May 1946, both Tjuplanov (Head of Propaganda) and Bokov (Member of the Military Council) warned the Central Committee members Pieck, Ulbricht, and Grotewohl of "Trotzkyite" elements within the party and urged them to undertake countermeasures.[7] Even the head of the Berlin party group of the SED, Hermann Matern (later chief of the party control organ) was concerned about this problem. In September 1946 he replied to a direct question from the first representative of the head of the Division for International Information, Panjuschkin, whether former rightist Social Democrats or former leftist Communists posed more of a danger to party unity by remarking: "The Ultra-Leftists.... [They do] not have their own organization, but they work in factions.... The greater danger lies with the left, both organizationally and ideologically."[8]

After the forced integration of its biggest opponent was successfully completed, the KPD-dominated party leadership immediately started considering steps for developing instruments and methods to meet both real and imagined internal party threats. The "Defense" division with the Section for Party Personnel (PPA) in the party ZK formed the institutional link between the defensive measures of the KPD and the SED's methods of party control. At its founding, the SED did not possess an adequate political or social basis within the populace. Its membership was also unreliable. Such failings seemed to justify measures of repression and ideological indoctrination from above, which were also quickly approved by the Soviets. Stalinists within the party leadership found these techniques to be the most effective way of realizing their goals of shaping both the party and society as a whole. The Defensive Division collected material about oppositional groups within the SED, in part with clandestine methods (and with the help of KPD contacts they also gathered information on the other zones within occupied Germany). The material was collected by informants who had infiltrated such groups or who were recruited from their ranks. Before the great organizational restructuring and wave of purges that took place between 1948 and 1952, such information, if it was not used immediately for disciplinary measures or to justify arrest by the occupation authorities, was filed away for later use.

The open Stalinization of the party – with the goal of transforming the SED apparatus into a well-disciplined mass party – that began after May 1948 was carried out largely by the Central Party Control Commission (ZPKK). Based on their declaration from July 1948 regarding the "Purging of Hostile and Degenerate Elements from the Party," SED leaders followed the course established by the new COMINFORM[9] and interpreted any straying from the party line as enemy activity and the work of foreign agents. Isolation and terrorist disciplinary measures were the most direct strategies of Stalinist control during the purges of 1949 to 1951. Most of the victims of the proclaimed battles "against the Tito-Fascists," Trotskyism and Social Democracy, " imperialist spies and agents" and "Zionist conspiracies" were not attacked for their oppositional activities. Rather, they became hostages of Stalinist disciplinary measures due to their political biographies and because of the changing Soviet foreign policy interests (especially in Eastern and Southeastern Europe) during the early stages of the Cold War.

After Krushev's revelations at the 20th Party Congress had led to a reconsideration of the Stalinist purges, the party leadership had to accommodate this shift in perspective while continuing to hold on to the logic of internal discipline developed during the constitutive phase of Stalinism in the SBZ–GDR. In 1956, those who had been responsible for purges within the SED had to fear being confronted by comrades in their own ranks for the unbroken lines of personal continuity at the upper levels of the party. Although the SBZ–GDR did not experience show trials like the Rajk–Slánský spectacles, the SED was nevertheless forced to deal with the issue, especially when after 1954 a series of secret trials resulted in draconian punishments (such as those against Friedrich and Anna Schlotterbeck, Bruno Goldhammer, Fritz Sperling of the KPD, Hans Schrecker, Paul Merker, and Max Fechner). Since the party purges of 1949 to 1951 were still fresh in everyone's minds, the next step was to replace the terrorist techniques of party control with more differentiated forms of repression. These were to be carried out with as much consistency as the most repressive Stalinist measures. The new disciplinary tactics – largely implemented by party control organs – developed in conjunction with the changing political challenges of the late 1950s and 1960s. They served as before mainly to secure the party leadership's monopoly and to protect the party from all forms of suspected or actual opposition.

Though old-style purges had become obsolete, party leaders still had to prevent frustration with party control measures and disciplinary action. It therefore became imperative that the party rid itself of its Stalinist ballast and move ahead with steps to maintain the "unity and purity of the party." After 1958, the party's policy goal of the "battle against revisionist tendencies" established a less than consistent course of de-Stalinization that ultimately aimed at the preservation of the Politburo's power and authority. This phase of reconstruction, which insured the party's arrogant monopoly of power, determined repressive measures well into the 1960s. The 1957 trial of the Harich circle exemplifies this course. The condemnation of the group around Schirdewan, Oelßner, Selbmann, Wollweber, and Ziller (falsely accused of being a "faction") further strengthened this trend. Yet this circle's oppositional policies were not factional but merely an expression of internal party conflict regarding the proper techniques of rule. Beyond such demonstrations of party strength, which served to underscore publicly the illegitimacy of any form of criticism, the party leadership slowly began to turn to methods of appeasement.

In the early 1960s, the party developed more moderate and even self-critical methods in dealing with its own members. Party leaders still wanted to avoid any questioning of their authority, but in spite of the unquestioned success of their earlier repressive policies, they hoped to develop more modern and effective techniques of party discipline. This meant a public departure from "older methods" of rule as part of an effort to gain trust and respectability. Previous beliefs that had stressed the necessity of continued repressive measures aimed at ideological control had to be re-formulated. These efforts were combined early on with more critical reflections about prior methods of party discipline. Further proof of this trend toward moderation can be found in such measures as the ordinance on the administration of justice issued by the State Council in 1961, the State Council ordinance on the responsibilities and methods of the judiciary system of 1963, as well as steps taken to make the judiciary independent of direct party control. Implicit in all of these changes was a criticism of the misuse of exceptional clauses which resulted in breaches of socialist codes in criminal investigations and of general legal norms. This included the activities of state security organs and the lapses in the public prosecutor's responsibility for them. These measures, aimed at partial liberalization, were accompanied by a somewhat more liberal communal voting law, more realistic youth and educational policies, and after 1962–63 more liberal cultural and media policies (up until 1965).

The party's change of course was first and foremost a direct expression of the limited effectiveness of terrorist measures of control within the new conditions of post-Stalinist development. The consolidation of the regime from 1961 to 1965 provided a good starting point for more flexible policies of social control which found expression in markedly improved social conditions for wide segments of the population. Party leaders placed increased emphasis on integration, rather than ideological coercion, and developed more flexible approaches to meeting real needs instead of authoritarian indoctrination. All of these measures created the basis for the economic reform of the 1960s. These new techniques could only function within the limits of the developing post-Stalinist party bureaucracy, which drew its authority from the uncontested monopoly of party rule legitimated only by itself.

The transformation of the Stasi's defensive policies from pure oppression into more sophisticated methods of surveillance is a perfect expression of this shift in the techniques of government. Of course, this change also found expression in internal methods of party control. Political and social isolation, achieved by obstacles to professional advancement or even complete exclusion from a career, which had previously been considered necessary as secondary or back-up measures, now became the principal instruments of repression, especially when the political costs of imprisonment seemed too high. The "Czech crisis" served as an example of how successful the double strategy of reintegrating dissidents while removing any potential for opposition with massive and demonstrative intimidation had become. Since protest – both within and outside of the party – could find neither conceptual or social support within society, it was extremely limited in breadth and width. Periodic flare-ups of internal party opposition or resistance were neither politically nor organizationally stable.

Tolerance as Method of Rule in Communist Society

The role of Stalinism within real existing socialism is contested by scholars. Many authors from different ideological camps agree that Leninism and Stalinism are closely linked, and point to the common constitutive attributes that result from the socialization of society and single party rule. Others define Stalinism as a system *sui generis*, and argue that it combines the most significant methods of exploitation within one system: workers and intellectuals are exploited by state capitalism, peasants are exploited in a relationship akin to feudal dependence, and prisoners in the camps are exploited under conditions nearing slavery. In this context it appears meaningless to consider tolerance as a method of rule.

Tolerance characterized and characterizes principally pre-bourgeois societies. The Edict of Toleration issued by Joseph II in 1781 guaranteed religious freedom to Protestants in Austria, but did not grant the Protestant church the same rights as the Catholic state church. The tolerance edict issued by Friedrich Wilhelm IV of Prussia in 1847 should be viewed in a similar light – namely as a political instrument of "enlightened absolutism."

In the Soviet Union under Lenin, one can hardly speak of tolerance as an essential element of politics. The Council of Peoples' Commissars combined repressive measures with policies aimed at granting smaller groups, such as ethnic minorities, emancipation. But the regime's anti-Zionist policies between 1917–18 and 1922 were relatively tolerant. While Zionist parties were not treated as political enemies, Zionist emigration to Palestine was not outlawed, and Zionist agricultural colonization projects won limited support.[10]

After Stalin's death, previous methods of systematic and thorough terror in the Soviet Union (and even more in its satellite states) were replaced by a mixture of controlled repression and tolerance. Yet those freedoms granted by party and state leaders were limited, and could be revoked at any time. How this tolerance actually functioned can be seen in changing policies toward various minorities – especially toward minorities who had served as scapegoats under Stalinism and had suffered accordingly.

Policies toward *religious* minorities ran the gamut from continued repression in Stalinist Albania to more measured oppression,
such as in Czechoslovakia, or even accommodation, as in the GDR
or Rumania. In Poland, the state party recognized the importance
of the Catholic Church and granted it so much autonomy that one
can almost speak of a "dual power" within the cultural infrastructure of society.[11]

Policies toward *social* and *cultural* minorities also encompassed
a variety of different approaches. For example, attempts were made
to reduce the Jews to a mere religious minority and to assimilate
the non-religious segments of the Jewish population. When these
failed, the Polish regime reacted in 1968 with forced expulsion,
while in Rumania some steps toward liberalization were undertaken. In the Soviet Union, tolerance toward the Jews had relatively fixed limits until 1985.[12]

The GDR, with its National–Socialist past, presented a special
case in the Soviet bloc. Scholarly attempts to understand the Holocaust have focused largely on how the international workers' movement, specifically its Communist arm, treated the Jewish question.[13]
Such approaches have emphasized the political and social dimensions of anti-Semitism and Jewish emancipation, while paying little
attention to its ethnic and religious components. The uniqueness
and largely irrational nature of the motives behind Auschwitz have
largely been ignored.

The GDR's policies toward the regime's small population of Jews
were, however, largely determined by the Soviet Union. Repressive
Stalinist measures toward the Jews, as they were practiced in the
USSR since 1949, were also extended, in somewhat milder form, to
the GDR. Stalinist anti-Semitic policies ended an initial phase of
SED policies toward the Jews that was not only characterized by
tolerance, but by active engagement. Jews were to have been integrated into all levels of society, and their social and religious life
supported. But the anti-Semitic campaign initiated by the Soviets
in 1952–53 put a stop to this process. Jews were not persecuted in
the GDR as Jews. Quite the contrary – SED leaders protested
against Western claims that they were carrying out anti-Semitic
policies. But the campaign against "cosmopolitanism" affected
Jewish (and non-Jewish re-emigrants from the West) much more
than other segments of the population.[14]

Five of the eight leaders of the Jewish community therefore fled
to the West. SED leaders nevertheless refused to stop financial support to the religious communities, although the Stasi suspected
them of being "agents of our class enemies." The SED adopted the
anti-Semitic rhetoric of the Prague Slánský trial[15] while simultane-

ously undermining individual outbursts of anti-Semitism in the populace.[16] Stalin's death finally brought to an end the specific brand of anti-Semitism, associated with his person, that was disguised as a fight against Zionism and "cosmopolitanism."

Thereafter the SED was able to introduce a policy of tolerance toward the Jewish community and toward secular Jewish practices. The memory of the NS genocide was disseminated, if somewhat one-sidedly, throughout society. The Jewish community was expected to comply with official policy, but was not forced to come out in open opposition to Israel. In the 1980s, this measured tolerance was replaced by active support of Jewish culture and religious practices. The reasons for this shift are to be found in more general overtures toward the U.S., increased prestige in the eyes of the FRG, and new freedoms resulting from changing Soviet policies (Gorbachev was decidedly against any form of anti-Semitism). These developments created more space for all minorities, even those of a nationalist nature.

German minorities in Eastern Europe were also used as pawns in the political battle with the FRG, particularly in Rumania. Tolerance and support of social and cultural institutions, and the ability to emigrate were linked to financial demands on the Federal Republic. Other developments were possible as well, and the Zhivkov regime in Bulgaria moved from tolerance to repression in their policies toward the Turkish population there. In the face of increasing financial difficulties, they became scapegoats. These periodic lapses into Stalinist policies show among others things how much or how little nominally socialist societies after 1956 had been able to overcome their Stalinist heritage.

Policies toward minorities were strongly influenced by different historical traditions. Homosexuals in Bulgaria were therefore existentially endangered. The ruling techniques that were supposed to secure popular loyalty were increasingly unsuccessful in those areas where a minority was not content with its minority status. Attempts to isolate youth subculture failed, and indeed the values of change were victorious, particularly in the area of culture.[17]

Policies of tolerance proved to be difficult to take back, once established. The question of tolerance became central during attempts at social emancipation "from above." The farthest-reaching concept of tolerance was formulated by the reformers of the Prague Spring in 1968. This effort to achieve socialist democracy based on majority rule was destroyed by Soviet tanks. The second attempt, Gorbachev's perestroika, came too late to mobilize a majority for a "reform of socialism above and below" (August Thalheimer).

Notes

1. Isaac Deutscher, who does not subscribe to totalitarianism theory, wrote in 1949, "Stalin's view on the role of political force, reflected in his deeds rather than his words, oozes the atmosphere of twentieth-century totalitarianism. Stalin might have paraphrased the old Marxian aphorism: force is no longer the midwife – force is the mother of the new society." Isaac Deutscher, *Stalin. A Political Biography* (London, 1961), 344.

2. The literature on this topic is vast. For a discussion of the emergence of a post-Bolshevik elite out of the terror of the mid-1930s see John Arch Getty, William Chase, and Sheila Fitzpatrick in *Stalinist Terror: New Perspectives*, ed. John Arch Getty and Roberta T. Manning (New York, 1993), 225–60. For the vehement debate on this structuralist approach see Robert Conquest in *Times Literary Supplement* (11 February 1994) and Conquest's reply, in ibid. (11 March 1994). Various interpretations are mapped out chronologically according to different schools in Chris Ward, *Stalin's Russia* (London, 1993); Guiseppe Boffa, *The Stalin Phenomenon* (Ithaca and London, 1992).

3. Robert Vincent Daniels, *The Conscience of the Revolution: Communist Opposition in Soviet Russia* (Cambridge, 1960). For more recent discussions see Theodor Bergmann and Mario Kessler, eds, *Ketzer im Kommunismus – Alternativen zum Stalinismus* (Mainz, 1993) with numerous essays about the confrontations between Stalinist and anti-Stalinist Communists.

4. The main criticism of totalitarian theory focuses on this point. See Wolfgang Wippermann, *Totalitarismustheorien* (Darmstadt, 1997).

5. Thomas Klein, "Widerstand und Verfolgung von Kommunisten während der Stalinisierung," *Utopie kreativ* 81/82 (1997): 123–34; idem, "Zu Opposition und Widerstand in der SED," *Die SED. Geschichte, Organisation, Politik. Ein Handbuch*, ed. Andreas Herbst et al. (Berlin, 1997), 60–69; Thomas Klein, Wilfriede Otto, and Peter Grieder, *Visionen. Repression und Opposition in der SED* (Frankfurt/Oder, 1997).

6. Stalin to his German guests Ulbricht, Ackermann, and Sobottka before the Soviets approved the founding of political parties in their zone. See also Jochen Laufer, "'Genossen, wie ist das Gesamtbild?' Ackermann, Ulbricht und Sobottka in Moskau im Juni 1945," *Deutschland-Archiv* 32 (1996): 355ff.

7. Rolf Badstübner and Wilfried Loth, eds, *Wilhelm Pieck, Aufzeichnungen zur Deutschlandpolitik 1945–1953* (Berlin, 1994), 73f.

8. Soviet Party Archive, RTsKhIDNI, f. 17, op. 128, d. 151, 1.120–36. For a translation see Elke Scherstjanoi, in *Beiträge zur Geschichte der Arbeiterbewegung* 38, no. 3 (1996): 59–88.

9. With its Anti-Tito Resolution, passed in June 1948, the COMINFORM increased the rigid course of Stalinizing all Communist parties within the Soviet sphere of influence.

10. Mario Kessler, *Zionismus und internationale Arbeiterbewegung 1897–1933* (Berlin, 1994), 106 et seq.

11. Francois Fejtö, *A History of the People's Democracies: Eastern Europe since Stalin* (Harmondsworth, 1974), 436–48 offers an overview of the religious institutions in Eastern and Central Eastern Europe.

12. For communist policies toward the Jews in the former Eastern bloc, see Peter Bettelheim et al., eds, *Antisemitismus in Osteuropa. Aspekte einer historischen Kontinuität* (Vienna, 1992); Jan Hancil and Michael Chase, eds, *Anti-Semitism in Post-Totalitarian Europe* (Prague, 1993).

13. Mario Kessler, *Antisemitismus, Zionismus und Sozialismus: Arbeiterbewegung und jüdische Frage im 20. Jahrhundert* (Mainz, 1994); Jack Jacobs, *On Socialists and "The Jewish Question" after Marx* (New York and London, 1992); Enzo Traverso, *The Marxists and the Jewish Question: The History of a Debate, 1843–1943* (Atlantic Highlands, 1994).

14. Mario Kessler, *Die SED und die Juden – zwischen Repression und Toleranz. Politische Entwicklungen bis 1967* (Berlin, 1995); Angelika Timm, *Hammer, Zirkel, Davidstern. Das gestörte Verhältnis der DDR zu Zionismus und Staat Israel* (Bonn, 1997); Lothar Mertens, *Davidstern unter Hammer und Zirkel. Die Jüdischen Gemeinden in der SBZ/DDR und ihre Behandlung durch Partei und Staat 1945–1990* (Hildesheim, 1997); Jeffrey Herf, *Divided Memory: The Nazi Past in the Two Germanies* (Cambridge, 1997).

15. Karel Kaplan and Frantisek Svátek, "Die politischen Säuberungen in der KPC," *Terror: Stalinistische Parteisäuberungen 1936–1953,* ed. Hermann Weber and Ulrich Mählert (Paderborn, 1998), 487–599.

16. See the reports about anti-Semitic remarks in Magdeburg, Gera and Frankfurt a.d. Oder and the measures of authorities in *Neues Deutschland* (29 January 1953).

17. Fejtö, *History of People's Democracies,* 429–35.

MEANS OF SOCIAL CONTROL

CREATING STATE SOCIALIST GOVERNANCE

THE CASE OF THE DEUTSCHE VOLKSPOLIZEI

Thomas Lindenberger

In order to understand the political system of the GDR, one cannot limit the field of research to those activities which correspond directly to the programmatic imperatives and orders of the power center. To find out to what extent and how society was practically "run" according to the party program and the decisions taken by the Politbüro, one should also look at the informal side of power, and in particular at relations on the micro-level of society. One must stress the interactive dimension of all processes of domination, its quality as social practice.[1]

It is important to focus not only on mechanical conformity to rules and orders – or on open defiance – but also on the vast realm of other forms of behavior such as compromise, bargaining, limited reciprocity, and shared interests between rulers and the ruled. This approach offers a different picture of the way in which the "actors" interpreted such practices, which meanings and what significance they had in mind while playing their roles in such power structures. This perspective aims at reconstructing the individuals' "sense of themselves," their *Eigen-Sinn*, a term, which Alf Lüdtke has introduced in the recent debates of social history and *Alltagsgeschichte*.[2]

Stressing the need to study the micro level of action, however, does not imply neglecting what was going on at the top level. In the case of state socialism, this would be particularly absurd, since a typical feature of its practice of government was the permanent obsession of top level functionaries with details of local incidents and circumstances. In principle and over the long run, both micro and macro perspectives have to be combined.[3]

In this study, however, I will concentrate rather on the state side, in particular on relations inside the East German police force, called *Volkspolizei*, which can be regarded as a microcosm in its own right.

The problem which I want to address more specifically is the nature of "governance" in early state socialism. For the SED leaders, "building the GDR state" was not limited to coming to power and repressing political opponents. The legitimacy of their power monopoly was founded on a vision of the socialist future that could only be reached under their leadership. In order to secure the permanence of their ascendancy and of the new state structure, other, relatively autonomous nuclei of power, which relied on a variety of historically given social networks and resources, had to be dissolved. The destruction of long established social and property relations had to precede or go along with the construction of new, "socialist" ones. During this process the SED had to establish a firm grip on the people going through this transformation in order to install a durable link between the power center and the individuals. This task created a practical dilemma: the more societal relations were dissolved or incorporated into the state structures, the more urgent the problem of directly controlling and "managing" the behaviors of the millions of "atomized" individuals became. This could not be done simply by issuing rules about what was forbidden or allowed and by punishing eventual infractions. Rather it implied techniques and methods of influencing people's behavior, which went beyond deterrence through punishment. The "conduct of the conduct" of individuals became a central dimension in establishing the party's influence over society.

"Conduct of the conduct" is a term borrowed from Michel Foucault's reflections on "governmentality." This concept seems to offer a promising approach for understanding some but not all features of the exertion of power within state socialism. Even if Foucault developed the notion while studying eighteenth-century literature on the art of government, it can be used to analyze political systems in other periods as well, as recent "neo-Foucauldian" debates among sociologists and political scientists have shown.[4] The concept aims in particular at state activities based on practices of producing knowledge about subjects with the aim of "managing" their behavior. "Governmentality" in the context of Foucault's analysis thus encompasses the "statesman's craft" of linking individuals and circumstances so as to make them act in a certain way, and to create an institutionalized complex of knowledge and power characteristic of late "cameralistic" absolutism. While it differs from earlier absolutist practice of hierarchically differentiated sovereignty, it is also distinct from liberal state policies, which were based on the assumption of a certain amount of autonomous self-regulation of the social realm. Transferred into the context of twentieth-century industrial society, the concept lends itself to analyzing the refined regulation practices which go along with the rise of the welfare state and its growing competence. The often stated affinities of state socialism with both the phenomenology of benevolent absolutism and the legacy of modern welfare state utopias[5] only underline the hypothesis that the concept of "governmentality" is suited to identifying key elements of domination inside GDR society. A "classic" instrument of behavior control, the modern, omnipresent uniformed police force, will now serve as test for this assumption.

Policing the People

Current discussions regarding GDR history are virtually completely silent about the "normal" police, the Deutsche Volkspolizei. Accounts of political repression and totalitarian features of the system are dominated by the secret service, the *Ministerium für Staatssicherheit* or *Stasi*, and, of course, the communist party, the SED, and the justice system. Public debates about rehabilitation and indemnification of justice victims, or about the purging of certain sensitive state institutions such as the education system, are almost completely focused on these institutions.

This lack of attention to the Volkspolizei reflects its subordinate status in the GDR state machinery, but this picture is accurate only for the last two decades of the system. During the 1970s and 1980s especially, the Honecker period, it was the Stasi, as the competing police institution, which expanded and intensified its grip on all areas of social life. A historical perspective from the beginning of the GDR's existence, however, shows the Volkspolizei in a much more powerful position: after all, this was the first institution of the East German state, even antedating the state itself by more than four years. It was created under Soviet control immediately after the liberation from Nazism in the summer of 1945, whereas the East German republic was founded only in the fall of 1949.[6]

Beyond this fact of pure chronology, the Volkspolizei of the late 1940s and early 1950s can also be regarded as the nucleus of all other repressive and armed state institutions of the GDR: the border police, the paramilitary barracked police force, which was eventually transformed into the national people's army, and the Stasi were offsprings of the Volkspolizei, both at the institutional and personnel level. No wonder that in the early anticommunist rhetoric of West German observers, the Volkspolizei played a much more important role than in the retrospective discussion. To understand the development of the GDR from its beginning, therefore, also requires taking the "normal" public police, the Volkspolizei, into account.

Moreover, the early Volkspolizei lends itself perfectly to studying the problems of building a new socialist state in a modern industrialized society, once the soviet type communist party has established its power monopoly. As a point of departure, this essay chooses 1952: it was in this year that the SED's second Party Conference decided to begin with "laying the foundations of socialism," leaving behind the more "neutral" stage of the antifascist democratic order. As a part of this program, all resources of the party, the mass organizations and, of course, the state institutions had to be mobilized. Because the state was considered as the most important "lever" in this process, its power had to be expanded at the expense of civil society. In particular the "collectivization" of the agricultural sector and its subsequent integration into the planned economy was one of the SED's major concerns during this time. Expanding state functions to further the construction of socialism, therefore, also implied intensifying the presence of the police in the countryside. The subsequent essay focuses on this theater, where humble village cops were doing their service amongst individual farmers, the majority of whom were not at all prepared to join one of the mandated agricultural cooperatives (LPGs, comparable to soviet collective farms).

Instead of giving an overall picture of the Volkspolizei during the 1950s, I will try to develop some important features of the exertion of power under state socialism on the basis of an analysis of the Volkspolizei in the countryside in the 1950s. One category of police officers merits particular attention, since it can be regarded as particularly characteristic of the Volkspolizei (and police forces in other states' socialist regimes as well). It is a position at the grass roots level of policing, which was introduced in 1952; from this time on, every GDR citizen had his or her *Abschnittsbevollmächtigte*, abbreviated as ABV, a term meaning approximately "section commissioner." Within his geographically defined section, the ABV was in charge of all police affairs, regardless of the particular branch or specialty. Initially, such a section was inhabited by up to 10,000 people inside larger towns, or a minimum of 1,000 people in rural districts, which often included several small villages. This meant that 5,000 ABV positions had to be created all over the republic in order to cover an average of about 4,000 inhabitants per section. After the June 1953 uprising, when the police force was increased considerably, the number of sections and ABVs was almost doubled. This system existed alongside the other police branches at the local level – those in charge of patrolling, traffic control, criminal investigations, registration and license affairs, etc.[7]

By its very definition, it was the ABV's supreme task to establish and cultivate a "close connection" with the population. He was obliged to reside in his section, and if necessary, to move there. He had to keep office hours, either in his home or in a public building, and was to be accessible by phone. He had to make regular visits to every household, or at least to every house. In order to gather all kinds of information, he had to be well informed on all economic, social, cultural, and above all, political features of his section. He was provided with precise instructions on how to collect such material and in particular how to put it down in "structure files," which could be used by colleagues in specialized branches of the police hierarchy. His fact finding activities were meant to produce an information base for criminal investigation as well as for the registration or the licensing offices, which had to be kept up to date. Whereas the first needed to keep track of the conduct of convicts or probationers, the second required material on the reliability of applicants for permission to travel to the West, while the latter, in charge of supervising associations and religious communities, was interested in the social activities of sporting clubs, church groups or other associations outside the official mass organizations that were regarded as potential seedbeds of political dissidence and nonconformism. To accomplish this broad task of information gathering, this policeman was bound to work as a kind of grass root sociologist on behalf of the state. Any higher government office which needed to get in contact with someone in a remote area would first consult the ABV or his "structure file" in order obtain the necessary background information.

The ABV's task to establish a "close link" with the populace included his duty to recruit, train and command a group of voluntary assistants: As many as fifteen people living in his section would help him in their free time to safeguard public order and provide all kinds of necessary information. Besides collecting material, the ABV also had to fulfill the normal tasks of a cop, familiar in noncommunist societies as well. He had to undertake some patrolling, traffic control, prosecuting of small scale offenders and criminals, and implementation of police measures at the local level on behalf of the specialized branches.

This enumeration hardly suffices to describe the ABV's tasks. The ABV was part of the police, and more generally, a party strategy to penetrate society at the very moment of the construction of socialism through the lever of state power. Representing the state, therefore, did not mean just supervising the citizens' conduct and reporting any disturbance of public order; it implied a far more active role, and taking the initiative: the ABV was above all to further new social relations in the place where he worked. In the countryside this meant his top priority was to guard the already existing units of socialist agriculture and to spur the foundation of new ones. In close cooperation with the party secretary, village mayor, director of the collective farm and other local notables from the "progressive," i.e., the socialist side, he had to consider how those farmers resisting collectivization could be convinced to give up their independence, how the influence of the local church community could be reduced, and how "bourgeois" and "hostile" elements could be held in check. But at the same time, it was also his duty to control his progressive partners and report grievances resulting from corruption, nepotism, and waste of resources in the already existing units of socialist agriculture to his superiors.

In the eyes of the planners in the central administration of the Volkspolizei, this ABV system was the most important policing innovation in the GDR. In a comparative perspective, it can be identified as belonging to the category of totalizing utopias, or rather dystopias, i.e., schemes of complete control through observation and information, which had informed nineteenth-century reform projects such as the prison system, psychiatric wards, educational classrooms, and finally, the police force.[8] One important difference should, however, be noted: this twentieth-century model of all encompassing surveillance implied a more active and responsible role of its personal representatives on the spot. It was also a dynamic concept that constantly blurred its own borderlines towards outside society, attempting to integrate the controlled into the activity of controlling. It is precisely at this point, that state socialist governance acquires a very specific quality and that is what makes a closer look at the lowest level of the political system particularly interesting.

Policing the Police

The files of the central administration of the people's police in the ministry of interior in Berlin indicate that most of the ABVs were hopelessly overtaxed by and under-equipped for their task. For instance, they lacked telephones, cars or motorbikes and often lived far away from their section due to the chronic housing crisis of post-war Germany. Superiors could be happy, if despite lacking political and professional qualifications, these village sheriffs had enough common sense and social standing in their communities somehow to manage their tasks without creating too many problems.

But there were also deeper reasons for the regular complaints about poor ABV work. The approach of penetrating society by total immersion could lead to close ties between the ABV and his surrounding population at the expense of those between the ABV and his superiors. In the countryside in particular, the ABV was "exposed to reactionary and bourgeois influences," as a central administration circular stated in 1957.[9]

During the fifties, when severe conflicts about collectivization divided the villages and rural population, two major techniques were used by the senior levels of party and police in order to overcome such intrinsic deficiencies of the system: the first were "instruction brigades" sent from the center into the countryside for fact finding and disciplining on the spot; the second was the forced ideological mobilization by the collective ritual of *Aussprache*, an intensive quasi-confessional discussion. Not surprisingly, these measures were imported from the practice of political institutions, namely the communist party.

"Instruction brigades" were a very popular practice in all state socialist systems.[10] Coming from the power center and often visiting the lowest level of hierarchy in a community, a group of instructors had to carry out a fact finding mission, combining two tasks. First, they had to gather information on the local case by investigating and producing an analysis of the state of affairs, including suggestions for improvement or new regulations in the future. Second, they had to control and, if necessary, correct the performance of local functionaries during their mission. The results of such brigade missions were laid down in detailed reports. Since one of the explicit functions of instruction brigades was to short-circuit the routinized and euphemistic communication from the bottom up to the top, their accounts often are full of blunt descriptions of fundamental weaknesses and abuses.

The first series of such reports about the activities of the ABV dates from December 1953.[11] The traumatic events of the 17 June uprising in the same year had revealed not only a considerable lack of support for the SED among industrial workers, but also widespread opposition among the rural population.[12] A brigade of top level functionaries both from the central committee and from the ministry of interior visited five ABVs from different regions of the republic, spending almost a week in the field, questioning the ABVs and their superiors, the village mayor, the local party and state security officials, scrutinizing files in the county police department, and evaluating the information at the end of the mission. Both the investigation and the final reports were structured according to the principles of the ABV system, laid down in the instructions of the Chief of the Volkspolizei. Thus, they can also be read as concrete interpretations of these rules, derived from the exemplary situations encountered during the instruction visits.

Following the tenets of Marxist–Leninist theory, the reports begin with extensive descriptions of the "objective" situation of the respective village and county. Data about the geographical location, occupation, economic and class structure are followed by a breakdown of political affiliations among the population, the strength of religious communities or other associations, ending with detailed descriptions of well known local "class enemies" and other "negative" persons: a priest preaching religious freedom, or a wealthy farmer polemicizing against collectivization, or a lazy laborer who always spouts Nazi slogans after getting drunk in the village pub, and so on. Also instances of "immoral conduct" such as illicit sexual relations are reported, and above all, anything which might point to contacts with West Germany or former noble estate owners, who had been expropriated during the land reform in 1945. Last, but not least, the strength, or often more accurately the weakness, of the "progressive" camp is assessed, which is attributed either to individual shortcomings of local functionaries, to structural deficits in the community, or to both.

Apart from yielding detailed insights into the village microcosms during the 1950s, reflecting the gossip and infighting characteristic of such rural communities, this part of the brigade reports is of importance for the following reason: it maps out those elements of social reality which were regarded as important and thus considered directly relevant for the SED's policy in general and at the local level. While carrying out the task of checking the ABV's performance in his village, the instructor was following the same schema that was laid down in the ABV's regulations. In producing a report on the ABV's section he was reproducing the basic assumptions underlying the concept of policing through the ABV system. This perspective assumed the ABV system to be a practicable approach to social reality, which in turn supposed a more general level of legitimacy of state socialist rule. Such reports showed the party's claim to be an omniscient authority above society to be valid. There was no local constellation or situation which could not be broken down to a set of "objective" factors regarding economy, society, and above all, politics, so that the party could then apply its political tenets and measures. And the same could therefore be expected from the local police officer, since he was supposedly educated and trained according to the principles of Marxism–Leninism, and was in most cases also a party member, a *Genosse*.

Why the situation was rarely this rosy, and why most of the local ABV did not live up to such high expectations, is the main topic of the second part of the reports. In a similarly comprehensive manner, it discusses the personality of the ABV. This part contains first of all his biography and social background. In particular, political affiliations in the past and social contacts in the present are of importance. Both of these elements offer important clues for an answer. For instance, comrade A is an ABV in a Saxon village, near the city of Meißen. His problem is that, although he has "good relations with the population," he "tends to underrate the outward manifestations of class struggle and regard them as harmless manifestations of every day life." Moreover, like his fellow ABV in the county, he knows too little about the local collective farms and political organizations, and thus represents a "serious danger," "lagging behind in his political and professional qualification." The following indicates that he shares even more with his fellow policemen: most of them are former social democrats, since the SPD had been the stronger party in this particular county, before it merged with the communists in the Socialist Unity Party in 1946. The implicit subtext of this description, well understood by anyone familiar with the Leninist stereotypes is that comrade A's political qualification is suffering from so-called "social democratism" and "reconciliationism."

On the other hand, comrade B, an ABV in a village in Mecklenburg, is a communist party veteran who had joined before 1933, having spent all twelve years of the Nazi period in prison. He is very aware of the class struggle in his village, his relations to all relevant socialist organizations are excellent, because he is a board member of most of them, and all relevant gatherings of the progressive forces are taking place in his home. But his relations with the private farmers and therefore the majority of the population are suffering from these commitments: he remains isolated from the social life in the village without taking measures against it. Here one can easily identify the subtext of an attribution of so-called "sectarianism", implying that comrade B is highly motivated, working eagerly as a policemen, but very inefficiently, nevertheless.

Every ABV is described as having good intentions and being in principle a loyal, politically correct and committed officer. Though the ABVs want to be good socialist policemen, for this or that individual reason, they are unable to be. Apart from a lack of material and equipment, the shortcomings in their performance have to be attributed to peculiar aspects of their personalities. It is not psychological traits such as character and intelligence, but socially attributed and acquired qualities, such as class origin, political socialization and education, that are regarded as the practical prerequisites of the new policing. The relevance of bringing together such information from individual biographies lies in the discursive circumscription of an empty space: it is not by his own effort, from his own individual potential, that the visited police officer may be able to fulfill his duties, even if his equipment could be improved. Rather, relief has to come from above, from the party. Blame for his shortcomings is to be laid on the party and police officials at the next higher level, since it is only to this level of hierarchy that the suggestions for solutions refer. The superiors are reproached for underestimating the importance of the ABV system and for neglecting the regular personal instruction and control of their ABV. These mid-level functionaries, both in the party and in the police, should spend more time with supervising and mentoring the ABV, which would require not only more political indoctrination, more assistance with problems on the spot, but also greater solicitude for individual problems of the ABV, such as housing, family troubles, and the like.

The principle of personalizing the political, and of politicizing the personal, already observed in the description of the class enemy at the local level, thus also applies to the analysis of the functionaries of one's own camp. Due to the deterministic assumptions of Leninist class theory, deficient individuals were always dependent on the helping hand of the party in order to improve their performance. Therefore, all the blame for such shortcomings was put on the intermediary levels of the hierarchy, which were criticized for having neglected their tasks as superiors and educators.

In this example of an instruction brigade, top level officers from Berlin sought the lowest level of hierarchy in order to find out what had gone wrong with police work in the countryside. But it is important to note that this technique was applied also to other levels of the hierarchy, as long as it followed the downward direction of control and instruction. In the case of the ABV system, it was even institutionalized two years later by the creation of an additional level of control officers, termed rural district instructors. Their only task was to control and mentor five to ten ABVs on a permanent basis.[13]

The above evidence suggests, as a first hypothesis, that the practice of instruction brigades can be regarded as containing a central element of governmentality under state socialism. The production of knowledge is combined with the reproduction of the party's monopolistic responsibilities in such a way that the socio-political biographies of individuals become the preferred object of investigation, the chief source of explanation and the main starting point for solutions to be applied exclusively by the party. It is in this sense that one can also speak of the state socialist political system as a "biocracy," to borrow a term recently coined by Lutz Niethammer to describe the enormous importance of politically "tuned" biographies in GDR social and power relations.[14]

Discussing Collectivization

The picture given so far is restricted mainly to the downward perspective inside the police apparatus, that is to the concepts that informed high level planners when designing new ways to police the construction of socialism, and to the manner in which they implemented this system. But power relations in a state socialist institution would be ill-conceived if the other perspective, that is the views of the ABV themselves, were left out. The regular articulation of these views was a routine in meetings and conferences of ABVs, a practice which gained particular importance when the party decided to accelerate the process of collectivization in 1957–58.[15]

Every county had to hold special meetings that were obligatory not only for the ABV and their immediate superiors, but also for higher officers and "guests" from the local party organization, the county council, and of course, the Stasi. Following guidelines from the central administration, their program started with a lengthy speech by the county police chief which laid out the principles of collectivization, including the specific situation of the agricultural sector in the county. Then, it was the ABVs' turn to open the "discussion," to unburden themselves regarding the practical problems with collectivization in their individual sections. Since the whole event was accurately written down and reported to the next higher authority, these documents show how the social and political conflicts aroused by the party's harsh collectivization course was debated among simple policemen and their superiors.

The fourteen protocols of such meetings in the Potsdam district in March and April 1958[16] yield a rather dichotomous, contradictory picture of policing at the bottom level of society. On the one hand, the superiors and the Stasi specialists invoke a horror scenario of the institutions of socialist agriculture being beleaguered by class enemies and their agents trying to undermine the construction of socialism wherever they can. Since any malfunction or setback on a collective farm or a machine-tractor station (MTS)[17] inevitably had to be attributed to activities of the class enemy, it was the task of every police officer, in particular of the ABV, to detect these activities even if they were hidden under the surface of apparently "unpolitical" phenomena such as "heavy drinking," "beer hall rows," or simple "negligence."

On the other hand the ABV also talked about the difficulties of the socialist sector of agriculture from quite a different angle: instead of finding agents of the class enemy behind every "incident," they identified structural and personal deficits as responsible for the poor reputation of socialism in the countryside inside the socialist sector itself. For instance they mentioned lack of material for safeguarding machines, crops or cattle, poor wages for laborers in the state-run, "people-owned estates" (VEG), and in particular, the immoral conduct of the responsible functionaries of these institutions, such as LPG presidents or VEG and MTS directors and brigadiers. They depicted these people as either incompetent managers, corrupt egoists, notorious drunkards, or all of these. Rarely did any of the ABV give details on individual farmers or class enemies such as *Großbauern* and priests. Obviously they had interpreted their task to further socialism in a very specific manner: instead of concentrating on the those farmers still running their businesses individually, they focused their observations on the socialist sector of agriculture. As a consequence, they registered the sources of setbacks and malfunctions without resorting to the demonologies and conspiracy theories of the official party discourse. Instead of personalizing the sinister underground activities of the class enemy, they personalized the weaknesses of socialist agriculture. Thus, in the midst of the so-called period of intensified class struggle in the countryside, the ABV reproduced all the arguments against joining the LPGs, which the individual farmers articulated throughout the 1950s in order to justify their reluctant attitudes towards the collective farms.

Confronted with these divergent accounts, the superior officers in turn questioned the very capacity of the ABVs to notice activities of the class enemy. This was considered a particularly urgent problem when it came to debating unresolved criminal cases and offenses which seemed to be "unpolitical," such as petty thefts, heavy drinking, etc. Following the official line of "reading" of realities, they had also be categorized as "hostile activities." "Nevertheless," a high ranking officer declared, "it is from the countryside that the smallest number of class enemy crimes was reported, although it is there that the class enemy is acting most vigorously." Therefore, the transmitter of such a message had to be criticized: reports like those of comrade X, always saying "everything is quiet, there is peace and harmony in my section..." are an expression of the fact that comrade X does not have the proper connection to the population. Otherwise, he would have heard something, and then criminal action would have been identified. Also, the good reputation of one of the cooperatives in X's section could not prevent the following verdict: "In my opinion, it is not due to him that the LPG is doing so well. It cannot be, since he is not a member of the party. He and his wife are working for the big farmer and he is also eating there."

Other ABVs were criticized because of their ambivalent attitude towards the church. As long as they themselves and their families were still members, they would not obtain the "clarity" required for the task "of transforming consciousness of the rural people." Finally, ABV attitudes towards the priority of collectivizing agriculture were challenged. Had they really put pressure on their relatives with landed property to join the cooperative, as was their duty as class-conscious representatives of the new socialist order? One ABV, who had refused to join as long as his business was doing well, was even known to own a small farm himself.

Such conferences were not mere exchanges of information. Their key function was the ritualized production of subjective accounts leading to subjectification. Those who articulated their own unfiltered observations about the state of public order in their section could be immediately corrected and put under pressure by being accused of lacking class consciousness. Only a few who had largely internalized the vision of the class enemy were able to present impeccable stories of class struggle in their sections and thus avoided the risk of being targeted in that personal way. The majority of statements, of course, held a middle position between these extremes, but they were influenced by subjective experience which had to be processed in a politically correct way while being presented to the forum of colleagues and comrades.

These "discussions" again show the personalizing of political imperatives and vice versa. The politicization of the personal experience bears all the weight of transforming the program into action. The peculiarity of such interactive procedures lies in the participation of those to be controlled; they were obliged to deliver a politically correct account of their own personality, experience, and behavior. Such regular and protracted rituals of participation of people in subaltern positions can be regarded as one of the key features of the practice of state socialist domination. The very term *Aussprache* points to the underlying concept of forming individual behavior. The reflexive verb *sich aussprechen,* from which it is derived, entails the connotation of "declaring oneself," including its emotional aspect of "unburdening oneself." The collective demands a transfer from an individual's inside to the outside in order to transform the shortcomings of subjective perception into objectivized class consciousness.

The affinity of such rituals of collective confession with the practices of pastoral power that Foucault has identified in the *longue durée* tradition of occidental techniques of subjectification is obvious.[18] In a secularized fashion, criticism and self-criticism were incorporated by earlier labor movements into their culture of organization and sociability, and transformed again into a means of internal discipline and control by Bolshevist parties.[19] Their extension to the realm of state machinery, production units, and mass organizations, in short, any institutionalized social relation under the dictatorial power of the communist party, can duly be regarded as a further element of state socialist governmentality.

Making the Personal Political

Some of the patterns found at the end of the 1950s pertain to the development of the GDR's political system in general. As long as the police had to cope with such a conflict-ridden situation as the rural communities during the collectivization campaign, there always remained the risk of ABVs who "collaborated" with the "wrong" side, preferred to live in peace with the big farmers of their villages instead of isolating themselves by displaying too much commitment to the socialist cause. In the eyes of the party, this dilemma could only be overcome by finally straightening out the situation in the villages themselves. Only after collectivization was brought to an end would the villages be fully cooperative, meaning that all farmers were organized inside cooperatives, and no private owners had economic importance. Now the self-government structures of the cooperatives could take over some of the burden from the policemen, since it also had to perform some security and disciplining functions, which now covered all people active in the agricultural sector.

The completion of the social transformation did not alter the very modes in which the imperatives of the socialist state were linked to the lives and behavior of individuals, one might even say, they were constantly converted into each other. On the contrary, practices such as the instruction brigades and the quasi-confessional *Aussprache* remained key elements of socialist governmentality, to be expanded and refined in subsequent years. The more society was organized following the state socialist model, the more these practices could be adopted at all levels of the hierarchy, not just inside the state bureaucracy, but in all other social areas which were penetrated more and more by the state. In an uninterrupted chain of control and instruction, this "conduct of the conduct" of individuals linked together the whole socio–political body, from the top leadership down to its most mundane brigades in workplaces, school classes, voluntary associations, and neighborhood activities. This process of dissolving social autonomy was dependent on knowledge and power practices by which the personal could constantly be rendered political and vice versa.

Thus the well known Leninist–Stalinist principle, "the cadre question is the central question" or "political questions are cadre questions," was not just about putting the right people in the right positions. It implied, above all, constant work with their personalities once they were put in office, that is, the continual shaping of their minds. According to the motto popular among party functionaries during the late 1950s, "working with the human being," not just with the representative of a category or function, can be regarded as one, if not *the,* characteristic feature of state socialist governmentality.

After the construction of the Berlin Wall, one could no longer escape from such pressure, which led to a certain pacification in social relations. This development is also reflected in the loss of graphic detail in such reports, accounts, and protocols found in source material: once the socialist state was fully established, the lack of open contradiction and conflict rendered its analysis more complicated and boring. Permanent practices of "education" – instead of open punishment and confrontational "discussion" – become the preferred paradigm of disciplining and governing people's behavior, thereby rendering the late GDR a kind of "educational dictatorship," always backed by a minimum of direct physical repression. The ways in which this paradigm was codified, institutionalized, and actually practiced in and by the Volkspolizei (as one among other institutions), could be analyzed as a further element of state socialist governmentality. Nevertheless, studying developments in the early phase of "laying the foundations of socialism" during the 1950s yields some insights into the very nature of state socialist practices of domination.

It has to be stressed that this essay could only touch in a preliminary fashion on the way in which those practices were appropriated and handled by those in subaltern positions. Nonetheless, some hypotheses may be derived from the evidence. The example of the ABV "discussions" shows that the actual content of such ritualized exchanges was not necessarily determined in advance. They could also be used on occasion to articulate interpretations of social reality following the ABV's own perceptions and concepts of what was or was not to be regarded as orderly, and what could be considered as proper police work. Far from constituting anything like "resistance" or "opposition" to official polities, talking about social reality as the grass root police officers did displayed their interpretation of their job, their practice of policing the small sector of socialism instead of the larger territory still held by the "class enemy." This *Eigen-Sinn* brought them into some fierce controversies with their superiors, and the abundant record of removals, dismissals, and disciplinary measures taken against ABVs corresponds to the constant tension between politically defined expectations from above and pragmatic self-control from below. But it never questioned the police or political system as such. Assessing the relevance of this articulation of *Eigen-Sinn* for the initial stability and subsequent erosion of state socialist power structures thus requires going beyond the mapping of its governmentality.[20]

Notes

1. See Alf Lüdtke, "Introduction," in *The History of Everyday Life. Reconstructing. Historical Experiences and Ways of Life*, ed. Alf Lüdtke (Princeton, 1995).
2. See Alf Lüdtke, "Geschichte und Eigensinn," in *Alltagskultur, Subjektivität und Geschichte. Zur Theorie und Praxis von Alltagsgeschichte*, ed. Berliner Geschichtswerkstatt (Münster, 1994), 139–53; Geoff Eley, "Labor History, Social History, Alltagsgeschichte: Experience, Culture, and the Politics of the Everyday – A New Direction for German Social History?" *Journal of Modern History* 61, no. 2 (1989); and Thomas Lindenberger, "Die Diktatur der Grenzen. Zur Einleitung," in: *Herrschaft und Eigen-Sinn in der Diktatur*, ed. Thomas Lindenberger (Cologne, 1999), 13–44.
3. Thomas Lindenberger, "Alltagsgeschichte und ihr möglicher Beitrag zu einer Gesellschaftsgeschichte der DDR," in *Die Grenzen der Diktatur. Staat und Gesellschaft in der DDR*, ed. Richard Bessel and Ralph Jessen, (Göttingen, 1996), 298–325.
4. Graham Burchell, Colin Gordon, Peter Miller, eds, *The Foucault Effect. Studies in Governmentality* (London, 1991). For recent Foucault-inspired studies on communist power structures see Ágnes Horváth, Árpád Szakolczai, *The Dissolution of Communist Power. The Case of Hungary* (London and New York, 1992); Jochen Hellbeck, "Fashioning the Stalinist Soul: The Diary of Stepan Podlubnyi (1931–1939)," *Jahrbücher für Geschichte Osteuropas*, 44 (1996): 344–73; Peter Holquist, "'Information Is the Alpha and Omega of Our Work': Bolshevik Surveillance in Its Pan-European Context," *Journal of Modern History* 69 (1997): 415–50; Stephen Kotkin, *Magnetic Mountain: Stalinism as a Civilization* (Berkeley, 1997).
5. See Jarausch in this volume.
6. On the early Volkspolizei see Richard Bessel, "Police of a 'New Type'? Police and Society in East Germany after 1945," *German History* 10 (1992): 290–301. For a general overview see Thomas Lindenberger, "Die Deutsche Volkspolizei (1945–1990)," in *Im Dienste der Partei. Handbuch der bewaffneten Organe der DDR*, ed. Torsten Diedrich, Hans Ehlert, and Rüdiger Wenzke, (Berlin, 1998), 97–152.
7. This summary description of the ABV system is based on files of the Hauptverwaltung der Deutschen Volkspolizei (HVDVP) in the Ministry of Interior, Bundesarchiv Berlin (BArchB), DO-1, Best. 11; and BArchB, DO-1, Best. 2.2, Weisungsbestand des Ministerium des Innern der DDR (in the following referred to as Weisungsbestand). For more detailed references and analysis of the ABV system see Thomas Lindenberger, "La police populaire de la RDA de

1952 à 1958. Une micro-étude sur la gouvernementalité de l'État socialiste," *Annales HSS* 53 (1998): 119–52; idem, "Der ABV als Landwirt. Zur Mitwirkung der Deutschen Volkspolizei bei der Kollektivierung der Landwirtschaft," in *Herrschaft und Eigen-Sinn*, 167-202.

8. See Michel Foucault, *Discipline and Punish: The Birth of the Prison*, trans. A. Sheridan (London, 1977); Clifford Shearing, "Reinventing Policing: Policing as Governance," in *Privatisierung staatlicher Kontrolle: Befunde, Konzepte, Tendenzen*, ed. Fritz Sack et al. (Baden-Baden, 1995), 70–87.

9. Chef der Deutschen Volkspolizei, 14. 3. 1957, an die Chefs der Bezirksbehörden, Anlage zu Befehl 152/52, Weisungsbestand.

10. For Hungary see Horváth and Szakolczai, *The Dissolution*, passim.

11. Abteilung für Sicherheitsfragen, 5. 1. 1954, Zusammenfassung der Berichte über die Überprüfung der Arbeit der Abschnittsbevollmächtigten in den Kreisen Meißen, Fürstenwalde, Rathenow, Hagenow und Merseburg, BArchB, DO-1, Best. 11, no. 23, Bl. 71ff.

12. On the June uprising see the essay collection in Kowalczuk, et al., eds, *Der Tag X – 17. Juni 1953. Die "innere Staatsgründung" der DDR als Ergebnis der Krise 1952/54* (Berlin, 1995), esp. Armin Mitter, "'Am 17. 6. 1953 haben die Arbeiter gestreikt, jetzt aber streiken wir Bauern.' Die Bauern und der Sozialismus," ibid., 75–128.

13. Thomas Lindenberger, "Der ABV im Text. Zur internen und öffentlichen Rede über die Deutsche Volkspolizei der 1950er Jahre." in *Akten. Eingaben. Schaufenster. Die DDR und ihre Texte*, ed. Alf Lüdtke and Peter Becker (Berlin, 1997), 137–66.

14. See Lutz Niethammer, "Biografie und Biokratie. Nachgedanken zu einem westdeutschen Oral-History-Projekt in der DDR fünf Jahre nach der deutschen Vereinigung," *Mitteilungen aus der kulturwissenschaftlichen Forschung*, 1996, no. 37: 370–87.

15. Christel Nehrig, "Landwirtschaftspolitik," in *Die SED. Geschichte-Organisation-Politik. Ein Handbuch*, ed. Alf Lüdtke and Peter Becker (Berlin, 1997), 294–305.

16. See Protokolle der ABV–Konferenzen in den vierzehn Kreisämtern des Bezirks Potsdam, Brandenburgisches Landeshauptarchiv, Rep. 404/15, no. 25, Bl. 104–241.

17. A "machine-tractor-station" was a state-run service station, designed to assist farmers, preferably those already collectivized, with modern agricultural machinery.

18. Michel Foucault, "Omnes et Singulatim," in *The Tanner Lectures on Human Values*, ed. Sterling McMurrin (Salt Lake City, 1981), vol. 2, 225–54.

19. For rituals of critique and self-critique in the Weimar KPD see Pamela Swett, "Neighborhood Mobilization and the Violence of Collapse: Berlin Political Culture, 1929–1933," (Ph.D. Thesis, Brown University, 1998); for the Stalinist purges, see Berthold Unfried, "Rituale von Konfession und Selbstkritik: Bilder vom stalinistischen Kader," in *Jahrbuch für Historische Kommunismusforschung*, 1994: 148–64.

20. See further contributions in Thomas Lindenberger, ed., *Herrschaft und Eigen-Sinn* (Cologne, 1999).

CHAPTER 8

FOOD SUPPLY IN A PLANNED ECONOMY

SED NUTRITION POLICY BETWEEN CRISIS RESPONSE AND POPULAR NEEDS

Burghard Ciesla and Patrice G. Poutrus

Supplying the GDR population with food was always a key issue for the SED leadership. It was clear to East German rulers from the very beginning that the GDR system would have no mid-range or long-term stability unless the populace was provided with adequate food and experienced constant improvements in the standard of living. Since the founding of the GDR in 1949, two tasks were therefore central to SED food policies: meeting consumer demands and supplying those needs from domestic production. The theoretical considerations behind this twofold goal were as follows: the projected collectivization of agriculture would result in overproduction, producing a surplus in foodstuffs and increasing the overall availability of goods. Marxist theory also predicted that "socialist forms of production" would be fundamentally superior to capitalism. Confident in this belief, SED leaders felt that supply problems and shortages would solve themselves over time. At the Second SED Congress in 1952, Walter Ulbricht, announced an acceleration in the development of socialism: "As a result of the double enslavement by American and West German monopoly capitalism, the living standard of the West German population will continue to sink, while in the GDR and the democratic sector of Berlin material and cultural conditions of the working people will improve according to plan."[1]

Soon after this announcement, the GDR, however, began to experience a social crisis that culminated in the mass protests of 17 June 1953, threatening the existence of SED rule. This trauma played a central role in determining SED food policies, and added another dimension that would have serious, destabilizing effects in the long run This element was a "paternalistic" concern, with which SED leaders attempted to placate East Germans' social dissatisfaction. Thereafter policy was formulated from the premise that any expression of discontent should not be allowed to go beyond what was considered "manageable." This was particularly true considering that popular expectations could never be quieted by promises of more prosperity, such as those expressed in the slogan "As we work today, so we will live tomorrow!"

In the interest of maintaining the system's stability within the framework of the Cold War, leaders felt it imperative to meet popular demands for better food supplies, regardless of the economy's actual ability to produce them. Until the GDR's demise, the basic rule of thumb was to avoid any abrupt changes in prices, work loads, or salaries. In the Honecker era (1971 to 1989), this principle proved to be a grave liability, since Honecker himself – due to his own personal experiences – had internalized a simplistic model of socialism which he wanted to see realized "at any price." In his world view, the average GDR citizen needed a warm, dry apartment, cheap basic food, and steady work. According to Honecker, once these needs had been met, socialism was bound to progress and flourish. The very paternalism that was originally a stabilizing element became an inflexible structure that inhibited the dynamic development of popular consumer needs.[2]

But where did these dynamic consumer needs actually come from? According to János Kornai's classical economic analysis, the GDR was actually a shortage economy (*Mangelwirtschaft*), a system that had little room for innovation. Instead, scarcity was the distinguishing feature of daily life, and shortages were pervasive, frequent, intensive, and chronic. In their capacity as both consumers and producers, East Germans experienced "numerous frustrations and foiled attempts to purchase products, long lines, forced substitutions, a continual search for goods, and postponement in purchases on a daily basis."[3] GDR citizens lacked the consumer sovereignty possessed by buyers in market economies. Instead, the basic rule was: the less likely it seemed that certain products or goods would be available, the more consumers should hoard. It is important to note that the GDR was not a "buyers' market" as in capitalist systems. In the planned economy, sellers (state-run retailers, marketing agencies, and industry) were not forced to compete for the trust and favor of buyers on an open market. The removal of market mechanisms meant that the two most important instruments in the competition for buyers, improved product quality and product innovation, were practically non-existent. Questions about consumption in the GDR were always secondary, only receiving government attention when it became necessary to deal with supply shortages, or crisis situations that had gone beyond what was considered "manageable."

The geographical and informational proximity of West Germany was also influential in creating consumer needs that placed pressures on the East German state. The West was omnipresent – via information gleaned through the media, in special stores, through the availability of Western products in the East, in the shape of private contacts or relatives. In other words, consumption served as a way of approaching the standards of the West. Although the differences between the two economic systems in the East and West remained fundamental, consumption shows how, with some time lag, Western mass culture found its way even into the GDR.[4]

The system of industrial and commercial distribution within the GDR's planned economy could not keep pace with more dynamic Western developments. Ultimately, food supply policies in the GDR were merely directed at providing the populace with sufficient amounts of products that often did not fulfill its wishes. The SED leadership attempted to bridge the ever-widening chasm between demand and supply among other things by concentrating on self-sufficiency. By implementing a strategy of economic isolation during the Cold War years, the SED hoped to offset the effects of Western trade embargoes and to achieve relative independence. But it became increasingly clear that this strategy would not work. In practice, claims to self-sufficiency were constantly contradicted, resulting in a strange paradox. While the state continually explained that it was necessary to become independent of Western imports, it simultaneously bought, traded or "managed" to get know-how from the West and to imitate Western styles. Preparations for the Leipzig trade fair in the fall of 1968, for instance, included a "plan for licensing" which asked the food industry to focus on licensing as a central element of supply, in order to save domestic capacities.[5]

Licensed production, barter, and joint ventures were used to improve supply, to reduce existing purchasing surpluses, introduce Western standards and attain foreign currency. Starting in the 1970s, chain stores, mail-order houses, and companies such as Triumph, Pepsi-Cola, Nestlé, Schiesser, Blaupunkt, or Salamander attempted to increase production in the GDR, and used the East as a cheap market and producer. Business in East Germany was just what many Western firms needed to gain advantages over their competitors. Coca Cola, for instance, tried repeatedly in the 1970s to expand into the East German market. Their competitor, Pepsi-Cola, proved to be more successful in these ventures. But Pepsi and the GDR regime mutually agreed to break off business relations after Pepsi proved to be a huge flop in the East.[6] GDR foreign trade policies played Western competitors against each other. This happened, for instance, in 1981, when in negotiations with the Swiss food manufacturer Nestlé, the GDR discussed the possibility of importing Nestlé products into the GDR at the cost of imports from the FRG (Triumph).[7]

As a result, GDR citizens could buy Western products, most of which were much more expensive than normal GDR goods. A bottle of Pepsi in 1974, for example, cost three times as much as the domestic, GDR-produced cola drink.[8] In the face of the limited range of articles, especially in the lower or mid-range price categories, consumers were forced to buy imported products. Most were available only in specialty shops, such as the *Delikat* chain, or the "Intershops" (where only foreign currency could be used), or in stores in large factories or state institutions. In this manner, the SED continued the policy of a two-class system of customers that stemmed from the 1940s and 1950s. From 1948 on the SED had established State Trade Organizations (HOs) that for Eastern tastes seemed very Western and were often called "a piece of the West in the East." There customers could buy rationed goods freely, and compared with the difficulties encountered on the open market, there was a veritable abundance of goods. This system largely reduced the ideological claims about sharing prosperity among all members of society to absurdity. In this manner, the contradictions inherent within the SED's "welfare dictatorship" deepened, and by the 1970s at the latest, the internal "logic of failure" (Diedrich Dörner) had become painfully evident.

Proceeding from this framework, the following two case studies on the introduction of frozen food in the fish industry and poultry farming intend to illustrate the tensions between state supply policies, industrial food production, everyday effects, and demands for a more modern consumer society. These examples illuminate patterns of supply that are typical of other areas in food production by raising the following questions: How did the SED's claims to self-sufficiency influence production? What mechanisms did the party leadership employ? How did producers and consumers react to these policies? The first case study of chicken farming focuses on the establishment of mass production in the poultry industry by examining "fried chicken," and following state policies in this area.

The second case study focuses on the fish industry to detail the introduction of a new product, frozen fish sticks. Proceeding from the industry's use of resources, this study examines the structural conditions that preceded and accompanied this product.[9]

The Case of the "Goldbroiler"

The introduction of fried chicken is, in comparison to the tale of GDR fish sticks, more than an agricultural success story. The account of this success – which was unique in GDR agriculture – began in 1965, when the first production facilities for poultry farming were opened in Königs Wusterhausen and Möckern. From an initial investment of 51.3 million GDR marks, 55 percent of which were hard currency funds,[10] the industry had a return of 1.7 billion marks. Overall, the eleven factory farms (*Kombinate Industrielle Mast*, or KIM), as well as other state farms and special production facilities, built over 2,000 chicken houses and processing plants for the production of fryers and eggs.[11] The leading facility of the "Chicken Producers of the GDR," as the VVB Industrial Animal Farming was called, employed 6,000 people in the plants under its charge in 1972.

The VVB also organized marketing through direct and door-to-door sales, as well as in specially outfitted restaurants, aptly called "Goldbroiler" (*Zum Goldbroiler*).[12] By 1978, over 142 such restaurants had been established all over East Germany.[13] The press praised the KIM plants as examples of the triumph of scientific-technological progress in the system of socialist agriculture.[14] From 1968 to 1971, East Berlin media celebrated each opening of a Goldbroiler restaurant like the winning of an Olympic gold medal. Finally, there were thirteen restaurants in East Berlin, and the newspaper *BZ am Abend* announced in 1972: "12,000 roasted chickens are consumed daily in the capital."[15] But despite the tremendous increase in poultry consumption, East German citizens – similar to Germans in the West – continued to eat mainly pork and potatoes (Table 8.1).[16]

The introduction of factory farming methods and the rise of a culture of dining out had a great impact on the habits of East Germans. These changes were a successful adaptation of Western patterns that did not easily correspond to existing structures in the GDR. In other words, compared to other areas, poultry production played a special role in the GDR's economy.[17] What were the circumstances that led to such an exceptional development, and why did it not trigger further innovations in East German agriculture or the GDR economy as a whole?

Table 8.1 *Consumption of Food Products per Capita (1960–1989)*

Selected Products	1960	1970	1975	1980	1985	1989
Beef and veal (kg)	18.0	22.3	22.2	22.5	24.2	25.1
Pork (kg)	33.3	38.7	48.0	57.8	61.9	63.8
Poultry (kg)	3.7	5.1	7.6	8.9	10.2	10.4
Fish and fish products (kg)	7.0	7.9	8.5	7.4	7.7	7.6
Potatoes and potato products (kg)	173.9	153.5	142.1	148.1	150.3	158.0

Source: "Zur Ernährungssituation in der DDR zwischen 1980 und 1990. Eine Materialsammlung," *Ernährungsforschung* 41 (1996): 153.

Following the lines laid down at the Fifth Party Congress of the SED in 1958, the East German state carried out a massive collectivization of agriculture, continuing until 1960.[18] This administratively orchestrated transformation of infrastructure led to a sharp decline in agricultural production[19] as well as a dramatic rise in state subsidies for the economically weak collective farms (LPGs), despite Walter Ulbricht's contrary prediction (Table 8.2).

The ensuing production shortages, and agriculture's inability to provide the population with the necessary foodstuffs, put the SED in a difficult spot. The impasse was complicated by the fact that the SED, with the West serving as a thorn in its side, had promised at the Fifth Party Congress to end all food rationing. As a result, grocery stores experienced an unexpected increase in sales.[20] Due to various price regulations and changes in the wage system, GDR citizens also simultaneously had more money at their disposal. However, the limited supplies available in stores were unable to absorb increased buying power.[21] Pressures on existing food supplies, freed from ration controls, suddenly increased.[22] Despite food imports and attempts to offer substitutes,[23] collectivization became an even

Table 8.2 *State Subsidies by Sector*

	1956	1961
Subsides for LPGs	91,300,000 Mk	765,000,000 Mk
Price subsidies	2,115,800,000 Mk	4,928,600,000 Mk
Social insurance subsidies	79,800,000 Mk	324,400,000 Mk
Credits/Loans subsidies	664,000,000 Mk	1,132,000,000 Mk

Source: "Hausmitteilung der Abteilung Planung und Finanzen des ZK der SED an das Büro Dr. Mittag, vom 8. September 1962." SAPMO-BArch, DY 30 IV A. 2.2021 No. 713, Bl. 178.

more serious threat to supplies after 1960.[24] Butter, milk, meat, and potatoes were particularly hard to find. They could only be purchased in retail stores via so-called "customer lists." In spite of official measures to remove ration controls, a kind of de-centralized rationing system, therefore, continued to exist.

The building of the Wall in 1961 brought no relief, since agriculture, already seriously weakened by the collectivization drive, was further handicapped by the effects of a bad harvest.[25] Spurred by fears of international tension, GDR citizens turned to hoarding.[26] These developments came to a head in 1962, breaking out in a full-fledged supply crisis. The gap between supply and demand continued to widen,[27] and the departments dealing with "party organs" and "security" within the Central Committee of the SED reported repeatedly that these grave food shortages would lead to serious unrest in areas of the GDR. In some cases workers even threatened to lay down their work.[28] They were criticizing not only the lack of foodstuffs, but they questioned the social policies of the party, especially the SED's collectivization measures in agriculture.[29] To defuse this dangerous situation, the SED ordered increases in food imports and the use of state reserves set aside for crisis situations.[30]

The orientation of the SED's Sixth Party Congress towards industrial methods of agricultural production should therefore not be dismissed as a utopian vision,[31] but be interpreted as a pragmatic reaction to a crisis created by the party itself. In the ensuing period, the leadership continued to search for solutions to fill the "meat gap" (*Fleischlücke*) with the GDR's own domestic resources. Comparative studies of animal feed, work patterns, investment need, costs, and necessary raising time made the introduction of large-scale animal farming appear promising.[32] Experiments with domestic duck farming, or raising chickens in mines were soon rejected in favor of industrial chicken farming, or abandoned entirely.[33] Although the GDR Academy of Agricultural Sciences had long collected data on poultry farming through domestic experiments[34] and research projects,[35] as well as cooperation with similar institutes in the COMECON,[36] and possessed remarkable scientific knowledge about the techniques of chicken breeding,[37] the state was nevertheless incapable of creating a production-ready technology for industrial poultry farming.

In late 1964 the SED's Office for Agriculture decided, therefore, to form a staff of agricultural experts and managers under the direction of the State Purchasing Committee.[38] This "Central Organizational Group" was charged with establishing pilot plants for industrial animal production that would meet international standards and reduce the need for expensive imports. Their plans focused on industrial production sites for poultry, but also included breeding and rearing facilities for cattle and swine.[39] The result of the Central Organizational Group's measures was the licensing – via Yugoslavia – of Dutch, West German, and British technologies in state-operated plants.[40] From this time on chicken farming concentrated on creating a particular type of chicken out of various breeds – the fryer. The short maturity time of fryers of only about fifty days and their large holding facilities made it possible to slaughter them regardless of the season.[41] Starting in 1966, a Yugoslav construction firm built the first of many large chicken houses near the East Berlin suburb of Königs Wusterhausen.[42] These formed the core of the people's owned (VE) KIM Königs Wusterhausen, founded on 1 January 1967, which in turn served as the model for several other projects in different regions. The goal of this investment was to provide "centers of the working class" with adequate fresh poultry and eggs.[43] This was especially important given that there were still serious problems providing adequate amounts of meat.[44]

In 1967, the state opened the "Goldbroiler" restaurants and special poultry shops in order to distribute the increased poultry production to urban households.[45] In spite of extreme shortages of meat, supplies had often sat undelivered in previous years due to lack of adequate transport, or would rot because of inadequate refrigeration.[46] Hence the state bypassed the wholesale distribution system of refrigeration and transportation, delivering directly to retailers. The outlets were modeled after the Austrian restaurant chain "Wienerwald." Such fast-food "grill restaurants" were more simply furnished than normal restaurants, which further reduced investment costs.[47] Yet the integration of these investments into the GDR economy did not proceed without friction, since the permanent ties to Western firms resulted in a great deal of mistrust from economic experts and party bureaucrats.[48] Because of this suspicion, the staff within the State Purchasing Committee was dissolved in 1968, and responsibility for the poultry industry was transferred to the VVB Animal Breeders Paretz.[49] In 1971, the legally independent VVB Industrial Farming of Berlin was formed, with central authority over all KIM plants.[50] This organizational change marked the high point of the development, and afterwards investment stopped expanding, merely maintaining the status quo.[51]

The consequences of the Goldbroiler success story can be summarized as follows:

1. Once the VVB ITP was founded, state meat producers quickly lost their special position within the GDR economy. After the KIM

plants had been established, factory-style animal farming was increasingly concentrated in the large agricultural production collectives (LPGs).[52] It also soon became apparent that the recipe for success, so effective in the poultry industry, could not be repeated with other small animals. Large-scale experiments with so-called "broikas" (fryer *Kaninchen,* or "fryer rabbits") ended with veterinary catastrophes and were terminated, despite the large amounts of money invested. Other projects aimed at processing or refining chicken also failed, due to a lack of investment from the West.[53]

2. Though successful in the late 1960s and early 1970s, Gold-broiler restaurants could not maintain their status as novelties for long. In addition to the usual complaints about unfriendly service, the chain's popularity soon became a problem itself. Several press reports noted that the restaurants, originally seen as a welcome gastronomic addition, soon lost their appeal due to large crowds. They quickly became unkempt and inhospitable fast food joints, rather than simple but clean restaurants.[54] The director of the State Purchasing Committee also noted in 1971 that not enough grills existed to allow a much-needed expansion of Goldbroiler restaurants.[55] Since the Goldbroilers were generally not placed in new locations, but consisted of re-furbished and re-opened old ones, even the increase in the number of new Goldbroilers could not stop the continual decline in the number of restaurants overall.[56] Obviously, funds were lacking for further expansion or renovation. Ultimately, school lunch programs and worker's canteens had priority over fast food chains.[57]

3. Public advertising campaigns and reports about the new Gold-broiler product constantly emphasized that chicken had less fat than pork and was therefore an important part of a healthy diet.[58] This argument was linked to a particular development: During the food shortages in the 1960s, the use of animal fats and meats of lesser quality had risen dramatically, so that experts at the Institute for Nutrition at the GDR's Academy of Sciences feared that large segments of the population would become obese.[59] Low-fat chicken was meant to counter these trends, especially in the face of chronic shortages of fruit and vegetables. But these considerations did not change behavioral patterns of the average GDR citizen. Although chicken, touted as "healthy," was consumed and seen as a welcome addition to the limited supply of meat, it was never perceived as a substitute for pork. In spite of medical warnings, "good," i.e., opulent, food continued to enjoy great popularity. Nutritionists see in this preference a continuity with earlier eating habits.[60]

Fish Sticks as an Alternative

Immediately after the end of the war, the desperate food situation compelled a search for alternate sources of supply. One of these alternatives was fishing. Fishing also assumed strategic significance due to the Soviet interest in feeding their troops.[61] But the limited coastal fishing carried out in the SBZ in 1946–47 could hardly meet these demands. Between 1948 and 1950, proposals were therefore made regarding the establishment of a real fishing industry. The SED also wished to strengthen the weak and underdeveloped infrastructure in the north of the SBZ–GDR in order to ease social and economic disparities between North and South. Aside from shipping and trade, a fishing industry seemed to offer the promise of economic recovery for the structurally weak coastal regions.

The construction of a fishing industry was basically completed by the mid-1950s. Afterwards, the fleet was expanded with new types of ships, since earlier boat models (loggers, trawlers, and cutters) only allowed fishing in certain seasons. Large portions of previously land-based processing technologies were also transferred onto the ships, which combined both nets and processing equipment. These investments made possible a transition from individual fishing to industrial fleet fishing, which began in about the mid-1960s. At the end of the decade, high sea fishing possessed an extensive fleet, which more than tripled its catches between 1960 and 1970 from about 89 to approximately 276 kilotons. Simultaneously, the import of fish and fish products was cut back by two-thirds, and the seasonal nature of the industry was visibly reduced. The industry thereby came very close to meeting the SED's demands for self-sufficiency.[62]

At the same time, however, it became clear that internationally, fishing was entering a period of decline. The worldwide over-use of resources led to a crisis in the 1970s, which culminated in the establishment of two-hundred-mile economic fishing zones. Areas rich in fishing near the coasts were now off limits. GDR fishing was especially hard hit by these restrictions, since 90 percent of the fleet's previous fishing grounds were no longer available. During 1978 totals, therefore, sank below the 1964 levels, and reserve stocks were only 80 percent of the levels from 1975.[63] This ever greater crisis of resources resulted in shortages, and until 1980–81 East Germans faced a real decline in the availability of fish. Although the industry would recover to some degree in the 1980s, the development of fish consumption that had started in the 1960s either stagnated, or became peripheral.

During the second half of the 1960s, planners within the GDR fishing industry hoped to increase supplies of kitchen-ready, customer-friendly, packaged, and refrigerated products.[64] This turn to frozen foods was largely influenced by developments in the West, since GDR leaders also realized such products belonged to the most significant innovations in Western food consumption habits. The changes associated with refrigerated food affected household practices, eating patterns, and thought processes. Frozen foods had become a standard in West Germany in the early 1960s. The West had long overcome the barrier of the lack of refrigeration technology that hampered the spread of frozen goods in the GDR, by introducing frozen foods in supermarkets and equipping a large number of households with refrigerators.[65] By 1964, West German retail stores possessed over 100,000 freezer units, and in 1962–63, 52 percent of all homes had refrigerators.[66] In comparison, at the beginning of the decade East Germany had only twelve refrigerators for every 100 households, catching up with West German standards of the early 1960s only by the end of the decade.[67] East German retail stores were similarly behind Western norms, so that in 1962–63, only 20 percent of the 1,692 specialty fish stores had refrigeration. Although with 39,247 square meters the fish industry possessed vast amounts of storage and transshipment space (in 87 delivery warehouses), only 12 percent of it was usable for refrigeration. And only 6 percent of that amount could be used for the storage of products below minus 18°C. Lack of adequate transport facilities and difficulties in producing the machinery needed for processing and refrigeration only worsened the situation.[68]

The early introduction of refrigeration in the West meant that starting in the late 1950s, the fishing industry could offer frozen food in retail stores. Frozen fish proved to be an attractive alternative to fresh fish, because it could be stored for longer periods and was easier to prepare. During the 1960s, the market share of frozen fish among all fish consumed in the FRG rose significantly from 27 percent in 1966 to 44 percent in 1970.[69] West German trade papers praised frozen fish as an article for the future that "makes cash registers ring."[70] Surprisingly, fish consumption in the South, traditionally lower than that of the North, began to climb slowly. This development was due to increased sales of frozen fish and the ability to transport it over longer distances. A closer look at consumption reveals a reversal of earlier patterns – the further south an area, the higher the fish consumption.[71]

The same development was evident in the GDR, although the number of products, their quality, and variety all lagged behind Western standards. GDR consumption of frozen foods in 1988 was only 20 percent of the consumption in the FRG.[72] In the same year, the per capita consumption of fish in the GDR at 4.8 kg was higher

Burghard Ciesla and Patrice Poutrus

than that in the FRG at 4.1 kg. But the variety of products processed by the GDR's fishing industry – 81,000 tons – differed significantly from the FRG's. In the GDR, preserved fish made up 43 percent of all products, followed by canned fish (28 percent), smoked fish (25 percent), and special products (4 percent). The consumption of smoked fish was much higher in the GDR than in the West; Easterners also ate more preserved (40 percent) and canned fish (18 percent) than Westerners. However, consumers were only rarely offered frozen fish which is subsumed under the 4 percent share of special products. It is clear that products that were more processed – frozen or ready to make items – ranked below other foods. Other basic, subsidized, cheap foods, such as potatoes, meat, or pasta were substituted for fish products. At the same time, the subsidies of fish prices, linked with specific marketing problems led to an "excess demand" for less processed products such as preserved or smoked fish.[73]

Frozen food production led to the realization of the "law of industrial mass production" worldwide. According to critics, mass-produced frozen foods "influenced daily eating habits, the variety of products offered, and reduced taste to a serialized level."[74] In the GDR fish processing industry, which was distinguished in the 1960s by a high degree of manual labor, frozen foods seemed to offer a chance to meet SED demands for increased mechanization, automation, and product standardization.[75] The Institute for Deep Sea Fishing and Fish Processing in Rostock-Marienehe, an industry research center, began to investigate the possibilities of such processes in the early 1960s.[76] The production of fish sticks seemed to offer optimal conditions for assembly line production techniques and product standardization.[77] Around 1966, the necessary technology had been acquired, and production procedures were ready to be introduced. Production finally commenced near the end of 1968. Three products were introduced in packages of five and ten pieces each: Rostock Fried Fish Sticks (pre-fried), Rostock Red Snapper Fillets (pre-fried and breaded), and Rostock Breaded Fish Sticks (pre-fried and breaded).[78]

At that time, fish sticks had already become a "classic" in the West German market. The Langnese–Igloo company had introduced the product early in the 1960s. Although sales were slow at first, the "fish sticks" (as they were called in the U.S., or "fish fingers," as they were referred to in Great Britain), became the biggest frozen food hit[79] in the Federal Republic. While in 1965 preparations were underway in the GDR to start producing fish sticks, the Purchasing Society of the Association of German Retail Stores (EDEKA) could announce triumphantly: "We have created a new bestseller with fish sticks."[80]

Fish stick production began in the East in 1969, and slowly began to reach a peak during the course of 1970, despite the vagaries of the catch. But in the summer of 1971, alarm bells began to sound in the Ministry for Regional Industry and Food Industry (MBL) after a report from the Schwerin Fishing Trade surfaced. This letter revealed that 38 tons of Rostock fish sticks, produced in November and December of 1970, were sitting in the firm's facilities, in danger of rotting. The amounts of stored fish sticks would, so the authors feared, "increase continually over time due to planned deliveries that will add to stocks and a general lack of sales." Despite this problem, Rostock continued to deliver large amounts to the firm, much like Goethe's sorcerer's apprentice. The MBL ordered that 40 percent of the 38 tons of Schwerin surplus be "shipped immediately for consumption." The remaining 23 tons of fish sticks had to be quality tested first.[81] But even the remaining fish sticks fit for consumption never made it to market. Instead, they were marked for further processing – now destined to become ingredients in future "fish salads."

The 1971 "fish stick mountain" marked the beginning of a steady decline in production, from 905 tons in 1970 to 109 tons in 1975. Grave setbacks in catches in 1977–78 and new types of fish that proved more difficult to process allowed only limited production.[82] In addition, consumers had serious reservations about the quality of GDR fish products. They suspected that fish of lesser quality (*Fischmus*, or fish mush) was being hidden under the breading. Called, among other things, "sawdust" by the populace, fish sticks seemed to resemble nothing more than wood shavings that had been pressed together and fried.[83] In official reports, coverage of the Rostock fish sticks breaks off around the mid-1970s, and their further history is difficult to reconstruct. According to information from contemporaries, fish sticks were still available in stores in the 1980s, but infrequently, and in relatively limited amounts. However, they were no longer marketed under the name "Rostock Fish Sticks."

The "decline" of fish sticks was also influenced to a large degree by increases in licensed production at the end of the 1970s. The GDR bought processing plants from Western companies, as well as practical know-how and the necessary packaging materials, hoping to finance the modernization of its plants with sales from products abroad. The fishing industry, as well as many other areas of food and consumer production, served in this manner as "extended workbenches" for the West. Yet exporters and representatives of the fishing industry argued paradoxically from a standpoint that emphasized autonomy, maintaining that once refinancing was complete, the production lines and know-how would belong to the GDR, permitting imports from the West to decline. East Germany's high seas fishing fleet would supply expensive fish as raw material in the process.[84]

These products were also available domestically, and could be bought as so-called "specialty items" in Intershops for foreign currency or in the specialty store *Delikat* at inflated GDR prices. Though the production of such delicatessen items remained modest, with a volume of 3.5 kilotons, the availability of delicacies (fish, sausage, chocolate, tea, coffee, spirits, etc.) played an important role in exhausting buying power and in supplementing the normal range of products.[85]

But why could the West German fish stick success story not be repeated in East Germany? How did the "cash register boom" of West German frozen foods become an East German sales debacle? The seemingly simple answers to these questions rest on a wide spectrum of internal and external circumstances. External factors, such as the international expansion of fishing boundaries and the resultant limitations on fishing have already been mentioned. The internal factors regarding fish stick production are related to the following: initially, problems with fish sticks had less to do with the quality of the fish caught as with the difficulties in attaining the capital and infrastructure needed to market the product. In the case of the fish stick mountain mentioned above, ten tons had been set aside for the Leipzig branch office. But Leipzig refused to accept the goods because it lacked the refrigeration needed for storage. Fish retailers did not possess enough refrigerated cars for transport, and retail stores did not have adequate freezer storage. In the early 1960s, only 40 percent of the existing 1,450 grocery stores and 84 percent of fish specialty shops had freezers.[86]

Even when stores did have freezers, they often had problems with this technology. A technical journal of 1972 noted: "Lack of knowledge regarding temperature levels, or amounts of ice thickness have resulted in a lack of quality and waste. Proper use and maintenance of freezers has been neglected. Defrosting is carried out irregularly; cooked food is inadequately cooled before being frozen, often creating disturbances in the highly sensitive machines, leading in some cases to breakdowns in cooling aggregates."[87] In the face of permanent shortages and lack of replacement parts, the latter meant that machines, when broken, were out of service for long periods of time. Where freezers were in use, they were often used for other foodstuffs, such as poultry. Ice cream was given priority, because it was thought to "attract business." In earlier years, the fact that there were serious gaps in the chain of refrigeration from producer to consumer was probably decisive for the failure of fish sticks. And finally, fish sticks were offered at inflated prices which were two and a half times more expensive than normal frozen fish fillets. Both large suppliers as well as families, therefore, avoided buying fish sticks. The problem was compounded by the fact that buyers could purchase less expensive, subsidized basic food products.[88]

Consumption in Socialist Society

The patriarchal policies of the GDR dictatorship were aimed at controlling "basic dissatisfaction" in the population. The ever present shortages of the planned economy and the lack of consumer sovereignty as well as the externally fueled dynamics of consumer desires produced frustration in the daily lives of GDR citizens. These factors influenced a complex development, in which the smallest disturbances, the simplest decisions, or corrective measures had ever more fatal and counter-productive consequences. In this manner, the GDR was driven to the limits of stability. Consequently, the decisions of SED leaders and the developments associated with them became irreversible, since they could not meet the pull of the other great attraction, the West, with any substantive alternative.

Both case studies have traced these mechanisms at work. They have shown how East German economic leaders attempted to introduce two different Western consumer products into the East and how they planned to alleviate chronic food shortages by industrialized food production – specifically chicken farming and fleet fishing. At the same time, the preparation and processing of animal products offered good prospects for implementing mechanization, automation, and standardization in the food industry. These studies exemplify how the agents within the planning system functioned under the circumstances of a static economy and a lack of market mechanisms in attempting to copy the consumer levels of the West, without being able to foresee the fatal "side effects" of these new products. This should have been possible, in view of freezer capacities. But there were false projections about the capacity of a closed freezer chain, extending from producers to consumers. Gaps existed everywhere: from the frozen storage capacities needed for production and transport, the supply of adequate packaging, and the availability of freezers for stores and restaurants, down to providing households with freezers. These problems could only slowly be remedied which had a negative effect on the spread of consumption and the differentiation of eating habits. In the face of a chronic lack of foreign currency, Western imports could not be relied upon to assist in the establishment of food production. The result was compensation and improvisation, which in turn triggered wild swings in supply that could only lead to dissatisfaction among East German citizens confronted with Western models.

These difficulties should not cloud the fact that East Germans viewed increased supplies of poultry and fish as an improvement in their normal fare, especially the establishment of special restaurants such as the "Goldbroiler" chain or the "Meals of the Sea"[89] fish restaurants, which met consumer demands for a more sophisticated eating culture. This was also behind the trend towards fast food restaurants with bars – eateries based on the principles established by American fast food and family restaurants. While the Goldbroiler chain became a success story, the fish restaurants enjoyed only initial success, since the fishing crisis of the 1970s limited expansion. Despite their varying degrees of success, both cases were influenced negatively by the East German distribution system as well as traditional eating patterns. Also influential were widespread suspicions of the state's attempts "to bring eating customs in line with existing possibilities" by educating the populace. The attempts of industry, trade, and gastronomy to influence eating habits were ultimately doomed to failure, since the problems associated with an expansion of food consumption and improvements in restaurant culture could not be met under the conditions laid down by a dogmatic, patriarchal system of supply.

The issue of supply in a planned economy is closely tied to such terms as autarchy, independence from world markets, self-sufficiency, or a provisional economy. But the SED's repeated calls for self-sufficiency and its attempts to achieve this goal in various areas of the food industry should not lead to the conclusion that the GDR was a self-sufficient economy. These case studies have shown that the opposite was true, that the GDR used its claims to self-sufficiency in a paradoxical attempt to copy Western consumer society.

Notes

1. Walter Ulbricht, *Die gegenwärtige Lage und die neueren Aufgaben der Sozialistischen Einheitspartei Deutschlands. Referat und Schlußwort auf der II. Parteikonferenz der SED Berlin, 9. bis 12. Juli 1952* (Berlin, 1952), 89.
2. M. Rainer Lepsius, "Die Institutionenordnung als Rahmenbedingung der Sozialgeschichte der DDR," in *Sozialgeschichte der DDR*, ed. Hartmut Kaelbe, Jürgen Kocka, and Hartmut Zwahr (Stuttgart, 1994), 24ff.
3. János Kornai, *Das sozialistische System. Die politische Ökonomie des Kommunismus* (Baden-Baden, 1995), vol. 29, 263–64.

4. S. Haustein, "Westeuropäische Annäherung durch Konsum seit 1945," in *Gesellschaft im Vergleich. Forschungen aus Sozial- und Geschichtswissenschaften, Komparatistische Bibliothek,* ed. Hartmut Kaelble and Jürgen Schriewer (Frankfurt am Main, 1998), vol. 9, 353–90; and Kornai, *System,* 257 ff.

5. Bundesarchiv Berlin-Lichterfelde (BArch), DG 5, no. 0806, "Konzeption für die Lizenztätigkeit in Vorbereitung und Durchführung der Leipziger Herbstmesse 1968," 11 June 1968.

6. For the talks between the GDR and Pepsi-Cola and Coca-Cola see the following files in the Ministry for Regional Industries: BArch, DG 5, Nos. 6283, 6284, and 6286.

7. "Reise Schweiz – Zurich/Vevey", 30 April 1981, BArch, DG 5, no. 6292.

8. The comparison is based on 0.25 liter bottles. BArch, DG 5, no. 6284.

9. Burghard Ciesla, "Eine sich selbst versorgende Konsumgesellschaft? Industrieller Fischfang, Fischwarenkonsum in der DDR," in *Herrschaft und Eigen–Sinn in der Diktatur. Forschungen zur Gesellschaftsgeschichte der DDR* (Cologne 1999), ed. Thomas Lindenberger; Patrice G. Poutrus, "'Mit Politik bekomme ich die Tennisbälle nicht groß!' Das Kombinat Industrielle Mast und seine Arbeiterinnen," in ibid.

10. Technisch-Ökonomische Zielstellung, Part 1, BArch, DK 107, A17, no. 23/1.

11. Landesarchiv Berlin (hereafter LAB), Rep 635, no. 130, Geflügelwirtschaftsverband der DDR.

12. KIM VEB Kombinate für Industrielle Mast, Werbematerial, LAB, Rep. 635/120. The term "broiler" was imported from English to denote the grilling of "fryer" chickens.

13. "Erhebung der Zentralverwaltung für Statistik beim Ministerat der DDR zum Gaststätten- und Küchennetz per 31.12.1978," BArch, DE 2, Box 30743, no. 0043716.

14. "Eier und Broiler am laufenden Band," *Neues Deutschland,* 18 September 1971.

15. *Berliner Zeitung* (BZ), 31 January 1970, *BZ am Abend,* 24 August 1970 and 13 October 1970.

16. I. Schön, "Wandlungen in den Verzehrgewohnheiten bei Fleisch von 1945 bis zur Gegenwart," in *Vom Hungerwinter zum kulinarischen Schlaraffenland. Aspekte einer Kulturgeschichte des Essens in der Bundesrepublik,* ed. W. Protzner (Wiesbaden, 1987), 107.

17. André Steiner, "Beständigkeit oder Wandel? Zur Entwicklung der Industriestruktur der DDR in den sechziger Jahren," *Jahrbuch für Wirtschaftsgeschichte* 2 (1995): 101ff.

18. Ch. Nehring, "Landwirtschaftspolitik," in *Die SED. Geschichte – Organisation – Politik. Ein Handbuch,* ed. Andreas Herbst et al. (Berlin, 1997), 299f.

19. *Statistisches Jahrbuch der Land-, Forst- und Nahrungsgüterwirtschaft der DDR* (Berlin, 1982), 125f.

20. "Bericht über die Auswirkungen der Abschaffung der Reste der Lebensmittelrationierung in den Haushalten von Arbeitern und von Angestellten der Industrie und der Bauindustrie," 14, BArch, DE, no. 1642.

21. Peter Hübner, *Konsens, Konflikt und Kompromiß. Soziale Arbeiterinteressen und Sozialpolitik in der SBZ/DDR 1945–1970* (Berlin,1995), 154ff.

22. Joerg Rösler, "Privater Konsum in Ostdeutschland 1950–1960," in *Modernisierung im Wiederaufbau,* ed. Axel Schildt and Arnold Sywottek (Bonn, 1993): 290–303.

23. "Information vom 19. Juni 1959 über Volkswirtschaftsplan der Lebensmittelindustrie für 1959," SAPMO-BArch, DY 30, J IV 2/3 A, no. 664; for substitution, see Joerg Rösler, "Butter, Margarine und Wirtschaftspolitik," *Jahrbuch für Wirtschaftsgeschichte* 29 (1988): 33–48.

24. "Informationbericht Nr. 34 zur Versorgung der Bevölkerung vom 9. September 1960," SAPMO-BArch, DY 30, IV 2/2.023, no. 53.

25. "Probleme die sich aus der Ernte für die Entwicklung der Produktion der Landwirtschaft und der Versorgung der Bevölkerung mit Nahrungsgütern im Jahr 1962 ergeben," SAPMO-BArch, DY 30, IV 2/2, no. 73: 96 f.

26. "Information über Hamsterkäufe vom 14. Oktober 1961," SAPMO-BArch, DY 30, IV 2/610, no. 28: 58.

27. For the shortages see Hübner, *Konsens*, 163ff.

28. "Hausmitteilung vom 14. August 1962, Diskussionen zur Versorgungslage und Feindarbeit im Bezirk Halle," SAPMO-BArch, DY 30, IV 2/610, no. 28: 266 f.

29. "Kurzinformation über die Durchführung der Lenkungsmaßnahmen für Fleisch- und Wurstwaren vom 28. Juni 1962," SAPMO-BArch, DY 30, IV 2.o23, no. 5: 85–9.

30. "Beschluß des Politbüros zur Sicherung der Versorgung mit Fleisch, Fisch und Eiern vom 21.August 1962," SAPMO-BArch, DY 30, IV 2/610, no. 17: 212 ff.

31. *Protokoll der Verhandlungen des VI. Parteitages der SED*, Bd. IV, (Berlin East, 1963), 349f.

32. "Einschätzung der Produktivität verschiedener Fleischarten hinsichtlich ihrer Ökonomie," SAPMO-BArch, DY 30, IV A 2.o23, no. 35: 42.

33. "Hinweise zur Deckung des Geflügelfleischbedarfs," SAPMO-BArch, DY 30, IV A 2.o23, no. 35: 43f.

34. "Protokolle der Arbeitsgruppe 'Intensivgeflügelhaltung' 1959–1962," BArch, DK 107/189, no. 190, vol. 1,"Protokolle der Arbeitsgemeinschaft 'Geflügelzucht' 1962–64," BArch, DK 107/A1, no. 21, vol. 1.

35. "Jahresbericht 1963 des Institutes für Geflügelzucht Rottenau der AdL," BArch, DK 107/236, no. 32.

36. "Liste der Themen auf dem Gebiet der Land- und Forstwirtschaft der sozialistischen Länder (Stand Dezember 1962), aus dem Reisebericht zur Konferenz über die wissenschaftlichen Grundlagen der Broilerproduktion am Institut für Geflügel Ivanka (CSSR)," Appendix 2, BArch, DK 107/A177, no. 65: 34 f.

37. "Aufbau der Broilerproduktion," Part 1, *Probleme der intensiven Geflügelwirtschaft*, 1 (Series of the Institut für Geflügelwirtschaft Merbitz, [Berlin East, 1963]).

38. "Bericht über den Stand und Vorbereitungen des Aufbaus von Anlagen für die schrittweise Einführung industriemäßiger Produktionsmethoden in der Landwirtschaft. Vorlage zur Sitzung des Büros für Landwirtschaft beim Politbüro, vom 14. Dezember 1964," SAPMO-BArch, DY 30, IV A 2.o23, no. 277.

39. "Entwurf eines Beschlusses des Präsidiums des Ministerrates über den Aufbau moderner Großanlagen für die industrielle Produktion von Schlachtvieh, Schlachtgeflügel und Eiern in der DDR. Protokoll der Sitzung des Präsidiums des Ministerrats vom 20. Mai 1965," BArch, DC 20 I/4, no. 1132.

40. "Information der Zentralen Aufbaugruppe vom 16. April 1966," SAPMO-BArch, DY 30, IV A 2/7, no. 174.

41. "Zum Aufbau und zur Organisation der industriemäßigen Anlagen," in *Industriemäßige Geflügelproduktion – Lehrbuch für die berufliche Spezialisierung*, Autorenkollektiv (Berlin East, 1975).

42. "Maßnahmen zum forcierten Aufbau eines modernen Broiler-Legehennen-Kombinates," SAPMO- BArch, DY 30, IV A 2.o23, no. 175.

43. "Grundgedanken zur prognostischen Entwicklung der Gefügelwirtschaft in der DDR bis 1980," SAPMO-BArch, DY 30, IV A 2.o23, no. 36.

44. "Zu Fragen der Versorgung der Bevölkerung, Hausmitteilungen an das Büro Mittag, vom 21. November 1964 und 20. Juni 1967," SAPMO- BArch, DY 30, IV A 2.o21, no. 712.

45. "Maßnahmen zur Gestaltung der Versorgungssysteme." 129 ff., LAB, Rep 113. no. 526.
46. "Verluste an Lebensmitteln tierischer Herkunft 1964," SAPMO-BArch, DY 30, IV A 2.023, no. 54
47. Speech of Werner Jarowinski, Secretary of the Central Committee of the SED, at the meeting to evaluate the Sixth Party Congress regarding socialist domestic trade, 12 May 1967 in Schömkwitz/Werder, SAPMO-BArch, DY 30, temporary no. 35446/1.
48. "Bericht vom 16. August 1968 der Inspektion Landwirtschaft der ABI über Probleme beim Aufbau der Beispielanlagen/Geflügel," BArch, DC 14, no. 220.
49. "Über die Zuordnung der Betriebe, Institutionen und Einrichtungen auf dem Gebiet der Landwirtschaft vom 11. Dezember 1968," LAB, Rep. 514, no. 3045, Copy of Order no. 5.
50. "Statut der VVB ITP," LAB, Rep. 635, no. 112.
51. "Bericht über den Stand der Störfreimachung der plan- und außerplanmäßigen Versorgung mit Import-Ersatzteilen, Vorlage für die Dienstberatung beim Generaldirektor der VVB am 3. Mai 1971," LAB, Rep. 635 no. 6.
52. "Geflügelwirtschaftsverband der DDR," LAB, Rep. 635, no. 130.
53. "Verschiedene Vorlagen zur Dienstbesprechung des Generaldirektors 1971," LAB, Rep. 635 no. 5.
54. "Pech-Broiler," *Berliner Zeitung*, 9 September 1968. "Teller mit Säge," *BZ am Abend*, 27 January 1971; "Nicht alles Gold was Broiler heißt," *Berliner Zeitung*, 18 January 1973.
55. Letter from Dr. Koch to the Politbüro member Grüneberg of 10 June 1971, SAPMO- BArch DY 30, IV A 2.o23, no. 37.
56. 1960: 34 423; 1964: 33155; 1966: 37160 (after this year plant canteens were included); 1968: 34235; 1973: 33360; 1976: 32816. See *Statistisches Jahrbuch der DDR 1979* (Berlin East, 1979), 225.
57. "Konzeption für die Entwicklung des Absatzes von warmen und kalten Hauptgerichten in den Einrichtungen des Zweiges Gaststättenwesen in der Hauptstadt der DDR, Berlin," LAB, Rep. 113, no. 527: 7 ff.
58. For example: *Goldbroiler und Ei* (Markleeberg, 1973).
59. Material der Abteilung Ernährungssoziologie des Deutschen Instituts für Ernährungsforschung, Ordnungszeichen 63/2, 10 ff., "Verbrauchsprognose für Nahrungsmittel bis 1970, Teil 2. Ernährungssituation in ernährungsphysiologischer und -soziologischer Sicht."
60. "Zur Ernährungssituation in der DDR zwischen 1980 und 1990."
61. Nikolai Aleksandrovich Antipenko, *In der Hauptrichtung* (Berlin East, 1973), 304–5.
62. Ciesla, "Die Ausgangslage und Entwicklung der zentralgeleiteten Fischindustrie in der SBZ/DDR von 1945 bis 1989," in *Unternehmen zwischen Markt und Macht. Aspekte deutscher Unternehmens- und Industriegeschichte im 20. Jahrhundert*, ed., Werner Plumpe and Chr. Kleinschmidt (Essen, 1992), 160–62.
63. Ciesla, "Fischindustrie," 164.
64. "Die Entwicklung der Fischwirtschaft der DDR in den Jahren 1966 bis 1970" (n.d., probably 1970), BArch, DG 5, no. 2568.
65. Michael Wildt, *Vom kleinen Wohlstand. Eine Konsumgeschichte der fünfziger Jahre* (Frankfurt am Main, 1966), 145 ff.
66. Wildt, *Wohlstand*, 124, 146.
67. *Statistisches Jahrbuch 1990*, 53; Archive of the Statistische Bundesamt, Zweigstelle Berlin der Staatlichen Zentralverwaltung für Statistik der DDR, no. 08030602, "Statistisches Jahrbuch des Lebensstandards 1966."

68. Landesarchiv Greifswald (hereafter LAG), Rep. 246, "Programm der Fischwirtschaft der DDR, 10. August 1963." 9–10.
69. *Lebensmittel Praxis,* 1973, no. 11: 108.
70. "Fisch bringt frischen Wind ins Geschäft," *Lebensmittel Praxis,* 1969, no. 3: 224.
71. See fn. 69.
72. Thomas Müller, *Wege von der Planwirtschaft zur Marktwirtschaft in der Nahrungsmittelindustrie. Das Beispiel Ostdeutschland* (Konstanz, 1993), 5: 70.
73. Müller, *Nahrungsmittelindustrie,* 172.
74. Wildt, *Wohlstand,* 147.
75. "Fischverarbeitungsindustrie 1964," 6ff., LAG, Rep. 246, no. 291.
76. "Rechenschaftsbericht für das 1. Halbjahr 1964 des Instituts für Hochseefischerei und Fischverarbeitung," LAG, Rep. 246, no. 51.
77. BArch, DG 5, no. 2568.
78. *Die Verpackung,* 1970, no. 2: 54.
79. Wildt, *Wohlstand,* 147.
80. Cited according to Ibid.
81. "Notiz für Genossen Dr. Wange über erhöhte Bestände an Fischstäbchen im Bezirk Schwerin" (n.d., probably between 12 and 17 August 1971); and "Information über erhöhte Bestände an Fischstäbchen im Bezirk Schwerin" (n.d., probably 10 August 1971), BArch, DG 5, no. 11685.
82. "Geschäftsbericht des VEB Fischkombinat Rostock 1975 vom 13. Februar 1976," 36f., LAG, Rep. 246, no. 651.
83. Interviews with contemporaries, summer 1997.
84. "Gestattungsproduktion Fischerzeugnisse, VVB Hochseefischerei, 1979–1982," BArch, DG 5, no. 6356.
85. "Zur Ernährungssituation in der DDR zwischen 1980 und 1990. Eine Materialsammlung," *Ernährungsforschung* 41 (1996): 124f.
86. BArch, DG 5, no. 1685.
87. "Kälte und ihr Nutzen. Rationeller versorgen mit Gefrierkost," *Gastronomie,* 1972, no. 2: 23.
88. BArch, DG 5, no. 1685.
89. See for more details Ciesla, "Konsumgesellschaft," passim.

CHAPTER 9

THE MYTH OF FEMALE EMANCIPATION

CONTRADICTIONS IN WOMEN'S LIVES

Leonore Ansorg and Renate Hürtgen

This article will try to link the issue of female emancipation in the GDR to the question of whether East German society can be characterized as a "modern dictatorship." While examining the supposed or actual emancipation of women in East Germany, as well as women's own understanding of this process, we will not explicitly engage in a discussion of the term "modern dictatorship." Instead, we would like to ascertain how and in which manner the ambivalent features of "modern dictatorship" were reflected in women's work. To put it differently: by describing processes and understandings of female emancipation in the GDR, we hope to find a way of capturing the specificity of East German society. Our work eschews a compartmentalization of the behavior and experiences of East German women into separate categories of distinct "modern" or "dictatorial" nature. Rather, we argue that women's values, behavior, or mentalities that resulted from distinct patterns of socialization in the GDR, together, formed a contradictory, but unified, whole.

In the following we address only one element of women's experience, namely *women's work*. Our assertions and arguments are, therefore, somewhat restricted, and our generalizations remain conditional. If we were to discuss other dimensions of social life, such as reproduction or reproductive policies, our study would most likely include different aspects, modifications and perhaps even contradictions of our argument. But we maintain that our choice of topic is, nevertheless, legitimate for the following reasons. First, the GDR was a "working society," and not just for men. With 91 percent of all women active in the labor force in 1988–89, the significance of women's work cannot be overemphasized (although such numbers say little about the effects of such labor or women's relationship to their work). Second, we assume that women's patterns of thought and behavior, which were determined by their double roles both at home and the workplace, can be found in distilled form in their working lives. At the same time, working women were active in areas of society dominated by the party and state, so that responsibility for the family and patterns of working life were expressed in a way particular to GDR society. Third, we chose working women because we feel that the literature on the topic, as well as popular perceptions of the same, have been marked by an uncritical, if not hagiographic attitude that we do not share. And finally, we maintain that our choice of subject allows us to present a methodological perspective that offers unique insights into the nature of East German society.

This essay will explore the question of work's effects on GDR women in the following steps: (1) It will begin with a short explanation of the general use of terms, especially the concept of "emancipation" itself, which forms the basis of our research. (2) It will continue with a discussion of current interpretations of the significance of women's work in the GDR and approaches towards "emancipation." (3) It will then proceed to an examination of specific structural prerequisites for women's work in the GDR, based on the example of an industrial plant. (4) Finally, it will conclude with an analysis of East German women's own understandings of emancipation and of themselves. The conclusion will consider the question of the relationship between "modern" and "dictatorial" elements of women's work in the GDR. Our characterizations of women's work and women's self-understandings are based on two empirical case studies regarding female work in a Prignitz textile factory as well as women's roles in the East German labor union FDGB.

Meanings of Emancipation

Everyday uses of terms rarely take into account their historic specificity. It therefore comes as no surprise to note that the current use of "emancipation" focuses exclusively on women without referring to "general emancipation" or to the emancipation of a particular social group, such as freedom from feudal ties. Today's understanding of the word is a thoroughly modern one, linked to a certain stage in the rise of industrial production and the resultant reordering of relationships between the sexes. The emancipation of women first received the significance it now possesses with the advent of "modernity." The possibility and necessity for women's work led to calls for "equality" and "emancipation." Thus industrial labor in general and women's industrial work in particular demands general, equal rights, which could call gendered notions of work and the very nature of social structures into question. In spite of today's situation, in which the problematic nature of factory work has become quite obvious, this development remains an emancipatory aspect of industrial labor that at most leads to a questioning of wage labor as such. The correlation between labor and emancipation provides a historical standard by which we can measure the specific case of East Germany – within the framework of modern industrialization. Yet in order to determine the *specifics* of "emancipation" in the GDR, we must first establish commonalties that transcend borders. East German women's understanding of emancipation can only be described on the basis of this broader definition.

In the following we will indicate how the term emancipation is currently used in developed industrial societies. Interestingly enough, the word's definition at a general level is hardly distinguishable from official GDR ideology. It is striking that emancipation as defined in the leading German dictionary *Duden* is discussed as two distinct phenomena: "1. freedom from a condition of dependence; independence; 2. legal and social equality (of men and women)."[1] Similarly the encyclopedia *Meyers Universallexikon* (GDR) of 1978 defines the word as "freedom from ... social dependence and ... equality."[2] Although these two uses are generally subsumed under one term, the different social levels and political–ideological dimensions of the term persist.

Emancipation most often refers to calls for equality. These entail the establishment of equal chances for women in societies divided along gender lines that distribute opportunities unequally between the sexes. Demands for equality often include claims for parity and equal rights on the job market, in organizations or political parties, as well as equal opportunities for social advancement. This emancipatory claim remains within the framework and possibilities of a society that assigns jobs asymmetrically between the sexes. It focuses on the conditions necessary to create equal participation for women within structures organized along patriarchal lines. The advancement of women, state social policies, and the establishment of quotas are thus all judged according to whether or not they are capable of supporting the individual choices of women on their way to equality and parity.

This catalog of demands points to the second definition of emancipation which categorically calls into question the endless cycle of quota filling, aiming instead to abolish the very social structures under discussion. In her study of emancipation, Cynthia Cockburn speaks of the problem of women's emancipation in terms of "practices of freedom."[3] In this sense, emancipation does not ask how women can alter patriarchal structures for their benefit, but rather how they can do away with them altogether. This second definition of emancipation places more emphasis on individual efforts, on transgressions, on breaking with traditional structures. According to this interpretation, there can be no such thing as an "emancipation from above," no state-led initiative, not the least because state institutions and structures are marked by an inability to change.

It is not always clear which version of the concept emancipation is meant in any given context. As long as family and labor, the private and public spheres, are separate and distinct, and as long as women continue to be structurally discriminated against in the job market, efforts will focus on how to improve women's chances within any given system. But in the face of the present restructuring of industrial labor resulting from its so-called feminization, the goals of emancipation have begun to change. Standards that are based on male stereotypes have become less acceptable. This definition of emancipation is associated with clear demands for change. In any case, varying emphases in terminology point to the different social and political conditions underlying any given approach.

For our study – an investigation of the emancipatory nature of labor and the "emancipatory understanding" of GDR women – a reference to the generally held current understanding of emancipation should suffice. It ought to be evident that the "modern" term of female emancipation, although not always clearly delineated from "equality" or "parity," contains elements of active behavior, self-determination, a questioning of given roles, and a search for independence. The commonalties in labor and women's work shared by different industrial societies make an application of this term to the GDR possible. Once we have established this more general definition of emancipation, we can examine the specific situation of women in East Germany, and thus better understand their positions in a world marked by distinct and singular conditions.

Evaluating Women's Work in the GDR

Critics of East German society, such as those who attempt to address the position of women within the GDR, generally focus on the glaring contradictions between party and state claims to have solved the "woman's question" on the one hand and the reality of a situation which saw neither equality nor emancipation for women on the other. As in other studies of industrialized societies, the focus of this criticism remains on work and the job market. In order to prove these discrepancies between claim and reality, scholars often contrast official "wishful thinking" about women's work with the actual position of women in society or with women's own self-perceptions. They also emphasize the relationship between changing policies towards women and the economic necessities of the job market. In light of this divergence between the ideological self-representations of the GDR state and the actual social realities of East German women, historians have spoken of a "myth" of emancipation and equality.[4]

Despite a boom in studies on East Germany, scholars have not addressed these issues at any length, restricting themselves to more traditional areas of women studies. When historians, sociologists, or political scientists do examine the situation of women in the GDR, they tend to make more moderate statements, emphasizing the East German state's role – if only a formal one – in promoting progress for women, and note that in comparison to the Federal Republic, women's emancipation in the GDR made considerable headway. In this essay we would like to ask how scholars can make such judgments that over the years seem to have become part of a public lore we would like to call, somewhat polemically, a "new myth of emancipation." Such assessments are also connected, in our view, with an approach that contrasts the political and ideological sphere with the experiences of women, without mediating between the two.

Such unquestioned assumptions about the "woman's question" in the GDR should not be confused with interpretations made with the transparent intent of defending East German society. Here we find the old "mystification" of the situation of women in the GDR in new clothing. The worsening opportunities for women in today's job market make the existence of "positive aspects" of work and life in the GDR seem plausible. Yet these assessments are not accurate. They are based on an ahistorical understanding of the past that conflates very concrete social behavior, such as women's conflict-avoiding strategies, or early pregnancies, with unchanging and essentialist female values.[5] But even when such arguments do not advance biological explanations of behavior, scholars, especially those who emphasize the positive aspects of women's lives in the GDR, are forced to present their evidence piecemeal, removed from the larger contexts in which they function. According to Irene Dölling, "achievements" such as the creation of state social policies are "taken on their own terms and judged in a positive light," without "being related to the complex relationships of women within 'real existing' socialist society." The result therefore remains "theoretically inadequate."[6]

Another interpretation of women's emancipation in the GDR (that cannot be accused of attempting to create a nostalgic vision of the East German past) proceeds on the assumption that there was a great contradiction between pretense and practice, but tenders a different interpretation of this paradox. In this view, the policies of equality formulated by the party and the state and carried out with great financial costs did lead to advances for GDR women, especially when compared to women in the Federal Republic. This development however, stands in contradiction to the "backwardness of the East German population in the area of emancipatory *consciousness.*"[7] In other words, progress resulted neither in real equality for GDR women, nor could women develop an emancipatory consciousness relative to their political possibilities. By emphasizing a potential that was never realized, this approach places responsibility for failure squarely on the shoulders of women themselves.[8] The "removal of gendered social inequalities from above left no traces in the psyches" of individuals.[9] Mentalities and behavior did not keep step with social structural developments.

A group of sociologists has offered similar arguments, praising the "creation of a culture of equality at the level of official norms, values, and models," while wondering why real equality and emancipation of women in East Germany did not follow suit. They also find the answer to this contradiction at the individual level. "These stumbling blocks in the creation of equality between the sexes are a result of the continued existence of patriarchal beliefs and patterns of behavior in the *private sphere.*"[10] Whether intentionally or not, these authors accuse women of not having taken advantage of the chances for equality offered to them in the political sphere. Due to their supposed psychological shortcomings or an inability to change, these women could not take advantage of the political opportunities presented to them.

We feel this rather problematic argumentation does not provide a satisfactory explanation. It is not the contradiction between legal or political developments and their unrealized potential that led to a lack of emancipation in the GDR, but rather the very contradictory nature of this possibility or claim itself.[11] We question the utility of approaches that focus on the supposed deficits of social change that contradicted official state ideology. Instead, we would like to draw on the more fruitful analysis offered by Regina Becker-Schmidt, whose term "ambivalent conflict" emphasizes that "the simultaneous existence of contradictory claims, behaviors, and feelings" can be traced back to larger structural contradictions within society as a whole.[12]

Women's Working Conditions in a Textile Plant

Scholars researching many areas of women's history have concluded that women's work is not synonymous with emancipation. Although occupation in "labor societies" (such as the GDR) serves as a prerequisite for further social equality, any claims regarding levels of emancipation must be based on concrete empirical studies.[13] In addition, when formulating questions about emancipation, it is necessary to examine women's work at home and in the family, since activities there generally had a negative effect on behavior in the workplace.[14] This approach emphasizes the contradictions between work and family, between production and reproduction.

While our study shares these assumptions, it centers more on the *nature of labor itself*. On the one hand, we are interested in the question of how the contradictory aspects of women's work can be compared to industrial labor in general and which "modern" elements it might encompass. On the other hand, we want to explore how labor was influenced by a centrally organized economy and dictatorial methods of political control. Our central question focuses on the specificity of women's industrial work under a political dictatorship, which we will explore based on two empirical case studies. Our first case study concerns a textile factory founded in the Prignitz, a rural region of East Germany,[15] and the second example analyzes the behavior and mentalities of women elected to the first workers' and personnel councils during the transformation of 1990.[16] Both studies are based on written sources as well as numerous extensive interviews with women (the latter with women from five different organizations in industry and government).

We would first like to emphasize that women's work in the GDR developed according to traditional gendered divisions of labor, both vertically and horizontally.[17] Thereby it reproduced and cemented typical gender roles characteristic of modern industrial societies. At the same time, paid employment was a necessary precondition for unpaid reproductive labor, carried out by women in the private sphere. Despite their entry into the job market, women in the GDR remained responsible for reproductive tasks. Almost all of the sociopolitical measures of the SED state related to the family were aimed at working women.[18] This double responsibility structured women's everyday experiences and influenced in turn their relationship to their jobs, because their type of employment was primarily determined by the reproductive demands of family life.

Division of labor along gender lines in the GDR was not merely a product of this society's earlier capitalist development, but was consciously promoted by the East German state. This is particularly evi-

dent in the Prignitz region, located in the present state of Brandenburg, that had previously remained untouched by industrial developments. The textile factory founded in this unspoiled countryside
produced synthetic fiber for clothing, employing predominately
women no longer needed in agriculture. A short time after the textile plant's founding, another factory was established in the area.
This metalworking factory hired males with the purpose of providing families for the women at the textile plant in order to establish
a permanent recruiting pool. In this manner the state organized the
industrialization of an agricultural region along traditionally gendered lines. Although the Prignitz region did not have a long-stand-
ing tradition of textile production, the factory's output target was
determined by a centralized, state-formulated plan. This plan did
not take into consideration the factory's recent origins and the new
recruitment of its employees. Greatly surpassing the plant's abilities,
the target schedule had serious and direct repercussions for the factory's employees. The women at the plant, unaccustomed to the
technical procedures of factory work and unfamiliar with labor conditions such as shift schedules and piece work, were forced to fill
quotas they could meet only with the greatest difficulty. Shortfalls
led to demands for increased productivity, which in turn produced
hectic working conditions and faulty output. These resulting product deficiencies had a negative impact on women's pay.

In order to fill production plans, the factory initiated overtime
shifts that had only further negative effects on the health and available leisure time of women who worked there. In addition, labor conditions at the plant were generally very poor. Most of the women
worked in large, windowless halls that were poorly ventilated and
filled with noise and heat. These conditions were especially hard on
women who had previously been active in agriculture and were unaccustomed to factory work. The plant was also poorly outfitted and
materials were of inferior quality. By the middle of the 1970s one-
third of those employed, largely women, were exposed to extremely
unfavorable working conditions, despite the factory's recent origins.[19]

The fact that production plans could not be met, in spite of all
efforts by the employees, led to low morale and a poor work
atmosphere. Such conditions also did not favor the formation of a
job-specific consciousness. Instead, women found a source of pride
and satisfaction in the relatively good pay they could receive by
exceeding their targets. This in turn influenced women's positions
in the private sphere, where they often earned more than their hus-
bands who still worked in agriculture.

The lack of democratic methods of regulation or control left
women without any real chance to influence the centrally orga-

nized production plans, to address the poor working conditions within the plant, or to initiate change. The labor organization FDGB, as well as other factory organizations (such as the youth group FDJ), echoed state demands to reach production goals and pressed women to work overtime and special shifts. In urging an increase in women's efforts, these organizations were generally following orders sent down by the SED-factory party organization or the higher SED offices responsible for "party control" and charged with the task of insuring that production levels were fulfilled. In this manner, factory policies meshed with political demands, so that employees could extricate themselves from them with only the greatest of difficulties. Women's work thus received a political dimension and refusal to work overtime could be interpreted accordingly as politically "negative" behavior.

Most women developed a sense of resignation and hopelessness as a result, and felt unable to make an impact on social or working conditions. Many attempted to solve their problems at the individual level by one to one contact with their superiors. They also reacted to stressful working conditions by refusing to work at all, or by slowing down work (violating work morale), and in some cases even left the plant. Throughout the period of our study the factory experienced an extremely high rate of employee fluctuation. Women often found other positions in the service industries related to the textile branch and the infrastructure of the region, but other, more far-reaching, alternatives for employment did not exist.

This example of a textile factory shows how "modern" elements of industrialization combined with political methods of dictatorial control. These extended from rigid enforcement of a centrally conceived state production plan from "above" on those "below" (and failure to meet quotas resulted in the firing of six different plant directors), which women felt as an increased pressure to produce. Without any means of labor organization, these women also experienced various forms of discipline through the political control of different "social organizations." Particularly since work itself had become a political value (since the duty to work was codified in law) and interpreted as a profession of faith in the socialist state, labor was connected to politics in a manner that translated into the appropriate pressure to perform. Economic labor relationships therefore became political ones.

Emancipatory Self-Perceptions of Women

The hierarchical organization of East German factories and lack of democratic structures in the GDR led principally, but not exclusively women to retreat to the small, restricted space of "the group" (*das Kollektiv*). There, political abstinence was the rule, a familial atmosphere dominated, questions related to work or society in general (with the exception of the task of getting provisions) were not discussed, and social problems relegated to the perimeter. The price of such harmonious relationships within the collective was a refusal to address social contradictions. Policies from above focused on what most patriarchal societies define as women's "natural" proclivities for "interpersonal relationships." These policies favored women who acquiesced, who concerned themselves with the collective without breaking any rules. Our study of thirty women has shown that "neutrality" and "conformity" were the qualities they most admired in themselves.[20] They wanted to "get along" with everyone and wished to avoid conflict at all costs.

It therefore comes as no surprise that the position of FDGB labor spokeswoman, a lower level job concerned with good relationships within the group, was preferred by women. It promised them on the one hand a small radius of activity and a few privileges, and on the other precisely those opportunities for care and human warmth that GDR women had learned to foster. We have observed that entry into the workplace did not weaken or change behaviors that women had developed as a result of the gendered nature of family life, but rather strengthened them instead. In particular, "negative experiences with democracy," or incidents which taught women that standing up for one's own interests or the interests of one's colleagues did not have much chance for success, did not offer women any grounds to alter their strategies of non-involvement.[21]

In order to come to terms with the double demands of a modern industrial society under dictatorial rule, women in the GDR developed quite a unique understanding of emancipation. Caught between responsibility for family and the demands of the workplace, emancipation for East German women meant finding the best way to fulfill their different role expectations. GDR women applied the emphasis on performance, characteristic of industrial labor, to all areas of life, even if their behavior actually failed to correspond to these standards. Emancipation for our interview partners did not mean a repudiation or questioning of their roles, but rather the subordination of their own interests to "a higher purpose." Typical for the women we spoke with is the statement: "I was emancipated because I never lost a day of work, despite my three kids, illness, and my divorce." Consequently, these women did not recognize any structural conditions for gendered hierarchies in the GDR. Most believed that it was each woman's private affair to determine how gender roles were defined and negotiated. In the face of grievances they shared in common with working men, they directed their complaints at those in control "up there," against whom men and women alike were helpless.

The "paternalistic welfare provisions" of the GDR state for "its women" faded into the background in the representations of the women we interviewed. This may be due in part to the self-evident nature of this policy, and the fact that *Fürsorge* was not limited to women. It may also be a result of a development that began at the latest in the 1980s in which the state increasingly failed to live up to its "duty." Younger women especially complained about the problems of trying to coordinate the demands of work and family, and they pointed to problems in shopping for their families. Older women often felt neglected by the government. The East German state, while viewing its citizens as mere recipients of its policies, attempted to repress any cases of individual independence, seeking instead to create a passive citizenry (and passive women). These activities, however, should not be denoted with the term "welfare," which overlooks a web of relationships that clearly imply domination.

Political practices in East Germany allowed women to interpret their successes and failures on an *individual* level. They could view their choices as resulting from their own actions, within their sphere of responsibility, and open to change. The logic of industrial society includes the belief that behavior is based on individual thoughts and actions. But the existence of a public sphere which would allow citizens to inform themselves was missing in the GDR. East Germans were therefore completely unfamiliar with forms of collective behavior. The best known example of this was the rejection of the introduction of quotas for women after 1989. Another was the belief that women had always done their duty, and those women who did not "make it" were just not good enough. At the same time this view made it hard for women to recognize the causes for the shortages and roadblocks in their working lives that could be ascribed to social, political, or patriarchal structures.

Instead, women assumed responsibility for everything – if they made it, they had earned it, and if not, they faulted their own personal shortcomings. Individual autonomy and "going it alone" were among the most important elements of the self perceptions of women we interviewed. Those elements typical of modern industrialized societies – the pressure to perform and the atomization of the individual – were carried to the extreme in East German women. Interestingly, West German managers have realized that GDR women possess these characteristics and, therefore, have sought to hire them, particularly during the present phase of restructuring.

The particular demands of industrial labor, combined with the continued existence of gendered tasks and responsibilities, led to a

wide and contradictory spectrum of values, mentalities and patterns of behavior in East German women. They were simultaneously family and performance oriented; they were good mothers
and workers; they were against elitism and for equality, yet nevertheless proud of what they had achieved on their own. These
women rejected on the whole demands for women's equality. Supporting social justice and the "ordinary folks," they sought harmony
in their relationships with others, while receiving support from their
superiors or "the state." They wished to make a difference, but they
did not see social conditions resulting from larger structures, and
felt instead that they were related to individual actions. We could
list numerous other, similar contradictions which would underscore
how this "dowry and inherited burden" worked together in practice.

Our examples of the mentalities and behaviors of East German
women that stem from their work have remained somewhat undifferentiated in this brief exposition. Two possible dangers in interpretation should therefore be mentioned. At closer examination it
becomes clear that these patterns could be different for women of
varying generations or social classes. Our representation, which is
meant to serve as a demonstration of a particular approach, is not
intended to add to clichés about "typical" East German women.
Our own studies have shown that the socialization processes of
women of the "founders" (*Aufbau*) generation of the 1950s are
very different from those of younger generations. Yet surprisingly,
many commonalties also cross generational lines.[22] Women's
retreat to the private sphere increased during the 1970s and 1980s
and was related to the more general mood of stagnation prevalent
in GDR society. We also left unexamined how women from various
social classes experienced work and possessed different self-perceptions.[23] Since GDR society in the 1970s and 1980s was characterized by limited social mobility between classes and workers, this
perspective needs to be considered, even if women within our sam-
ple shared many characteristics that crossed class boundaries.

Secondly, we could not show here how the "double socialization"
of GDR society influenced women's lives. We have neither examined
the effects of women's work on their increased social relations or on
their chances for advancement, nor have we considered the effects
of work on women's lives at home. Neither have we explored the
results of the contradictions between ideology and the actual experiences of women in East Germany. And lastly, we see the thoughts
and behavior of GDR women as a part of a whole set of practices
which are also not all that different from those of men.

In the emancipatory understanding of GDR women, modern
aspects of industrial work combined with the effects of society in a

patriarchal and dictatorial state to form a contradictory pair whose two sides formed a whole. To borrow a metaphor from Bourdieu,[24] who said that separating class and gender characteristics is as easy as distinguishing the yellow of a lemon from its sour taste, we argue that these two aspects cannot be considered in isolation from each other. When thinking about women's willingness to perform in the workplace, we must also include their simultaneous retreat into the private sphere; when talking about their familial and harmonious work life we need to reflect on their unwillingness to criticize problems at the workplace or address grievances in society. The benefits and costs of GDR socialization – both positive and negative effects – cannot be divided up into separate elements. Only in their entirety can they reflect the distinct quality of women's experiences in the GDR.

Women's lives were characterized by the fact that, once they started working, their horizons – previously limited to the family – were suddenly broadened. The large numbers of women entering the workplace marked a social process that reordered gender roles, as well as altered the social practices and self-perceptions of women. But this modernization was relativized (and in this article we could only touch upon this rather cursorily) by the concrete structural conditions women found themselves in. Particularly the lack of collective action and a public sphere meant that women acted at an individual level. This favored a development that strengthened traditional roles and ways of thinking – in spite of women's work. We would like to speak of this development in terms of a "blocked modernity." This places GDR society into the context of modern industrial societies, but also points to the destructive elements inherent within them.

Notes

1. *Duden. Fremdwörterbuch* (Mannheim, 1995).
2. *Meyers Universallexikon* (Leipzig, 1978), vol. 1, 623.
3. Cynthia Cockburn, "Blockierte Frauenwege," *Argument* (Hamburg, 1993), Special Issue 212: 271.
4. Grit Bühler, *Mythos der Gleichberechtigung in der DDR* (Frankfurt am Main, 1997).
5. Ursula Schröter, "Frauen in den neuen Bundesländern – Go West," in *Umbruch. Beiträge zur sozialen Transformation in den alten und neuen Bundesländern*, ed. Katrin Andruschow, Renate Hürtgen, Rita Mersmann (Berlin 1996), vol.11, 15–27.
6. This argument is taken from Irene Dölling, "Zum Verhältnis von modernen und traditionellen Aspekten im Lebenszusammenhang von Frauen in der DDR," in *Unter Hammer und Zirkel. Frauenbiographien vor dem Hintergrund ostdeutscher*

Sozialisationserfahrungen, ed. Zentrum für interdisziplinäre Frauenforschung der Humboldt-Universität Berlin (Berlin, 1995), 23.

7. Rainer Geißler, *Die Sozialstruktur Deutschlands* (Opladen, 1996), 301.

8. Geißler argues that women from the East German states currently have more reservations about typically male occupations or about women in leadership positions and are in favor of women being responsible for the raising of children. Ibid., 301.

9. Rainer Geißler, *Sozialer Umbruch in Ostdeutschland* (1993), 65f.

10. Karl-Ulrich Mayer and Martin Diewald, "Kollektiv und Eigensinn: Die Geschichte der DDR und die Lebensverläufe ihrer Bürger," *Aus Politik und Zeitgeschichte*, 1996, no. 46: 14.

11. To illustrate the contradictory nature of this "claim," official party and state policies towards women need to be examined in light of the necessities and goals that guide various alternatives.

12. Regina Becker-Schmidt, "Ambivalenz und Nachträglichkeit: Perspektiven einer feministischen Biographieforschung," in *Was heißt hier eigentlich feministisch? Zur theoretischen Diskussion in den Geistes- und Sozialwissenschaften* (Bremen, 1993), 81f.

13. Our results stem from a microhistorical study of a textile factory in the Prignitz region in the present state of Brandenburg. They are based on an examination of SED sources of different organizational levels as well as printed sources of mass organizations. We also carried out interviews with women employed at the textile factory.

14. See the recent publication by Gunilla-Frederike Budde, ed., *Frauen arbeiten. Erwerbstätigkeit in Ost- und Westdeutschland nach 1945* (Göttingen, 1997).

15. Leonore Ansorg, "Der Fortschritt kommt aufs Land. Weibliche Erwerbsarbeit in der Prignitz," in *Frauen arbeiten*, ed. Gunilla-Friederike Budde, 78–99.

16. Renate Hürtgen, *FrauenWende – WendeFrauen. Frauen in den ersten betrieblichen Interessenvertretungen der neuen Bundesländer* (Münster, 1997).

17. See the following chapter by Dagmar Langenhan and Sabine Roß, "The Socialist Glass Ceiling: Limits to Female Careers" this volume.

18. Heike Trappe, *Emanzipation oder Zwang? Frauen in der DDR zwischen Beruf, Familie und Sozialpolitik* (Berlin, 1995).

19. "Bericht zum rationellen Einsatz des gesellschaftlichen Arbeitsvermögens in ausgewählten Zweigen und Betrieben des Bezirkes vom 10. October, 1975," BLHA, Rep. 530, Nr. 5070.

20. Interviews with thirty women who were voted into the first factory and personnel organizations during the 1990 transformation form the basis of this section. The results are therefore not necessarily applicable to all GDR women. See Renate Hürtgen, *Frauen Wende – WendeFrauen*, 37f.

21. Birgit Bütow, "Politische Nichtpartizipation von Frauen?" in *EigenArtige Ostfrauen. Frauenemanzipation in der DDR und in den neuen Bundesländern*, ed. Birgit Bütow and Heidi Stecker (Bielefeld,1994), 262f.

22. Heike Trappe, *Emanzipation oder Zwang?* passim.

23. Petra Frerichs, "Klasse und Geschlecht 1. Arbeit. Macht. Anerkennung. Interesse," *Sozialstrukturanalyse* 10 (Opladen, 1997).

24. Pierre Bourdieu, *Die feinen Unterschiede. Kritik der gesellschaftlichen Urteilskraft* (Frankfurt am Main, 1982), 182.

CHAPTER 10

THE SOCIALIST GLASS CEILING

LIMITS TO FEMALE CAREERS

Dagmar Langenhan and Sabine Roß

If, in the communist society we have yet to create in the distant future, *all* members of society, women as well as men, are to enjoy social equality, and if *everyone* in the work force, women as well as men, are to develop intellectually and physically to their fullest potential, then it is clear that steps to achieve these goals need to be undertaken now, in the period of the early stages of the establishment of a socialist society.[1]

This 1979 statement of Ingeburg Lange, head of the Division for Women in the Central Committee of the SED and the GDR's most prominent "woman's representative" demonstrates (albeit indirectly) how elusive legal and social equality were for East German women. When she was speaking in 1979, both goals had already been officially achieved for some time. Not only did party and state organs take credit for the accomplishment in official proclamations, but the majority of GDR women also believed in the reality of those claims. As such, they constituted an essential element in the self-legitimization of the GDR state.

This distorted picture had its origins in the fact that the socialist vision of equal rights and opportunities was restricted to integrating women into the workforce. SED rulers merely applied categories of labor associated with the processes of professionalization in modern industrial societies to women. Despite numerous attempts to regulate and control conditions in order to secure equality for women in all areas of society, traditional gender roles remained intact, as did – in somewhat modified form – gendered divisions of labor. Such gendered notions limited women's chances at real social equality. The path towards the socialist dream of women's equality was paved with very real stumbling blocks, because both the internal tendencies of modern industrialized societies "to divide work along gender lines"[2] as well as the paternalistic policies of the SED made the realization of such dreams difficult.

Along those lines, the following essay, based on two contrasting case studies, addresses questions about equal rights in the workplace and social equality for women in general. Equal rights in the workplace encompass the formal, legal definitions of rights and opportunities for both sexes on the job; social equality refers to how these equal rights and chances were realized in daily practice. These terms need to be distinguished from the concept of women's emancipation, which is concerned more with the psychological and cultural dimensions of equality, or with the consequences of women's positions in the political and social sphere. Since they were discussed in Chapter 9, we will not address such questions in this study.[3] Instead, our interests are focused on the question of female careers, and we examine the possibilities and limitations women experienced in their professional advancement under SED rule. The study focuses on two groups located at opposite ends of the scale of the degree of possible state and political influence – those women at the top (within the state bureaucracy) and those at the bottom (in the countryside). The time period under consideration extends from the 1970s to the 1980s, which saw a radical change in SED policies regarding equal rights and opportunities in the job market.

Legal Equality

Political, legal, and social equality in the GDR had always been defined in an economic context, and was expressed constitutionally in these terms as well. On the one hand this definition drew on the traditions of the Marxist workers' and women's movement, which saw the question of women's rights linked to the "realization of the historic mission of the working classes" that could only be achieved in "a common battle of men and women for social progress."[4] This prior subordination of the women's question under the broader question of workers' rights continued in the GDR.[5]

On the other hand this injunction also paid tribute to the new power relationships established after the end of the war. On 17 August 1946, the SVAG's order No. 253 guaranteed women equal pay for equal work. This order not only applied Soviet "legal premises" to the Soviet occupation zone, but it also met demands made by the women's committees formed in May and June 1945, that partially drew on the traditions of the bourgeois women's movement.

The normative element of legal equality was part of the first GDR constitution of 1949 (and in the following ones from 1968 and 1974). For the first time in German history, a constitution proclaimed the equality of men and women, both in their right to work, as well as their right to "equal pay for equal work."[6] But these demands could never be fully realized, since "equal work" was difficult to guarantee. Women's lack of qualifications and other hindrances in the workplace, to be discussed below, made such equality a distant goal.

The "Law regarding the protection of mothers and their children and the rights of women" of September 1950 further elaborated the constitutional basis of the legal equality of men and women.[7] Women were to be assured that they could participate in political, social, and cultural life by being allowed to take jobs outside traditional women's work and having the opportunity to train for new careers. Although representatives of the Democratic Women's League (DFD) played an important role in drafting the relevant passages of the law, it soon became clear that the SED was interested in a policy of women's equality not *with*, certainly not *from*, but merely *for* women.[8]

The Family Code of December 1965, as well as the Labor Code of June 1977 were both based on the earlier law from 1950. While the Family Code could still speak of legal equality for men and women who were to arrange their relationships so that both would have the "right to develop their abilities for their own and society's interests,"[9] the Labor Code laid out the rights and duties of women on the job and within the family. The state was obligated to create conditions that would allow women to "adjust better to their equal status on the job and in their careers and to be able to coordinate their careers more successfully with their tasks as mothers and with their responsibilities within the family."[10]

The shift from policies aimed at helping women to policies aimed at helping families that began in the 1970s meant that it became easier for women to balance the demands of their career with the needs of their families. But the rules associated with the "family *and* career model" were focused on women, which meant that traditional gender roles and work patterns were not transformed, but instead, reinforced.[11] The regime's equality policies should be understood in their contradiction not only as an *opportunity*, but also at the same time as paternalistic *protection* and *limitation* of women's lives.[12] GDR legislation posited a particular model of both men and women, thereby significantly reducing individual choices and possibilities. This severely limited a modern policy of equal opportunity. In the face of the social and economic situation in East Germany, this meant that for women and their careers, the modernizing effects of the 1960s had come to an end.

Social Equality

The policy of equal opportunity, motivated by economic considerations and political ideology, consisted of three different levels. These included especially:

1. the establishment of absolute SED control by including women in the workforce;
2 the use of women as workers within larger state economic policies to meet chronic labor shortages; and
3. economic independence, possibility for career advancement and improvement of women's social status.

Among these aims, the third goal predominated in the self-perceptions of working women. As many studies and polls have shown, these women accurately reflected the demands they were faced with from many different fronts. But in most cases, what was central to them was qualified work – without excluding traditional perceptions of career and family. Differences between the generations do exist; for instance, the entry of women of the so-called "founding generation" into the workforce was dominated by the task of having to overcome the results of the war. The reasons for these perceptions are to be found in the shortage of male workers, as well as in the party's social program aimed at integrating women into the newly founded state. For women themselves, what was most important was ensuring their own existence. This contradiction between the politically organized attempts to rule from above and individual interests was typical for most women's lives until the end of the state in 1989.

The second generation of women, the so-called "building generation" (*Aufbaugeneration*) of the 1950s and 1960s, got better job training and could enjoy greater social mobility. Typical for these women was that many received their education via a "second path" (that is, they were generally non-traditional students who entered the system by the backdoor), and they made the transition from paid piecework to lifelong careers. The "granddaughter generation" of the 1970s and 1980s saw a group of women entering the workforce who were products of the state's educational policies that had promised equal educational chances for all since the 1950s. Their perceptions of themselves as women in secure careers determined their life choices.[13]

These generational differences correspond to changing paradigms and self-perceptions of women.[14] While in the 1940s and 1950s the idea of women workers was most important, the 1960s praised the self-confident and successful career woman as role model. Due to the continued lack of qualified personnel, emphasis was placed on the qualifications of (not only) women and their place in the productive process. This picture began to change in the beginning of the 1970s. What now became important was how best to combine careers with motherhood – and social-political measures were taken to ease the load (nurseries, mothers' leave, etc.). Between these generational differences, changing role models, and the above-mentioned laws and regulations of the workforce, as well as state policies regarding women, there existed a common thread and some obvious temporal parallels. In these aspects, the GDR was similar to other modern industrial societies, whether of the Western or Eastern type.

If one considers general indicators such as the numbers of female workers or qualification levels, the picture of social equality of women in the GDR is confirmed. From 1950 to 1989 the number of women in the workforce rose steadily (except in agriculture) from 40 percent to 49 percent; by 1989, over 91 percent of all women of working age were either employed or in training.[15] The GDR therefore was in the front rank of international attempts to realize the "right and duty to work for all." Only France and the Scandinavian countries showed similar advances, while the US was just beginning to move in this direction. With its policies the GDR did create modern social conditions that allowed women to pursue careers in combination with family life.[16]

But these numbers tell us nothing about what kind of work women were engaged in. In spite of high levels of employment, the gender-specific and traditional, vertical segmentation of work continued to exist through the 1970s and 1980s. Although in the 1960s women did enter careers previously limited exclusively to men, their overall representation in these jobs remained marginal.

In education and training, women's experiences gradually became more similar to those of men. For instance, in the 1980s the number of women without a degree of some kind dropped from 41 percent to 12 percent (44 percent in 1971).[17] What had led to this equality were measures aimed at providing job-specific training opportunities that firms were obligated by law to offer. Women of the founding and *Aufbau* generations took advantage of these opportunities, since by acquiring formal training they could increase their wages. This training also increasingly became a prerequisite for further advancement, and a necessary component of social mobility.

If one examines women's positions within the workforce, the positive picture of social equality in the GDR is somewhat relativized. The higher the pay status or influence of any position, the less women were represented. Thus, "real-existing socialism" also continued previous horizontal segregation based on gender that extended beyond qualifications or training.

The qualifications needed to enter managerial positions were fixed for both men and women. They were based on specific technical requirements relative to the position. The paternalistic and caretaking policies of the SED allowed women to achieve the necessary qualifications via training courses and continuing education, and thereby pursue successful careers. The increasing technical competence of women and ensuing professionalization can be considered as modernizing aspects of the regime. Yet factors unique to the GDR, such as state control of career choices, state-regulated gender quotas in different fields (and the hurdles established that effectively closed certain careers to women, especially starting in the 1980s), as well as the basic duty to participate in training all point to the ambivalences of the modernization process in the GDR in regards to gender.[18] The early 1970s saw a closing of career paths and a decrease of women in leading positions, both of which were related to an excess of qualified applicants. Party membership increasingly became the determining factor in deciding advancement.

In spite of increases in the number of qualified women, the "right to work for all" did not translate into the "right to the same job" for women. The *Frauenreport '90* summarized after the fall of the GDR: "In no other area of work was social discrimination against women as high as it was in management."[19] If in modern, industrialized countries the representation of women in various managerial positions serves as a general indicator of the importance attached to these areas within society,[20] then the following can be concluded about the GDR: the closer to the real loci of power, the less women were represented in leading positions.[21] It is true that one-third of all managerial positions in the GDR were occupied by women – but these were definitely on the lower and middle levels. For instance, women were seldom directors of plants; and within the entire GDR industry at the end of the 1980s, there were only four female CEOs.[22] Among the deputy directors or division heads 8 percent were women, while only 3 percent of all *Kombinate* were led by women, and these primarily managed plants with fewer than 500 employees.[23]

Women also were excluded from equal participation in managerial positions within the state apparatus. The bureaucracy, directly controlled by the party at its various levels, was responsible for the control and planning not only of the economy, but of most areas of society. The most important task of the government was the implementation and realization of party directives.[24] This should have meant – at least theoretically – that laws related to equality would lead directly to the advancement of women into managerial positions. Although women were more frequently represented within the state apparatus than in the party or the economy, cadre membership in the 1980s consisted of "only" 34 percent women in leading positions.[25] Fourth-fifths of these women had a university or technical degree, a figure that was about 10 percent lower than their male colleagues.

In those ministries that included industry and construction, the number of women rose by 1989 to approximately 25 percent, while in those ministries concerned with the economy and non-productive areas their share averaged around one-third. It was particularly in the latter area where the differences were most noticeable; for instance 40 percent of leading positions in education were occupied by women, in trade and food supply 48 percent, and in the area of health and medicine 57 percent in 1989. Women in higher positions were confronted with the rule that the more rigid the hierarchies, the fewer of them were present. Ascending from the level of section heads to division chiefs and deputy leaders of other central state organs all the way up to ministers, state secretaries and deputy ministers, the number of women represented sank from 17 percent to 1.5 percent.

Very few women occupied positions of real power in the area of the executive. Only one woman was appointed as head of a District Council (*Rat des Bezirks*) at the end of the 1980s (Irma Uschkamp in Cottbus), and only one woman belonged to the Council of Ministers of the GDR in the 1980s (Margot Honecker). In the mid-1980s out of the about 200 different state secretaries and representative ministers, there were only four women. The percentage of women within the State Council was 20 percent at the beginning of the 1980s.[26] In comparison, at the municipal level the presence of women was much higher, and about one third of all mayors were female in 1989. The size of the communities needs to be specified, however, since women were generally mayors of smaller towns.[27]

The number of leading party cadres who had occupied their positions for longer than ten years continually grew in the course of the GDR's history. This also held true for women. But surprisingly, at the end of the 1980s there were just as many women who had only been in their positions for two to five years. The age differences of these groups also reflect the aging of the populace as a result of career blockage. During the 1980s, the average age rose overall, especially in the group of women over 55 years of age. But only 12 percent of women in general belonged to this group, while 25 percent of all male leaders fell into this category.[28] Overall, the 1970s and 1980s saw de-modernizing tendencies in leading positions that found expression in growing self-recruitment which led to sinking social mobility. This is also demonstrated by the drastic decline in leading personnel under the age of 25 years.

For women, this process of closure within the leading groups in the 1970s and 1980s was apparently not as drastic as it was for men. Whether this should serve as proof that the modernizing effects for women ended later; whether this indicates a parallel process of closure and non-closure, which would speak for the existence of gender-specific waves of modernization; whether this merely reflects a time lag; or whether the continued recruitment of female leaders in the 1980s was a result of the peculiar patterns of bureaucracy remains to be clarified further in empirical studies.

In those areas of society where the SED did not have such a great influence as in the state apparatus, women's career chances developed in a similar manner. Thus work and life patterns in traditional work, such as agriculture,[29] approximated those of women in other areas during the 1980s, but some older traditions also continued. Due to its contradictory demands for modernization of agriculture and claims to self-sufficiency in food supply, the SED leadership was in a constant battle to secure its own dictatorial ascendancy and to insure agricultural production. Therefore, the formal, legal proclamation of socio-political equality for rural women occurred later, since the party's control in these areas was limited by people's property.[30]

Rural women also experienced characteristic modern industrial trends, such as sinking numbers of workers in the primary sector and the simultaneous reduction of quantitative work and the increase in levels of qualification. Until 1989 their numbers in agriculture sank much faster (by about 60 percent to about 316,000) than those of men (by about 40 percent).[31] This is one indication that it was particularly younger women who left for jobs outside of agriculture. Since 92 percent of all women (and 94 percent of men) had concluded some kind of professional training (*Berufsabschluß*) in 1989, the level of qualification was higher than in other areas of the economy.[32] North–South differences between the industrialized and agricultural regions were also significant. Approximately every fifth leading position in agriculture was occupied by a woman.

Women were especially represented in the middle (about 75 percent) and upper managerial levels (about 40 percent).[33]

Generational differences were more marked in agricultural work than in other areas. In the 1970s and 1980s, leading positions occupied by women were primarily in the hands of the *Aufbau* generation. These women entered the workforce in the 1950s and 1960s largely because of SED policies that were aimed less at winning rural women as workers than entry into a collective farm to advance the "socialist transformation of agriculture." In this instance, labor problems and the state's claims to rule came together in a particular manner. The collective farms offered women a lifelong perspective for work outside of the home. The SED had also initiated a unique training campaign that gave women a chance at qualified work and opportunity for social mobility within changing agricultural structures. In so-called village academies, winter schools, and women's special courses, particularly older women and mothers with no particular qualifications, who had previously only helped out in a pinch as family members, could now acquire a high school equivalency or even a technical or university degree in special study courses. In contrast to only 8.5 percent in 1963, 62 percent of the women working in agriculture had received some sort of training by 1970, although only 1.3 percent had a university or technical degree (6.3 percent of men).[34]

This distribution reflects the fact that rural women of this generation favored qualifying courses that allowed them to combine the duties of their careers and their families while allowing them to better themselves financially. Education at universities or schools in places other than where these women lived and worked, therefore, posed more serious hurdles to their careers than to men's. At the same time, semi-technical knowledge in the agricultural field, which was hardly acquired by schooling, and based on traditional methods, favored the careers of women. The women of this generation took over leading positions in the agricultural plants and in the state apparatus and remained there until 1989 – as brigade leaders, heads of LPGs, VEG directors, agricultural secretaries in the regional bureaucracy – and then their careers usually broke off.

Rural women of the "granddaughter generation," who entered the workforce in the 1970s and 1980s with complete and continuing training, therefore stood before closed doors and had little chance of advancement. Alternatives existed for them in jobs outside of agriculture within the collective farms where they normally also chose "typically" female jobs. The percentage of women active in administrative and white collar positions was 12.5 percent, and in cultural and social positions they accounted for 5.3 percent (in 1989).[35]

Most women were, however, employed in the production end of agriculture, especially in "manual labor" with little chance of advancement. The introduction of new technologies in the 1960s seemed to promise a change in the allocation of jobs according to gender.[36] Yet what happened was that the more certain jobs were professionalized and won higher status, the more women were likely to be elbowed out of them into non-mechanized areas. In addition, due to the seasonal character of agricultural work, a large portion of women were only part-time employees (35 percent in 1970). This percentage decreased steadily with increased specialization (23 percent in 1989). De-qualification and lack of opportunities associated with temporary employment remained exclusively a problem for women.[37]

The form of job qualification set limits to careers as well. The separation of plant and animal production reduced job possibilities for those women who entered the job market after the 1970s. Industrially organized agriculture had no need for prior general qualifications. Other developments – such as the decline of the multigenerational family, the employment of the "grandmother generation," long working hours and commuting time to and from work, time pressures caused by "social duties," deteriorating supplies and services, and the spread of individualized farming – raised even in agriculture "the pressure of daily problems on individuals in the 1980s [that was expressed] as an increase in pressure on women."[38]

Limits to Female Careers

The under-representation of women in leading positions, compared to the official claims of the GDR, can be traced back to a series of system-immanent, all-encompassing, culturally constructed and gender specific factors, which – due to their complexity and magnitude – cannot all be discussed here.

The opportunities for career advancement (with the necessary qualifications) were determined above all by the conflict between career and family. Independent of their positions within the system, women always made decisions about their careers based on their ability to combine family duties with the demands of their jobs; they found themselves in a "double-bind situation" even in the GDR. The resultant pressures influenced state policies and their realization in individual careers. The GDR's model of family and career, which in reality was a severely limited three phase model, set as many implicit limits to equality as the family versus career or the "classic" three phase models of other (mostly Western) industrialized societies. One important factor leading to the under-representation of women in higher positions was the amount of time spent on the job. Women were increasingly part-time employees (in 1989: 27 percent), and based on their qualifications, worked in positions that were below their abilities.[39]

The gendered nature of work distribution was not only a central obstacle to women's career possibilities. The fact that women continued to be responsible for work within the home also represented a problem specific to the GDR regarding their position within society as a whole. Without "endangering the stability of the family and the reproduction of the populace" women were supposed to be educated "as effectively and systematically as possible about the practices of a masculine labor market."[40] This meant, among other things, that choices for leading positions were made based on the criteria of the cadre system. Since the responsible agencies were dominated by a generation of men, influenced by more traditional perceptions of women's roles, women's chances for advancement were limited on many fronts.

GDR studies regarding "women and management" give the impression that women needed to be "led by the hand," and forced to their own happiness. Similarly, the literature described policies for the advancement of women as "development aid." What was seen as needing further development was not the organizations or their leaders who were responsible for discrimination, but "the women who were subjected to this discrimination."[41] Even in the GDR the working world was gendered masculine, and the organization of work, management structures, planning, and workload demands were all tailored to male socialization and conduct. Working mothers were, in most cases, unable to meet demands for regional mobility and flexibility of work hours. The structural conditions created by the SED leadership were too inflexible to assist women. Indeed, women became a risk factor in those plants with a high number of female employees, further limiting their career chances.

VEBs were extremely unwilling to invest in employees (by paying for training courses) who would be likely to break off their careers at a later time. Particularly since the new social measures of the 1970s, women were considered "unreliable employees," whether they actually wanted to have children or not. In 1987 the magazine *Für Dich* noted sarcastically that qualified women were simply not fit for managerial positions because of "biologically-based risks."[42] This attitude resulted both in a "marginalization of women's work" and also helps explain the barriers women encountered along their career paths.[43]

Another cause was women's peculiar relationship to work, which was influenced by their socialization. This in turn determined the choice of careers (already heavily structured by the state) and influenced their desire to advance in a career. Even if the family was not the main focus in women's lives, women might develop an inner distance to their careers that was difficult to overcome, especially when state policies in their official intentions often had the opposite effect, since they made it easier for women to found families and interrupt their careers.

Moreover, the values and mentalities of women often did not match those behaviors and characteristics demanded of managers and leaders. This was another contradiction women encountered in their career – the discrepancy between the applicability and application of official objectives and the realization of their own private goals and plans. This raises the question of women's relationship to such things as their "careers," "power," and "the exercise of power." Under the conditions of the SED regime, career advancement for both men and women generally meant more responsibility, more time invested in one's work, sometimes a higher income, but in any case more social and political influence and control. Interviews and studies, however, give the impression that women seem to have viewed the exercise of power in light of the content of its responsibilities, and preferred a more "participatory and collegial style of leadership."[44] Even in the GDR, where conditions aimed at achieving equality, such leadership qualities were neither desired nor rewarded. Women obviously displayed less interest in pursuing careers and interpreted success more as a result of accidents or state paternalistic policies than as an expression of their own "goal-oriented activities."[45]

The lives of men and women and their daily experiences were therefore very different from one another. Even "real existing socialism," with its policies aimed at helping women, did little to change this discrepancy. Traditional discriminatory structures continued to exist. Gender therefore needs to be interpreted as a structural characteristic that influenced both the vertical and horizontal segregation of the workforce, and that determined traditional roles within the family which were passed on to the next generation. Transformations within the job market could not change gender roles, which were characterized by a great deal of inertia, nor could they fundamentally alter the chances for women in a career.[46]

The high degree of gender equality in the GDR is often cited as an indicator for its relative modernity. An analysis of the number of women in managerial and leadership positions shows, however, that old structures remained intact – patterns that were based on traditional models of gender roles that belonged to the cultural traditions of both German states after 1945, and which continued to have lasting influence in both.

Attempts made by the SED regime to free women from the class constraints of gender roles resulting from industrialization – which forced women to have full-time, life-long careers – were only partially successful. The party's measures were based on an understanding of modernization that hearkened back to the early days of industrialization, which could not meet the more differentiated demands of the second half of the twentieth century. The party did not attempt to help *remove* the divisions between household work and careers for men and women, but merely tried to help women *combine* their careers and family duties.

Insofar as the regime's policies in later years increasingly attempted to create institutions and structures based on a gendered division of labor, they acted as a barrier to the social mobility of women. This reveals the ambivalent results of a paternalistic regime that manifested itself in the contradictory developments which, while allowing women to participate in the job "market," still blocked their attempts to take over managerial or leadership positions. The fact that some women could rise to the upper levels shows that, in the wake of delayed modernization, even the GDR experienced changes in traditional gender roles, due largely to the increased numbers of women in the workforce and the ensuing social conditions. This was not synonymous, however, with legal and social equality of the sexes in the working sphere.

Notes

1. Ingeburg Lange, *Die Verwirklichung der Beschlüsse des IX. Parteitages der SED zur weiteren Förderung der Frau. Vorlesung und Schriften, Parteihochschule "Karl Marx" beim ZK der SED* (Berlin, 1979), 8.
2. Ulrich Beck, *Risikogesellschaft. Auf dem Weg in eine andere Moderne* (Frankfurt am Main, 1996), 174.
3. See the preceding chapter by Leonore Ansorg and Renate Hürtgen in this volume.
4. Herta Kuhrig and Wolfram Speigner, "Gleichberechtigung der Frau – Aufgaben und ihre Realisierung in der DDR," in *Wie emanzipiert sind die Frauen in der DDR?* ed. idem (Cologne, 1979), 14.
5. Irene Dölling, "Über den Partiarchalismus staatssozialistischer Gesellschaften und die Geschlechterfrage im gesellschaftlichen Umbruch," *Utopie kreativ* 7 (1991): 25–32.
6. *Verfassung der DDR*, Article 24, GBl. 1949, no. 1: 4.
7. GBl. I, no. 111: 1037. See also Virginia Penrose, "Vierzig Jahre SED-Frauenpolitik: Ziele, Strategien und Ergebnisse," *Frauenforschung. Informationsdienst des Forschungsinstituts Frau und Gesellschaft* 8, no. 4 (1990): 60–77.
8. Since women's role models and perceptions closely corresponded, while legal and social equality were to be reached by means of constitutional mandates,

no independent women's movement developed in the GDR. Under the influence of the SED, the DFD was reduced to a "transmission belt" for party orders.

9. *Familiengesetzbuch der DDR vom 20. Dezember 1965, i.d.F des Einführungsgesetzes vom 19. Juni 1975 zum Zivilgesetzbuch der DDR*, Paragraph 2 (GBl. I, no. 27: 517).

10. *Arbeitsgesetzbuch der DDR vom 16. juni 1977*, Paragraph 3 (GBl. I, no. 18: 185). Especially important for this development was the drastic decline in births starting at the beginning of the 1970s.

11. Heike Trappe, *Emanzipation oder Zwang? Frauen in der DDR zwischen Beruf, Familie und Sozialpolitik* (Berlin, 1995).

12. Hildegard Maria Nickel, "'Mitgestalterinnen des Sozialismus' – Frauenarbeit in der DDR," in *Frauen in Deutschland 1945–1992*, ed. Hildegard Maria Nickel and Gisela Helwig (Bonn 1993) 233–56.

13. Interviews carried out by Dagmar Langenhan as part of the project "Continuity and change in rural societies" (University of Potsdam).

14. Ulrike Enders, "Leitbilder, Frembilder, Selbstbilder oder: Was Frauen in der DDR am beruflichen Aufstieg hindert," in *Fremdbestimmt. Selbstbestimmt?*, ed. Magdalene Deters and Susanne Weigandt (Berlin, 1987), 28–32.

15. Gunnar Winkler, ed., *Frauenreport '90* (Berlin, 1990), 63.

16. The FRG has a lower level of women in the workforce than the Scandanavian countries, France, or the GDR. See Uwe Becker, "Frauenerwerbstätigkeit – Eine vergleichende Bestandsaufnahme," *Aus Politik und Zeitgeschichte*, 1989, no. 28: 23.

17. Gisela Helwig, "Frauen im SED–Staat," *Materialien der Enquete-Kommission "Aufarbeitung von Geschichte und Folgen der SED-Diktatur in Deutschland"* vol. 3, no. 2 (Baden-Baden, Frankfurt am Main), 1253.

18. Irene Dölling, "Zum Verhältnis von modernen und traditionalen Aspekten im Lebenszusammenhang von Frauen," *Berliner Debatte Initial* 4 (1994): 30.

19. Winkler, *Frauenreport*, 93f.

20. Beck, *Risikogesellschaft*, 166.

21. Gerd Meyer, "Frauen in den Machthierarchien der DDR oder: Der lange Weg zur Parität. Empirische Befunde 1971–1985," *Deutschland Archiv* 19 (1986): 294–311.

22. Helwig, *Frauen im SED-Staat*, 1256.

23. BA, DC 20, Pers. 12.

24. Gerhard Schulze, "Der Ministerrat, die Ministerien und andere zentrale Staatsorgane," in *Verwaltungsstrukturen der DDR*, ed. Klaus König (Baden-Baden, 1991), 91–108.

25. For this and the following, see BA, DC 10, Pers. 12.

26. Gabriele Gast, "'Frauen,'" in *DDR Handbuch*, ed. Bundesministerium für innerdeutsche Beziehungen, vol. 3 (Cologne, 1985), 449.

27. BA, DC 20, Pers. 37, Presse-Information, no. 18 from 10 February 1989: 5.

28. Women could retire at 60 years, while men had to work to 65 (in the age group of 55 to 60 year olds there were 14.5 percent men and 9.6 percent women).

29. "Rural women" is used as a general term for women whose working and personal lives were determined by independent or dependent work in agriculture.

30. The realization of state regulations within LPGs was the responsibility of the largely elected leadership.

31. *Statistisches Jahrbuch der DDR* (Berlin, 1990), 19.

32. Figures based on ibid., 127ff.

33. Winkler, *Frauenreport*, 91.

34. Figures based on *Statistisches Jahrbuch: 1990*, 217.

35. Statistisches Bundesamt, ed., *Sonderreihe mit Beiträgen für das Gebiet der DDR* (Wiesbaden, 1995), no. 26: 17.

36. Ina Merkel, "Leitbilder und Lebensweisen von Frauen in der DDR," in *Sozialgeschichte der DDR*, ed. Jürgen Kocka, Hartmut Kaelble and Hartmut Zwahr (Stuttgart, 1994), 379.

37. Statistisches Bundesamt, *Sonderreihe*, 14ff and 54.

38. Iris Häuser, "Gegenidentitäten. Zur Vorbereitung des politischen Umbruchs in der DDR," *Studien zur DDR-Gesellschaft* (Münster, 1996), vol. 3: 141.

39. Winkler, *Frauenreport*, 83.

40. Susanne Diemer, "'Ich bin Sekretärin, schön und gut, aber ich bin auch ich, ich bin Rosa S.' Weibliche Erwerbstätigkeit in der DDR – eine Betrachtung der Dokumentarliteratur," in *Qualifikationsprozesse und Arbeitssituation von Frauen in der Bundesrepublik Deutschland und in der DDR*, ed. Dieter Voigt (Berlin, 1989), 129.

41. Karin Hausen and Gertraude Krell, "Perspektiven einer Politik der Gleichstellung von Frauen und Männern," in *Frauenerwerbsarbeit: Forschung zu Geschichte und Gegenwart*, ed. Karin Hausen and Gertraude Krell (Munich, 1993), 9.

42. *Für Dich* 2 (1987).

43. Gertrud Pfister, "Die Grenzen der Emanzipation – Aufstiegsbarrieren für Frauen in der DDR," in *Elite in Wissenschaft und Politik: Empirische Untersuchungen und theoretische Ansätze*, ed. Dieter Voigt (Berlin, 1987), 215.

44. Deters and Weigandt, "Karrierechancen," 21.

45. Deters and Wiegandt, "Selbstbilder karriereorientierter Frauen. Bundesrepublik Deutschland und DDR im Vergleich," in *Qualifikationsprozesse*, ed. Voigt, 167f.

46. Hausen and Krell, "Perspektiven," 11.

CULTURAL DIMENSIONS
OF DOMINATION

DICTATORSHIP AS DISCOURSE

CULTURAL PERSPECTIVES ON SED LEGITIMACY

Martin Sabrow

There is...a true lie." Stephan Hermlin, 1996[1]

The further the former East German state slips into the past, the more difficult it is to understand how the GDR system could function, noted one of Germany's leading weekly magazines seven years after German reunification.[2] Paradoxically, the more information we have about the SED dictatorship – its techniques of power, its economic system, and social structure – the less we seem to understand how it could continue to exist for over forty years. The state's ideological rhetoric, its Manichean patterns of thought, and the ritual acts that shaped the daily lives of its citizens all appear hopelessly foreign to us, even incomprehensible.

Both critics and supporters of the past regime share this sense of incomprehension and are unable to explain the GDR's sustained legitimacy. In 1998 a former Politburo member who has radically distanced himself from his prior policies spoke on TV with some astonishment about the barriers in his head, and was unable to justify why it had never occurred to him before 1989, not even when he was in the West, to read the books of communism's critics such as Arthur Koestler or Wolfgang Leonhard.[3] And the ex-pastor Joachim Gauck, who certainly cannot be accused of excessive loyalty to the state, has asked himself how he could have been unwilling for such a long time to confront the true nature of the East German state.[4] Even Erich Mielke, head of the state security system and keeper of all state secrets, could provide no explanation for the sudden erosion of the chains that had tied the populace to the dictatorship, and asked, "How could it happen that we simply gave up our GDR, just like that?"[5]

All these questions revolve around the same problem – how to explain the internal force that held communist regimes together in the twentieth century. Unlike the NS state, socialist rule in East Germany did not grow from within, but was imposed from without. It never enjoyed the support of the majority of the population, and at no time could the regime establish a substitute legitimacy through such incentives as social mobility, economic prosperity, or national identity. Indeed, unlike other states within the Eastern bloc, it faced a permanent rival in all of these areas in the Federal Republic, a state that claimed the same national identity and whose citizens spoke the same language. The political, social, and cultural influence of West Germany was undeniable and constant throughout the GDR's entire existence. "We are here, and over there at the Brandenburg Gate is the enemy," warned Kurt Hager, responsible for ideological questions, in his attempt to dismiss academic resistance to a radical politicization of the historical profession in 1956.[6]

The GDR could never meet any of the requirements formulated by Max Weber in his ideal types of legitimate rule. Traditionalism or bureaucratic legality fit a dictatorship in a society that was experiencing rapid social change, a partially de-professionalized administration, and numerous novel and informal stabilizing mechanisms as little as the charisma of its leaders. In short, the "builders of socialism"[7] were no *Führer*. And yet, the "majority of East Germans did not question the legitimacy of their state," as Jens Reich has rightly pointed out.[8] It is possible that one of the main causes for the long-term stability of socialist regimes (which varied for different countries within the Soviet bloc) as well as one of the reasons for their sudden and unexpected collapse can be traced back to their inner binding force and its slow erosion. This form of compensatory legitimacy, not (or not solely) based on ideology and more than mere reluctant loyalty, has not yet been adequately addressed by scholars.[9]

Studies that examine the GDR in terms of the historical development of its dictatorship offer few starting points for considering the widespread social acceptance of the regime which granted it a more permanent quality and secured its daily existence. Those scholars who employ totalitarian theory to emphasize the repressive nature of the regime measure the GDR – either openly or not – against the backdrop of the achievements of liberal democracies. This approach reduces analysis of the GDR to assigning varying degrees of abnormality to the regime. Such analysts describe the

SED dictatorship as trapped in a permanent state of emergency, and fail to analyze those elements in GDR society that at least internally, made SED rule less like a dictatorship, or not entirely a dictatorship. Because this approach sees the GDR "from above," it concentrates on static and unchanging intentions or goals, rather than focusing on the actual practice of rule. This limits historians' ability to understand the regime's acceptance in society and the ways in which methods of rule were internalized by the populace. It also does little to explain the sudden, almost noiseless implosion of the regime that ended Germany's second dictatorship almost as dramatically as the first.

The term "modern dictatorship" attempts to address these short-comings, but it has not yet been able to remedy them effectively. In the context of modernization theory, the dictatorships of the twentieth century cannot seriously be considered in terms of their modernity. The relative modernity of the second German dictatorship is in any case highly contested, particularly in light of the fact that the regime collapsed precisely because of its modernizing deficits vis-á-vis the West.[10] The term "modern" is further problematic in and of itself, as long as it is seen not as a historical category but as a teleological end, meant to shape a particular present and form of its ruling values. One could also argue that describing the national socialist and communist dictatorships as modern follows the very definition of modernity forwarded by those regimes themselves, which robs the term of its analytical usefulness.[11]

Yet all dictatorships of the twentieth century are different from "pre-modern" forms of dictatorial rule; they all attempt to drape their power in the cloak of legitimate, plebiscitary rule. They counter those problems associated with individualization in the democratic age with visions of communal utopias; they base their rule on mobilization and aim at mass participation. Nevertheless, they are not people's democracies, but *people's dictatorships*, based on a shared or forced identification between the rulers and the ruled. In concrete applications of the term "modern dictatorship," however, the instruments of this mobilizing form of legitimacy – such as "propaganda, repression, seduction, and terror" – nevertheless mirror (or borrow from) classical totalitarian theory.[12]

A cultural historical approach seems to offer more promising avenues of analysis. It would examine the non-material structures of East German realities which shaped patterns of action and thought over a period of forty years. From such a perspective, the important question about the GDR becomes whether the dictatorship could create a form of normalcy that provided its citizens with a specific identity. This normality secured acceptance of the regime and was rooted in a particular discourse that dovetailed with the state's interests and methods of rule. No other field promises a more fruitful analysis of the methods of such a construction than the regime's relationship to the past, and the manner in which historians created a particular GDR history and defined historical truth.

Truth in Historical Scholarship

Judged by general professional norms, the standards of internal research organization, public exchange of information, and international prestige, the historical profession in the GDR only partly and incompletely resembled that "normal scholarship" which many of its proponents after 1989[13] and a slowly growing number of West Germans claimed for it before 1989. If one looks more closely at the internal rules of the profession and East German professional discourse, one can see that ideological norms of "socialist science" not only influenced daily encounters with the past, but determined a level of thought beyond individual professional analysis. GDR history was, according to its own standards, a *political* history that saw its symbiotic relationship with the interests of the SED not as an enslavement of scholarship, but as a way of freeing history from the chains of bourgeois convention. Historians were not only aware of the political dimension of their work, they believed that the influence of party decisions, the pronouncement of significant historical "turning points," and the shifts of political course were vital elements of their profession. In the theoretical reflections of the introductory textbook by Eckermann and Mohr, the party itself was portrayed as the ideal historian.[14] The separation of politics and science very typical of the West, however much it may form the basis of a moral evaluation of GDR history, cannot provide an adequate explanation of this unique brand of politicized history.

Professionalism was not seen as opposed to partisanship, but it was rather the combination of both that was typical of history in East Germany. According to the internal logic of their profession, GDR historians believed that history did not have to lose in empirical veracity what it had gained in political significance. The unique blend of partisanship and objectivity appeared in practice, not as an ideological struggle with the truth or as a blatant manipulation of the facts, but seemed merely the result of a brand of inquiry structured along different lines. Professional historians and politicians agreed in their belief that empiricism and partisanship could be united. Kurt Hager was certainly not in danger of becoming a laughing stock when he commented to the "leading comrades of the historical profession" in 1971: "History is an active factor in the realization of the party's politics. These politics are to learn from the past, and to act on these lessons. This has nothing to do with pragmatic simplification, but rather, it is objective truth."[15]

To meet such demands, the discursive field of GDR historiography had to be quite different from that of the West. GDR historians worked within a scholarship that countered Western criteria such as plausibility, plurality, and skepticism with the "ideal of the proper realization." This was based on the belief that "historical science ... [is able] to give an exact picture of the entire historical process."[16] The force of a partisan definition of the truth within socialist science allowed historians to do away with contradictory evidence or judgments, when necessary, and to deny potential detractors any basis of criticism, without injuring the scientific nature of their discourse. In the case of a conflict between partisanship and objectivity, the "veto power of the sources" was only limited. Research results that met the standards of historical *Quellenkritik* could be dismissed in East German-speak as overly "objectified" or "facticist" whenever they contradicted party positions.

This combination of partisanship and objectivity which formed a new brand of historical truth extended far beyond the borders of history, replacing the categorical distinction between fact and fiction with a contrast between internal and external discourses, or GDR science and enemy science. The borders between fact and fiction became increasingly unclear over time – as for example when a cabaret satire of petitions in the GDR was treated not as a satire, but as a petition, or when the Institute for Marxism-Leninism in the ZK, the keeper of party history, was also made responsible for controlling literature when novels addressed any problems or themes associated with the workers' movement. Lines were also blurred when Walter Ulbricht himself censored and updated his own speeches for publication. Party objectivity and "bourgeois objectivity" were set in diametrical opposition, such as when a professional review criticized a work dealing with the Berlin crisis after 1945 because its "very detailed focus on the organization and technical side of the 'airlift' ... [has reduced] insight into the true nature of this provocation."[17] Or it was obvious when a work about the Hamburg uprising of 1923 was condemned because the author, presumably under the spell of the sources, had portrayed Ernst Thälmann's actions almost as putsch-like activities. His work was therefore judged "facticist" and banned because its author had merely "busily collected material."[18]

An analysis of dissertation reviews, meetings of historians on controversial questions, assessments of the Central Institute for History or working reports from the end of the 1950s to the middle of the

1980s – all show how effectively the categorical framework of the second German historiography, once in place, determined even the daily practice of history. The controversies that did flare up occasionally after 1958 were isolated incidents, occurring when the rules of partisan scientific discourse had been disregarded, or when a historian, in the words of East-speak, had either become a victim of the suggestive power of the sources or, in ignoring the rules of partisanship, had fallen under the spell of the enemy. The lack of conflict and the power of rules that are evident in the files of the Academy Institute for History can be explained less as the result of any particular cowardice or inherent corruptibility of East German historians than as an expression of the height of the walls of their "discursive prison." Socialist historical discourse staked out the profession's field of study, privileged certain approaches over others, was based on other criteria than history in the West, and was, for a long time, able to repress and withstand competing points of view not only in its dealings with the outside world, but internally as well.[19]

GDR history was therefore, in its internal logic, not any less dynamic, inquisitive, or capable of development than its Western counterpart, but it possessed an entirely different structure. In other words, GDR historiography was not successful in dealing with those "blank spots" of its cultural map that outsiders were quick to point out because it was shaped and formed by constant political pressure. Rather, to continue the metaphor, GDR history was successful precisely because it used a different map altogether. As such it represents a special type of "fettered science" that gained legitimacy by "transforming realities into fiction" (Hannah Arendt). This was achieved not by the declaration of a permanent state of emergency, but rather by a specific normality which allowed it to become established as a "ruled normal science" and gave it an inner legitimacy that explains the discourse's long stability.

Closed Society and Its Borders

The second reality of the socialist view of the past was as artificial as the state it served. The profession's main goal was to defend the state against both external and internal enemies. To achieve this end, East German history employed two basic, interrelated strategies of identity building: establishing an enemy without, while attempting to close ranks within. Outwardly, GDR history branded the "bourgeois" competitors in the West as the "objective opponents," whose threat was independent of their subjective goals. The creation of this trope of an enemy allowed East German discourse to become *immunized*, as it was able to condemn non-Marxist accounts and narratives as "unscientific" without having to address their actual claims. It also *universalized* the profession's self-understanding by projecting its own partiality and instrumentality onto the West, ascribing to West Germans those characteristics of political control and uniformity that characterized the GDR itself. And finally, it *homogenized* GDR discourse by framing internal disputes as dangerous attacks of the enemy on the "history front," and using the growing appeal of hostile viewpoints as a justification for continued and constant vigilance.

The inner conformity of GDR history was expressed in daily practice by an unusual zeal to expose and erase even the smallest signs of ideological co-existence. This was also evident in the rituals of criticism and self-criticism that did not end with a mere recognition of "weakness" or "straying," but were only complete after each individual had publicly recognized his failings and recanted the offending remarks. One can distinguish several different dimensions by which the organized preoccupation with the past functioned in the GDR.[20] First, the profession was based on *spatial conformity* and the absolute validity of a particular GDR vision of the past, which resulted in a rejection of all suspected "revisionist" or "bourgeois" narratives.

This claim to totality also had a *temporal dimension*, encompassing past, present, and future at once, leading to a historical presentism. This phenomenon had a variety of consequences; for instance, Wilhelm Pieck's speeches were published only after steps were taken to remove all "contemporary comments" from the book, or editors of the collected works of other figures referred to them as "currently complete." No remark better captures the power of this historical presentism than the comments made by a reviewer who, in his capacity as a censor, had been forced to deal with the bothersome "stubbornness" of historical sources: "Historical studies are often not very gratifying objects. Few readers appreciate how much trouble they are, and many forget how difficult it is to come to conclusions that are generally valid.... In addition – and this can hardly be overemphasized – the fact that the sources of our historical studies were not created by representatives of historical materialism makes it tough as well. One constantly has to interpret them differently from how they were written, and that is very difficult."[21]

Socially, the holistic, closed approach influenced the identity of controllers and the controlled, professional historians and historical functionaries. This found expression in the career paths of both political leaders and historians, whereby individuals frequently switched careers. For instance, Ulbricht described himself as a "hobby historian." Within East German professional discourse, it was not so much scholarship that complained about being instrumentalized by politics as politics that complained about being instrumentalized by scholarship – and politicians often remarked that they were left with the responsibility of having to make all historical decisions.[22] And fourth, Marxist–Leninist theory insured *ideological conformity* by ruling out any compromise between socialist and bourgeois ideology.

Evidence from examining the practice of history also contradicts the thesis of the GDR as an extinct or dying society. The second reality of socialist historical thought did not replace public discourse, nor did it rule out internal development that could go against the wishes of those in charge. A look at the role of "scholarly debate" in East German history is helpful in this context. This phrase had a very different meaning from the Western concept of "pluralism" and its lack in the East was a source of repeatedly voiced concerns. Kurt Hager, for instance, demanded in 1971 that historians "not continue to discuss the underdeveloped state of the scientific exchange of ideas, but should instead start with scientific discussion." With this demand he questioned the ideal of the so-called "proper insight": "If the enemy notices that we argue amongst ourselves, this should not be seen as a hindrance.... It is not necessary to have only one publication on a single topic that is then treated like the Bible."[23]

But because the ideal of "proper insight" determined professional discourse, the exchange of ideas within history remained artificial, and party calls for increased "truthful discussion" went unheeded. The result was a pretense of scientific exchange, without any real content.[24] Although professional journals and historical institutes routinely reported on the "development of scholarly discussion," this was not meant as open debate. Instead this characterized (and this was the basic contradiction of history as practiced in the GDR) a science dependent on public space for the completion and dissemination of a socialist view of history, while denying such space any real power, and compensating for this lack with a system of planning, review, and control. These steps were necessary because the *ideal of a closed public sphere* in the GDR suffered from the same contradictions as the construction of a partisan objectivity.

This becomes even more clear at the edges of socialist professional discourse. The socialist model of science was at all times artificial, and hardly synonymous with the realities of the profession. It was in constant need of "political guidance," and remained a discourse imposed from above that did not survive a day beyond the collapse of the regime. History had to fight daily to preserve its artificial existence against the open or hidden traditions of the profession, against outside influences that were difficult to control, as well as against the discipline's own internal development. And finally, history had to struggle with the historical sources themselves. The disparity between proclaimed norms and perceived reality was expressed in never ending battles between competing positions, in calls to arms against foreign intrusion and "objective influences," as well as cries for continued ideological vigilance. Perceived threats to the profession influenced the identity of social science no less than historians' belief in their presumed superiority. Attempts to reach a "new type of truth" found expression in battles against individual "weaknesses" and foreign intervention.

Beyond the basic contradiction between public posturing and private beliefs, historical practice was marked by dual demands of partisanship and objectivity that were impossible to reconcile. This division resulted in various types of historians, from the cadre writer who toed the party line, to the "pure scholar" who only conformed externally, or to the most common type of professional, the "compromise historian." The latter attempted to follow the divergent imperatives of party loyalty and scientific objectivity that were almost impossible to reconcile. They compensated for their failure to do so with numerous tactical maneuvers, defending their positions while hinting at other, hidden meanings, venturing forth at times and retreating at others. They masked their intentions with vague formulations and double-speak that determined both historical teaching and research in the GDR.

Yet history's discursive field remained strong enough to defend the legitimacy of the discipline both internally and externally, and could so repel any attempts to question the authority of the profession as a whole until the very end of the regime. These measures, combining defensiveness and partial retreat, were largely successful, except in a few cases when certain discourses could not be integrated, or when the ideals of party objectivity could not overrule cold, hard realities. Some prominent examples of these failures can be found in the history of German-Soviet relations during the NS regime or histories of the communist party. In those cases, historical professional discourse had one last weapon in its arsenal that can be called the "principle of cognitive exclusiveness," which awarded historians special access to knowledge while combining this privilege with demands for silence justified by a sense of responsibility.[25]

The Erosion of Historical Discourse

Despite these measures, historical discourse in the GDR remained ephemeral at best. After consolidation was completed in the 1960s, this discourse began to lose its coherence and momentum, and during the mid-1980s at the latest, a very definite process of erosion had set in. A telling indicator of this development was the growing lack of trust in the profession's own discourse. Paradoxically, this distrust increased as history became more stabilized. Thus, while in the 1950s historians discussing chapters of a planned textbook on German history could make appeals for more public participation, at the end of the 1960s, historians involved in a project on the history of the German people were urged to keep the details of their meetings behind closed doors.

The 1970s saw the return of Western scholarship, banned from GDR discourse, that functioned in many areas both as a challenger and a potential ally. This development blurred the previously very clear distinctions between "bourgeois" and "socialist" interpretations of the past. The Honecker era experienced a discursive conflict between international integration of the profession and national disintegration, as any increase in prestige in the West translated into a dismantling of internal discursive walls in the East. Many different factors played a role in this development, such as West German historians' attempts to integrate GDR history and increased contacts with the West, especially after the cultural exchange program of 1986 began to have an impact on all areas of life.[26] Equally significant were increased differences within socialist historiography in East Central Europe, and paradigm shifts in socialist historical discourse, which replaced earlier interpretations of stark black and white divisions with the concept of a "struggle for peace" that united all behind a common goal – that of world peace. Finally, the delayed changing of the guard, which became highly visible in the political sphere during the last years of SED rule, also had an impact, making the divisions and distinctions between the new and old generation that much more apparent.

These developments were expressed within historical discourse in terms of a perceived threat to GDR historiography's immune system with "bourgeois" history as a dangerous virus. In 1981 the yearly report of the Academy Institute for History expressed with some concern: "The express intentions of BRD bourgeois historians to construct a 'common German historical consciousness' and to play GDR historians against each other have resulted in greater ideological demands. These attempts must be met with more decisive measures."[27]

Five years later, against the backdrop of Soviet *perestroika*, GDR historiography grew more defensive, as different areas began to be touched by change. The one-time opponent that had been deemed too "bourgeois" for serious consideration now became a real competitor. Those GDR historians who were sensitive to change complained more frequently about restrictive research policies, or – even worse – made taboo-breaking observations about contemporary history in order not to be outdone by the West. Internal reviews (the necessary prerequisite for publication) began to judge works according to their level of complexity and fairness, criticizing them for "simplifications" or "one-sidedness." Widespread calls for increased differentiation, meant to bridge the gap between GDR and international scholarship, became more pronounced. "From a party viewpoint, we have begun to make more differentiated judgments, and have thus extended our previous knowledge to a great extent,"[28] concluded a work on Eastern agricultural workers. The wording underscores the efforts involved in trying to come to terms with two very different understandings of scholarship. Later in the 1980s, demands became even more pronounced, so that an evaluator could criticize a textbook by arguing, despite all efforts to simplify and shorten the material, it should not ignore the fact that "something can and should be done in order to further differentiate the results."[29]

Other texts of the period reveal similar patterns. Travel reports of 1988–89 often say less about the authors' own internal views of history in the outside world than about the crisis of legitimation they found themselves in when confronted with it. "The main problem that I met everywhere had to do with Soviet development under Stalin. I was told about the recent issue of the journal *Sputnik* that I had not heard about in the GDR.... It needs to be said in all clarity that we can no longer avoid existing problems. Restrictions or confiscations of property can only be seen as short-term, but hardly effective long-term solutions," reported a traveler returning from the FRG in November 1988 who had previously distinguished himself by his loyalty to the party and his willingness to conform. The extremely cautious director of the Academy Institute for History had already made similar remarks in 1985:

> In any case, things can't go on like this; we can't continue to become more differentiated in all classes and strata, with only one exception – the leadership of socialist society. If something doesn't change, we'll have to apply the brakes, since this development is so obvious to our enemies that I'm actually surprised that they remain so polite, friendly and pleasant instead of bringing these deficits to our attention on a daily basis. But the question remains – how should we deal with the traditions of the workers' movement? Because otherwise the enemy – people like [the West German historian Lutz] Niethammer – will take over. [30]

If one replaces the suspected machinations of a West German historian with the more real danger to a historical world view that depended on artificiality and isolation for its continued existence, then the fears expressed by the director of the Academy were as justified as the warnings of the Stasi about the dangers of German–German cooperation. In 1988 an internal report had warned that encounters with the enemy (no longer classified "imperialist" or "bourgeois," but more neutrally deemed "non-Marxist") would have far-reaching consequences. "The demands made on our scholarly and political abilities in this process have risen considerably."[31] What was meant by this sentence is revealed in internal reports that expressed concern about the conceptual deficits and general backwardness of Marxist historical research. The perceived potential threat posed by the West was revealed in an East German reaction to a German–German conference on social history in 1988.

> Our Hagen colleagues questioned our understanding...of transitional periods and a common revolutionary process..., class and strata distinctions within the working class and the intelligentsia; workers' interests; the relationship between material and ideal interests,...the unity of economic and social policy, the relationship between economic and social progress. Niethammer criticized what he felt was Hübner's simplification of workers' interests to elementary needs (bread and wages). He argued that broad political developments had not been adequately considered and that the events of June 17, 1953 had not been addressed.[32]

The disintegration of the once-powerful vision of the class enemy in the West accompanied and accelerated the erosion of scholarly discourse within GDR historiography. No one was a better witness to the dramatic consequences of this erosion than Kurt Hager himself, who analyzed the second SPD–SED historians' forum held in May 1989 (before the ideological commission of the ZK) by stating "we have advanced in areas we had previously ignored."[33] What this meant became more evident in the conference minutes that noted, without comment, how the Westerners had expressed the desire "to discuss so-called blank spots, such as the rehabilitation of Communists killed under Stalin, or the question of the German-Soviet Non-Aggression Pact of August–September 1939."[34] The director of the Academy Institute remarked with some surprise "that there was no direct reaction from the Division of Science of the ZK of the SED." And further, Kurt Hager's response to the same question revealed that professionals in the East (up to the highest levels of the ZK) had already assumed the enemy's language, even in their very manner of thought. "On the question of future discussion topics, he noted that obviously too little had been done in the past to show what we have already done to address such blank spots."[35]

Theoretical Implications

What can these results about East German history tell us about the nature of the second German dictatorship? First, they correspond to many of Hannah Arendt's thoughts on totalitarian rule. The same "transformation of fact into fiction," the same fictionalization of the real that she saw as typical of the NS regime also characterized the construction of historical reality under communist rule.[36] No other interpretation marks so clearly the fundamental difference between socialist and non-socialist societies in the twentieth century. No other theory better characterizes the nature of a particular form of rule that knew no limits to its power, and aimed at absolute control of human life, a system that erased the boundaries between individuals and society as a whole, rulers and the ruled, fact and fiction, truth and falsehood so thoroughly that in the end it became impossible to distinguish between repression and freedom.[37] One critic of totalitarianism grudgingly praised the GDR during the period of détente by stating, "It is difficult ... to do without the term totalitarianism, which is generally deplored as partisan and polemical.... The term totalitarianism is able as no other to capture one of the main characteristics of Marxist-Leninist, and especially SED ideology, which claims to be complete, whole, without contradiction, and completely homogenous."[38]

Yet totalitarian theory is limited by the fact that it declares its own reality to be the only existing one, ruling out the possibility of deviation. An approach that follows Hannah Arendt in making the "emancipation of reality and experience" one of the main traits of totalitarian rule[39] closes off the possibility of recognizing other "realities." It makes it impossible to see how they are constructed, and how plausible or durable they might be. And it is precisely in the creation of an "intermediary world" of beliefs, thought patterns and experiential horizons – in effect the invention of a second reality – that East German socialism could believe (as Jens Reich has noted) in its own legitimacy. It was in this area as well that, in a slow process of internal erosion, the GDR ultimately lost this very legitimacy. Only with the collapse of the dictatorship did the fictional nature of this second reality become obvious. And what Hannah Arendt had already noted for the first German dictatorship became true for the second – that after the end of totalitarian rule "nothing remained from the doctrinal system that had any relationship to reality."[40]

If this example of the mechanisms involved in the construction of historical reality can be generalized, we can say that the truth *about* the stability of the GDR state lies in the fact that truth *in* the GDR regime could be defined more successfully in its own terms and much longer than it now appears in retrospect. Similarly, the gradual erosion of socialist professional discourse can be interpreted as a continuing process in which those bonds that tied the populace to the regime slowly unraveled. This produced that combination of inner legitimacy and outward loyalty characteristic of the latter phase of the regime, which led to a loss of international and domestic guarantees. In an analysis of the inner stability and later sudden collapse of the regime it is therefore not enough to examine repressive measures and the ideological potential of such systems of rule. Nor can one merely consider the relative modernity or non-modernity of various techniques of rule.

Only a cultural approach that examines how the state created entire systems of meaning and indeed how reality was constructed within the regime as a whole will allow scholars to comprehend the deeper levels of consensus in socialist "consensus dictatorships." This type of rule was marked by cooperation and understanding between above and below, between the avant-garde and the masses, the leaders and the led, and the party and the people. The acceptance of dictatorship was created, in large part, by this kind of consensus building – by conviction, repression, and (self-)deception, in short by the creation of a particular form of historical and social reality.

Notes

1. Stephan Hermlin, "Spiegel-Gespräch," *Der Spiegel*, 1996, No. 41: 258.
2. Andreas Zielcke, "Spion in der Hitparade. Geheimdienststreß im Strom der DDR–Trivialitäten: das schwere Los des Werner Schönfelder," *Süddeutsche Zeitung* (29–31 March 1997).
3. Günter Schabowski in the TV discussion on "Schwamm drüber? – Zum Umgang mit DDR-Unrecht," ARD, 10 June 1998.
4. Stéphane Courtois, ed., *Schwarzbuch des Kommunismus. Unterdrückung, Verbrechen und Terror* (Munich, 1998).
5. Erich Mielke, "Spiegel-Gespräch," *Der Spiegel*, 1992, No. 46: 39.
6. Stenographic protocol of talks by Prof. Kurt Hager with comrade historians on 12 January 1958, SAPMO BArch, DY 30, IV 2/9.04/133.
7. This was the title of a propaganda film on Walter Ulbricht in 1953 that was never shown.
8. Jens Reich, "Gespenster von morgen. Wie können die Gesellschaften im Osten mit ihrer Vergangenheit fertig werden – mit Widerstand, Verrat, und Gleichgültigkeit?" *Die Zeit* (21 February 1997): 4.
9. Mary Fulbrook, *Anatomy of a Dictatorship. Inside the GDR 1949–1989* (Oxford and New York, 1995), 22, 139 reduces the actions of leaders to a "curious com-

bination of paternalism and paranoia" while referring to the reactions of the ruled as a "combination of conformity and grumbling."

10. For this problem, see the chapter by Detlef Pollack in this volume.

11. Mitchell Ash, "Wissenschaft, Politik und Modernität in der DDR – Ansätze einer Neubetrachtung," in *Wissenschaft und Politik – Genetik und Humangenetik in der DDR (1949–1989)*, ed. Karin Weisemann, Peter Kröner, and Richard Toellner (Münster, 1997), 1–25.

12. Jürgen Kocka, "Ein deutscher Sonderweg. Überlegungen zur Sozialgeschichte der DDR," in *Vereinigungskrise. Zur Geschichte der Gegenwart*, ed. Jürgen Kocka (Göttingen, 1996), 104 as well as, "Nationalsozialismus und SED-Diktatur im Vergleich," in ibid., 93. See also Kocka's article in this volume, which discusses various objections to the term.

13. Kurt Pätzold, "Die Geschichtsschreibung in der Deutschen Demokratischen Republik (DDR) in der Retrospektive – ein Diskussionsbeitrag," in *Die Mauern der Geschichte: Historiographie in Europa zwischen Diktatur und Demokratie*, ed. Martin Sabrow and Gustavo Corni (Leipzig, 1996), 187.

14. Walther Eckermann and Hubert Mohr, eds, *Einführung in das Studium der Geschichte* (East Berlin, 1966), 95. "Besides the fact that the party and especially its leadership know how to apply materialist dialectics and historical materialism creatively to the analysis of historical events, the historical work of the Marxist party has the further methodological advantage that its scientific analyses are constantly subjected to decisive criteria of determining the truth – namely the practice of class warfare or socialist development."

15. "Protokollnotiz vom Erfahrungsaustausch leitender Genossen der Geschichtswissenschaft mit Genossen Prof. Kurt Hager am 27.9.1971, 14.10.1971," Archive of the Berlin-Brandenburg Academy of Sciences (hereafter ABBAW), ZIG 614e. "In my opinion it first must be determined that history actually needs to be written as it occurred. That means that the objectivity of historical research is a necessary requirement…. On the other hand we always approach history from the perspective of the working class, from the standpoint of the battle for the victory of socialism, that is, in a strictly partisan fashion."

16. Eckermann and Mohr, eds, *Einführung*, 70.

17. Karlheinz Gerlach, Review of the book "Kalter Krieg um Berlin…," 17 November 1978, ABBAW, AV 2776. The practice of refuting any argument by pointing out its popularity with the "enemy" was continued as late as the 1980s.

18. Heinz Habedank, *Zur Geschichte des Hamburger Aufstandes 1923* (Berlin 1958). For background information, see Martin Sabrow, "Der staatssozialistische Geschichtsdiskurs im Spiegel seiner Gutachtenpraxis," in Sabrow, ed., *Verwaltete Vergangenheit. Geschichtskultur und Herrschaftslegitimation in der DDR* (Leipzig 1997), 41ff.

19. Hannah Arendt describes the same process when she argues that the term of self-deception is analytically useless because it "assumes the ability to distinguish between truth and falsehood, between facts and fiction." Hannah Arendt, *Wahrheit und Lüge in der Politik*, 2nd ed. (Munich, 1987).

20. Frank Wilhelmy, *Der Zerfall der SED-Herrschaft. Zur Erosion des marxistisch-leninistischen Legitimitätsanspruches in der DDR* (Münster and Hamburg, 1995), 188ff.

21. Friedrich W. Stöcker, Betr. Wolfgang Rudolph, "Die Insel der Schiffer, Zeugnisse, Erinnerungen und Geschichten von rügischer Schiffahrt," 7 September 1961, SAPMO BArch, DR 1, 5065.

22. "Johannes Hörnig über Aufgaben der Geschichtswissenschaft [after September 1963]," SAPMO-BArch, DY 30, IV A 2/9.04/134. "Historians have, as Walter Ulbricht expressed it at the 16th plenary in his concluding remarks, 'tactfully

avoided addressing' all the questions that have to do with the creation of the strategy and tactics of the KPD. This, comrades, is a serious criticism of party leadership directed at historical scholarship. We do not wish to deny that this has to do with extremely complicated political problems. But in the eyes of the party the responsibility for solving such issues lies with the historical profession."

23. "Protokollnotiz vom Erfahrungsaustausch leitender Genossen der Geschichts-wissenschaft mit Genossen Prof. Kurt Hager am 27.9.1971, 14.10.1971," ABBAW. ZIG 614e.

24. Ernst Hoffmann, "Zum Artikel des Genossen Jürgen Kuczynski," *Einheit* 12 (1957): 612–24: "What use does scholarly debate have for achieving objective truth, when one concedes that *all* scientists and writers – even bourgeois philosophers, historians, and political economists – are striving to reach the truth? Obviously this would only seriously damage objective truth and schol-arly debate." Cf. also Klaus Zweiling, "Einige Bemerkungen zur Diskussion über Meinungsstreit und Dogmatismus," in ibid.: 879–88: "Behind this point raised by Comrade Kuczynski is the question... who will decide which schol-arly debate is 'acceptable' and which not? Naturally not the personal con-sciousness of an individual comrade scientist, but the organized consciousness of the working class, of the party (of which even we comrade scientists are a part, but only one single part!)."

25. The principle of cognitive exclusivity could lead to absurd consequences, such as the reprimand that the "representation of the 'secret clause' [of the Nazi-Soviet non-agression pact]... is not suited [but not false!] for publication in this work." Ernst Engelberg, "Diskussionsbeitrag in der Mitgliederversamm-lung der SED-Grundorganisation des Instituts für Geschichte, 15.6.1965," SAPMO BArch, DY 30, IV A2/9.04/331. Cf. Stefan Wolle, *Die heile Welt der Dik-tatur. Alltag und Herrschaft in der DDR 1971–1989* (Berlin, 1998): 137ff.

26. "Protokollnotiz über die Abschlußbesprechung (zum Diskussionsforum von Historikern der DDR mit Historikern der Historischen Kommission beim Parteivorstand der SPD in Berlin am 30.–31. Mai 1989) am 19.7.1989," ABBAW, ZIG 167/4.

27. Ibid., ZIG 682, Yearly report 1981, Zentralinstitut für Geschichte, 30 December 1981.

28. ABBAW, AV 2892, Hübner, Evaluation of the manuscript "Lage und Kampf der Landarbeiter im ostelbischen Preussen."

29. Fritz Klein, Evaluation of history textbook for the eighth grade (chapters 4–8), 5 August 1986 (in the author's possession).

30. ABBAW, ZIG, 091/6, Diskussionsprotokoll zum Tagesordnungspunkt 1 der Dienstbesprechung vom 15.5.1985.

31. Landesarchiv Berlin, 00205, Zentralinstitut für Geschichte, GO der SED, Rechenschaftsbericht, October 1988.

32. ABBAW, ZIG 703/9, WB DDR-Geschichte im ZIG der AdW, Bericht über das Arbeitstreffen in der Fernuniversität Hagen (BRD), 30 September to 10 Octo-ber 1988.

33. See note 26.

34. Ibid.

35. See note 26.

36. Hannah Arendt, *Elemente und Ursprünge totaler Herrschaft* (Munich, 1991²): 654f.

37. For the field of literature see Simone Barck, Martina Langermann, and Siegfried Lokatis, *"Jedes Buch ein Abenteuer." Zensur-System und literarische Öffentlichkeiten in der DDR bis Ende der sechziger Jahre* (Berlin, 1997): esp. 188ff. Cf. Martin Sabrow, "Das Wahrheitsproblem in der DDR-Geschichtswis-senschaft," *Tel Aviver Jahrbuch für deutsche Geschichte* 25 (1996): 233–57.

38. Hans-Peter Waldrich, *Der Demokratiebegriff der SED. Ein Vergleich zwischen der älteren deutschen Sozialdemokratie und der Sozialistischen Einheitspartei Deutschlands* (Stuttgart, 1980), 79.
39. Arendt, *Elemente*, 723.
40. Arendt, *Elemente*, 574 described the collapse of totalitarian systems of thought by using the NS state as an example: "If the movement collapses outwardly for whatever reasons, and if the 'terror of organization' disappears, from one day to the next its supporters stop believing in the dogma and fiction for which they had been willing to give their lives just the day before." See also Wilhelmy, *Zerfall*, 191f.

CHAPTER 12

THE FETTERED MEDIA

CONTROLLING PUBLIC DEBATE

*Simone Barck, Christoph Classen
and Thomas Heimann*

Twentieth century dictatorships have been distinguished by the manner in which they can avail themselves of the technical and cultural potential of methods of mass persuasion. Using modern media, they perpetuate their rule and instrumentalize and establish hegemony through institutionalized ideologies. Societies of the "Soviet type,"[1] such as the GDR, generally fit this description. During the GDR's existence, the SED party and the state apparatus utilized traditional and modern forms of mass media and their institutional, substantive, and argumentative forms of control to secure and further their power. The media's potentially stabilizing effects are obvious, and have been remarked upon by authors who subscribe to totalitarian theories of rule[2] as well as by representatives of more critically oriented theoretical models.[3] While the former focus on aspects of centralized control and analyze the processes by which the state can implement canonized points of view to the exclusion of dissenting opinions, the latter emphasize those aspects of centralized forms of media that are "seductive," and capable of mobilizing the masses. Both perspectives are not necessarily exclusive, and are in fact interdependent.[4]

The historical "modernity" of the GDR as a particular form of dictatorship cannot be captured exclusively in these terms. Methods of media control were not just highly functionalized and orchestrated from above. Instead, media politics in the GDR were

complex and ambiguous, composed of different, and at times, contradictory elements such as planning, control and party evaluation. The result of these policies was the appearance of "censorship
without censors."[5] By establishing certain standards of behavior
and other mechanisms of control, the state and the party could del-
egate censorship downwards to journalists, artists, and politicians.
These individuals became in the process both rulers and the ruled,
integrated as they were within the apparatus of power and simultaneously faced with the representations of social reality they
encountered on a daily basis.

At the same time, claims to "totalitarian" rule inevitably lead to
questions about their actual limits, and point to the possibility of
resistance, the existence of oppositional or contradictory developments, and the significance of internal conflicts inherent within the
system itself. These contradictions stem largely from the fact that
media have unintentional results that are often extremely difficult,
if not impossible, to control. In the following essay, the authors will
describe the mechanisms of regulation and control in the GDR and
analyze the influence of West German media in the East to discuss
the dimensions of control, resistance and transgression in East German press, radio, TV, film, and literature.[6]

Instruments of Regulation and Control

Not only the GDR press, but East German radio, television, film, as
well as publishing and the book trade were all centrally organized
monopolies. Producing and distributing their products on a large
scale, they were part of a differentiated, complex system of manipulation and regulation that secured claims to total control through
various means. Within this complex, roughly four different systems
of rule can be distinguished: first, the practice of repressive personnel policies and restrictive recruitment; second, the establishment of a centrally organized institutional structure with a
multilevel planning system; third, the distribution of current topics
and programs as well as the regulation of language (so-called
weekly "arguments"); and finally methods of surveillance through
censorship and Stasi activities.[7]

Radio and Television

East German radio and television stood under a particularly strict
system of party control. In the immediate aftermath of the collapse
of NS rule, the Soviet military administration in Germany (SVAG)
had subjected radio to a system of censorship and review before

and after broadcasting (pre- and post-censorship). These authorities gradually transferred responsibility for radio into German hands until 1949.

In 1952 a "State Radio Committee" was established within the Council of Ministers (SRK) which was based on Soviet models. This committee replaced the previous general board of management and became the central instrument of control for radio, and until 1968 for television as well.[8] At the same time the federal states had to give up their own stations and cancel their own programming, thereby reducing them to mere regional studios. They were replaced by three centralized programs, produced by so-called "cross-sectional" editors. All of these measures were aimed at securing effective control of the media. But radio became less popular due to omnipresent political propaganda and the uniformity of programming. Starting in spring 1953, therefore, the state reversed some of these measures. Programming was reorganized along more horizontal lines with three relatively independent stations, forming a stable organization that was to remain in place from 1956 until the GDR's demise.[9]

The Planning System, set up as early as 1950, was an important instrument in the concrete realization of specific programming. In conjunction with the Division for Press and Television, the SRK laid out guidelines scheduling programming up to six weeks in advance. According to the rules established by the "Central Guidelines," the editors were to draw up their own programming in conjunction with the SRK, which then had to approve the contents. This mid-range planning was supplemented by short-term scheduling that had to be approved two weeks before programs were aired. The amount of air time that editors actually had at their disposal was therefore very limited.[10]

Another important means the SED had at its disposal to transform radio into an instrument of rule was personnel policy. Appointments were linked to ideological criteria. In the years 1949–1952, radio saw a comprehensive purge that removed "class enemies and questionable elements." Those affected were many former western emigrants in leading positions accused of the "English disease" (i.e., liberalism and pluralistic tendencies) or "ideological negligence" (i.e., criticism of conditions and developments in the GDR or the Soviet Union and the use of Western sources).[11] These measures also affected numerous lower-level employees, technicians, and musicians, who refused to move to the Eastern sector of Berlin or who displayed any disdain at all for Stalinist policies. These steps were typical for the period, related as they were to the SED's restructuring as a "party of the new order" and to the Stalinist purges. Their scale nevertheless illustrates how significant the party thought of journalists as "functionaries of the working class."

Starting in the 1960s, such "harsh" disciplinary actions were replaced with a system of punishments and rewards aimed at integrating journalists into the ruling apparatus. Well into the 1980s the party punished any straying from the official line, nonconformist thought, or "moral lapses" with sanctions that had potentially damaging consequences. Nevertheless, criminal prosecution or public humiliation of suspected offenders were more the exception than the rule. Instead, the party actively promoted conformity in an attempt to avoid public controversy, and officials sought to steer individuals in the right direction through preventive "career talks."[12]

The recruitment and socialization of a new generation of professionals was another element of the party's personnel policy that subordinated radio to the ruling party. Starting in the 1950s, almost all journalists had to complete their studies at Leipzig University.[13] Admission was limited, while ideological concerns took center stage. This emphasis on indoctrination stood in direct conflict with demands for more objective qualifications. The state determined individual career paths and job choices once studies were completed.[14] Journalists' ideological leanings also played a key role in their relationship to the party and other organizations. At least two thirds of all journalists were members of the "Association of East German Journalists" (VDJ).[15] A large percentage also belonged to the SED and could be directed through party groups. The threat of party hearings often squelched potential criticism at a very early stage.[16]

Hindered structurally by these mechanisms, opposition and dissidence could not easily find expression in East German radio. But even those journalists who toed the party line were not always capable of recognizing and following the intentions of party leaders. To meet this need, weekly "arguments" were organized by leaders of the party's agitation division starting in 1952. Officially these meetings, which all of Berlin's chief media editors attended, were designed to provide answers to recent debates and controversies. In reality, however, the meetings functioned as instruments for the creation of binding rules of discourse, identifying those subjects considered off limits as well as those issues the party wished to emphasize. Supplied with detailed specifics and formal rules of procedure, editors were charged with realizing these goals in their programming, even if these specifics were euphemistically deemed mere "recommendations."[17]

As these examples illustrate, East German media manipulation was not based on pre- or post-broadcast censorship in a classical sense. The reasons for this practice are obvious: the range of media available in an industrialized society made wide-ranging censorship impossible. Such censorship was unnecessary, since the lack of political independence and the effectiveness of preventive measures made direct censorship superfluous. Concentrated efforts from above were seldom necessary.[18] The one exception to this rule were the church newspapers, because they were removed from open political influence. At the same time, however, a complex system of permanent controls secured the preventive effects of most indirect methods of rule.

The role of the state security system in the media remains unclear.[19] Officially the Stasi was responsible for the "operative security" of all technology, such as the prevention of acts of sabotage against radio transmitters or newspaper presses. The Stasi was not generally responsible for substantive issues, unless printing mistakes or broadcasting errors were interpreted as deliberate acts. The most important means of control at their disposal was the "political-operative" subordination of personnel carried out at two different levels. Employing methods similar to those implemented in other institutions, the Stasi upheld official contacts to "leading cadres" and also worked with unofficial informants. A 1969 directive that called for the examination of journalists for "ideological lapses," "the spread of oppositional views," or questionable "moral behavior" was probably related to events surrounding the Prague Spring.[20]

Printing and Publishing

Books belonged, as did newspapers and magazines, to the so-called "basic needs of the population," and thus were supported by considerable state subsidies. Starting in the 1960s, a specialized publishing system consisting of about eighty different publishing firms produced 6,000 titles per year, with about 1,200 in the non-fiction category. The State Commission for the Arts, much hated by producers for its dogmatic and often incompetent decisions, was abolished in the reforms following the events of 17th June 1953. The responsibilities for central control and direction were taken over by the Ministry of Culture in January 1954. In a complicated process that extended over a number of years, an independent Office for Literature and Publishing, created in 1951, emerged.[21] Still part of the Ministry of Culture in 1956, it became the Chief Administration for Publishing and the Book Trade by 1963. With a staff of a few dozen it planned and controlled the production, distribution, and reception of books until the fall of the East German state. Its chief instrument of control was the five-year and one-year plans which established various cultural "themes" and "accents."

The most important measure at the disposal of the *Hauptver-waltung* was the so-called "reviews." The word *Begutachtung* was an invention of real-existing socialism and stands for the censorship that had been officially banned by the constitution. These reviews applied to all areas of publishing, from children's books and educational materials, to novels, poetry, dramas, and even calendars.[22] The complex process of covert censorship was termed the "printing approval process." It followed the established rules of cultural politics, that is it demanded socialist–realist literature follow party lines. Decisions were based on an "aesthetics of the choice of subject matter and heroes,"[23] while literature with militaristic, pornographic, "decadent," or "modernist" content and form was forbidden. The ZK division responsible for culture and science, the SED's representative in this area, provided the necessary political and ideological guidelines.

Conflicts did occur between politics, ideology, and the economy when state-sponsored literature – such as the so-called factory reports – had to be pulled because of their realistic portrayal of actual working conditions. Some stories were canceled when apologetic or affirmative literature proved to be economically less than lucrative. These tensions attest to the contradictions between "planning and censorship."[24]

The print media were constantly plagued by shortages in the paper and printing industries. Problems worsened dramatically starting in the 1970s. The GDR did have a high number of publications relative to its population, but the state could not meet its printing demands to produce daily and weekly newspapers and illustrated magazines. In the mid-1980s, for instance, the popular journal *Wochenpost* could not fill its 100,000 orders.[25]

The Film Industry

In order to control the complicated processes involved in film-making the state had created central direction and control agencies in 1949. These soon proved to be extremely ineffective in maintaining the industrial and technical infrastructure, implementing political strategies, planning, realizing and controlling production, and in distribution.[26] Hampered by excessive bureaucratic centralization and rigid ideological norms, film production sank in the years 1952 and 1953. Studios produced only six and then eight films per year.

In the wake of the June 1953 crisis, the Chief Office for Film (HV Film) was created in the newly founded Ministry for Culture. This office was responsible for the development of yearly production and "thematic" guidelines for projects. It could thus control the content and form of studio productions (for feature-length movies, documentaries and shorts, popular scientific movies and animated films) made under the DEFA monopoly (Deutsche Film Aktiengesellschaft). These plans also had to be approved by the Politburo. Special sections of the HV Film reviewed specific film projects in conjunction with the Central Committee, handed out licenses for filming, set the number of copies for each film and even regulated the number of allotted cinema showings. When films had particularly political messages, such as the two-part, feature-length movie on the Communist hero Ernst Thälmann, representatives of the Politburo even "reviewed" the scripts and the films. The Division for Agitation in the SED's Central Committee was generally responsible for the cinematic weekly news show "The Eyewitness," as well as for documentaries. This division also supervised the distribution of films in conjunction with the Distribution Commission. HV Film finally was co-responsible for the different divisions within the state broadcasting system, such as the dramatic arts (two-thirds of all DEFA films produced in the 1970s and 1980s were made-for-TV movies).

During the 1950s, the different studios developed a system of control and review to guide them in searching for material and in evaluating future film projects. These procedures involved a complicated process of checks and negotiations between artists and the control agencies of the studios on the one hand and with the film agencies and responsible party divisions on the other. Borrowing from practices established in the theater, studios making feature films and documentaries (as well as different divisions of television) hired "politically reliable" dramaturgs. In their central positions within the studios, these dramaturgs could ensure a high degree of pre-broadcast censorship. Projects were looked over by the studio leadership before being sent to the HV Film for "review." In cases of particular political significance, these sessions could even take place in the presence of ZK members.

The centralized nature of film production and distribution included many different factors and the Ministry of Culture was not the sole administrative control agency. The HV Film had to cooperate with other ministries and agencies, and work through party channels up to the highest levels of the leadership. This influenced the availability of financial and technical resources, the training of artistic and technical personnel, as well as the support of competent bureaucrats within the film agencies. Such procedures not only had an impact on marketing strategies, but also determined how movie theaters were equipped and films distributed. Lastly this structure also guided mass produced works in community centers and film clubs, party and mass organizations, and even international cultural exchanges.

Western Media Influence

The role which Western media played in the GDR can hardly be
over-emphasized, since it constituted a kind of "second" media that
constantly influenced and subverted the "first", i. e., official GDR
media. Consequently, GDR media were increasingly forced into a
defensive position vis-à-vis their challengers from the West that
belied their public claims to superiority. This "double media landscape"[27] permanently undermined the credibility of SED information policies and strengthened popular acceptance of Western
media. Despite the party's elaborate and complicated process of
control, the SED was constantly in an inferior position. Instead of
setting their own agenda, they were forced to respond to issues and
measures established by the Federal Republic.[28] The roots of this
defensiveness were to be found East Germany's unique situation
that set it apart from all other communist-ruled systems in Central
and Eastern Europe. In spite of claims to the contrary, the state
never had a monopoly of the media in the GDR. It is commonplace
to note that radio waves and satellite signals transcend borders.

Decisive for the situation in the GDR was that the Western
media did not have to overcome cultural or language barriers.[29] It
was a daily habit for most GDR citizens to inform themselves about
the West, but also about their own country, from a variety of
sources. They took divergent, and often contradictory pieces of
information and pieced them together to form a whole.[30] West German television and radio programming occupied a central position
in this process, because they offered valuable information about
the West that citizens could not obtain otherwise due to the restrictions on travel. Western sources also reported on those events and
processes in the GDR that went unreported in the East. Perceptions
about the West were not exclusively formed by information
gleaned from the media, however. Reports from people with travel
permits, memories of life before the Wall, and other sources of
information also played an important role.

No official data exist concerning the spread or acceptance of
Western radio programs in the GDR. But the audience-share
reached by GDR stations can allow us to speculate about the large
dissemination and acceptance of Western programs in the East.[31] In
the early years of television, in the late 1950s, approximately 60
percent of GDR citizens could theoretically receive Western programming.[32] In the 1980s this number had risen to 80 percent.[33]
Only the northern-most areas of East Germany around Rostock and
southeastern areas near Dresden remained unable to receive programming, and these regions were therefore popularly referred to

as the "valleys of the clueless." West German radio could be received in wide areas since the 1960s. The actual use of Western media was widespread at all times.[34] In the Federal Republic, on the other hand, due to technical difficulties, only about 15 percent of all households could view GDR television. And only a small minority (16 percent) actually took advantage of this opportunity daily or several times a week.[35]

From the beginning, competition between the Federal Republic and the GDR was carried out on the air. During the Cold War both sides sought to win over the population of the other side and to discredit their "opponents" by often highly exaggerated propaganda claims.[36] Nevertheless, the West soon gained an advantage, while East German media were increasingly forced into the defensive. This defensiveness not only characterized the provision of the necessary technical infrastructure, but also forms of programming and their conceptualization, as well as program content.

The government was repeatedly forced to mobilize extra resources to stop Western stations from supplying the East with programming, or receiving better quality signals than GDR programs. The forced expansion of television in the East was also linked to previous developments in the Western zones.[37] The GDR was continually behind – whether in broadcasting technology, the number of receivers in use, or in the implementation of new standards such as FM radio, stereo, or color television – and always trying to catch up with the "big brother" in the West who continued to set the standards.[38]

The situation regarding program content was marked by similar difficulties. In TV's early years, producers could hardly make enough shows to meet demand. Producers in the Federal Republic solved this problem by distributing the burden of the first state television channel among the members of the federally structured ARD network (*Arbeitsgemeinschaft der öffentlich-rechtlichen Rundfunkanstalten der Bundesrepublik Deutschland*). In the GDR television was centralized for political reasons. Although GDR TV aired the first official test program a few days before that of its competitor in the West (21 December 1952, as opposed to 26 December 1952), the transition to regular programming took place a full year later than in the FRG.[39] It was October 1969 before the GDR could implement a second television channel (the FRG already had three channels), and it still did not possess the necessary production capacities.[40]

Many GDR television programs, especially in the area of light entertainment, copied successful West German formats (that were in turn often copies of successful American shows). But political programs also often borrowed formally from West German models.

Thus the news program *Aktuelle Kamera* was based on the West German *Tagesschau*; the roundtable discussion entitled "Meeting Point Berlin" with foreign journalists copied Werner Höfer's "International Breakfast"; the critical news show *Prisma*[41] had both *Panorama* and *Report* as spiritual godfathers, while Karl-Eduard v. Schnitzler's famous "Black Channel"[42] also had a western precursor – "Red Spectacles" by Thilo Koch.[43]

Just how much the hegemony of the East German media was undermined by the West becomes even more clear when considering the level of content. The bloody repression of the Chinese student protest movement at Tienamen Square in summer 1989 was at first not noted in the GDR media. But a large portion of GDR citizens was informed about events through Western television or radio. In reaction to Western coverage, GDR media attempted to interpret the event as a victory over "counter-revolutionary forces."[44] This reaction probably led the East German public to question the credibility of GDR media further. In any case, the state's continued claims to an absolute information monopoly had grown absurd. East German reporting was continually forced to react implicitly or explicitly to Western sources, although the media often used vague formulations to avoid directly quoting the West.[45]

SED media policy was faced with an additional problem: the goal of "mass solidarity" could not be achieved by programs with political–ideological content. In other words: entertainment and advice shows – which at least formally had little ideological content – enjoyed the highest ratings, while propaganda broadcasts such as the "Black Channel" had a limited viewership that continually declined over time. Their formal and empty nature was a hindrance to public acceptance. Owing its longevity to political circumstances, this rhetorical style proved to be an internal weakness that could not be remedied, despite repeated complaints about the unattractiveness of GDR news shows.[46] GDR media enjoyed its greatest successes in terms of viewership when programmers abandoned their claims to spread propaganda, and when shows closely followed Western formats.[47]

The GDR state's claim to speak for all of Germany – a policy upheld until the beginning of the 1970s – only intensified this problem. Programming ostensibly had the goal of convincing citizens in the West of the superiority of Ulbricht's brand of socialism. To achieve this goal, three radio programs and a series of different television shows targeted Western audiences. These programs competed directly with Western shows. The resulting contradictions could not remain hidden for long, as can be seen by the example of the pirate radio "Freedom Station 904." Functioning in the West as the voice of the banned Communist party, the station used popular music programming, modeled on Radio Luxembourg.[48] Internally this policy increasingly came under attack. It appeared paradoxical to forbid the reception of Western channels while simultaneously offering a program similar to precisely what had been forbidden. Gerhart Eisler's response to this criticism was apodictic – it was not the music, but the words, that determined the quality of any given radio program.[49]

The fact that GDR media were increasingly put on the defensive also stemmed from a policy dictated by ideological premises. In the 1940s and 1950s, as communist rule began to stabilize, first the press and radio, then television and film were part of the larger system of domination.[50] Following classical Marxist thought, these media were instruments that would, through propaganda and agitation, spread the ideology of the party as a "collective organizer." This concept, originating with Lenin, was unsuited to the postwar German situation for several reasons. First, it falsely assumed media's direct and linear effect. Second, it did not differentiate between audio-visual and print media, but relied at times almost exclusively on the press. Third, it did not consider the possibilities of a media that could cross political borders. And fourth, it ignored public demands to be "entertained."[51] Despite these limitations, the state persisted with such a "normative communication policy" until the middle of the 1960s.[52]

At times policies towards the media were accompanied by attempts to restrict reception of Western programming. This included sending out disruptive signals, or campaigns against roof antennas directed towards the West. Citizens were encouraged to turn in and denounce neighbors and co-workers suspected of watching Western television. Such measures peaked with the erection of the Wall in 1961, but were abandoned shortly thereafter. Although the reception of Western shows was never explicitly forbidden, listeners and viewers could be persecuted for "spreading inflammatory information" or "conveying information threatening to the state." Yet the leadership consistently refused to outlaw viewing directly or to install widespread technical measures hindering reception because of their fears of popular protest or unrest.[53]

Starting in the 1970s a relative reorientation in media politics occurred. The reception of Western programming was officially approved, television and radio were recognized as service and entertainment industries and actively supported in the 1980s. However, this new outlook could not alter the larger, underlying problems. Centralization and government control of media hindered necessary reforms and developments, such as much-needed regionalization. Most importantly, the party retained its claims to "guide" press and radio directly. In the fall of 1989 the editors of *Aktuelle Kamera* complained that until the end of the GDR programming had been treated like a "preview of the *Neues Deutschland*," while the specific nature of a news show, namely its topicality, had been consistently ignored.[54] Even more damaging was the fact that in the face of a worsening economic and social crisis, Eastern media continued its course of "journalistic optimism," while Western sources conveyed a negative, more ambivalent portrait of GDR society.[55]

In retrospect it seems that journalists provided politicians with exactly the picture of the East German state the latter wanted to see. The *Aktuelle Kamera* and other politically-oriented programs increasingly became "target shows" for functionaries in the state and party bureaucracy. They provided leaders with important information, orientation, and identification. For the majority of the population, however, they offered a representation of reality that was radically different from daily perceptions, and delivered political messages that were simplistic and without substance. The result was a fundamental lack of credibility: viewer ratings for the *Aktuelle Kamera* sank between 1981 and 1988 from 14 percent to a mere 9.5 percent. And on 1 May 1989, ratings for the program *Schwarzer Kanal* reached a new nadir of 0.5 percent.[56]

Viewer rejection of GDR offerings cannot simply be explained away with references to the competition offered by Western media. The so-called "uses and gratification approach"[57] offers a more helpful explanation. This perspective interprets the use of resources according to the gratification they provide. Most East German people did not expect any gratification from the media. In fact reality as presented there created a certain cognitive dissonance in the face of personal perceptions that completely contradicted media images.[58] This theory also helps explain why many viewers rejected programs with explicit political content, while continuing to watch entertainment shows and self-help programs. Such shows helped people come to terms with the demands of daily life, if only by enabling them to put such cares behind them for a brief moment.[59]

The Arts and the Public

In accordance with the dictatorial nature of GDR society, the publics created by the arts were thoroughly permeated by state control.[60] Since the term public sphere cannot be applied in the Habermasian sense – democratic and normative – to East Germany, it must be used in a neutral, descriptive, empirical, and historical sense. Such terms as "system immanent,"[61] "party public,"[62] "official public spheres under party control,"[63] or "socialist public sphere"[64] have been used by historians and social scientists in an attempt to describe the complicated system of communicative spaces in the GDR. The public sphere is a complex network with various fragmented and interrelated dimensions. We have already discussed the second dimension that existed in East Germany, namely the competing public created by West German media. GDR sub-culture and counter-cultures made up a third dimension. The infiltration of these cultures by the state security system was not revealed until after the collapse of the East German state, and how this infiltration actually affected the production of art remains a contentious issue. Churches and their associated public spheres, with their sanctioned tolerance of medial and interpersonal forms of communication, represent another special case. In the 1980s, various political, social, and cultural groups used these spaces as public spheres.

The public spheres created by the arts should be conceptualized as "partial public spheres" that represented "contested areas of control" because they were "placed in a central position in the antechamber of power."[65] But in the area of artistic and cultural production the internal rules of art production could result in tendencies that stood in opposition to official norms and dogmas. Cultural public spheres in the GDR were marked by ideological and aesthetic concepts of struggle (socialist realism, decadence), the universalization of discourses, and a distinct lack of public and open discussion.

The less audio–visual media and the press concerned themselves with the interests, needs and experiences of GDR citizens, the more other forms of expression gained in significance. Therefore the fine arts, literature, film, and the theater (and the sciences, as well) assumed informal and communicative "substitute functions"[66] that determined their rather significant position in society and secured for their producers and publics a large degree of prestige. Here also lie the roots of general public attitudes that saw literary intellectuals as "representatives" who could speak for those without voices.

Partial public spheres depended to a large degree on local, medial, institutional and organizational as well as individual factors. Questions about who could write about what subject, when, in which literary journal, and in which manner said a great deal about the degree of control as well as the development of individual styles. A literary discussion about a single work could take on many different forms, depending on whether it was carried out by the writers' association, the Academy of Arts, or within the party apparatus itself. An empirical study addressing these issues has yet to be written.[67] It also remains to be considered how the various partial publics were related to each other and whether one can speak of "disjointed partial public spheres."[68] In the polyfunctional practice of art and culture, the compensatory, social–therapeutic, emancipatory, and anticipatory functions of art increased in the course of the 1970s, while the apologetic, politically affirmative and integrative effects of production steadily declined. This was reflected in literature and film, and in exhibition culture[69] and the theater.[70]

Movies and the Cinema

Due to their particular mimetic and visual qualities and their "collective" reception, feature length and documentary films represent a particular communicative field, separate from previously discussed structural factors and different from the individual reception of television. In the GDR, films were shown not only in cinemas, but at such venues as community centers, at mass events, and in film clubs. Due to claims for the "mass effects" of film, even industrial plants set up special showings or organized film prizes. Next to regular theater showings, distribution plans also included thematic film festivals and factory showings, such as the annual "Week of Soviet Films" or the "People's Democratic Films" meant to awaken the interest of the viewing public.

In contrast to television, the influence of the SED on DEFA's production of feature length and documentary films was less direct. It would be interesting to consider whether film production was on the whole more sensitive to changes within the domestic scene than television, which remained tied to its propagandistic functions. It does seem that filmmakers had greater leeway in making their movies, although this varied from project to project and from director to director. Nevertheless, the state monopoly of the DEFA remained, in the last instance, part of the larger system of direction and control. Caught within a net of mostly informal (thus unknown to those being watched) informants of the Stasi, the DEFA functioned within limits established by the state.[71] Film production illuminated a particular dilemma of dictatorial rule in the area of artistic production: how to use the productive potential of artistic individuality while holding more critical tendencies in check.

Despite the state's "caring supervision" of film production, statesponsored films could, according to their form, content, or cultural political context, have other, unintended results. These meanings could be independent of such films' official purpose and in some circumstances even stand in opposition to them. It seems that many films possessed ambivalent, and at times even subversive significance for some viewers, who often read between the lines. When the control boards felt that films might not deliver their intended results, they often planned "test viewings" in front of a pre-selected audience.

Looking back, however, GDR films' failings (both in content and form) were immense, and cumulative. Film producers were kept from addressing international aesthetic discourses or "sensitive topics" touching upon aspects of daily life, such as the presence of Soviet troops in East Germany. Any even remotely critical stance towards the Stalinist roots of the SED regime was barred by taboos and censorship. Institutionalized mistrust and a "continuity of suspicion" on behalf of the party and state apparatus towards the production of films often culminated in "collective" campaigns. In 1957, in the wake of the SED's "cultural political offensive," a movement against "revisionist" and "neutral" tendencies targeted the influence of Italian "neorealism" and the new Czech and Polish cinema.[72] Even those Soviet films that dared to express cautious criticism of Stalinist measures were restricted by suspicious GDR authorities.

In December 1965 the Eleventh Plenary of the Central Committee of the SED passed judgment on twelve DEFA feature films, which made up a large portion of the studio's yearly production. The event was unique in the history of DEFA and left a lasting impression on the artists involved. Those singled out by the party were film makers, actors, and mid-level managers who had dared to criticize the stagnation in society and politics prevalent in the GDR. The party's actions put an end to a discursive practice that could have worked against the basic affirmatory tendencies of GDR film.[73] These so-called "banned films" were shown in public only at the end of SED rule. The positive reactions of viewers to such critical views of society should not be overemphasized, yet they point to massive deficits in the communicative system of the GDR dictatorship.[74]

Nevertheless, the shift in the 1970s and 1980s towards everyday experiences in prose, theater, or DEFA films had its own long-term dynamic that was difficult to control. If on their way through the layers of bureaucratic control, film projects survived attempts to smooth out contradictions and erase criticisms, a not inconsiderable number preserved elements of "residual" social relevance. Topics previously not addressed (daily experiences such as youth criminality, aging, disease, death, poor housing conditions, homosexuality, or alternative lifestyles) began to be discussed in the 1970s. With postulates such as "the socialist way of life" or "general development" cultural differences could be addressed and expressed in new aesthetic forms.[75]

This was true not only for GDR feature films, but to a greater extent for documentaries which – as art forms – possessed more social relevance in the GDR than in West Germany.[76] Makers of documentaries may have had more difficulties than their colleagues in feature-length films in opposing the ruling paradigms of propaganda and agitational rule through nonfictional DEFA productions. But some documentaries could – at least compared to television with its largely affirmative message or feature films that enjoyed more attention from the party – offer a more critical view of GDR realities.[77]

On the other hand, established mechanisms of power did not prevent production of sometimes quite effective media events that crossed genres. It would be interesting to examine the effects of the adaptation of works of literature as radio programs, television films, or movies. So-called "TV novels," which drew on the narrative and aesthetic norms of feature length films and adapted them to television formats, were especially popular among viewers (such as the antifascist TV drama "Awakened Conscience" of 1961, or "Dr. Schlüter" of 1965–66).[78] Such attempts to create a particular television aesthetic and to experiment with dramatic forms remained undeveloped, especially during the second half of the 1960s when television dramas were reintegrated into the SED's party canon. "Ambitious party journalists, state functionaries or ZK members" assumed responsibility for writing TV dramas with relevant messages, and artistic projects were restricted largely to the adaptation of literature to television.[79]

After television became a true means of mass communication in the GDR, film producers at DEFA could develop specific forms of controlled entertainment and means of control. Their methods of production and program planning were highly flexible, although artistic innovation, particularly when compared to Western standards, remained relatively low. With varying degrees of success producers appropriated Western genres (love stories, science fiction and Westerns) that enjoyed wide popularity. These types of films generally followed concepts less susceptible to propagandistic messages and were often governed by economic interests (made for export).[80] Yet a shift in possible discourses allowed a more differentiated use of popular genres (especially in regards to antifascist themes or literature adaptations).

The SED viewed entertainment in the visual media as an ideological instrument of mass rule. This was more true for television than for film. But the state also saw visual media as a means of spreading knowledge about art and science to the people. Further studies are needed to determine the true integrative potential of GDR film and would need to focus more intensely on content and program analysis as well as consider popular reception.[81]

Conflicts that GDR filmmakers experienced between the opposing elements of "foreign influence and self-determination"[82] were built into the very system of DEFA's film production. Unwilling to tolerate any institutional attempts to introduce pluralistic methods, the state did allow at times some timid steps in that direction. Decentralized film production groups, such as DEFA's "Artistic Workshop," consisted of a fixed cast of directors, cinematographers, dramatists, and actors. However, the repressive *Kahlschlag* Plenum of the SED's Central Committee in 1965 robbed such groups of their relative and partial economic independence. Restructured along party lines, they were often restocked with more "trustworthy" party members.[83]

The 1980s saw one last attempt to decentralize and liberalize film production. A group of young DEFA filmmakers – surrounded by "informal informants" of the state security system – worked out a plan for an alternative studio. The proposal of this "lost generation" had, however, already failed before it came before the public in 1988 at the last meeting of GDR filmmakers and television workers.[84]

The party's total control determined most of the associational activities of those working in film and television. The Association of Film and Television, founded in 1967, did offer a certain forum for communication among its members, but no fundamental critique of the basic forms of film production was possible. The GDR Academy of Arts allowed more room for discussion. There the president of the Academy Konrad Wolf, a DEFA film director, granted literature, poetry, and painting the same standing as film and television.

The most important forum for film in the GDR was the Documentary Film Festival in Leipzig, which had enjoyed international acclaim since 1957. A film festival for feature films similar to the West German Berlin *Berlinale* did not exist in the East. The Leipzig festival, therefore, had a rather ambivalent position from the very start. It served as advertising for the cultural policy of the GDR while simultaneously offering artists and those interested in film in the GDR a window to the international world of film. Open criticism of the system was not tolerated: "One never learned in Leipzig anything about the crimes of the past in socialist countries, or about what in other 'friendly states' of the Eastern block was already being served up as the truth," complained Christiane Mückenberger, former director of the festival. As late as 1988 organizers were not allowed to show Soviet programs containing elements of "Glasnost." The festival generally functioned as a catalyst between critical tendencies within DEFA documentaries and a small, elite public.[85]

After television had replaced the cinema as the leading visual medium, the 1960s saw the beginnings of local and university film clubs that functioned as communicative spaces. Initially charged with propagandistic goals, these clubs were meant to form public taste in the service of the party. With time, however, such clubs organized individual programs aimed at specific groups and offered films different from regular cinema fare. Particularly starting in the late 1970s such clubs became increasingly critical. Within ten years their numbers had doubled, so that by the middle of the 1980s these "alternative" showings had more than 200,000 viewers.[86] It goes without saying that forbidden films were not included in the catalog of the State Film Archives for the film clubs.

Such partial public spheres may have done their part in encouraging and furthering critical readings of films and expressive methods of filmmaking. They were limited, however, by their exclusive nature (in the case of the festival) or as "sheltered" spaces (sheltered by self-censorship, social control, the Stasi, or control of the press) and were unable to achieve wider influence.

Literature

The public sphere associated with literature presents a special case, because "literature [was] one of the few links between the private and public spheres in the GDR."[87] As an "intermediary space,"[88] literature could function as a "substitute source of information" or as a kind of "substitute public sphere." Drawing on the tradition of social democratic pedagogy that placed emphasis on the spoken and printed word as a means of educating workers, literature enjoyed a high reputation in East Germany. Self-representations of the GDR as a "literature society" and "land of readers" as well as catch-phrases such as "an educated nation" underscore the cultural revolutionary claims of the SED regime. They also help to explain the characterization of the GDR as an educational and educating dictatorship.[89] The more problematic political culture became, the more literary culture – which had remained "a place of socialization and ideological legitimization" – became burdened by functions unrelated to literature.[90]

Studies carried out in the 1990s regarding daily encounters with culture in both German states have emphasized the differences between East and West that point to the lasting influence of cultural socialization and behavioral patterns inherited from the GDR dictatorship. Although the exaggerated claims to a "reading society" have proven untenable, it does deserve to be noted that East Germany had an "extensive reading public," distinguished from readers in the Federal Republic by its interests, range, purchasing practices, and library use.[91] The fact that the GDR enjoyed an extensive library system (97 percent of all communities had a state or communal library, including many exclusively for children or adolescents) which disappeared in the wake of reunification should be seen as the basis of this broad interest.

The more GDR literature could emancipate itself from party claims, the more readers turned to it as an essential "guide." The wide acceptance of literature and literary activities (whether in the FDJ, the trade unions, work brigades, domestic communities, in clubs and community centers, in the city, or in the country) had its roots in this development. Literature became a communicative object, a way to discuss individual and social problems. The more texts could critically address GDR realities, the more resonance authors and publishing houses enjoyed. This naturally resulted in an increased measure of control and surveillance, which was carried out broadly starting in 1969.[92]

In her short story "What is left," written in 1979 but published in 1990, Christa Wolf describes how secret surveillance and threat of control ruined creativity and communication. Her tale also highlights the discursive power of the public reading of any given text, which allowed participants of the public to find their own voices, despite their own fears. "In the last row a young women rose and introduced the word "future" into the discussion – a word against which we are all helpless, a word that is capable of changing the atmosphere of any room and moving any gathering. And if the words "Growth – Prosperity – Stability" had appeared in large bright letters on the wall, nothing could have helped more, because then the really important questions would have been addressed, the questions we live for and without which we could die."[93]

Claims to a "literature society" also implied the existence of a lively literary scene, boxed in between political mandates and official taboos. Stereotypical calls for more open discussion and a "free exchange of opinions" remained a staple in real-socialistic literary life. Actual controversial debates in the daily papers (such as those surrounding Erwin Strittmatter's *Ole Bienkopp* or Christa Wolf's *Der geteilte Himmel*) only took place in the 1960s, although calls were repeatedly made to revive them. The democratizing aspects of these discussions caused ruling dignitaries to view them as threatening. We have already seen by the example of the *Wochenpost* how "letters to the editor" could function as a substitute for democracy.[94]

The professionalization of literary criticism that had its roots in the 1960s reflected the political norms and canon of socialist realism, but with its more scientific and aesthetic criteria it resulted in an emancipation of GDR literature from simplistic propaganda. Starting in the 1970s authors turned to the realities of the concept of socialist realism, interpreting it in more open ideological terms and with literary originality.

In the forty years of their rule, GDR leaders preferred a literature of monosemy and were suspicious of lyrical or satirical genres. Literature of the Bitterfeld school with its all too realistic portrayals was also to prove a large stumbling block. Any criticism of the system was viewed as an "unfortunate occurrence" by GDR rulers and a "happy coincidence" by the ruled.

Ironies of Control

1989 saw the end of the GDR, and with it, the end of a system of fettered media that had determined the viewing, listening, and reading habits of the East German public. The SED, tied to antiquated, classically Marxist concepts of the late nineteenth and early twentieth centuries, could not effectively harness mass media in the service of its rule. The party's assumptions about the possibility of the "direct" and linear effects of the media proved to be inadequate. Nor could the party properly judge the actual situation of the media in East Germany and the growing import of audiovisual means of mass communication that cut across political borders and resulted in a highly differentiated and changing public.

The "supersystem"[95] erected by the SED state was characterized by a high degree of centralization and a complex structure of regulation and control that allowed little room for independent subsystems (typical of democratic societies) to develop. The state's methods of control determined and maintained a centrally organized media landscape that hindered change, differentiation, or adaptation. The SED's lack of flexibility and the continuity of its media policies attest to its concern for media's potentially disruptive powers.[96] It was typical for a "closed" system, such as that of the GDR, that calls for more public information became loudest during crisis situations, such as the June 1953 crisis. It was then that the state demanded a new media policy that would adequately serve the experiences and needs of the populace. Since media were considered the "party's best weapon," political concerns always won out over economic ones.

GDR media were therefore, in the end, deficient. Particularly in the face of international (Western) communicative standards and a growing sense of disbelief on behalf of the GDR population, these deficits increased tensions within society. The democratic aspects of modern mass culture (already noted by Walter Benjamin)[97] were held in check by the system's rigid structures and through internalized ideological criteria, which only emphasized the liberating effects of Western media for those in the East. Artistic public spheres, therefore, were of special significance in the GDR. But, as this essay suggests, there were numerous frictions there as well. In radio and television, where the methods of control were strict and all-encompassing, Western media continually won "the war of the airwaves," though they could only be interpreted on an individual basis. When performers in other media such as literature, film, theater, cabaret, or painting attempted to address deficits, the state reacted with measures that continually threatened what little room for expression and artistic standards had been achieved.

The basic contradiction between the media's ideological and political functions and methods of control, as well as the necessity of understanding viewer reactions and interpretations, could never be satisfactorily resolved. The fact that narrow propagandistic methods of rule became increasingly obsolete is in large measure due to the very expansion of mass media and other modernization processes. The need to come to terms with the demands of a modern industrial state – which included the spread of audio-visual media – was in this sense (however unintentionally) incompatible with claims to totalitarian rule. It is in this manner that one can speak of an "interrupted or broken modernization" in the area of the media.

Attempts to interpret the SED's patterns of rule in the area of media exclusively under the aspect of total control are, however, too simplistic. Assuming that (particularly in the latter stages of its existence) the GDR repeatedly saw "rudimentary, individual elements that pointed to the possibility of a civil society,"[98] future research needs to concentrate on the inner dynamics, contradictions, and dysfunctionalities of the media in East Germany that we have laid out in this essay. Further, more concrete studies also need corresponding theories that address the fact that the GDR "was not a homogenous, socially undifferentiated society, but a fragmented one marked by deep divisions and ruptures."[99] Along these lines it would be useful to examine the existence of partial public spheres and their meaning in society, or to ask questions about the means by which political culture was reproduced in the GDR. More empirical studies should also analyze the special nature of public spheres in East Germany that were subjected to constant restructuring and change.[100]

At the same time, the differences between various forms of the media need to be examined more carefully, particularly in terms of their relative acceptance or rejection within the population. Such studies could help to formulate a more precise historical understanding of the problem of modernity. For the case of the GDR, questions about how the characteristics of a pre-modern, monocratic society (such as immobility, homogeneity, conservatism) could and did interact with the modern characteristics of an industrial society (differentiation, mass production, mass communication and mobilization of the masses in the service of an abstract vision of the future) would be extremely useful.[101]

And finally, the role and mentality of those actors involved in this system need to be explored more fully.[102] At present we believe that an approach combining the triad of structure, mechanisms, and agency offers the best possible method to gain new insights into the actual nature of East German communication and help us understand the specific institutional and individual spheres of media in the GDR.

Notes

1. Sigrid Meuschel, *Legitimation und Parteiherrschaft in der DDR. Zum Paradox von Stabilität und Revolution in der DDR 1945–1989* (Frankfurt am Main, 1992), 104.
2. Horst Möller, "Sind nationalsozialistische und kommunistische Diktaturen vergleichbar?" *Potsdamer Bulletin für Zeithistorische Studien* 2 (1994): 14.
3. Jürgen Kocka, "Nationalsozialismus und SED-Diktatur im Vergleich. Ein deutscher Sonderweg," in *Vereinigungskrise. Zur Geschichte der Gegenwart* (Göttingen, 1995), 93, and idem, "Überlegungen zur Sozialgeschichte der DDR," in ibid., 104.
4. Heiko Zeutschner, *Die braune Mattscheibe. Fernsehen im Nationalsozialismus* (Berlin,1995).
5. Gunter Holzweißig, *Zensur ohne Zensor. Die SED-Informationsdisktatur* (Bonn, 1997), 15.
6. Jürgen Wilke, "Medien DDR," *Fischer Lexikon Publizistik Massenkommunikation*, ed. Elisabeth Noelle-Neumann et al. (Frankfurt am Main, 1994), 219–44; Wolfgang Mühl-Benninghaus, "Medienpolitische Probleme in Deutschland zwischen 1945 und 1989," in *Mit uns zieht die neue Zeit.... 40 Jahre DDR-Medien,* ed. Heide Riedel (Berlin, 1993), 9–20.
7. Gunter Holzweißig, *Zensur ohne Zensor*, and Peter Strunk, *Zensur ohne Zensoren. Medienkontrolle und Propagandapolitik unter sowjetischer Besatzungsmacht in Deutschland* (Berlin, 1996).
8. The establishment of separate boards for both television and radio in 1968 reflected the growing importance of television.
9. Konrad Dussel, "Die Sowjetisierung des DDR-Rundfunks in den fünfziger Jahren. Die Organisation des Staatlichen Rundfunkkomitees und seine Leitungstätigkeit," *Zeitschrift für Geschichtswissenshaft* 45 (1997): 992–1016.
10. Adelheid von Saldern and Inge Marßolek, eds, *Zuhören und Gehörtwerden (II). Radio in der DDR zwischen Lenkung und Ablenkung* (Tübingen, 1998).
11. Ansgar Diller, "Der Rundfunk als Herrschaftsinstrument in der DDR," in *Materialien der Enquete-Kommission, "Aufarbeitung von Geschichte und Folgen der SED–Diktatur,"* ed. Deutscher Bundestag (Frankfurt am Main, 1995), Vol II: 1214–42.
12. Holzweißig, *Zensur ohne Zensor*, 124–26.
13. Brigitte Klump, *Das rote Kloster. Als Zögling in der Kaderschmiede der Stasi,* 2nd ed. (Munich, 1991).
14. Stefan Pannen, *Die Weiterleiter. Funktion und Selbstverständnis ostdeutscher Journalisten* (Cologne, 1992), 32–34.
15. Arne Kapitza, *Transformation der ostdeutschen Presse. "Berliner Zeitung," "Junge Welt," und "Sonntag/Freitag" im Prozeß der deutschen Vereinigung* (Opladen, 1997), 65.

16. Pannen, *Die Weiterleiter*, 30–32.
17. Ulrich Bürger (alias: Ulrich Ginolas*), Das sagen wir natürlich so nicht! Donnerstags-Argus bei Herrn Geggel* (Berlin, 1990).
18. Post-publication censorship did occur at least partially in the agitation division and in the press division. This forged a link with more preventive measures.
19. Ansgar Diller, "Massenkommunikationsmittel im Klassenkampf. Der Staatssicherheitsdienst der DDR und die Medien," *Rundfunk und Geschichte* 20 (1994): 107–120, and Holzweißig, *Zensur*, 89–91.
20. Ibid., 94.
21. Siegfried Lokatis, "Vom Amt für Literatur und Verlagswesen zur Hauptverwaltung Verlagswesen im Ministerium für Kultur," in *Jedes Buch ein Abenteuer. Zensursystem und literarische Öffentlichkeiten in der DDR bis Ender der sechziger Jahre*, ed. Simone Barck, Martina Langermann, and Siegfried Lokatis (Berlin, 1997), 19–36.
22. Ernst Wichner and Herbert Wiesner, eds, *Ausstellungsbuch Zensur in der DDR. Geschichte, Praxis und 'Ästhetik' der Behinderung von Literaur* (Berlin, 1991).
23. Simone Barck, "Leseland als Auslaufmodell – ein Workshop am ZZF Potsdam," in *Potsdamer Bulletin* 8 (1996): 47; and Gerhard Dahne, "Vom Blick über die Mauer," in *Das Loch in der Mauer. Der innerdeutsche Literaturaustausch*, ed. Mark Lehmstedt and Siegfried Lokatis (Wiesbaden, 1997), 311.
24. Simone Barck, Martina Langermann, and Siegfried Lokatis, "Die DDR – eine verhinderte Literaturgesellschaft?" in *Die DDR als Geschichte, Fragen – Hypothesen – Perspektiven*, ed. Jürgen Kocka and Martin Sabrow (Berlin, 1994), 155.
25. Gunter Holzweißig, ed., "DDR-Presse unter Parteikontrolle. Kommentierte Dokumentation," ed. Gesamtdeutsches Institut, Bundesanstalt für gesamtdeutsche Aufgaben, *Analysen und Berichte* no. 3 (1991): 122–39.
26. Thomas Heimann, "DEFA, Künstler und SED Kulturpolitik. Zum Verhältnis von Kulturpolitik und Filmproduktion in der SBZ/DDR 1945–1959," *Beiträge zur Film- und Fernsehwissenschaft*, vol 46: 89–183.
27. Roland Reck, *Wasserträger des Regimes. Rolle und Selbstverständnis von DDR-Journalisten vor und nach der Wende 1989/90* (Münster, 1995), 325.
28. Joseph E. Naftzinger, *Policy-Making in the German Democratic Republic: The Response to the West German Trans-Border Television Broadcasting* (Ph.D. Dissertation, University of Maryland, 1994).
29. Similar situations have not occurred in those areas where cultural barriers are non-existent – North and South Korea, for instance, have different television broadcasting systems.
30. Kurt R. Hesse, "Ständiges Puzzlespiel. Tele-Visionen und persönliche Erfahrungen prägten die ostdeutschen Vorstellungen vom Westen," *Die Bundesrepublik Deutschland im Spiegel der DDR-Medien*, ed. Bundeszentrale für politische Bildung (Bonn, 1997), 37–40.
31. Christa Braumann, "Fernsehforschung zwischen Parteilichkeit und Objektivität. Zur Zuschauerforschung in der ehemaligen DDR," *Rundfunk und Fernsehen* 42 (1994): 526f.
32. Peter Hoff, "Organisation und Programmentwicklung des DDR-Fernsehens," in *Institution, Technik und Programm. Rahmenaspekte der Programmgeschichte des Fernsehens*, ed. Knut Hickethier (Munich, 1993), 246.
33. Ibid., 246.
34. See the figures in Kurt R. Hesse, *Westmedien in der DDR. Nutzung, Image und Auswirkungen bundesrepublikanischen Hörfunk und Fernsehens* (Cologne, 1988), 128.
35. Günter Bentele, Otfried Jarren, Dieter Storll, "Elektronische Medien in Berlin (West) – Interesse und Nutzung," in *Der SFB in der Berliner Medienlandschaft*.

Eine Bestandsaufnahme, ed. Sender Freies Berlin (Berlin 1986), 31, quoted in Hesse, *Westmedien,* 129.

36. Christoph Classen, "'Guten Abend und Auf Wiederhören.' Faschismus und Antifaschismus in Hörfunkkommentaren der frühen DDR," in *Verwaltete Vergangenheit. Geschichtskultur und Herrschaftslegitimation in der DDR,* ed. Martin Sabrow (Leipzig, 1997), 237–55.

37. Peter Hoff, *Organisation,* 245.

38. Thomas Beutelschmidt, *Sozialistische Audiovision. Zur Geschichte der Medienkultur in der DDR* (Potsdam, 1995), 105–7.

39. Peter Hoff, "Die Jahre der Unschuld. Zur Vor- und Frühgeschichte des Deutschen Fernsehfunks/Fernsehens der DDR," *Rundfunk und Fernsehen* 42 (1994): 555–80.

40. Peter Hoff, *Organisation,* 269.

41. Susanne Pollert, "Wo Licht ist, fällt auch Schatten. Das zeitkritische Magazin 'Prisma' im Kontext der DDR-Fernsehgeschichte," in *Zwischen Service und Propaganda. Zur Geschichte und Ästhetik von Magazinsendungen im Fernsehen der DDR 1952–1991,* ed. Helmut Heinze and Anja Kreutz (Berlin 1998), 18.

42. The "Black Channel" (1960 to 1989) was a program that tried to prove to viewers in the East that Western reporting was systematically manipulated and falsified.

43. Thilo Koch, "Westlicher Blick," *Mit uns zieht die neue Zeit,* ed. Heide Riedel, 125–29.

44. Kurt R. Hesse, "Fernsehen und Revolution. Zum Einfluß der Westmedien auf die politische Wende in der DDR," *Rundfunk und Fernsehen* 38 (1990): 331.

45. Georg Schütte, "ABC-Berichterstattung. Das Bild der Bundesrepublik Deutschland in der 'Aktuellen Kamera',," *Die Bundesrepublik Detuschland im Spiegel der DDR-Medien,* ed. Bundeszentrale für politische Bildung, 9–25.

46. Stefan Heym, "Je voller der Mund, desto leerer die Sprüche. Leben mit der Aktuellen Kamera," *So durften wir glauben zu kämpfen… Erfahrungen mit DDR-Medien,* ed. Edith Spielhagen (Berlin, 1993), 93–100. Cf. Odilio Gudorf, *Sprache als Politik. Untersuchung zur öffentlichen Sprache und Kommunikationsstruktur in der DDR* (Cologne, 1981), 133.

47. Gerhard Gmel, Susanne Deimling, and Jürgen Bortz, "Die Nutzung des Mediums Fernsehen in der DDR vor und nach der Wende," *Rundfunk und Fernsehen* 42 (1994): 542–54.

48. Jürgen Wilke and Stefan Sartoris, "Radiopropaganda durch Geheimsender der DDR im Kalten Krieg," *Pressepolitik und Propaganda. Historische Studien vom Vormärz bis zum Kalten Krieg,* ed. Jürgen Wilke (Cologne, 1997), 285–382.

49. Rolf Geserick, "Wettkampf der Systeme. Hörfunk und Fernsehen in der DDR von 1952 bis 1989," *ARD-Jahrbuch 91,* ed. ARD (Hamburg, 1991), 44–55.

50. Hans Poerschke, "Gedanken zur Journalismus–Konzeption der SED in den fünfziger Jahren," *Ansichten zur Geschichte der DDR,* ed. Dietmar Keller et al. (Bonn, 1993), vol. 1, 237–55.

51. Axel Schildt, *Moderne Zeiten. Freizeit, Massenmedien und "Zeitgeist" in der Bundesrepublik der fünfziger Jahre* (Hamburg, 1995), 222.

52. Rolf Geserick, *40 Jahre Presse, Rundfunk und Kommunikationspolitik in der DDR* (Munich, 1989), 41ff.

53. Naftzinger, *Policy Making,* 300f.

54. Schütte, "ABC Berichterstattung," 15. See also Peter Ludes, "Das Fernsehen als Herrschaftsinstrument der SED," in *Materialien der Enquete–Kommission,* vol. 2, no. 4: 2195–217.

55. Schütte, "ABC Berichterstattung," 23.

56. Braumann, "Fernsehforschung," 536, 541.

57. P. Palmgreen, L. A. Wenner, and K. E. Rosengren, "Uses and Gratifications Research: The Past Ten Years," *Media Gratificatons Research*, ed. P. Palmgreen, L. A. Wenner, and K. E. Rosengren (Beverly Hills, 1985).

58. Gmel, Deimling, and Bortz, "Die Nutzung," 553f. Cf. Doris Rosenstein, "Zuschauer als Partner. Ratgebersendungen im DDR-Fernsehen," in *Zwischen Service und Propaganda*, 402.

59. Ibid., 550.

60. Alf Lüdtke, " 'Helden der Arbeit' – Mühen beim Arbeiten. Zur mißmutigen Loyalität von Industriearbeitern in der DDR," *Sozialgeschichte der DDR*, ed. Hartmut Kaelble, Jürgen Kocka, and Hartmut Zwahr (Stuttgart, 1994), 188–213; and Jürgen Kocka, "Eine durchherrschte Gesellschaft," in ibid., 547–53.

61. Simone Barck, Martina Langermann, and Jörg Requate, "Kommunikative Strukturen, Medien und Öffentlichkeit in der DDR. Dimensionen und Ambivalenzen," *Berliner Debatte. Initial* 4/5 (1995): 27.

62. Peter Hohendahl, "Recasting the Public Sphere," *Octobre 73* (1995): 45.

63. David Bathrick, *The Powers of Speech. The Politics of Culture in the GDR* (Lincoln, 1995), 34.

64. Marc Silberman, "Problematizing the 'Socialist Public Sphere': Concepts and Consequences," *What Remains? East German Culture and the Postwar Public,* ed. idem (Wisconsin, 1997), 1–37.

65. Jürgen Gerhards and Friedhelm Neidhardt, "Strukturen und Funktionen moderner Öffentlichkeit," *Öffentlichkeit, Kultur, Massenkommunikation,* ed. Stefan Müller–Dohm and Klaus Neumann–Braun (Oldenbourg, 1991), 40.

66. Antonia Grunenberg, "Bewußtseinslagen und Leitbilder in der DDR," *Deutschland Handbuch. Eine doppelte Bilanz 1949–1989,* ed. Werner Weidenfeld and Hartmut Zimmermann (Bonn, 1989), 221; and Meuschel, *Legitimation und Parteiherrschaft*, 309f, 428.

67. Roland Reck, "Wasserträger des Regimes," and Klaus Polkehn, *Das war die Wochenpost. Geschichte und Geschichten einer Zeitung* (Berlin, 1997). See Kapitza, *Transformation der ostdeutschen Presse,* passim; Ulriche Kluge, Steffen Birkefeld, and Silvia Müller, *Willfährige Propagandisten. MfS und Bezirksparteizeitungen: Berliner Zeitung, Sächsische Zeitung, Neuer Tag* (Stuttgart, 1997).

68. Alex Demirovic, *Demokratie und Herrschaft. Aspekte kritischer Gesellschaftstheorie* (Münster, 1997), 181.

69. Günter Feist, Eckhardt Gillen, and Beatrice Vierneisel, eds, *Kunstdokumentation SBZ/DDR 1945–1990. Aufsätze, Berichte, Materialien* (Berlin, 1996).

70. Ralph Hammerthaler, "Die Position des Theaters in der DDR," *Theater in der DDR. Chronik und Positionen,* ed. Christa Hasche, Traute Schölling, and Joachim Fiebach (Berlin, 1994), 246–55.

71. Axel Geiss, *Repression und Freiheit. DEFA-Regisseure zwischen Fremd- und Selbstbestimmung,* ed. Brandenburgische Landeszentrale für politische Bildung (Potsdam, 1997).

72. Neimann, *DEFA, Künstler und SED-Kulturpolitik*, 255–322.

73. Christiane Mückenberger, ed., *"Prädikat besonders schädlich." Filmtexte mit Vorwort und einem dokumentaren Anhang* (Berlin, 1990); Joshua Feinstein, *The Triumph of the Ordinary. Depictions of Daily Life in the East German Cinema 1956–1966* (Ph.D. Thesis, Stanford University, 1995).

74. Klaus Wischnewski, "Die zornigen jungen Männer von Babelsberg," *Kahlschlag. Das 11. Plenum des ZK der SED. Studien und Dokumente,* ed. Günter Agde (Berlin, 1991), 171–88.

75. Klaus Wischnewski, "Träumer und gewöhnliche Leute," and Elke Schieber, "Anfang vom Ende oder Kontinuität des Argwohns," in *Das zweite Leben der Filmstadt Babelsberg. DEFA–Spielfilme 1946–1992,* ed. Filmmuseum Potsdam

(Berlin 1994), 212–63 and 264–327. Cf. Wolfgang Haible, *Schwierigkeiten mit der Massenkultur. Zur kulturtheoretischen Diskussion massenmedialer Unterhaltung in der DDR seit den siebziger Jahren* (Mainz, 1993), 15–41.

76. Eduard Schreiber, "Zeit der verpaßten Möglichkeiten 1970–1980," *Schwarzweiß und Farbe. DEFA-Dokumentarfilme 1946–92*, ed. Filmmuseum Potsdam (Berlin, 1994), 128–79. See also Wilhelm Roth, "Dokumentaristen. Wege zur Wirklichkeit," *Film in der DDR*, ed. Peter W. Jansen and Wolfram Schütte (Munich, 1977), 167–202.

77. Günter Jordan, "Von Perlen und Kieselsteinen. Der DEFA-Dokumentarfilm von 1946 bis Mitte der fünfziger Jahre," *Deutschlandbilder Ost*, ed. Peter Zimmermann, 61f. See also Filmmuseum Potsdam, ed., *Schwarzweiß und Farbe*.

78. Käthe Rülicke-Weiler in *Film- und Fernsehkunst der DDR*, ed. Hochschule für Film und Fernsehen (Berlin, 1979), 197–214; and Inge Münz-Koenen, *Fernsehdramatik – Experimente – Methoden – Tendenzen* (Berlin, 1974), 49–61.

79. Hans Müncheberg, "Zur Geschichte der Fernsehdramatik in der DDR," in *Mit uns zieht die neue Zeit*, ed. Heide Riedel, 101.

80. Heinz Kersten, "Enwicklungslinien," in *Film in der DDR*: 7–56, esp. 44. Cf. Lothar Bisky and Dieter Wiedemann, *Der Spielfilm. Rezeption und Wirkung. Kultursoziologische Analysen* (Berlin, 1985).

81. Heinz Niemann, *Meinungsforschung in der DDR. Die geheimen Berichte des Instituts für Meinungsforschung an das Politbüro der SED* (Cologne, 1993); and idem, *Hinterm Zaun. Politische Kultur und Meinungsforschung in der DDR – Die geheimen Berichte an das Politbüro der SED* (Berlin, 1995).

82. Axel Geiss, *Repression und Freiheit*, 9.

83. Joshua Feinstein, *Triumph of the Ordinary*, 154–63; and Klaus Wischnewski, footnote 74.

84. Freunde der Deutschen Kinemathek, eds, *DEFA NOVA – nach wie vor? Versuch einer Spurensicherung* (Berlin, 1993), 82.

85. Christiane Mückenberger, "Fenster zur Welt. Zur Geschichte der Leipziger Dokumentar- und Kurzfilmwoche," *Schwarzweiß und Farbe*, 374.

86. "Filmspiegel," 22 (1986): 30.

87. David Bathrick, *Powers of Speech*, 44.

88. Marc Silberman, "Problematizing," 3.

89. Simone Barck, Martina Langermann, and Siegfried Lokatis, "The German Democratic Republic as a 'Reading Nation.' Utopia, Planning, Reality, and Ideology," *The Powers of Intellectuals in Contemporary Germany*, ed. Michael Geyer (Chicago, 1999).

90. David Bathrick, *Powers of Speech*, 35.

91. Stiftung Lesen, *Leseverhalten in Deutschand 1992/1993. Repräsentativstudie zum Lese- und Medienverhalten der erwachsenen Bevölkerung im vereinigten Deutschland* (Mainz, 1993).

92. Joachim Walther, *Sicherungsbereich Literatur. Schriftsteller und Staatssicherheit in der DDR* (Berlin, 1996), 140–267.

93. Christa Wolf, *Was bleibt* (Berlin, 1990), 66f.

94. Klaus Polkehn, *Wochenpost*, 240–42.

95. Arne Kapitza, *Transformation*, 32.

96. Rudolf Reinhardt, *Zeitungen und Zeiten. Journalist im Berlin der Nachkriegszeit* (Cologne, 1988), 161–76.

97. Walter Benjamin, *Das Kunstwerk im Zeitalter seiner technischen Reproduzierbarkeit. Drei Studien zur Kunstsoziologie* (Frankfurt am Main, 1963).

98. Meuschel, *Legitimation und Parteiherrschaft*, 15.

99. See Detlef Pollack, chapter two in this volume. Cf. Modernität und Modernitätsblockaden. See Pollack, "Religion und gesellschaftlicher Wandel," in *Der*

Zusammenbruch der DDR, ed. Hans Jonas und Martin Kohli (Frankfurt am Main, 1993), 246–49.

100. Marc Silberman, "Problematizing," 1.
101. Ibid., 17.
102. Roland Reck's work, based on interviews, allows a reconstruction of the motivation and perceptions of participants, but his comparison of the GDR and the Third Reich, by examining the "Wochenpost" and "Das Reich," also points to the problems inherent in such an approach.

CHAPTER 13

CRITICISM AND CENSORSHIP

NEGOTIATING CABARET PERFORMANCE AND BOOK PRODUCTION

Sylvia Klötzer and Siegfried Lokatis

In the cabaret sketch "Little Moritz and the Press,"[1] we meet a young trainee on his first day on the job in a newspaper office. The news comes in over the wire that "Sicily has drifted away from Italy and is now stranded on the western coast of England." In the paper the next day, no mention is made of the event. Instead, the headlines read, "Harvest Saved." "Notice," the chief editor says to the astonished young man, "our newspaper's task is not to inform our citizens, but to confuse our class enemies."

This skit about censorship never appeared on stage. Yet it serves as a model of the regime's censorship policies. In the GDR, even the word "censorship" was censored. One spoke instead of "recommendations" and "procedures to approve publication." In the following, the term "censorship" serves as a way of describing the pervasive system of information control that encompassed archives, films, newspapers, ministries, and ZK offices as well as cabaret and literature. The two areas of the spoken and the printed word will be used to examine certain aspects and individual practices of censorship in the GDR.

Satire and Censorship

The main goal of the state's censorship of satirical criticism (that had the GDR itself as its object) was to limit the public's access to it.

The general rule of control was: the smaller the venue and the tinier the public, the larger the (limited) freedoms allowed.[2] In 1957 the DEFA used material from the repertoire of the East Berlin Cabaret "Thistle" for a film in a series of satirical short films called "The Porcupine." The film, entitled "House Lighting,"[3] portrays the end of an apartment house meeting, in which a functionary is expounding upon the "pressing questions of the day." The camera moves from the speaker's voluminous manuscript to pan across the assembled residents who have long lost any interest in the speech and have nodded off. When awakened to discuss the problem, "What moves you, when you look at the world today?" they can finally ask the questions that they find so pressing: "When will the lighting and the broken stairs finally be repaired?" "But friends, those are trivialities....We must look at the bigger picture," answers the functionary, in an attempt to move back to his speech. "But we can't do that without any lights!" comes the response from the audience, and the speaker is brought back down to earth by the laughter of his spectators. The satirical criticism of this scene is directed at the empty formulas of political rhetoric. They are taken literally and confronted with concrete realities, and the promise of a "brighter future" with socialism is contrasted with the lack of light in the building's stairwell. At the end of the film, the speaker falls down the broken staircase in the unlit hall. The satirical message of the film is clear: socialism has no future if the problems of its "residents" are not taken seriously.

This scene, which was allowed on stage, was forbidden on film. Even after numerous changes, the Chief Office for Film (*Hauptverwaltung Film*) in the Ministry of Culture refused to approve the "Porcupine" episode in April 1957. Only the cabaret could satirize SED propaganda which contradicted daily experiences. Cabaret alone could play a "game" with a "series of holy and important terms,"[4] and show disrespect towards party solutions. With the argument that GDR "enemies"[5] could use the film without any changes, "House Lighting" was placed on the index. The renewed fears of self-criticism that surfaced after the short-lived de-Stalinization "thaw" doomed experimental, satirical film to failure. In 1959, DEFA stopped numbering the films in the "Porcupine" series, since gaps between the installments made the missing numbers too obvious. In 1963, production for the series was drastically cut back. The satirical elements in the movies gave way to lighter, and more humorous, entertainment. After this conceptual change of pace, it was only a matter of time before the series was canceled altogether which finally occurred two years later.

The logic behind banning satire and reducing it to mere comical entertainment becomes apparent in a fundamental debate about the role of satire under socialism, revolving around the "Porcupine" series.[6] The resistance and distrust of SED cultural leaders towards these films found expression in a critique of a particular aesthetic form. On the one hand, SED leaders expressed a desire basically to forbid satirical criticism; on the other, they wished to make satire a part of the educational and propaganda goals of the party, thereby bringing it under their own control. Party leaders based their wish to ban satire on their belief (which was not easy to disprove) that satire was a potential "attack on the system." They attempted to disarm satire by giving it a permanent target, one that satire was to fight continually to defeat – class society. According to this logic, it could be argued that satire had no further function in socialism, in a classless society. This position could not be maintained, however, and satire was never officially deprived of its right to exist. But the basic distrust of it as an art form remained.

A more subtle method of deflecting satirical criticism was to control and partially limit satire. The SED's declaration that it had a "new function" under socialism intended to direct satire to "do its part by the means it has at its disposal to solve the problems posed by the party and the state, or to put it bluntly – [to assist] in the realization of socialism."[7] The kind of satire the party desired and demanded can be seen in the regulations for film satire. "Biting" satire was to be directed at the "main conflict" – the confrontation with the West. But GDR topics which were defined as "minor conflicts" required that "the artistic means [be] differentiated," and satiric elements be toned down. "In order to educate the public and to teach the populace, satirical methods are less fitting than the more mild form of humor or irony."[8] And lastly, drawing on "socialist realism" in literature, satire was supposed to be infused with a general optimism. Reality, seen in a critical light, was to be shown[9] "in its revolutionary development."[10] The term used in this context, "positive satire," which was as vague as it was meaningless, reveals the leaders' intentions of reducing the critical, "negative" elements of satire to mere positive "turns of phrase," especially by replacing them with comical ones.

The new mass media of TV, which had a much larger viewing audience, harbored many more reservations about critical reflections on GDR society from the start.[11] At no time were there any serious satires on television, but instead examples of the more comedic "substitute" satire. When GDR television began the new entertainment series "A Mixed Bag," it presented the cabaret trio, "The Three Dialecticians." The disparity between expectations associated with the word "cabaret" and what was actually offered in the show was so great that the monthly *Eulenspiegel* noted angrily, "One should finally draw conclusions from the undeniable fact that not even the authors and actors can laugh about the appearance or substance of the Dialectician trio. That would be nice to the public and dialectic."[12]

By defining the purposes of satirical criticism and tying these to party goals, the SED created the conditions necessary for using satire for their own interests. This meant first, that they wanted to remain out of its range and protect the state from criticism. Second, they wished to control and regulate satire in their function as patron. And third, they wished to enjoy and use satire in small doses. This explains why the formal tasks satire was to fulfill were never clearly laid out. Official rhetoric masked the party's desire to rule. Until 1989 the battle against the "enemy" was repeated time and time again in unending monotony, while calls were made for patience with domestic problems, and optimism demanded for the future. At the same time however, particularly in the cabarets, sketches had long since developed a satirical practice that frequently undermined or went against these official goals.

The Cabaret as Local Satire

Since satire was kept out of film and television, it moved into regional capitals, where new cabarets were being founded once again.[13] During the short period of reform after June 1953, the first three GDR cabarets were opened,[14] the Porcupine film series was initiated, and the satirical newspaper, "Fresh Air," was replaced by the more attractive *Eulenspiegel*. When the number of professional cabarets tripled between 1973 and 1980, only the smallest form of satire was supported by the state.

The 1980 statutes of the new Potsdam "Cabaret at the Obelisk," echoed older demands: satire was, above all, meant to "reveal class enemies and their policies" and then "in a light-hearted, satirical, and playful manner, point out and attack anachronisms in socialist life, especially those thoughts and behaviors not appropriate in socialism."[15] While the original version of the text, written by Heinz Düdder, the first cabaret director, had argued that cabaret should "criticize backward things and backward thoughts...and work as a motor for change,"[16] this call for criticism was struck by the District Council. This action underscores the SED's wish to make "its" cabaret deal only with those themes or phenomena which the party itself defined as "backward" or "foreign." These aims were contradicted by the self-assured goals of the cabaret members: "Our first commandment [is to] stage new, contemporary, and original political and satirical criticism in the form of cabaret."[17]

The program "How we hedge and shuffle,"[18] written in 1979 and premiered in February 1981, was the first production to discuss complex, multidimensional themes and contemporary problems in a more fundamental and varied manner than the traditional "potpourris." The plans for the show, which came to fruition the same time as the cabaret statute, show clearly the gap between official demands and actual results. Not only are class enemies not mentioned in the piece, but social problems, which could serve as examples of already outdated "individual events," were also not discussed. The dramaturg Inge Ristock sent the following text to the Council of the Region of Potsdam:

> Already the title reveals that the piece emphasizes thoughts and behaviors, such as mental acrobatics, opportunism, lack of courage, hypocrisy, window-dressing, etc. How we often talk around a subject rather than getting to the heart of any given matter when dealing with problems that don't fit into the picture painted of our idyllic world. How the representatives of public opinion hedge when it comes to having to make unpopular revelations public.... We need to show the causes, naturally... – that one gets ahead in this life exactly with this manner of hedging, and not by strength of character. We learn that empty praise often has more rewards than justified criticism....[19]

The cultural official (*Kulturrat*), in charge of supervising the cabaret, noted: "This view is unacceptable.... Discrepancy between upper – middle – lower. Cabaret has abandoned its task of revealing human behavior – which should serve as a measure for all." And he concluded: "This is not about human weakness, but about a society of broken people. We have landed at Biermann, Wegener, Wolf, and others."[20]

This remark reveals the party's vision of how the cabaret was to relate to the tensions of the times – it was to tone down individual criticism and avoid any portrayal of "human weakness" in order to paint a picture of an intact, homogenous society. This strategy attempted to deny the gap between party leaders and the people that had become manifest in the 1970s. The phrase "broken people" and the mention of Wolf Biermann and Christa Wolf make this evident. Biermann's expatriation had led to a protest of established artists, Wolf among others, who for the first time spoke out publicly against a Politburo decision. Authors who refused "party discipline" were later defamed in the GDR press as "broken people."[21] The function which the party had reserved for cabaret becomes clear – it was to ease tensions and remove their potentially destructive nature by addressing them in a moderate manner. While these tensions could result in dark, contemplative prose pieces, they were to be shown with a "happy face" on stage.

These intentions are evident in the revised plan for the show that came about after talks between the *Kulturrat* and cabaret leaders. "1. 'How we hedge and shuffle' – in the last thirty years we have accomplished much; not only in the consciousness of the people, but in economics as well. 2. Even though our class enemies hedge and shuffle, they cannot turn back the wheel of history. 3. No matter how much we hedge and shuffle, socialism exists in reality."[22] This text, which reads like a capitulation of the cabaret artists to official demands, should rather be seen as a tactical maneuver, meant to save the program's original concept. It framed the premise of the piece in terms of "positive satire" and removed any references to a "broken society." The viewpoint shifted from the main theme of "accommodation" in three ways. First, the piece received a more positive overall tone; second, the class enemy became the main target; and third, the phenomenon to be criticized was no longer interpreted as a social problem, but mere "individual weakness." "How do some people shuffle and hedge in order to gain a greater slice of the pie and win more status than the Joneses."[23] If this plan had actually been performed on stage, the cabaret would have renounced any reason for existence by proclaiming its distance from real life. In the media conception of the SED it would also have become a completely useless instrument. But at the same time this discrepancy allowed the censorship and control offices the possibility of interfering at any time: At any point well-formulated concepts could be contrasted with objectionable (or "failed") realizations.

The reference to "positive satire" served the same purpose as the obligatory Honecker quote at the beginning of any speech – it was a sign of loyalty to the SED. It was also the basis of a program that remained within the parameters of what was possible at the time, but nevertheless took on contemporary problems. "How we hedge and shuffle" proved its topicality in one sense by criticizing the kind of hypocrisy that had occurred during preparations for the piece itself. Though interference by state and party organs resulted in another revision, the staged program returned to the original plan but it pleased everyone. In the opening number,[24] the piece pokes fun at those opportunists who call a brown piano green just because a "leader" has defined it so. After a telephone call from a comrade, synonymous with "a change of party line," everyone immediately starts calling it blue. The discrepancy between reality and representation, which was always present in the GDR was revealed as arbitrary and false on stage.

The piece also passed review on GDR newspapers. Called to summarize the content of an article, one cabaret player confuses content with the goal of the GDR press by proclaiming, "We are – I mean – somehow... we are terrific!"[25] Especially well-received[26] was the appearance of a Martian, who wins the respect and admiration of GDR earthlings because he has a "phrase disabler" in his head that enables him to "avoid hearing or producing unnecessary and empty phrases... or even to think them." He is therefore incapable of understanding the "language of the GDR."[27]

Although this piece could bring up and laugh at daily hypocrisy and everyday distortions, expressions of desires – particularly the wish to travel – remained taboo. The sketch "A bird's eye view,"[28] though packaged in a "cute," "popular" wrapping, was struck out by the District Council at the first reading. In this piece two privileged swallows, "South-Flying Cadres," have a conversation with a family of ordinary sparrows, who have to stay in the GDR because they are too "flighty, and without purpose." The sketch not only criticized the fact that travel privileges were enjoyed by only a few, but the fact that educational chances were being denied to many. The sparrow father notes ruefully: "Sometimes I think...it wouldn't be half so bad for our education if we could fly around a bit."

The limits to possible arrangements between cultural functionaries, regional party leaders and cabaret players became obvious during the premiere of a later piece that opened in 1986, and was closed by the regional party leadership after three days. "Full steam ahead – but from where?" so the name given to the program by the dramaturg Uwe Scheddin in mid-1984, was to deal with "the establishment of the performance principle in our society." To serve as the basis for the material were, as Scheddin formulated cryptically, the "experiences with modern, developing (and still to be developed) socialist means of production, including all the relevant social processes....The form of this program is not to be as broad-ranging and multi-faceted as most topical, political pieces. We would like to have all the skits take place in one plant. Let the structure of the plant become the structure of the piece."[29] The unique quality of this concept lies in its dialectic – the cabaret players took the dictum that they should examine factory conditions at its word. The authors actually went to various plants, and the program was printed in the form of a factory newspaper (called "Safety-Valve"), and was even printed on a factory printing press. The "plant" was the GDR and its cabaret the valve to let off steam.

For the new and inexperienced *Kulturrat*, the concept that he was presented with was proof that "his" cabaret was bent on finding "inadequacies in the GDR economy," since he read the text within the parameters of official, optimistic party-speak. Since the dramaturg had quieted such apprehensions, the result was a debacle during the actual premiere in 1986. On stage, it became obvious that the slogan "Full steam ahead" could be read as, "Full steam – but where is it coming from?" The sketches presented a society without resources that had a media bent on spreading optimism. These two topics – economy and media politics – became the subject of a piece that highlighted the search for "inadequacies in the economy," which due to lack of substance could only be put on stage – by the media. The sketch, presented as a "factory cabaret," was accompanied by a "television team" that had come to the plant in expectation of a visit by "the delegation, headed by the Second Secretary" (while the "real," First Secretary, was watching the opening). The audience was forced to serve as a prop for the TV team and to practice clapping – "And now to your task during the speech. You will want to read the secretary's speech tomorrow in the newspaper. It is being printed right now, with all of your reactions, which we will now dictate to you. Spontaneously."[30] The announcement that the speech has already been printed, including the audience's own reactions, reveals to the viewing public the extent of their powerlessness. They are called to "give everything they've got" – not in their jobs, but in their expressions of support, which are directed by the camera team.

The theme of media politics was explored in other sketches as well. "Warrant"[31] discussed the discrepancy between media reporting ("Robot replaces two people") and reality ("Three people are in charge of servicing the robot, it stands motionless for 16 hours because the packer further down the assembly line is missing"). "Full steam ahead" also commented on the censoring of cabaret and poked fun at the official task of fighting the class enemy. In one scene, a "functionary" wants to "help out" a cabaret player. He expresses his regrets that "the class enemy always [gets away] unpunished" in cabaret. The performer answers, "I'm sorry, but how are we supposed to punish him? There is no class enemy present." And turning to the audience, he asks, "Or has one of you brought along a rich uncle from the West?" And he concludes, "The class enemy doesn't give a damn about our little factory cabaret!"[32] The message of the piece was clear: cabaret should study the problems of its own "factory" – GDR society.

The opening of "Full steam ahead"[33] took place in front of a silent regional party leadership. A Stasi report described the reaction of Günter Jahn, first secretary of the Potsdam district as "he clapped only once."[34] To fill the silence, the audience applauded long and hard.[35] On the very same evening, Jahn informed the players that "he was dissatisfied with the lack of engagement with [the problem of] imperialism," and that he felt "personally attacked because of the mention of the 'Bavarian House'."[36] This establishment was a historic pub that the Potsdam district leadership had declared an official party meeting place, thus barring the public. The cabaret had used this local example to criticize party privileges and "the public laughed its head off."[37]

Although the piece was completely rewritten and many sketches were removed entirely,[38] the resulting program not only registered the seismographic changes of the time, but actively called for changes along the lines of Soviet "Glasnost" reforms. This orientation was obvious in an earlier version that included the statement, "In the Soviet Union there will be some reforms, including some experiments."[39] The cabaret players, who had been developing as an ensemble prior to "Full steam ahead," were also willing to risk an experiment and explore their possibilities.[40]

While *kulturrat* believed he had supervised the program in the party's interests before the premiere, after the opening he abandoned the ensemble, since it had earned the obvious displeasure of the District Secretary. Without the *Kulturrat* as a connecting link, party officials in closed ranks could use the program to demonstrate the power of the party. The cancellation of "Full steam ahead" was a blow to the cabaret players and to the Potsdam "Hans-Otto-Theater," where open resistance to regional party policies had begun to form. The Ministry of State Security had already informed Jahn about "attempts" in the theater "to instigate a repertory that contradicts socialist cultural policies."[41] If cabaret could serve the party as a place where contemporary problems could be articulated openly, it also had to accept its function as a space where the SED could carry out its claims to censorship and control.

In this political situation, another outcome was possible – if the district leadership followed different interests, or if the District Council mediated more successfully. This can be demonstrated by a comparison with the situation in Dresden. There, Hans Modrow, Jahn's colleague, used his censorship powers in a different manner. The First Secretary of the Dresden District Organization let "It depends on you, not on everyone"[42] pass censorship at its opening – in spite of opposition by his own party organization, the Dresden District Council, and the Stasi. In his own region Modrow used the cabaret "Hercules' club" in order to vent internal party conflicts publicly, and to emphasize his own version of Saxon Glasnost vis-à-vis the party's headquarters in Berlin.

"It depends on you, not on everyone" parodied a conference of party delegates, and turned its contents on its head. The cabaret simulated the "First Outsider Conference of the Republic." In the foyer the delegates were greeted with critical songs and chants and with an exhibit about problems in the GDR. "Greetings" were sent by the line in front of the supermarket and by a pioneer group, called "Unbecoming Conduct."[43] While the text was being prepared, the Dresden District Council objected that "the frustrated authors want to insult the party and the state";[44] "the satire lacks the progressive element"; and "the piece leaves one with the taste of bitter regret."[45] The responsible official in Modrow's regional party organization deemed the texts "absolutely exaggerated." They "negate all accomplishments," raised "false charges," were "narrow-minded falsifications" and revealed "how little the authors understand and how much they miss."[46]

The cabaret, however, received support from two different sides – from the directly responsible city official for culture, Seltmann, and from the First Secretary of the District, Modrow. Seltmann refused to let the Stasi read the initial version of the text with the argument that the work was not yet completed.[47] What was decisive was his refusal to comply. The MfS had already demanded that it assist in editing the text after members of the cabaret had tested parts of the new program at a sanatorium. It had sent the transcripts to Modrow, asking that he "address the program, and make decisions about further steps," since the "goal of socialist cabaret [has] not [been] achieved" and "negative forces are set free for activities that are hostile to society." Modrow informed the Stasi that "only parts of the program have been shown up to now" and that "one ... should not take anything out of context."[48] Thus, "It depends on you, not on everyone" could make it to its premiere and remain on the playbill of the "Hercules' club," while at the same time the new Dresden production was judged "counter-revolutionary" and rumors of its cancellation abounded.[49]

The controversy surrounding the program from 1986 points to a "criticism of censorship," directed at the SED's monopoly over opinion. This criticism focused on increasing pressures from above that had been intensifying since the mid-1980s, and on various practices within the state and party bureaucracy responsible for cabarets. As the example of "Full steam ahead" showed in Potsdam, some cabarets attempted to reject the demands for more "positive" elements in satire, and criticized such optimistic portrayals as a kind of "socialist Hollywood." Rather than merely laughing at mistakes already overcome, fighting the enemy in the West, or easing tensions in everyday life by providing a sense of comic relief, cabaret presented biting satires. It attacked the leading hypocrisy – and its own hypocrisy as well, that distinguished between the internal acknowledgment of problems and the need to play them down in public, or even to deny their existence. Satire demanded that problems within society be discussed openly, while condemning the silences and the silenced public.

As the comparison between the Potsdam and Dresden productions of 1986 has shown, cabaret at that time was less interested in fighting for their programs with the "responsible party comrades" than in fighting for what was publicly allowed to be said. In retrospect it seems that there were various views regarding what was permissible within the SED after 1986. One place in which these debates were carried out was the cabaret. In the same measure that the SED began to lose control of the public sphere, its "safety valve" cabaret also became less easy to manage and control. An MfS report of 1988 after a production by the Potsdam cabaret, called "Parlour Games"[50] reinforces this point. The Stasi Major noted: "The [number] 'clown games'[51] received much applause. ...The message of this scene is: the police denies travel applications in an arbitrary and indiscriminate manner (on stage there is a raffle for a trip West due to 'urgent family matters');[52] representatives of the police registry are portrayed as ignorant; after a petition to the Upper Clown Council (the state leadership) a trip is approved, yet the applicant is treated badly by the police; the head clown (E. Honecker) also takes a trip to the West."[53]

The Modernity of Book Censorship

The central direction of over seventy large publishers responsible for book production was a much larger task than the control of the small cabaret stages. It took a huge party and state apparatus to achieve.[54] One of the most important criteria in book censorship was the relative degree of "modernity" of any given work. Judged by this high standard, works were denied because they were considered "backwards" in regards to "scientific communism." Countless requests for new printings were rejected on the grounds that such works were hopelessly outdated, and that social progress had long since passed them by. What exactly was meant by the term "modernity," was, however, not very clear. Two rival directions in literary theory were divided on this point. Authors such as Hemingway, Kafka, Sartre, and Proust, who for some were representatives of "modern literature," were for others (who saw "modernity" as resulting from "socialist development") representatives of a morbid "decadence" that was to be forbidden by censors.[55] This approach elicited scorn from many authors since campaigns against decadence and censorship often hid nothing more than petty prudishness and lowbrow dilettantism. The acts of censorship that took place during the 1950s provide a never-ending source of grotesque examples of such behavior.[56]

The GDR's system of censorship also revealed some feudalistic characteristics, and personal privilege and loyalty reigned. Leading functionaries provided "their" publishers with paper, and also occasionally allowed authors who were in political disgrace to publish their works. In light of these developments, the infamous publishing aspirations of the secret service[57] were merely a particularly sad case. The publicly attested lack of "ideologically trustworthy cadre authors," editors, and censors combined with a cultural bureaucracy that had invaded all social areas, organizations, ministries, and institutions to provide an astonishing amount of jobs for friends of publishers and their families. The literature system was endogenously structured. It was not unusual for an author to work as a censor, and for his wife to be in a publishing house, his brother in a literary organization, his aunt in radio, and his cousin in the Ministry of Culture. The GDR was a small country, where everyone knew everyone else. Without good connections, an author could wait a very long time for permission to publish. While clientelism was as widespread as it was in the West, this does not make the censorship system "modern" in any sense.

In the year 1965, the eight-volume "History of the German worker's movement" was nearing completion. Under the editorship of Walter Ulbricht, over 300 historians, organized in various working groups, had contributed to this "holy writ" of the SED. Each team received its own "stylistic editor," and a special style handbook was published to provide guidance for the authors. The eight different volumes, therefore, seemed to be written by the same hand, in spite of the number of individuals involved in the project. This approach made it possible to realize the concept of a modern master narrative, serving in the future as a measure of all things, as a source of all historical truth. Until Ulbricht's fall, every historical manuscript – even historical novels –was checked by censors to see if it corresponded to the "Eight Volumes" or not. The mechanisms of text control were also strictly organized. Every sentence was gone over with a fine-toothed comb. Entire ZK meetings were dedicated to a single work, and even the members of the Politburo devoted their precious time to reviewing texts. To give a work a final blessing and render it authoritative, all passages that might touch on Soviet interests were passed for review to Moscow. Since time was an issue, the head of the Institute for Marxism–Leninism drove a completed chapter to the Schönefeld airport. He was met by a trustworthy special courier. If the party comrades in Moscow were sober, the manuscript could be printed two days later.[58]

This example shows the significance granted to the printed word and the resources which the state was willing to invest in order to control it. Countless more or less scientific reviews, arguments, correspondence, and meeting protocols are to be found in the files of the censors and in publishing house archives. Starting in the 1960s, arbitrary, administrative directives became relatively rare. It is difficult to ascertain how exactly GDR censorship practices differed from Western procedures in large publishing houses or television broadcasting. One main difference is to be found in the degree of control, and the willingness to create numerous censorship positions and all sorts of agencies. A potentially explosive manuscript might – not counting the Stasi – have to pass ten stations, from the special editor to the head of the censorship agency. It could also be handed on up to the top, to the ZK or the Politburo. Since Soviet review methods were considered time-consuming and complicated, GDR censors did their best to avoid or shorten the process.

In the context of censorship the term "modernity" needs to be used with caution. If one considers the enormous political costs (not to mention the mountains of manuscript pages) involved in the loss of prestige if a head of state or communist leader were forced by Moscow to withdraw a book, then these precautions appear worth the effort. Since even years later, trucks filled with Brezhnev speeches could disappear for weeks in the Ukraine, the relative modernity of the flying censor becomes obvious.

In international comparison, GDR censorship was not only "modern," but starting at the end of the 1950s it took an uncontested lead. Dictators around the world had good cause to look with some envy towards East Berlin. Unfortunately, there is too little information about censorship in other Eastern bloc nations. While every book published in the GDR has its own file, complete with dates and reviews, little is known about the socialist lands to the East. When GDR delegates traveled to Warsaw, Prague, or Havana to study methods of censorship, they shrugged their shoulders over the lax, indiscriminate methods of control. Manuscripts from "fraternal countries" were therefore censored again in East Berlin, although this occasionally lead to official protests and diplomatic crises.[59]

To avoid misunderstandings, it needs to be emphasized that the ideological control at the border was originally directed against any liberal openings or the so-called "literature of the thaw," and served to secure a hard-line approach. But these policies could also serve the opposite purpose, to protect the reform attempts of the 1960s, to bar outdated Stalinist tracts or hard-line revisionist works under Brezhnev. Censorship granted the GDR a degree of sovereignty and room to maneuver. It worked as an "ideological floodgate" and a flexible instrument of control. In 1962, censors struck Stalin's name from hundreds of books and manuscripts – effectively carrying out a de-Stalinization with Stalinist methods.[60] Censorship was an instrument of power that was not tied to a particular course, but which provided the most effective method in making a course change and granting it visibility.

The leading position of the GDR in censorship was not merely due to its particular rigidity or mixture of communist orthodoxy, Stalinist inflexibility, Prussian thoroughness, and Lutheran-Pietist belief in the printed word. What made it unique was that the system saw itself faced with challenges that caused it continually to renew and modernize its methods. Its goal was to reeducate the entire population in antifascist thought through literature. While other countries, such as Poland, Czechoslovakia, and Hungary were protected by language barriers from any "ideological contamination" and could allow themselves a degree of tolerance, the GDR's "class enemy" shared a common language. In divided Germany socialist literature policy was also dependent on the enemy in many respects. It was impossible to draw the curtains. The state, therefore, had to differentiate between enemy products. While during some phases of censorship hardly a novel was allowed to pass the border, for much of the forty years an intense exchange of literary products flourished that was limited only by lack of hard currency.[61]

Methods of control and the creation of an entire ensemble of institutions aimed at monitoring the foreign trade of books had their origins in the 1950s. This decade experienced the founding of numerous new institutions, ranging from a central office, responsible for ordering, controlling, and distributing scientific literature and journals, a special organization for export, a "copyright office" in charge of licensing and foreign currency, or special bookstores in the West, finally to the "Edition Leipzig," a publishing house of books for export that sold special books for collectors.

Officials quickly learned to look the other way when dealing with income in the form of foreign currency. In the 1950s, pictures of saints were exported to Poland and pin-up photos to the Orient via a shadow company. The printing presses of the upscale Academy Publishing House reserved their glossy art paper for Swedish pornography. Many publishing houses even developed a kind of reverse censorship that removed many questionable phrases, peace slogans, or Lenin quotes with a view towards Western markets.

Whether dealing with the import of Soviet literature or the effective control of poster calendars, whether publishing children's books or establishing mechanisms of control – the learning processes involved in all areas of censorship were quite similar.[62]

First, one had to figure out when it was enough merely to add an epilogue or limit distribution. It took time to determine the best method of dealing with troublesome authors – ignore them, start a public campaign against them, or let them leave the country. It took time to weigh which texts should be sent to the Foreign Ministry for approval, and which should be forwarded to the feared Institute for Marxism–Leninism. Every "ideological slip-up" – whether it was an outdated Stalin quote or a badly touched up photograph – pointed to a previously overlooked gap in surveillance that needed to be closed, to an irresponsible editor, or a cursory review. One had to learn that the new generation of authors needed to be censored differently than Saint Augustine; when dealing with texts of the "classical heritage" and "world literature" it was best just to review the afterword and otherwise merely concentrate on winnowing out unwanted works at an earlier stage of publication. In this manner censorship functioned as a filter in the adaptation of foreign literature, constituting a strange cosmos of ideas, views and traditions, and a specific "social memory."

Each book published was also the result of a complicated political process and an expression of institutional pressure. When arguments took place behind closed doors regarding circulation, deadlines, or revisions, a censor needed to be informed about the formal and informal channels of influence which each author had at his disposal. Censors also had to know whether the CDU press could receive more paper at the expense of the NDPD, if a national award winner was more prestigious than the Institute for Contemporary Historical Studies, or if a new poet was possibly Walter Ulbricht's right hand man.

In the 1950s the system of censorship was structured, if at all, in a chaotic manner. Large publishing houses, such as the party publisher Dietz, the educational press *Volk und Wissen*, and the *Aufbau-Verlag* functioned as the showcases of GDR cultural politics and therefore enjoyed a special position that secured them relative independence from state censorship. Most belletristic houses (similar to the retail trade) were property of the SED financial division. This was merely one of six offices, more or less in competition with each other, responsible for literature within the ZK. It took over eighteen years to establish a stable state censorship agency, the Chief Administration for Publishing and Book Trade, within the Ministry of Culture, effectively ending the double rule of party and state apparatus. The censorship agency, founded as the "Office for Literature and Publishing,"[63] took over control of newspapers in 1952, people-owned publishing houses in 1956, libraries in 1958, and party presses and people's bookstores in 1963. The process marked the completion of a successful centralization of control.

The censorship agency's dealings with church presses,[64] and publishing houses of the various block parties, mass organization, and ministries, were political affairs. If a censor forbade a book published by the religious St Benno Press, the bishop might come calling. If a censor limited the amount of paper allotted to the CDU press, the party leadership would protest. The youth organization FDJ was adamant about receiving as much paper as the trade union press. Competition for the largest piece of the paper pie was a question of prestige and also one of finances. It took several years to set up a system of practice between the censorship agency and the organizational presses that reflected the distribution of power in society.

The beginning of the 1960s was marked by a significant push for codification. In 1961, for the first and only time, "Censorship Guidelines" were drawn up that prescribed the responsibilities of editors, publishers, reviewers, and censors.[65] Every step in the censorship process required a "scientific concept." Cybernetics was making headway in other areas of GDR society, and the system of censorship was also restructured along similar lines. Publishing houses were conceptualized as elements within a self-regulatory cycle. They were to discuss the criteria by which they would be censored. Planning agencies were established in which publishers, book retailers, ministries, and scientific institutes determined production.

The censorship agency became the economic planning office for book trade and publishing. Each censorship measure was akin to a shot in the foot. The later an intervention took place, the more expensive it was, since the text might already be type-set or printed. For this reason, control was concentrated in the planning stage. Censorship increasingly became similar to a consumer inspection agency that tested a finished product. This was necessary since the publication of books was a long and involved process. Once the book had been written, it was likely that a new political course, different from the line at the time of its conception, had changed the codes of speech or made it questionable to quote certain party leaders. Even the most orthodox or opportunist could not follow the twists and turns of the party line without the help of the censor.

The normal relationship between any given author and censorship was reversed in the GDR. An increasingly flexible method of planning combined with a shift towards placing the burden of censorship ōn publishers before the actual production process. In a sense, the tortoise and the hare switched places. Censors were no longer trailing behind authors, but ran ahead of them, urging them on. They pointed to certain topics or themes worthy of discussion, or let authors gather experiences in LPGs or *Kombinate*. If in the 1960s an author could not finish a book on schedule and needed to "grow ideologically," this was deemed a planning mistake, and chalked up to the bad control measures of the publishing house. By passing on responsibility for censorship to the presses, the censorship agency had less work and could also shift the burden of blame onto other shoulders.

In comparison to the 1950s, when "bourgeois" editors or uninformed party members were responsible for censorship, a new generation came to power in the 1960s that possessed special qualifications acquired at the university level. The quality of reviews improved substantially. Censors learned to distinguish between subtle nuances of fact and fiction, which ultimately gave more autonomy to texts and authors. Censorship became more broadly based, and was delegated downwards, towards the presses and reviewers. The chief administrative office for censorship within the Ministry of Culture became a mere coordination point for a wide-ranging system of control that encompassed archives, librarians, politicians, academicians, and even customs officials. Many authors and scientists functioned simultaneously as censors and reviewers, so that the boundaries between author and censor were less than clear-cut. Because censorship added an aura of scientific authority, interactions with censors became a part of daily scientific practice.[66] Even a guide for building model railroads was reviewed by over twenty specialists with the thoroughness one might expect in a work devoted to the November Revolution.[67]

Whether the subject was Lenin's works or mathematical formulas, whether books were intended for "planners and leaders" or a broad public, there was no room for publication of texts outside the official system of censorship. The creative process was directed at the unavoidable fight for publication. Which book was not written in light of later censorship? How many authors spent the majority of their time trying to outwit censors?[68] One of the greatest successes of the GDR's literature policies was making authors their own censors.[69] But self-censorship was not enough to guarantee publication. Authors needed well-informed editors, skillful reviewers, or a publishing house with artistic inclinations. Everyone involved in the publishing trade was part of an intricate process of negotiation and competition for publication permission, circulation, paper quality, or the approval of individual passages.

Confrontations concerning the publication of manuscripts were part of the logic of the bureaucratic system. The state approval for publication legitimated every book that appeared in the GDR, granting it political validity. Indirectly, all other books that were not approved became hazardous contraband and desired goods. Particularly books from the Soviet Union were potentially more dangerous than literature from the West (which was considered "hostile" anyway). Generally every published book served as a precedent for ones to follow. While one individual book could be deemed an "ideological breakdown," two books could equal a "new line." At the same time, every time a book was forbidden, publishers became uneasy, and the possible parameters of what could be said in public were reduced. Ideological course changes were often signaled by spectacular censorship cases, but everyday life was characterized by permanent haggling about the appearance of books, carried out behind the scenes or beyond the borders of the public realm.

Every decision was the result of a hidden political tug-of-war carried out by representatives of the various "social forces" in the GDR – organizations, ministries, scientists, and artists. In the process scientific, economic, financial, pedagogical, aesthetic, and political principles were discussed and determined. Censorship functioned not only as an administrative tool wielded from above, but was a process of give and take between different groups. As such it was influenced by social forces. Criteria could be determined (if the political winds were blowing from the right direction) by contemporary aesthetic and scientific developments. But much was left to chance. A narrow-minded official in the "HV Publishing and Book Trade," or the timid publisher could influence an entire discipline. The censorship agency was populated by some open and educated individuals who were willing to work with editors to save a "problematic book." The development of the GDR's "critical contemporary literature" in the form of works by Volker Braun,[70] Erwin Strittmatter and Christa Wolf would have been inconceivable without such support from the censorship agency.[71] The front did not always run directly between censorship and author, but often split the censorship agency and authors' associations within.

Censorship was, therefore, an omnipresent phenomenon, that dominated (in some cases positively) intellectual life in the GDR. By politicizing all texts, censorship became a motor for the leveling of social differences. At the same time it set off specific areas of control by marking formal disciplinary boundaries or creating special, de-politicized spaces. The files concerning the publication of Goethe's *Farbenlehre* contain the remark, "No objections. Approved." The differentiation of criteria used to judge works was one of the most important instruments of control. The political relevance of a work could be inferred from the publisher. The spectrum ranged from official party works of the Dietz press that were sharply controlled,[72] to the *Heimat* literature of provincial presses, the new style of novels of the *Aufbau* press that potentially challenged criteria of "social realism," or the just barely tolerated murder mysteries published by the *Greifen* press in Rudolstadt. Insiders were aware of all sorts of nuances. This provided an entire vocabulary to discuss different cases.

If the "leveling of sectoral differences" can be seen as criterion for modernization deficits, the role of censorship remained quite ambivalent. Politicization served to abolish social distinctions, only to reverse the process step by step, under constant state control. The result was a new cosmos, a beehive with more or less strictly controlled spaces, some of which were entirely free of censorship. The entire system had a unique institutional form that functioned according to the internal rules specific to the control of information.

GDR censorship was the target of almost unbroken criticism between 1945 and 1990. Time and again there were more or less official resolutions and protests from scientists and authors that found their echoes in the West German press. Hundreds of tricks were employed to circumvent official censors. Some authors could mobilize politicians on their behalf. Ulbricht and Honecker complained about censorship and used their names to promote certain authors. But even they were incapable of getting rid of censorship entirely. While the Soviets did their part to insure that certain themes were excluded from literature, the system's own internal dynamics drove the entire process.

This permanent criticism was one factor in repeated attempts to restructure and modernize methods of control. In the 1950s the state censorship agency was certainly the most unstable of all bureaucracies. At the same time, it was a source of innovation that surrounded and influenced the entire intellectual life of the GDR. The system delegated censorship and responsibility downwards, to publishing houses and reviewers, thereby largely veiling the censored nature of the publication process. The system was so effective in making authors their own censors that censorship seemed, on the surface, completely superfluous. But in reality there were repeated attempts to remove all state control of printing and publication and to decentralize censorship, to make publishing houses independent "responsible ideological centers." No reform period was without such initiatives. Most publishers were opposed to such attempts to increase their responsibility. They saw state censorship as a protection, since they could not be punished for printing books that had received official approval. Paradoxically but logically, attempts to abolish state censorship therefore originated largely from the censorship agency itself. Who would willingly want to assume such responsibilities?

Censorship and Dictatorship

It has often been said that dictatorships cannot function without censorship. This does not just mean the oppression of public criticism. If dictatorial rule is based on a mass party, censorship becomes an indispensable instrument of control. It defines the "party line." The disappearance of Trotsky, and not Stalin, from the history books showed the party where real power lay. Then Stalin was replaced by the "Soviet leadership." Whoever was deemed the new person out of favor could no longer appear anywhere by name or be mentioned in the same breath with Lenin. Naturally, all party members were aware of the absurdity of such symbolic gestures. But this absurdity influenced belief, making it clear who possessed power, and who could determine truth.

No one can say how the removal of the printing approval process would have affected GDR literature. There were many publishing houses with far stricter ideological guidelines than those followed within the censorship agency. But any decentralization of censorship was connected to the internal party democratization of the SED. A recognition of publishing houses as "independent ideological centers" would have allowed the creation of internal oppositional party platforms. This happened with the *Aufbau* Publishing House in 1956. The removal of state censorship was one of the main demands of the publisher Walter Janka[73] and the philosophy editor Wolfgang Harich. Shortly before the Ministry of Culture announced the official cessation of state censorship, both men were arrested.[74] The *Kahlschlag* party congress of 1965 ended any further discussion of the issue.[75] The area of cabaret productions shows a similar ambivalence between party control and protection that both hampered and inspired the conception of programs.

Earlier attempts at reform had always occurred within the parameters of the censorship system. What was open to debate was not whether censorship should be abolished altogether, but who had the power to wield it and invest his own texts with political validity. The mere existence of censorship made every book and every play a potential political weapon. Abolishing censorship would open the system to the vagaries of changing winds, setting forces free that, according to the logic of the system, would be impossible to control. Censorship in "real existing" socialism was omnipresent and everyday, and deeply anchored in social structures. Its rules were firmly tied to the logic of an entire system of control. No dictator could dictate them any longer.

Notes

1. Text of Ristock, Geier, and Rascher. Rat des Bezirkes Potsdam, Abt. Kultur. "Grundsatzmaterialien zum Aufbau des Kabaretts am Obelisk." Brandenburgisches Landeshauptarchiv (BLHA), Rep. 401, No. A/4390, Abg. 1993, B599, Carton 652.

2. "Satire" is defined as an "attack" on the "shocking realities" of life, carried out by hyperbole, irony, and biting criticism. See Ulrich Gaier, *Satire* (Tübingen, 1967).

3. The 98th number of the DEFA short film series "The Porcupine." Director: Ernst Kahler; story: Hans Harnisch. Copy MB 074, VK 0657 in the Bundesfilmarchiv, Berlin.

4. "Aktennotiz betr. Abnahme in der HV Film am 3.4.1957," SAPMO, Bestand DR-1-4458, HV Film.

5. Ibid.

6. See esp. the journals *Sonntag* and *Neue Deutsche Filmkunst* between 1953 and 1963.

7. Georg Honigmann, "Satire und Widerspruch," *Deutsche Filmkunst* 6 (1959): 162–66.

8. Ibid., 165; Hans Dieter Mäde, "Treffsicherheit – nach wie vor das Hauptproblem," *Deutsche Filmkunst* 8 (1958): 227–29.

9. For a rationalization see Frank Burkhard Habel, *Die Behandlung von Widersprüchen in der DEFA-Stacheltier-Produktion* (Diplom Arbeit, Potsdam Babelsberg, 1984).

10. Quoted in Hannes Hüttner, "Von der satirischen Methode," *Deutsche Filmkunst* 1 (1956): 19f.

11. Peter Ludes, "Das Fernsehen als Herrschaftsinstrument der SED," in *Material der Enquete-Kommission "Aufarbeitung von Geschichte und Folgen der SED-Diktatur in Deutschland,"* ed. Deutscher Bundestag, vol. 2/3 (Baden-Baden, 1995), 2194–217.

12. Hansgeorg Stengel, "Fernseh-Eule," *Eulenspiegel* 21 (1977): 6. Cf. Sylvia Klötzer, "'Volldampf woraus?' –Satire in der DDR. 'Eulenspiegel' und 'Kabarett am Obelisk' in den siebziger und achtziger Jahren," in Thomas Lindenberger, ed., *Herrschaft und Eigen-Sinn in der Diktatur* (Cologne, 1999).

13. As single exemption the cabaret "Die Kiebitzensteiner" in Halle was founded in 1967.

14. The first cabarets were the Berlin Distel 1953, the Leipzig Pfeffermühle 1954, and the Dresden Herkuleskeule 1955.

15. "Statut Kabarett am Obelisk," from 1 January 1980; BLHA, see fn. 1.

16. "Konzeptions-Entwurf für ein Kabarett in der Bezirksstadt Potsdam," from 6 April 1977 by Heinz Düdder. BLHA, see fn. 1.

17. Program "Startschüsse," ed. Potsdamer Kabarett am Obelisk, premiered in 1978.

18. "Wie wir uns drehn und wenden," directed by Gerd Staiger, book by Inge Ristock, artistic direction by Matthias Meyer. Premiered on 28 February 1981.

19. Inge Ristock, "Wie wir uns drehn und wenden. Konzeption zu einem Kabarett-Programm," BLHA, see fn. 1.

20. Handwritten note of the Potsdamer *Kulturrat* Grabe, BLHA.

21. "Brief von Dieter Noll an Erich Honecker," *Neues Deutschland*, 22 May 1979: 4.

22. "Wie wir uns drehn und wenden. Konzeptionelle Gedanken zum III. Kabarettprogramm des Potsdamer Kabaretts am Obelisk," BLHA.

23. Ibid.

24. Rigera, "Es grünt so blau," all the quotes from this piece in BLHA.
25. W. Hampel, "Vor uns neigt die Erde sich."
26. Christian Klötzer, "Kabarett-Eule" zu "Wie wir uns drehn und wenden," *Eulenspiegel* 39 (1981): 6.
27. Harry Fiebig, "Sternstunde."
28. "Vogelperspektiven," text by Dieter Lietz.
29. "Volldampf woraus. Arbeitskonzeption für das aktuelle politische Programm 1985," script by Uwe Scheddin.
30. "Volldampf woher?" (Entrance, part II), version by Andreas Turowski, script by Uwe Scheddin, final version.
31. Author: André Brie.
32. Uwe Scheddin, "Die Betriebsstörung," after Wladimir Majakowski, "Schwitzbad," third act.
33. Director: Gerd Staiger; premiere: 28 June 1986.
34. "Information über die Situation im Potsdamer Kabarett," 6 November 1986, BStU, MfS AOP 2123/87 (Potsdam), 140.
35. Interviews with Uwe Scheddin and Gerd Staiger in the fall of 1997.
36. "Operative Information über das Programm 'Volldampf woraus' des Potsdamer Kabaretts am Obelisk' vom 4. Juli 1986," BStU, MfS (Potsdam), Abt. AKG 360, 25.
37. Interview with Uwe Scheddin on 19 September 1997 in Berlin.
38. For example the sketch "Initiativoli" portrays factory competitions as a mere show, interesting for the workers only for the prize money. Private archive of Dieter Lietz.
39. "Arbeitskonzeption für das aktuelle politische Programm 1985," script by Uwe Scheddin.
40. Interviews with Uwe Scheddin, Gerd Staiger, Dieter Lietz, and André Brie in fall 1997 in Berlin.
41. "Information über einige die gegenwärtige Situation kennzeichnende Erscheinungen an den Theatern von Potsdam und Brandenburg," 21 February 1986, noted by Günter Jahn the next day, BStU, MfS (Potsdam) AKG 815, 19–22.
42. "Auf Dich kommt es an, nicht auf alle. Eine Außenseiterkonferenz von Peter Ensikat und Wolfgang Schaller," director: Gisela Oechelhaeuser together with Wolfgang Schaller, premiere on 20 December 1986.
43. Peter Ensikat and Wolfgang Schaller, "Konzeption für ein Kabarettprogramm 'Auf Dich kommt es an, nicht auf alle,'" of 6 September 1985, Sächsisches Hauptstaatsarchiv (SHStA), IV E, 2/9/02/570.
44. "Aktennotiz zur Sofortinformation betr. neues Programm der Herkuleskeule," from 24 June 1986, SHStA, IV E, 2/9/02/570.
45. "Information zum gegenwärtigen Stand der Vorbereitung des neuen Programms des Kabaretts 'Herkuleskeule' Dresden," from 14 July 1986. BStU, MfS (Dresden), AOP 3337/91, vol. I: 20.
46. Wolfgang Schaller's reaction to accusations of Dr. Cassier (Bezirksleitung Dresden, Abt. Kultur), 1 August 1986. SHStA, IV E, 2/9/02/570.
47. See fn. 45: 17–21.
48. BStU, MfS (Dresden) AKG/P1/127/86, "Information über ein beabsichtigtes neues Programm des Dresdner Kabaretts 'Herkuleskeule' im Herbst 1986," 23 May 1986: 1–9.
49. BStU MfS (Dresden) AOP 3337/91, vol. I, "Bericht zu Wolfgang Schaller und der gegenwärtigen Situation im Kabarett 'Herkuleskeule,'" 2 February 1987: 68f.
50. "Gesellschaftsspiele," director: Klaus Gendries a.G., premiere: 15 February 1988.
51. Authors: Hans J. Finke and Hartmut Guy.
52. "Reise in dringenden Familienangelegenheiten" – the criterion for a trip to the West.

53. BStU, MfS (Potsdam) AKG 360, "Einschätzung des Kabarettprogramms 'Gesellschaftsspiele,'" 5 February 1988: 119f.
54. Simone Barck, Martina Langermann, and Siegfried Lokatis, *"Jedes Buch ein Abenteuer!" Zensursystem und literarische Öffentlichkeiten in der DDR bis Ende der sechziger Jahre* (Berlin, 1997).
55. Simone Barck, "Das Dekadenz-Verdikt. Zur Konjunktur eines kulturpolitischen 'Kampfkonzepts' Ende der 1950er bis Mitte der 1960er Jahre," in *Historische DDR–Forschung,* ed. Jürgen Kocka (Berlin, 1993) 327–44.
56. The sources related to the printing approval of the Chief Office of Book Publishing and the Book Trade for the 1950s are located in the Bundesarchiv Berlin-Lichterfelde under the signatures BA–DR1, 5002–112. They are filed alphabetically by author's name.
57. Joachim Walther, *Sicherungsbereich Literatur. Schriftsteller und Staatssicherheit in der DDR* (Berlin, 1996).
58. Interview of 15 November 1996 with Professor Lothar Berthold, former director of the Institut für Marxismus–Leninismus. A documentation of the "Geschichte der deutschen Arbeiterbewegung" is now in preparation at the ZZF.
59. Siegfried Lokatis, "Sowjetisierung und Literaturpolitik. Von der Förderung zur Verstümmelung sowjetischer Literatur in der frühen DDR," in *Amerikanisierung und Sowjetisierung in Deutschland 1945–1970,* ed. Konrad Jarausch and Hannes Siegrist, 361–86.
60. Barck, Langermann, and Lokatis, *"Jedes Buch ein Abenteuer,"* 208f.
61. Mark Lehmstedt and Siegfried Lokatis, eds, *Das Loch in der Mauer. Der innerdeutsche Literaturaustausch* (Wiesbaden, 1997).
62. See for the following: *"Jedes Buch ein Abenteuer,"* 24–52.
63. Carsten Gansel, *Parlament des Geistes. Literatur zwischen Hoffnung und Repression 1945–1961* (Berlin, 1996), 132–41, 148–53; Siegfried Lokatis, "Das Amt für Literatur und Verlagswesen oder die schwere Geburt des Literaturapparates der DDR," in *Historische DDR-Forschung,* ed. Jürgen Kocka, 303–26.
64. Siegfried Bräuer and Clemens Vollnhals, eds, *"In der DDR gibt es keine Zensur." Die Evangelische Verlagsanstalt und die Praxis der Druckgenehmigung 1954–1989* (Leipzig, 1995).
65. Barck, Langemann and Lokatis, *"Jedes Buch ein Abenteuer,"* 188–96.
66. Siegfried Lokatis, "Wissenschaftler und Verleger in der DDR. Das Beispiel des Akademie-Verlages," *Geschichte und Gesellschaft* 22 (1996): 46–61.
67. BA DR-1, 5092, Gerhard Trost, 1959–1962.
68. For many examples, see Richard Zipser, ed., *Fragebogen: Zensur* (Leipzig, 1995).
69. Manfred Jäger, "Das Wechselspiel von Selbstzensur und Literaturlenkung in der DDR," in *"Literaturentwicklungsprozesse." Die Zensur der Literatur in der DDR,* ed. Ernest Wichner and Herbert Wiesner (Frankfurt am Main, 1993), 18–49.
70. York-Gothart Mix, ed., *"Ein Oberkunze darf nicht wieder vorkommen." Materialien zur Publikationsgeschichte und Zensur des Hinze-Kunze-Romans von Volker Braun* (Wiesbaden, 1993).
71. Barck, Langermann, and Lokatis, *"Jedes Buch ein Abenteuer,"* 171, 218f.
72. Siegfried Lokatis, "Dietz. Probleme der Ideologiewirtschaft im zentralen Parteiverlag der SED," in *Von der Aufgabe der Freiheit. Festschrift für Hans Mommsen,* ed. Christian Jansen, Lutz Niethammer and Bernd Weisbrod (Berlin, 1996): 533–48.
73. Walter Janka, *"...bis zur Verhaftung." Erinnerungen eines deutschen Verlegers* (Berlin and Weimar, 1993).
74. Carsten Wurm, *Der frühe Aufbau-Verlag* (Wiesbaden, 1996).
75. Günter Agde, ed., *Kahlschlag. Das 11. Plenum des ZK der SED 1965* (Berlin, 1991).

CHAPTER 14

THE PIVOTAL CADRES

LEADERSHIP STYLES AND SELF-IMAGES OF GDR-ELITES

Arnd Bauerkämper and Jürgen Danyel

> He must enjoy the trust of his own party; he must be able to master the
> tasks handed to him; he must have intimate ties to the people, he must
> possess their confidence so that he can count on the initiative of the
> masses when carrying out the policies of the party.[1]

Franz Dahlem's description of the new type of SED functionary in
1946 illuminates the contradictions inherent within the self-images
and leadership styles of the GDR's leading "cadres." In their self-perceptions, East German party and state leaders vacillated between an
egalitarian habitus that corresponded to the divisions within society,
and an elite image that drew upon Leninist understandings of the
party as a revolutionary "avant-garde" serving as the vanguard of
the working classes. Marx and Engels had demanded that the proletariat be led by a centralized leadership which would provide
them with the unity and power they otherwise lacked. Proceeding
from an understanding of state and society that saw the two as
inseparable, Lenin granted the proletariat a key role in the revolutionary process and in the necessary mobilization of the masses.

Marxist–Leninist thought therefore carried the system's seeds of
rule by party cadres that was later expressed within Soviet state
socialism and Stalinization. With its volunteerist elements, the
social utopia envisioned by the Soviets highly overrated the significance of the party "cadre" in political development. Stalin's remarks
from 1939 only underscore this fact: "If we could understand how

to arm our cadres ideologically in all areas and to steel them politically in such a way that they could situate themselves freely in the domestic and international scene; if we could understand how to transform them into truly mature Marxist–Leninists, capable of making the decisions related to the rule of the land without grave error, then we would have every reason to see nine-tenths of all of our problems already solved."[2] In reality, however, the entrenched system of cadre rule in the USSR (and in the GDR as well) stood in stark contrast to visions of an egalitarian communist society, without entirely replacing them as a basis of legitimation.[3]

"Elites," "Cadres," and "Intellectuals"

Strict followers of Marxist–Leninist party ideology within the SED were not alone in their rejection of "elites" as an obsolete social phenomenon. This aversion was shared by wide segments of GDR society. What East Germans disdained was not only the idea of an exclusive and privileged "elite" that should or could distinguish itself through its superior moral qualities, but also "functional elites," those "influential, more or less closed, social and political groups which remove themselves from larger and smaller strata by delegation or competition in order to take over a particular function in society or politics."[4] Marxist thought castigated the concept of "elites" as a bourgeois doctrine. Elites, "in their social and political nature as an expression of the will to power expressed by reactionary circles of the monopoly bourgeoisie,"[5] had supposedly been made obsolete by the "masses" in their role as "makers of history."[6] SED leaders could count on a broad consensus within society that viewed elites with some skepticism. Based on the roles played by traditional elites during the National Socialist "seizure of power" and during and after the collapse of the Third Reich, this skepticism was directed at both the competence and ethical qualities of elites. Such reservations have resonance even today, and help to explain why East Germans still view the word "elite" with great prejudice.[7]

The term "cadres," on the other hand, was largely positive, and referred in the GDR to those individuals who had distinguished themselves through "dedication to the party, knowledge, discipline, creativity, humility, and model behavior at home and the workplace."[8] Leaders in East Germany did not perceive of themselves, therefore, as "elites." They did demand a large measure of freedom to make decisions, and they derived their power and their new roles as leaders from their roots in the working class. Yet their self-perceptions were linked to claims of ideological infallibility that had ambivalent consequences. Party elites removed themselves from the general population through their ability to define the party's program and to set its agenda. This freedom was accompanied by a high level of expectations. With their ability to decide anything and everything, cadres possessed such a great degree of competence that overextension and self-blockage were the unavoidable result. The charged relationship between egalitarian claims and the system of cadre rule practiced by GDR elites had other sources beyond simple programmatic contradictions within Marxist–Leninist ideology. Tensions between the homogenization and leveling of East German society and the functional demands of a modern, industrial society built on a division of labor also contributed to such contradictions.[9]

These disparities also determined the relationship between "the workers" and "the intellectuals." Composed of members with a high rate of university and technical training, the term *Intelligenz* in the GDR referred to those experts who carried out intellectual and creative activities tied to special fields of knowledge and distinguished themselves from the working classes through a specific lifestyle. These "functional cadres" could not recruit to leadership positions – something only "positional cadres" could do. GDR "intellectuals" were made up of university-trained "cadres" that filled special positions in areas such as planning, science, research, education, and training. According to the tenets of SED ideology, this *neue Intelligenz* was meant to merge gradually with the working classes. In the 1980s, this ideal of social egalitarianism was rather unwillingly replaced with a recognition of social differences, and the "intellectuals" were granted an independent place within the development of real-existing socialism.[10]

Changing Leadership Self-images

Members of the SED elite, functionaries in the lower apparatus,[11] and regional leaders derived an aura of special exclusivity from the idea of belonging to the working class. The self-image of these "elites, who did not want to be elites,"[12] was not only based on old anti-elite sentiments, but at least in the 1950s, was fueled by the political wish to remove old bourgeois privileges (such as in the area of education). Additionally, many state and party functionaries who came to power in the SED in the late 1940s actually did have their roots in the working class. Many of the older party leaders could also point to their pasts as proof of their elitist self-images. Because they had opposed the Nazi regime, GDR leaders could feel morally superior to the majority of the population who had either supported or adapted to National Socialism.[13]

Following the social upheavals of the postwar period and the exchange of elites in the 1960s, professions of belonging to the "workers" and the "anti-fascists" increasingly became part of a highly stylized rhetoric. Such discursive rituals could only thinly disguise the party's absolute claims to power and the cadres' elitist decision-making practices. The egalitarian self-image of leaders not only reflected the party's attempt to legitimize its rule, but was also the expression of the homogenization of East German society and of the population's corresponding sensitivity regarding social distinctions. The SED could replace old elites and privileges with new groups because of their claims to create a new social order, to reeducate the people and make them into "socialist personalities" who would be loyal to the party, highly qualified, and blessed with sterling character.[14]

Due to denazification and land reform, large numbers of traditional elites had been removed from power as early as the summer and fall of 1945. Until the end of 1949, more than 7,160 owners of large land holdings had been dispossessed in the SBZ. The influence of such landowners within rural power structures and in society as a whole was drastically reduced by these measures. In the late 1940s and early 1950s, SED leaders also attacked other "large landowners," or farmers with more than about twenty hectares of land.[15] In the industrial sector, denazification measures affected directors and factory managers who had compromised themselves as "economic leaders" during the NS regime. Following the Saxon plebiscite of 30 June 1946, regarding the dispossession of Nazi and other war criminals and in the wake of similar plebiscites held in other provinces of the SBZ, many industrial plants were led by a transitional elite composed of former employees and managers. Previous plant employees rose in the ranks to become entrepreneurs, trustees, or "interim plant managers," effectively replacing the economic bourgeoisie who had held such positions in the past.[16]

The elite exchange of the late 1940s also had consequences for the educated middle classes. Bourgeois experts remained an integral part of the central state administration in East Germany up until the early 1950s. They were in demand because the SED's planned economic and social reconstruction of society depended on the expertise and knowledge of educated elites, since the next generation was not yet ready to step in. Still the party subjected such middle class experts in the central state administrative apparatus to strict controls in the late 1940s, even extending to their private lives, if the SED suspected them of disloyalty.[17] Changes were also slow within the universities, and for those careers with high qualifications, delegating workers to study, and creating new institutions such as the "preparatory schools" or "workers' and farmers' faculties" only made real headway in the 1960s. During the 1950s most professors still belonged to the educated middle classes, both in regards to their social origins and their lifestyles and habitus.[18]

For medical doctors, an opposing trend set in: although in the 1940s and 1950s new recruits from the working classes and farming families entered the profession, in the 1960s students increasingly came from the educated middle classes. Although doctors lost their corporate tradition of self-rule and became integrated into the state medical system, they did not suffer greatly from deprofessionalization. Instead, they could maintain their status consciousness, particularly since the SED granted them a high degree of social prestige with special awards and honors.[19]

The building of the Wall, the changing of the guard, and the training of a new generation of "cadres" helped create a "new technical intelligence" that took over the position in East German society once enjoyed by engineers. Nonetheless, the particular professional ethos of engineers could not be replaced fully.[20] Through regimentation of the academic professions, the SED could draw on traditions of state control and carry them to an extreme. Since the self-image of professionals, which was decidedly anti-liberal, was quite persistent, it was at least partly compatible with party rule.[21]

In the factories, technical personnel had to defer to the "cult of the proletariat" of the loyal "cadres," many of whom had risen from the factory floor. The command tone, associated with centralized production plans, tended to violate the status consciousness of highly qualified "functional elites," and this made them less willing to perform on the job. Their loss of prestige and authority was also a prime motivator in their increasing desire to flee the country. The exodus to the West, which began to develop a particular dynamic in the late 1950s, threatened to destabilize the entire SED regime. In 1960 therefore Ulbricht demanded that party and state officials practice "great tact, sensitivity, and magnanimity" vis-à-vis their subordinates.[22]

The *neue Intelligenz* of the GDR developed a specific social profile that expressed itself in leisure time activities and in the private sphere, extending even to the choice of partners or friends. "Functional cadres" socialized with each other, visited concerts or went to the theater together, or were socially active within their own communities. Most of their spouses also had university or technical degrees, which meant that many academic families could preserve a semblance of a bourgeois habitus. The SED recognized this need for social distinction by making material rewards and cultural offering group specific.[23]

In the 1950s the weakening of traditional elites and the subsequent development of new decision-making structures led to an increased demand for skilled leaders, who were largely recruited from the previously underprivileged classes. Loyal party cadres did not only rise from the ranks of crash courses at the newly established educational institutions, but rather social organizations such as the Free German Youth (FDJ) served as catalysts for the replacement of the elite.[24] New cadres were trained and established in state institutions like agriculture, where they worked in machine loan stations – the so-called MTS – or in the VEB. There they served as "strongholds of socialism in the countryside." As "new men" they acquired special training in the SED-established party schools, academies, institutes, and training courses. Party and state officials were obliged to appoint personnel according to their qualifications, "because one cannot let the qualities of cadre members go to waste." Their rapid path to the top intensified such new leaders' self-confidence and influenced their ruling styles. For example, many forced through changes in factories under their control against the will of the workers engaged there.[25]

The self-image of "cadres" in the 1950s and 1960s was characterized by an intense pride in its members' scientific training, an unbridled faith in progress, an idealization of rationality and modernity, as well as a deep-seated loyalty towards the party leadership. Such self-perceptions were a result of ideological conviction, idealism, privilege, and qualification. Special training of leaders was linked to political indoctrination. The number of university graduates increased significantly in the second half of the 1950s. From then on it became a prerequisite for any career to participate in the regional party schools of the SED or to take part in the training courses offered by the FDJ or the FDGB.[26]

The Influence of "Cadre Policies" on Leadership Styles

While the qualifications for leaders were significantly raised during the 1950s, "cadre politics" as such ran into structural roadblocks in the shape of the planned economy and the resultant shortages. SED regional party directives transferring cadres from state positions into party jobs hindered any continuity in the development of industrial or agricultural plants. Delegating people to schools for functionaries was not always clear-cut. Focused on the larger goal of meeting plan directives, factory managers were thus reluctant to risk introducing innovations in the production process and often not ready to allow much-needed specialists time off to qualify further, if they were needed in the factories. Party members who had been selected for additional training were often deemed "irreplaceable," or not allowed to qualify on the grounds that "these comrades might conceivably not want to return to their place of work."[27]

This structural problem was supposed to be compensated by a systematic "cadre policy" that selected, trained, and appointed new leaders. Based on plans for personnel needs and development, special divisions within plants were responsible for "cadre work," that encompassed the "direction, planning, organization, selection, development, and appointment of cadres." State and party authorities were to recruit new leaders, train them, and place them in a specific field that corresponded to their abilities. Personnel files accompanied these officials throughout their careers, serving as instruments of control, and as a way of directing these loyal and highly qualified individuals.[28]

Starting in the late 1940s, the GDR also took over the Soviet *Nomenklatura* system which included lists of leaders in the party, state bureaucracies, and the economy. Compiled by the SED's central party apparatus and the Ministry of the Interior, such lists existed as early as the 1950s for the upper levels of power (the Politburo, Central Committee and Council of Ministers and Council of State), as well as for regional party structures and *Bezirk*- as well as *Kreisräte*. This nomenclature also included a list of people who had been chosen to occupy certain positions by the appropriate "apparatus." GDR leaders were therefore co-opted, not delegated or elected. The institutional dualism of party and state within the nomenclature forced cadres into separate groups, reducing their activities to hierarchical, separate spheres of power.[29]

This dual structure of party organs and state agencies, bureaucracy, and economic controls also shaped the decision making and leadership styles of East German elites. Within the *Nomenklatura* system SED cadres were, however, simultaneously subjects and objects of rule. On the one hand they executed the party's policies, but on the other they were subject to the rigid, paternalistic control of the party commissions. "Leading cadres" therefore exhibited a particular symbiosis of ideological argumentation and the command tone of state directives. Their leadership style aroused protests, particularly among status-conscious leaders, contributing to their unwillingness to perform or follow. Although the significance of ideological factors in determining the actions of functional elites declined during the 1970s and 1980s, and was replaced by a more technocratic leadership style in the economy, this conflict threatened the limits of the regime. The entrenched mechanisms of cadre politics, combined with a wide spectrum of possible political sanctions, severely hindered the implementation of efficient styles of leadership based on modern management principles, and curtailed the development of professional autonomy. In general, "cadre politics" resulted in a singular combination of political loyalty and expertise.[30]

When the GDR faced increasing modernization pressures in the 1970s and 1980s, it became obvious that economic elites did not possess the necessary mental and organizational skills necessary for innovation and reform. Socialist managers had developed qualities in the course of their careers that enabled them to survive the vagaries of planned economics with its mixture of political directives, fictitious plan targets, various campaigns, extra-economic pressures and permanent shortages. A 1986 sociological study of the innovative abilities of economic elites came to the sobering conclusion that "the demands of scientific–technological progress... are not even remotely [present] in the thought of leaders."[31] The elites studied did not differentiate between the demands of routine tasks and innovative processes. They ranked such qualities as "operational flexibility," "self-discipline," and "perseverance and tenacity" first, closely followed by "effective political–ideological influence on the masses." Qualities such as "a willingness to take risks" or "questioning established practices" were ranked at the very bottom in a catalog of nineteen different qualities, in seventeenth and nineteenth place, respectively.[32]

The unwillingness of managers to take risks resulted from a lack of autonomy within East Germany's social subsystems. Despite the separation of party and state at the cadre level, the borders between both remained fluid in practice. Direct party interference in state agencies, as well as economic, social, and cultural processes was a matter of course. SED party leaders often took measures into their own hands, particularly when problems arose in the area of providing the populace with the necessary supplies or meeting production plans. Though this dictatorial style of rule could not address structural weaknesses within the system, it did shape the behavior of functional elites. "Continual interference from above, the concentration of decision-making powers in the hands of a small group at the head of the party hierarchy, the strain placed on upper decision-making levels and the resultant powerlessness of the lower levels – all of these practices persisted, and led to a general acceptance of formalism in bureaucratic and manufacturing relationships, as well as the avoidance of all conflict, accommodation, and a stifling of creativity and ethical behavior."[33]

In addition, most state and economic functionaries were also part of the political structure of the SED. In this capacity their own behavior oscillated between political–ideological motivation and technical expertise. Therefore, these structures produced a specific form of indecisiveness – and this behavior was supported by discrepancies between the demands of the job and relatively poor earnings. GDR crisis management was dominated by the tendency to blame shortages and planning problems on so-called "subjective factors," and not on structural deficiencies. Intervention "from above," which had to succeed because of the need to legitimize rule, often merely resulted in dramatic personnel decisions. Consequently, the specific "rationality" of the East German system of rule translated into an unwillingness to be too visible in conflict situations. In this sense, the leadership styles of East German elites contributed to the blockage of modernization characteristic of the GDR. An analysis of political elites at the regional or local party level or within the central party apparatus would reveal similar self-images.

Implications for Dictatorship Theory

Our present findings still are not sufficient to provide an answer to the question of the relative modernity of the GDR dictatorship. It would be helpful to differentiate between different phases of development in the GDR's history. In the West, the postwar break with pre-1945 elite traditions and the weakness of traditional elites can be seen as an indicator of modernization and democratization. West German elites were recruited from a wide sociological basis and came from various areas of expertise. If these criteria for modernity are applied to the GDR, the results are contradictory.[34] As recruiting became more liberal during the 1950s and 1960s – part of the phase of upward mobility in East Germany – some elements of modernity seem to have been present. However, this development was accompanied by an uprooting of traditional elites – a process that went far beyond the mere removal from positions of power of those elites who had cooperated with the Nazi regime.

The emphasis placed on the working classes as the basis of a new East German elite can also be interpreted as a renewed limitation of elite recruitment. The GDR possessed an elite largely determined by its origins, in both social and political aspects. Membership in the working class was not merely an ideological postulate, but defined the recruitment path of most new East German elites. The inflationary use of this criterion did expand the base of elite rule, but at the cost of accommodation, of accepting official paradigms and career models. In addition, East German social structures became much more rigid in the 1960s and 1970s, which meant that new recruitment occurred largely within established social groups. This led to a loss in mobility for elite recruitment as well.

The phase of East German economic reform initiated during the first half of the 1960s under Walter Ulbricht should also be seen in this light.[35] Attempts to make the centralized GDR economy more flexible increased the need for expert advice. Peter Christian Ludz has already described the transformation that occurred as a result of these developments in his study of "party elites in transition," which he has characterized as a form of "consultative authoritarianism."[36] The new recruits who came to power in the wake of these developments had a particular leadership style that has often been described in the literature as "technocratic." But a closer look reveals that what occurred was a symbiosis between the political claims of Marxist ideology and a contemporary euphoria for technology, science, and futurism. The enthusiasm of SED leaders for the systematic sciences and cybernetic prognostication is typical of such views. They were part of an attempt to reconcile communist beliefs in the creation of a new society with the demands of modernization through a technocratic style. Despite the predictions of many Western sociologists and political scientists that East German elites would be increasingly specialized experts,[37] such developments remained in their preliminary stages. They failed in the end due to the fact that SED elites were more ready to make economic adjustments than to implement the necessary political changes.

The influence of the GDR's political regime on East German elites is also evident in another area. In his portrait of the GDR as a "paternalist welfare" society,[38] Konrad Jarausch has pointed to the combination of dictatorial rule and egalitarian utopianism that was typical of East German society. This dual nature was also reflected in the behavior and self-images of elites. On the one hand official ideology posited common interests between the elites granted authority by the "workers' and farmers' state" and the social groups below them: "Socialist leadership styles differ from both authoritarian traits and liberal behavior, though some residues of such behavior can be found at times. Socialist leadership is characterized by the active participation of all group members and the removal of the contradictions between direction and implementation that are typical of most capitalist systems."[39]

Leading socialist cadres not only possessed singular functions within the larger hierarchy of rule but also played an important regulatory, educational, and welfare role for all areas of society. This reached beyond political organization and the workplace and touched individuals in their daily lives. It comes as no surprise that the *Handbook of Socialist Managerial Science: Leader, Collective, Personality* – a guide for economic managers – granted managers wide-ranging social authority. This charge reached from shaping the "collective" and the development of "workers" personalities through motivation, or character-building, up to serving spiritual needs or "promotion of physical culture and sport."[40] It is also now commonly known that party secretaries were expected to settle marriage crises or plant managers to find apartments for their employees.

In SED cadre policy, supportive concern for the problems of daily life was linked to elements of control and rule. The SED could draw on traditions of authoritarian–paternalistic rule particular to Germany that had contributed to the *Sonderweg* since the late nineteenth century. The party's demand that cadres possess exemplary characters and lead lives above moral reproach meant that deficits within the system of cadre politics were personified and moralized. When leaders were accused of shortcomings or lapses, party members would meet in order "to bring them back on the right track with everyone's support."[41] Criticism from higher levels was also generally directed at individuals accused of misbehavior or weaknesses. While such methods allowed the SED to control key positions during the 1940s and 1950s and occupy them with loyal party members, the personalized and moralizing approach to problems covered up the larger structural deficiencies within real existing socialism. Cadre policy contained no self-correcting measures, and party and state leaders were burdened with responsibilities they were in no way prepared to meet.[42]

In East German society, the individual – unless he resisted such attempts – was integrated into larger political or social communities. This also held true for GDR elites. This "collectivism" seems at first glance to go against hierarchical systems of rule and to undermine the theory of the homogenization of East German society. Status symbols and other differences in lifestyles played no great role in the definition of leading groups. But such differences did exist, and these were viewed quite critically in the face of egalitarian claims. Yet despite the *Wandlitz*-ghetto and the few high profile scientists and artists, most leaders in the GDR were not socially separate from other social groups. A closer look at the presence of such leaders in various areas such as the family, home life, or leisure associations reveals how much the regime had penetrated society. These arenas were to be used in coordination with other techniques and institutions to control the entire network of social relations. East Germans' attempts to remove themselves from such control by retiring to so-called "niches" can only be interpreted as flight from the welfare policies of the intrusive state.

The Problem of Generational Change

The cadre policy of the SED regime was closely tied to the various political "apparatuses" that were structurally independent from each other. Despite informal avenues of communication between the regional leaders, it was not easy to build a common culture and an *esprit de corps* based on shared values and norms. Not only was there a lack of horizontal integration, but vertical integration also suffered from the effects of the upward mobility of elites that occurred imme- diately after the war. Leaders were coopted regionally, and not – as in parliamentary democracies in pluralistic societies – elected or dele- gated. The younger generation of party cadres who took over posi- tions in the economy and society, starting in the late 1950s, was already trained and even socialized in the GDR. Since recruitment was linked to political loyalty, class or social identities were consis- tently undermined. As a result, biographical or personal traits lost their significance in the face of secondary socialization, which in turn influenced the leadership styles and self-images of GDR cadres.[43]

Some real distinctions can be made between leadership styles and decision-making competencies of political elites and functional elites at the lower levels. Top SED leaders who belonged to the older gen- eration saw themselves as actors in a social upheaval marked by the class warfare or communist resistance of their youth. Their political behavior was very similar to the organizational tenets of the com- munist movement. While political elites in bourgeois societies came from professions that allowed them some degree of autonomy and fitted them with the qualities necessary for "politics as profession,"[44] such foundations were completely lacking in the GDR. Those func- tionaries socialized in the KPD typically experienced career paths which quickly brought them to positions of power within the party. Party careers were the rule, and not the exception. In this process, East German elites learned a form of politics that emphasized the ability to mobilize the masses, follow ideological guidelines, and organize effectively. Political thought was greatly influenced by war propaganda and perceptions of the enemy that manifested them- selves in internal conspiracy theories, or obsession with deviation and external critiques of capitalism and fears of fascism – particu- larly directed at the FRG.

The next generation of the political elite – as well as the follow- ing generations – shared many of the convictions of the GDR's founding fathers, but were focused more on the concrete realities of East German society, which they attempted to address in the face of a loss of visionary faith. Until 1989 "the experience of battles to stay alive and survive elimination"[45] remained characteristic of most GDR elites. The resulting traits, such as "vigilance, a sensitivity for political intrigue and for threatening groups or coalitions,"[46] were also shared by those functional elites forced to negotiate between the expectations of the working class and the demands of central administrative political institutions.

The general subordination of East German leaders to politics had wide-reaching consequences. In the 1980s it resulted in their unwillingness and inability to challenge the course of the SED gerontocracy, although they shared much of the frustration of the wider population with the lack of reforms. Therefore, their participation in the revolutionary events in 1989 was minuscule – only under pressure from the opposition and the dramatic loss of public support resulting from the collapse of SED rule did they display any willingness to change.

The GDR lives on in these characteristics of its elites. The present discussion regarding the persistence of old mentalities and milieus in the new German states is also reflected in the values of leaders with East German backgrounds within the new German elites. These individuals, who at present enjoy much power, particularly in the media and within the academy, are more motivated by values such as community and welfare than their West German colleagues. They tend to place equality and justice above individual freedom and autonomy. As the "Potsdam Elite Study" published in 1997 shows, Eastern elites differ from West Germans in their understanding of the state and of democracy. They place greater emphasis on plebiscitary than on representative foundations of democracy, and attribute to the state more responsibility for the development of society.[47]

Thus some of the authoritarian values and statist traditions of the German *Sonderweg* continue to live on among East German elites who experienced the GDR "welfare dictatorship." In the pluralistic society and the parliamentary democracy of united Germany, such welfare state expectations might offer a chance to improve the responsiveness of elites vis-à-vis those groups who elected them or delegated power to them. This self-image of East German elites could thus strengthen the social foundations of all German elites by tying them more closely to the population and hindering the formation of an isolated "political class." Whether this social orientation, freed from the shackles of authoritarian rule, can reinforce democratic values in a united Germany or whether they will – similar to other characteristics from the pre-1989 period – simply fade away remains to be seen.[48]

Notes

1. Franz Dahlem, "Der neue Typ des Funktionärs der SED," *Einheit* 1 (1946): 199.
2. Josef Stalin, "Rechenschaftsbericht an den XVIII. Parteitag über die Arbeit des ZK der KPDSU 10. März 1939," in *Fragen des Leninismus*, ed. Josef Stalin (Berlin, 1955), 801.
3. Hartmut Zimmermann, "Überlegungen zur Geschichte der Kader und der Kaderpolitik in der SBZ/DDR," in *Sozialgeschichte der DDR*, ed. Harmut Kaelble, Jürgen Kocka, and Harmut Zwahr (Stuttgart, 1994), 348–53. For the "avant-garde doctrine," see Albert G. Meyer, "Historical Development of the Communist Theory of Leadership," in *Political Leadership in Eastern Europe and the Soviet Union*, ed. R. Barry Farrell (London, 1970), 5–16; Gert-Joachim Glaeßner, *Herrschaft durch Kader. Leitung der Gesellschaft und Kaderpolitik in der DDR* (Opladen, 1977), 53–78. See also Dieter Voigt and Sabine Gries, "Karriereangebote, Karrieremuster und Eliterekrutierung," *Materialien der Enquete-Kommission "Aufarbeitung von Geschichte und Folgen der SED-Diktatur in Deutschland,"* ed. Deutscher Bundestag, vol. 3/3 (Baden-Baden, 1995), 1947f.
4. Otto Stammer, "Das Elitenproblem in der Demokratie," *Schmollers Jahrbuch für Gesetzgebung, Verwaltung und Volkswirtschaft* 71, no. 5 (1951): 9. See Arnd Bauerkämper, "Die tabuisierte Elite. Problembericht, Fragen und Hypothesen der zeithistorischen Forschung über Führungsgruppen in der DDR," *Potsdamer Bulletin für Zeithistorische Studien* 9 (April 1997): 1f., 25–28.
5. Georg Assman, ed., *Wörterbuch der marxistisch-leninistischen Soziologie* (Berlin, 1977), 157.
6. Waltraud Böhme, ed., *Kleines politisches Wörterbuch* (Berlin, 1973), 191.
7. Hans-Dieter Klingemann, Richard Stöss, and Bernhard Weßels, *Politische Klasse und politische Institutionen. Probleme und Perspektiven der Elitenforschung. Dietrich Herzog zum 60. Geburtstag*, ed. Klingemann, Stöss, and Weßels (Opladen, 1991), 10. For the Nazi case, see Martin Broszat and Klaus Schwabe, eds, *Die deutschen Eliten und der Weg in den Zweiten Weltkrieg* (Munich, 1989) and Fritz Fischer, *Bündnis der Eliten. Zur Kontinuität der Machtstrukturen in Deutschland, 1871–1945* (Düsseldorf, 1985), 93–95.
8. Quoted in Böhme, *Kleines politisches Wörterbuch*, 420. See also Zimmermann, "Überlegungen." 323. For the use of the terms "elite" and "cadre" in the GDR see Arnd Bauerkämper, Jürgen Danyel, and Peter Hübner, " 'Funtionäre des schaffenden Volkes?' Die Führungsgruppen der DDR als Forschungsproblem," in *Gesellschaft ohne Eliten? Führungsgruppen in der DDR*, ed. Arnd Bauerkämper, Jürgen Danyel, Peter Hübner, and Sabine Roß (Berlin, 1997), 33, 56f.
9. Rainer Geißler, *Die Sozialstruktur Deutschlands. Ein Studienbuch zur gesellschaftlichen Entwicklung mit einer Zwischenbilanz zur Vereinigung* (Opladen, 1996), 104f.
10. Sigrid Meuschel, *Legitimation und Parteiherrschaft. Zum Paradox von Stabilität und Revolution in der DDR 1945–1989* (Frankfurt, 1992), 242–49. For the term *Intelligenz* see Günter Erbe, *Arbeiterklasse und Intelligenz in der DDR. Soziale Annäherung von Produktionsarbeiterschaft und wissenschaftlich-technischer Intelligenz im Industriebetrieb* (Opladen, 1982), 18–25, 45f; Irmhild Rudolph, "Kader – Intelligenz – Elite. Zu einigen herrschaftssoziologischen Aspekten der Sozialstruktur in der DDR," *30 Jahre DDR. Zwölfte Tagung zum Stand der DDR-Forschung in der Bundesrepublik, 5. bis 8. Juni 1979* (Cologne, 1979), 126–32; also Zimmermann, "Überlegungen," 346f.
11. For Lenin's conception of a new type of state apparatus based on the model of the Paris Commune, see George Labica and Gérard Bensussan, ed., *Kritisches Wörterbuch des Marxismus* (Berlin, 1983), vol. 1, 78f.

12. Irene Runge, "Eliten, die keine sein wollten," *Blätter für deutsche und internationale Politik* 41 (1996): 1165–70.
13. Günter Benser, "Zur sozialen und politischen Struktur der KPD und ihres Kaders (1945/1946)," *Beiträge zur Geschichte der Arbeiterbewegung* 39/4 (1997): 33.
14. Jürgen Kocka, "Eine durchherrschte Gesellschaft," in *Sozialgeschichte*, ed. Kaelble, Kocka, and Zwahr, 548f.
15. Wolfgang Bell, *Enteignungen in der Landwirtschaft der DDR nach 1949 und deren politische Hintergründe. Analyse und Dokumentation* (Münster-Hiltrup 1992), 46–60, 76–79; Arnd Bauerkämper, "Von der Bodenreform zur Kollektivierung. Zum Wandel der ländlichen Gesellschaft in der Sowjetischen Besatzungszone Deutschlands und DDR 1945–1952," in *Sozialgeschichte*, ed. Kaelble, Kocka, and Zwar, 122; and Bauerkämper, "Neue und traditionale Führungsgruppen auf dem Lande. Politische Herrschaft und Gesellschaft in der Sowjetischen Besatzungszone," *Berliner Debatte. Initial* 4, no. 5 (1995): 85–90.
16. Frank Schulz, "Elitenwandel in der Leipziger Wirtschaftsregion 1945–1948. Von den Leipziger 'sächsischen Industriefamilien' zu Kadern aus dem Leipziger Arbeitermilieu," *Comparativ* 5 (1995): 112–26.
17. Christoph Boyer, *"Die Kader entscheiden alles..." Kaderpolitik und Kaderentwicklung in der zentralen Staatsverwaltung der SBZ und frühen DDR (1945–1952)* (Dresden, 1952), 45–48, 53; Dirk Hoffmann, "'Umsiedler' in den Funktionseliten Brandenburgs 1945–1952," in: *50 Jahre Flucht und Vertreibung. Gemeinsamkeiten und Unterschiede bei der Aufnahme und Integration der Vertriebenen in die Gesellschaften der Westzonen/BRD und der SBZ/DDR* (Magdeburg, 1997), 238–48.
18. Ralph Jessen, "Professoren im Sozialismus. Aspekte des Strukturwandels der Hochschullehrerschaft in der Ulbricht-Ära," in *Sozialgeschichte*, ed. Kaelble, Kocka, and Zwar, 221–25, 239.
19. Anna-Sabine Ernst, *"Die beste Prophylaxe ist der Sozialismus." Ärzte und medizinische Hochschullehrer in der SBZ/DDR, 1945–1961* (Münster, 1997); idem, "Von der bürgerlichen zur sozialistischen Profession? Ärzte in der DDR, 1945–1961," in *Die Grenzen der Diktatur. Staat und Gesellschaft in der DDR*, ed. Richard Bessel and Ralph Jessen (Göttingen, 1996), 25–48.
20. Dolores L. Augustine, "Frustrierte Technokraten. Zur Sozialgeschichte des Ingenieurberufs in der Ulbricht-Ära," in ibid., 51, 56, 68f.
21. Hannes Siegrist, "Bürgerliche Berufe. Die Professionen und das Bürgertum," in *Bürgerliche Berufe. Zur Sozialgeschichte der freien und akademischen Berufe im internationalen Vergleich* (Göttingen 1988): 11–48; and Konrad H. Jarausch, "Die unfreien Professionen. Überlegungen zu den Wandlungsprozessen im deutschen Bildungsbürgertum 1900–1955," in *Bürgertum im 19. Jahrhundert*, ed. Jürgen Kocka (Göttingen, 1995), vol. 2, 200–22.
22. Quoted in Anna-Sabine Ernst, "Erbe und Hypothek. (Alltags-)kulturelle Leitbilder in der SBZ/DDR 1945–1961," in *Kultur und Kulturträger in der DDR. Analysen*, ed. Stiftung Mitteldeutscher Kulturrat (Berlin, 1993), 44.
23. Erbe, *Arbeiterklasse,* 200–3, Ernst, "Erbe," 46–48. For the term "habitus" see Sven Reichardt, "Bourdieu für Historiker? Ein kultursoziologisches Angebot an die Sozialgeschichte," in *Geschichte zwischen Kultur und Gesellschaft. Beiträge zur Theoriedebatte*, ed. Thomas Mergel and Thomas Welskopp (Munich, 1997), 74.
24. Gert Noack, "Das Führungspersonal der Freien Deutschen Jugend zwischen 1945 und 1955. Konzeptionelle Überlegungen zu einem Forschungsprojekt," in *Institut für zeitgeschichtliche Jugendforschung, Jahresbericht 1992* (Berlin, 1992): 91–102. Gert Noack, "Die Rolle der FDJ beim Elitenwechsel in der

SBZ/DDR," in *Aber nicht im Gleichschritt. Zur Entstehung der Freien Deutschen Jugend*, ed. Helga Gotschlich, Katharina Lange, and Edeltraud Schulze (Berlin, 1997), 133–38. See also Klaus Schwabe, *Arroganz der Macht. Herrschaftsgeschichte von KPD und SED in Mecklenburg und Vorpommern 1945–1952* (Schwerin, 1997), 159.

25. Stiftung Archiv der Parteien und Massenorganisationen der DDR im Bundesarchiv, Berlin (SAPMO-BArch), Sg Y 30/2154: 36–40. Quoted in Brandenburgisches Landeshauptarchiv Potsdam (BLHA), Bez. Pdm. Rep. 401, no. 1224: 726.

26. For this trend in agriculture see letter of 2 February 1947, BLHA, Bez. FfO. Rep. 601, no. 374; "Material für die LPG-Konferenz," 15 January 1958, Bez. FfO. Rep 601, no. 3746.

27. Report of 14 July 1970, BLHA, Bez. FfO. Rep. 730, no. 3184. Christoph Buchheim, "Die Wirtschaftsordnung als Barriere des gesamtwirtschaftlichen Wachstums in der DDR," *Vierteljahrschrift für Sozial- und Wirtschaftsgeschichte* 82 (1995): 208. See Hermann Martin, "Die Kaderpolitik im Staatsapparat," *SBZ - Archiv* 6 (1995): 195.

28. Quoted in Heinrich Bader, ed. *Ökonomisches Lexikon, H-P* (Berlin 1979): 166. Dieter Voigt, Werner Voß, and Sabine Meck, *Sozialstruktur der DDR. Eine Einführung* (Darmstadt, 1987), 245–60; Dieter Voigt and Lothar Mertens, "Kader und Kaderpolitik," in *Lexikon des DDR-Sozialismus. Das Staats- und Gesellschaftssystem der DDR*, ed. Rainer Eppelmann et al. (Paderborn, 1996), 322–24. See also Carola Stern, "Kaderpolitik in der 'DDR,'" *SBZ-Archiv* 5 (1954): 228–31; Martin, 193–95.

29. Erhard Schneider, "Nomenklatur," in Eppelmann et al., *Lexikon*, 437f. Eberhard Schneider, "Karriereangebote, Karrieremuster und Elitenrekrutierungen," in *Materialien der Enquete-Kommission*, 1715; Matthias Wagner, "Gerüst der Macht. Das Kadernomenklatursystem als Ausdruck der führenden Rolle der SED," in *Gesellschaft ohne Eliten?* ed. Bauerkämper et al., 87–108. For the Soviet model see Christoph Müller and George Hodnett "Kader," "Kaderpolitik," in *Sowjetsystem und Demokratische Gesellschaft. Eine vergleichende Enzyklopädie*, 3 (Freiburg, 1969), 458–61.

30. Ernst, "Erbe," 43, 46; Voigt and Gries, "Karriereangebote," 1909; Augustine, "Frustrierte Technokraten," 53, 69. See also Thomas Klein, "Die Herrschaft der Parteibürokratie. Disziplinierung, Repression und Widerstand in der SED," *Aus Politik und Zeitgeschichte*, 1996, no. 20: 3–12; Schwabe, 159–63; and the article by Keßler in this volume.

31. Günter Bohring and Klaus Ladensack, *Wie Leiter den wissenschaftlich-technischen Fortschritt bewältigen* (Berlin, 1986), 154.

32. Ibid., 153f.

33. Peter Hübner, "Industrielle Manager in der SBZ/DDR. Sozial- und mentalitätsgeschichtliche Aspekte," *Geschichte und Gesellschaft* 24 (1998): 78.

34. Martin Greiffenhagen, *Politische Legitimität in Deutschland* (Gütersloh, 1997), 124. See also Wolfgang Zapf, *Wandlungen der deutschen Elite. Ein Zirkulationsmodell deutscher Führungsgruppen 1919–1961* (Munich, 1965), 169, 195.

35. Monika Kaiser, *Der Machtwechsel von Ulbricht zu Honecker. Funktionsmechanismen der SED-Diktatur in Konfliktsituationen 1962 bis 1972* (Berlin, 1997).

36. Peter Christian Ludz, *Parteielite im Wandel. Funktionsaufbau, Sozialstruktur und Ideologie der SED-Führung* (Cologne, 1968), 258. See also Monika Kaiser's article in *Gesellschaft ohne Eliten?*, 253–64.

37. Ernst Richert, *Die DDR-Elite oder Unsere Partner von morgen?* (Reinbek, 1968).

38. See chapter 3 by Konrad Jarausch.

39. See *Leiter, Kollektiv, Persönlichkeit. Handbuch für die sozialistische Leitungstätigkeit* (Berlin 1982), 396; Erbe, *Arbeiterklasse,* 42–46.
40. Ibid., 368ff.
41. This rhetoric characterized the wide-ranging demands to determine lifestyle choices and steer social development. See BLHA, Bez. Pdm. Rep. 401, no. 1224: 232.
42. Boyer, *Kader,* 16f., 23, 50, 52, 54; and Buchheim, "Wirtschaftsordnung," 207–10. For the paternalist traditions of the *Sonderweg* see the literature cited in Jürgen Kocka, "Ein deutscher Sonderweg. Überlegungen zur Sozialgeschichte der DDR," *Aus Politik und Zeitgeschichte,* 1994, no. 40: 45.
43. Klaus von Beyme, "Elite," in *Marxismus im Systemvergleich. Soziologie,* ed. C. D. Kernig (Frankfurt am Main 1973), vol. 1, 154. See also Bauerkämper, "Die tabuisierte Elite," 19–33.
44. Max Weber, "Politik als Beruf," in *Gesammelte politische Schriften,* ed. Johannes Winckelmann (Tübingen, 1988), 505–60.
45. Wolfgang Engler, *Die zivilisatorische Lücke. Versuche über den Staatssozialismus* (Frankfurt am Main, 1992), 70.
46. Ibid., 71.
47. Wilhelm Bürklin, "Elitenforschung in der Bundesrepublik: historische Bedingungen und aktuelle Herausforderungen," in *Eliten in Deutschland: Rekrutierung und Integration,* ed. Wilhelm Bürklin et al. (Opladen, 1997), 29f., 33; Viktoria Kaina, "Wertorientierung im Eliten-Bevölkerungsvergleich: Vertikale Distanzen, geteilte Loyalitäten und das Erbe der Trennung," in ibid., 376, 378–80, 383, 387f. For remnants of paternalistic perceptions see Gert-Joachim Glaeßner, "Regimewechsel und Elitentransfer. Parlamentarisch-politische und Verwaltungseliten in Ostdeutschland," *Deutschland Archiv 29* (1996): 861f.
48. Klaus von Beyme, "Der Begriff der politischen Klasse – Eine neue Dimension der Elitenforschung?" in *Politische Vierteljahresschrift 33* (1992): 4–32; idem, "Brauchen wir eine Politische Klasse?" *Aus Politik und Zeitgeschichte,* 1991, no. 50: 3–13; Bernhard Weßels, "Zum Begriff der 'Politischen Klasse,'" *Gewerkschaftliche Monatshefte 43* (1992): 541–49. For responsiveness see Herbert Uppendahl, "Repräsentation und Responsivität: Bausteine einer Theorie responsiver Demokratie," *Zeitschrift für Parlamentsfragen 1* (1981): 123–34 and Helmut Köser, "Demokratie und Elitenherrschaft. Das Eliteproblem in der Demokratietheorie," *Die neue Elite. Eine Kritik der kritischen Demokratietheorie,* ed. Dieter Oberndörfer and Wolfgang Jäger (Freiburg, 1975), 149–92.

TEMPORAL
TRANSFORMATIONS

STAGNATION OR CHANGE?

TRANSFORMATIONS OF THE WORKPLACE IN THE GDR

Peter Hübner

One of the most contested questions about the nature of the "first German workers' and peasants' state" concerns the characterization of the SED regime as a "modern dictatorship."[1] Questions about the relative "modernity" of the regime help to locate the dictatorship within a specific historical context, while also problematizing the applicability and usefulness of modernization theory in general.[2] With its normative, structural approach, a modernization perspective makes a strong case for comparative studies, particularly those that address structural innovations and their internal consequences. Such a comparison should not only consider the differences between pluralist democracy and dictatorship, or compare the relative strengths and weaknesses of market vs. planned economies, but it must also examine the causes of innovation and stagnation, as well as their consequences.

The GDR deserves study because its development lies within a larger process of modernization with its roots in Imperial Germany. This process developed further in the Weimar Republic, and continued to exist in the Nazi state as "reactionary modernism"[3] (if not, as Hans Mommsen has shown, in all sectors of the economy or society).[4] It was particularly in the area of economics – specifically industrial production – where the ruptures of the postwar era made the lines of continuity between the GDR and earlier periods more visible. Such continuities lead to the question of how innovative the SED actually was in its claims to reshape society, how the party followed the road to modernization laid down in the first half of the century, and where its path diverged from this route.

In the dictatorial and state-run socio-economic processes by which GDR society developed, both innovative and stagnative tendencies existed side by side in a tense relationship with each other. This became especially clear in the area of work. Because labor possessed such central structural and ideological significance, but had simultaneously little practical value, the contradictions of East German society became most obvious in people's working lives.[5] This relationship was potentially explosive, but the political developments of the Cold War allowed the SED to gain some control by removing and externalizing the basic conflict between capitalism and socialism outwards onto the West.[6]

The working sphere has repeatedly shown itself to be the area within industrialized dictatorships of the twentieth century where the successes and failures of the regime became most quickly and clearly evident.[7] In the face of our present knowledge about the historical end of the "dictatorship of the proletariat" in Eastern and Central Europe, we need to ask in what measure labor and the economy served as innovative impulses without which even socialist regimes cannot exist. It is also important to consider how these spheres could become a source of weakness or lead to a lack of performance, stagnation, or erosion that made the post-1990 transformation much more difficult than other post-dictatorial transitions. What were the preconditions which resulted in massive deindustrialization, shrinkage of the labor force and unemployment in East Germany?[8]

Social Divisions in the "Workers' Society"

The main causes for this weakness are to be found in the nature of the GDR as a "workers' society." The term *Arbeitsgesellschaft* was originally coined by Hannah Arendt and used by sociologists to emphasize that East German society was integrated largely by labor and employment. This is evidenced by the role which industrial plants played as the most significant sites of socialization, as well as such factors as the GDR's high rate of employment, the ideological emphasis on work, and the centering of social policy on factories.[9]

The terms "labor," "workers," and "working class" were of central significance to the SED's system of rule, serving both as political legitimation and social orientation. They reflected GDR society's self-image as a modern, but also relatively closed, labor society. The party's social policies proceeded from the assumption that the working class functioned as the social, political, and cultural center of gravity, around which all other social classes and strata in East German society were arranged.[10] This model possessed immense political significance, legitimating as it did the rule of the party as the "dictatorship of the proletariat."[11]

In the Soviet zone, society and economy experienced dramatic transformations following the end of the Second World War. In the workplace individuals were forced to come to terms with changes instigated in the political sphere, and to learn how to interact with the socialist institutions of an implanted dictatorship.[12] Several waves of dispossession and collectivization between 1945 and 1972 led to dramatic changes in the primary and secondary sectors of the economy and the creation of state-owned or people-owned properties. This process even extended to the tertiary sector. Because traditional relationships of property holding and land ownership were destroyed, the dramatic social changes had egalitarian, as well as divisive, effects. This transformation was sped up by the SED's industrial and agricultural policies, and preference for large state-run or people-owned economic units. These attempts appear in retrospect as a kind of unique German–German social experiment, in which the market won out in the end.[13]

To explain these developments, scholars have begun to address problems associated with social differentiation and inequality. Heike Solga, for instance, has argued that the class structure of the GDR, once established in the years 1945 to 1961, stabilized itself between 1961 and 1970, only to enter a period of renewed differentiation between 1980 and 1989. Solga maintains that "the functioning of GDR society...can be explained productively in terms of its class structure" which is a structural source of social inequality. East German society was divided up by state socialist categories of class and the following "lines of inequality:"

1. the privileged who controlled state property (party elites and their servitors);
2. the politically and economically discriminated self-employed;
3. the increasingly marginalized holders of people's property (master artisans, and collectivized farmers); and
4. the working class as putative rulers and yet exploited group, proportionally the largest segment of the population.[14]

Although there were undeniable social inequalities in the GDR, this model places too much emphasis on property. Solga thus loses sight of other, and in this case more significant, considerations. Her distinction between various forms of property excludes the propertied middle class. The SED dictatorship possessed access to all the productive resources of the GDR – independent of property rights – and its system of economic planning represented an instrument of control without equal.[15]

Nonetheless, the working class continually pressured the regime for concessions and benefited most from its social policies. Some commentators have, therefore, spoken of the party's "courting of the working class."[16] This is only one indicator of the egalitarian effects of the party's revolutionary social policies. No doubt stratification and inequality continued to exist, and in its later years, the GDR experienced some re-differentiation, but their quality and scope are not enough to justify references to clear-cut class positions. Much evidence supports the argument that the GDR was a "society of workers and farmers, with egalitarian tendencies extending downwards, and not up towards the middle."[17]

These social divisions are quite significant for the relationship between innovation and stagnation in the workplace. They hold the key to understanding those egalitarian tendencies that were not merely a result of increased income or the spread of consumer goods, but were linked to the GDR's system of social control. The regime carefully regulated society from above, and those living conditions in the GDR which resulted in the greatest amount of dissatisfaction affected the majority of citizens, "regardless of the degree of their qualifications or their performance."[18] They were intricately linked to the social and cultural interests of the working class, were oriented towards these interests, and thus in turn influenced other social groups.

The resultant practical and cultural domination of the working class did not merely stem from the regime's emphasis on the factory as the basic unit in GDR society. Its roots lay further in the past. Due to Nazi economic policies and particularly the Second World War, the population of central Germany (later the GDR) was more "proletarian" than in other German-speaking regions.[19] After the Second World War, proletarian elements strengthened because of the great influx of war refugees and expellees which raised the number of workers in the workforce, and also increased the number of women at the same time.[20] These conditions aided the SED in instituting those steps needed for the realization of their political goals.[21]

The party's economic policies also insured that workers constituted a relatively high percentage of the entire working population. The main reasons were the demands placed on the economy by Soviet reparation policies and import needs, as well as an industrialization strategy based on import substitution, which included elements of autarchy.[22] The state's centralized planned economy meant that more workers were needed, because the lack of flexibility in planning and production made labor reserves more indispensable. It also became evident that the lack of investment in rationalization could be offset, at least in part, by a greater reliance on cheaper women's labor. Increasing militarization of GDR society and the establishment of a repressive state administration also severely affected labor resources. Official statistics give an unreliable picture of numbers, since many positions were included in the so-called secret areas of the military, police, state security, customs, or special factories. In 1989 some 727,000 individuals were employed in those areas.[23] Therefore it was precisely in its de facto full employment and in the centralized nature of the economy that the "workers' society" of the GDR proved to be a political construct.

Due to the stream of refugees and expellees from the former German lands to the East in 1945 to 1947, the SBZ won back the population it had lost during the war.[24] This dramatic development resulted in an increase in the number of workers and women in the work-force.[25] Even though the integration of these groups was masked by the exodus to the West in the late 1940s, it nevertheless coincided with the social goals of the SED (Table 15.1).

Increases in the number of self-employed and employed family members can be traced to short-term self-employment for those individuals unable to find work. This segment was a reservoir for later increases in the number of workers in the working population.

The SED's economic and social policies aimed at regenerating the working population, controlling it as thoroughly as possible, and quantitatively increasing the number of industrial workers.[26] The first Five Year Plan exemplifies the demand for an increase in

Table 15.1 *Employment in the Soviet Zone According to Position (in thousands)*

	Self-employed	Family members	White collar/ officials	Workers
1939				
Total	954	989	1376	4366
Men	799	141	990	2931
Women	155	848	386	1435
1946				
Total	1263	1041	1424	4411
Men	948	165	759	2593
Women	316	877	665	1818

Source: E. Beck, "Die Erwerbspersonen in der SBZ nach der Stellung im Beruf," *Statistische Praxis* 3 (1948): 187. "Family members" refers to help by kin in agriculture or business.

the numbers of employed by about 890,000 jobs out of a total of 7.6 million, while the number of industrial workers alone was to be raised by 448,000 to 2.8 million. At least in quantitative terms, therefore, the SED created the conditions for its social model, consisting of "two classes, one stratum, and others" (workers, collectivized farmers, intelligentsia, and others) which had an "apologetic and not sociological" purpose.[27]

This program nonetheless laid the groundwork for a far-reaching social leveling, which affected even the self-perceptions of GDR citizens. In 1988, 61 percent of all those employed in industry were defined as workers.[28] These statistics were based on a very broad definition of the designation "worker" that ranged from coal miners to hair stylists, from locksmiths to nurses.[29] Even if such categorizations exaggerated social realities, these self-definitions reveal how the GDR could be perceived as a "frozen" society. According to a poll taken in 1991 concerning subjective social position, 61 percent of East German respondents considered themselves to be working class, 37 percent middle class, and only 2 percent upper middle class. In West Germany, only 25 percent of those questioned considered themselves workers, 62 percent as middle class, and 13 percent as upper middle class.[30]

The steady stream of those who left the East – up until 1961 three million mostly younger and employable citizens – may have contributed indirectly to these developments.[31] The exodus drained the pool of available labor resources, but since the end of the 1950s, the mass flight also led to more social mobility, particularly for women. It was therefore possible to maintain the number of workers within the total workforce at a constant level, which was surprisingly close to pre-war figures (Table 15.2).

The reasons for this development can be summarized as follows:

1. The GDR territory was heavily influenced by the Nazi Four Year Plan and the industrialization associated with the war economy,

Table 15.2 *Workers as Percent of the Total Number of Employed in the GDR*

1939	56.8
1946	54.2
1950	52.1
1980	54.4
1990	52.4

Sources: Datenreport 1992/4. Zahlen und Fakten über die Bundesrepublik Deutschland, ed. Statistisches Bundesamt et al. (Bonn, 1992/4), 86, 99 f; Beck, "Erwerbspersonen," 187; *Statistisches Jahrbuch der DDR 1955* (Berlin, 1956); and Gunnar Winkler, ed., *Sozialreport 1990* (Berlin, 1990), 1: 75.

which resulted in large numbers of new jobs. Subsequent consolidation and expansion of industry meant a further need for workers.

2. The centralized planned economy created a new demand for workers. Just as large amounts of warehouse supplies were typical for many industries, these firms also built up reserves of paid workers in order to meet production plans that proceeded at an uneven pace.

3. The militarization of GDR society and the extension of state rule led to a drain on resources, but also to a large degree of concentration in areas related to military production.

Labor Law, Employment, and Social Policies

Wartime expansion, planning and militarization inflated the need for labor, which cannot be measured according to normal market standards. Since the GDR economy was "not at all aimed at a constant expansion of consumption,"[32] the right to work made up one of the main pillars of its labor policy. This right – perhaps one of the party's most important means of legitimation – was established as early as 1949 in Article 5 of the GDR constitution.[33] But this promise did not rule out short-term unemployment, and the right to a job did not exist as such. This was regulated by the Labor Code of 1961, which was accompanied by the stipulation that citizens also had a duty to work.[34] Article 24 of the 1968 constitution and the revised constitution of 1974 both emphasized that the right to work was linked to the duty to work.[35] It remained unclear whether this duty was of a juridical or moral nature, but the state in any case was obligated to provide jobs for its citizens.

Due to manpower shortages which began at the end of the 1950s, SED social policies began to target expanding jobs for women (Table 15.3).

Undoubtedly the primary aim of such policies was the mobilization of women workers.[36] But the process had significant secondary

Table 15.3 *Women in the GDR Economy, 1949-1989 as Percent*

Year	Production	Non-production	Industry
1949	38.2	59.4	25.5
1960	41.4	64.2	40.5
1970	43.6	70.3	42.4
1980	44.1	72.9	43.3
1990	42.5	72.6	41.0

Source: Statistisches Jahrbuch der DDR 1989 (Berlin, 1989), 18–19.

consequences, particularly since industry was forced to equip larger plants with child care centers, clinics, or doctors' offices, shops, and rest areas for women. In some cases, factories even provided vacation homes and so-called *Arbeiterversorgung*, or food for workers during work breaks.[37] In this manner, increased mobilization resulted in even more demands for new personnel.

The incorporation of women into the workforce had ambivalent results. On the one hand, the process served as a mobilizing factor for society, and yet on the other it preserved traditional social roles. Many women held lower paid positions and were employed in simple mechanical trades. In 1990 women's monthly net earnings were on average 825 marks; in comparison, men earned 1,131 marks.[38] Cheaper women's labor also relieved many plants from the burden of having to invest in rationalization. Although this was often effective as a short-term solution, it had fatal long-term consequences for the East German economy, severely limiting its competitive abilities.

The employment of individuals already past retirement age had similar consequences. Among the entire workforce (excluding apprentices), only 5 percent had entered retirement in 1950, while in 1964 this share had risen to 7.4 percent.[39] After reaching a high point at the beginning of the 1970s, the number of employed retirees declined steadily thereafter (Table 15.4).

It is important to note the manner in which economic, social and employment policies were interrelated. Conceptually, they were part of socialist economic planning, based on heavy industry and raw materials. While in the early phase of recovery this strategy may have been justified, its limits were clearly exposed by the end of the 1950s.

The early years of the GDR were filled with enormous economic problems: war destruction, dismantling, reparations, malnutrition, and a lack of housing, energy resources, as well as raw materials.[40] Considering these conditions, the economy of the SBZ-GDR developed relatively well. Even if official propaganda inflated the results of the Two Year Plan 1949-50 and the first Five Year Plan 1951-55,

Table 15.4 *Elderly in the Workforce as Percent*

Year	60-65 years old	65 years old and older
1969	7.9	6.2
1975	5.9	5.0
1979	3.4	3.9
1984	4.5	2.0
1989	4.6	1.7

Source: Statistisches Jahrbuch der DDR 1990 (Berlin, 1990), 131.

the accomplishments achieved by the mid-1950s were remarkable. According to official statistics, the GDR's national economy increased from 30.7 billion marks in 1950 to 49.8 billion marks in 1955.[41]

Even at this early stage, it was nonetheless evident that East Germany was lagging behind the productivity of other Western countries and the FRG. According to official accounts, GDR industry had surpassed industrial production of 1936 by 111 percent, and had grown more quickly than in the West. But Albrecht Ritschl has shown that this result was based on nominal figures, not adjusted for prices.[42] He estimates this value to have been only 87 percent, and emphasizes that even before the war the later GDR territory was not producing as much as areas in the West; this disparity only increased after 1945. The reason for this development cannot be traced to a deficit in technology. "In light of present results it seems plausible to argue that a large gap existed between East and West as early as 1950. This reflected only to a small degree a traditional lag of productivity, and cannot explain the disparity in production at the time of reunification. In any case, it seems that the transition to a planned socialist economy had a lasting shock-effect on the GDR's industrial productivity."

This argument seems irrefutable, especially since the effects of the shock were noted by contemporaries. By the mid-1950s, GDR economists had begun to discuss productivity problems openly. Friedrich Behrens, the head of the State Central Administration for Statistics, addressed the problem in a lengthy article for the journal *Wirtschaftwissenschaft*.[43] He argued that productivity per worker had increased more slowly than productivity per work hour, which pointed to a decline in labor intensity. Behrens concluded that even in a socialist economy, labor intensity played an important role. Therefore, material interests as related to salaries had to consider both positive and negative aspects. Any individual who did not work hard enough, who violated work discipline, was absent without excuse, in short, whoever did "not do his job according to society's normal, average intensity," had to reckon with a cut in pay. Unfortunately, practices such as "wage opportunism," and questionable principles such as "pay security" and "norm security" hindered such measures. Though Behrens argued that low work intensity was "seemingly a typical problem of the transitional period," he complained about the lack of lasting incentives: "Indeed there are workers today who resort to tricks once employed against capitalist piecework, and who keep their work intensity low, because they are no longer motivated by fear of unemployment or driven by capitalist overseers. In part, solidarity is still misconstrued as leveling."[44]

Behrens' remarks could be interpreted as a call to exploit the potentially explosive nature of social inequality within the framework of a socialist planned economy. But he was not willing to carry his argument to that extreme. If contradictions existed in the early phase of centralized planning between economic goals and social expectations, he felt they were largely rooted in the subjective failure of those involved. These actors often did not behave according to economic principles. Unsatisfactory production planning and organization were "one of the main shortcomings of our industry," which led to disruptions in work rhythms. "On the one hand there is a false production rhythm in our factories that is expressed in a threefold curve (monthly, quarterly, and annually) which limits the development of work productivity, contributes to stoppages, waiting periods, etc. and leads to a disproportionate increase in average pay and reduced production quality. On the other hand, we have an over-supply in production plans – not only in materials and half-finished goods, but also finished products. Further, there is an excess of buying power."[45]

Behrens' summary identifies those problems that were to plague the GDR during its entire existence. They were not merely the result of subjective failings, but can be traced to a "lack of efficiently allocated state resources and insufficient innovation within the economy."[46] This did not mean that resources were merely scarce on the over-regulated consumer end, they were also lacking, if not more so, on the investment side. Reparation demands at the beginning of the 1950s were one of the main causes of this lack of investment, which was intensified by the demands placed on the economy by the military and social expenditures of the 1980s. Irregular cycles of investment contradicted official proclamations about investment planning aimed at maintaining proper proportions.[47] The consequences of these developments were obvious in the workplace.

Just at the moment when the SED leadership believed it could develop the economic potential of a socialist economy behind the protection of the Wall and under the military umbrella of the USSR, the GDR entered a long and dramatic period of decline. Paul Kennedy has argued that what occurred was the collapse of multinational empires whose political aspirations stood in stark contrast to economic developments. "As the world economy began to shift its focus away from traditional industries to knowledge-based and consumer-oriented industries such as computers, electronics, automobiles, civil aeronautics, pharmaceuticals, and communications, the USSR was not in a position to follow suit."[48] At the same time the "long cycle of the Soviet economy" from 1928 to 1960 shifted from growth to decline, which was visible in the fall of the average GNP.

The GDR attempted to extricate itself from this downward spiral. While Ulbricht engaged in a risky economic reform, Honecker tried to overcome economic weaknesses by emphasizing social policies. Until the mid-1970s, it seemed as if the SED could at least keep pace with Western European standards. After that point, however, the GDR economy quickly became more like those of other Central and Eastern European states under Soviet rule.

Although economic planning targeted industrial investment, large segments of the political economy remained outside centralized control. Many jobs were technically outdated, and demanded a large degree of manual labor. In 1961, for instance, among workers in state and "partially nationalized" industries, only 43.8 percent were machine operators. Though one-half were engaged in largely manual labor, only one fifth had physically demanding jobs. Of the workers not at a machine, 66.3 percent performed manual labor without the help of power tools. In the transport sector, 73.5 percent of all workers were manual laborers or had few tools at their disposal. Fifty-five and one-half percent of repair personnel were manual workers.[49] Change came about very slowly. At the end of the 1980s, 40 percent of industrial workers performed largely manual labor, and among assembly line workers, the number was as high as 70 percent. Although the degree of mechanization increased from about 52 percent in 1970 to about 60 percent in 1989 and the degree of automation was raised from 6.6 percent to 13.2 percent, many antiquated positions remained.[50] Simultaneously, the condition of the infrastructure deteriorated further, and an ever higher share of capital goods became obsolete (Table 15.5).

The obvious pressures on the political economy led to unrealistic demands for new manpower. This resulted not only in egalitarian tendencies, but it also slowed down structural changes.[51] The expansion of the economy's tertiary sector typical of other modern industrial nations occurred much later in the GDR than elsewhere, and then only at a greatly diminished rate. This lag is expressed in the number of individuals employed in different sectors. While industry remained dominant despite the decline that began in the

Table 15.5 *Depreciation Quota in Percent*

Year	1975	1980	1985	1989
Industry	47.3	50.8	52.7	54.2
Trades and Crafts	32.3	46.7	55.0	61.3
Construction	52.9	56.4	67.2	68.6
Agriculture	49.8	56.7	63.0	60.8

Source: Statistisches Jahrbuch der DDR 1990 (Berlin, 1990), 121.

1970s, transportation and telecommunications saw only relatively insignificant increases in the number of new jobs, calculated without apprentices (Table 15.6).

GDR economy and society were distinguished by the relatively strong development of the primary sector and the absolute superiority of the secondary sector. The tertiary sector remained undeveloped; it fulfilled the functions of distribution and provision rather than services in a wider sense.

This industrial "conservatism" was also reflected in GDR products. The design and production of typical industrial products from 1945 to 1990, such as tools, office machines, synthetic fabric, and film drew from inventions, developments, and production procedures dating from the 1920s and 1930s. Such conservatism was not only a result of a policy of autarchy, but stemmed from a conservative mentality that party and state elites shared with wide segments of the populace. It was based on a linear perception of development in society, economics, and culture.

Social policies – mainly aimed at workers – had a great deal of influence on the East German job market.[52] Composed of a mixture of performance-based rewards and measures aimed at pacifying the public, such policies created an extensive social safety net. Their founding principles drew on ideas similar to those held by the Left in the Weimar Republic, while borrowing elements from Soviet social practices.[53]

The implementation of SED social policies in the GDR fundamentally influenced economic growth. Next to the goals of guaranteeing basic social needs and strengthening pronatalist tendencies, social policies, above all, mobilized resources to improve the performance of the economy. This was why factory-level measures were granted such a high priority.[54] Social policies developed over time from directives aimed at the protection of physical work reserves, via attempts focused on creating a system of performance rewards, to the measures of the 1970s and 1980s

Table 15.6 *Number of Employed by Economic Sector (in thousands)*

Year	1950	1960	1970	1980	1989
Industry	2098	2768	2855	3128	3187
Crafts and Trades	600	414	404	259	267
Construction	465	470	538	583	560
Agriculture	2005	1304	997	878	923
Communications	455	554	581	613	639
Trade	674	890	858	850	877

Source: Statistisches Jahrbuch der DDR 1990 (Berlin, 1990), 19.

that were instruments of crisis management and control.[55] State-regulated price subventions for "basic necessities," rents, and salaries for public servants constituted the second main pillar of the social system. A third pillar was provided by the state-financed welfare and medical systems.[56]

The social system did provide benefits, but in practice individual measures lost their efficiency within the relatively short span of two to three years. Thereafter they became routine, and were often subject to various forms of abuse. Correction was almost impossible since, for political reasons, the SED could neither take back existing regulations, nor did it desire to do so. At least since the slogan of "the unity of economic and social policy"[57] became the strategic guidepost of the 1970s and 1980s, the regime found itself in an uncomfortable dilemma. Attempts to control the situation further strained material resources, dramatically slowed investment rates, and gradually drained the economic power of the state. This type of social policy was doomed to failure not only because it carried the seeds of its own destruction in the form of growing costs, but even more problematic was the fact that, in its leveling effects, this policy weakened the innovative potential of GDR society. In the first half of the 1980s the sociologist Manfred Lötsch addressed the problem by emphasizing the dynamic effects of social differences.[58] Shortly before the end of the regime, the newspaper published by the Central Committee (ZK) of the SED, *Einheit*, attempted to conduct a public discussion about performance in socialism. Similarly, Otto Reinhold, ZK member and rector of the Academy for Social Sciences, indirectly pointed out one of the system's decisive failings by stating "performance comes before distribution."[59] This could be interpreted as a call for change. But the GDR was not a performance society, it was a distribution society.

Konrad Jarausch has asked whether the concept of "welfare dictatorship" might be able to describe the "radicalized welfare state" under real-existing socialism. Much evidence supports this claim, especially the intentions of party and state elites. SED functionaries were indeed heavily influenced by the philosophy of welfare.[60] But what might speak against this view is the uncaring practical application of economic and social policy by the SED. It was this course – admittedly implemented under difficult conditions – that destroyed its own foundations from the mid-1970s on. If one considers income structure and social regulation more closely, the unquestionably paternalistic nature of SED policies is tied to a fearful and opportunistic policy of distribution. Its chief goal was not social welfare, although this was significant, but rather the securing of the party's political power.

Interests, Conflicts, and Milieus

The SED's social policies resulted in numerous, often explosive conflicts. Their effects on the relationship between stagnation and innovation within the GDR's workforce is difficult to determine. The dispossession, collectivization, and nationalization of property between 1945 and 1972 affected farmers and small businessmen particularly. Artisans and traders became marginalized. Their attempts at protest and resistance were too weak and diffuse to force the regime to take any corrective measures. While the GDR's economy won little from nationalization and collectivization, it lost a stratum of innovators and private entrepreneurs that could have served as dynamic factors.[61]

The intelligentsia was in part marginalized by the exchange of elites in 1945; while many were willing to cooperate with the regime, others chose to leave for the West. During the 1950s and 1960s a new, socialist "intelligentsia" existed side by side with the old bourgeois "remnants." Largely employed in salaried positions, the members of this group were often forced into expressions of loyalty for the sake of their careers, which ruled out the possibility of a direct confrontation with the SED.[62]

The relationship between party leaders and the working class was entirely different. Workers occupied an ambivalent position in GDR society, at once strong and yet weak. Their strength stemmed from the fact that the SED remained more economically than politically dependent on their loyalty. Their weakness was rooted in the circumstance that workers were deprived of any independent organizations, while trade unions became subjected to the will of the party after 1947-48.[63] Workers thus had little opportunity to organize or articulate their own interests.

The wave of strikes and protests that broke out around 17th June 1953 was of central significance. The regime's attempts to cut back in social services and increase regulative controls led to a conflict with the working class that had historic lessons for both sides. In the event's aftermath, the search for socio–political agreements became a strategic goal of most social policy. The SED avoided antagonizing workers through its wage policies. The workers were at first hesitant, but then more willing to accept production competitions initiated from above. What motivated them was not ideology but the promise of rewards and social services at the workplace. The cover of "socialist competition" was actually a method of dividing up social resources. Until the regime's demise, the SED had no other choice than to come to terms with divergent workers' interests in the area of wages and social policy.[64]

The fact that factories in the GDR became important instruments of state social policies offered management the means to diffuse social conflicts.[65] Such methods included cash rewards, prizes, special treatment outside of the market, reduced work schedules, vacation time, or the allotment of factory-owned apartments. These instruments were a mixture of legally inscribed regulations and internal practices that in times of need could move outside the sphere of legality. The extra-legal establishment of the five-day work week long before 1965 is such an example.[66]

Most workers were motivated by the demands of daily life and short-term and mid-range goals focused on "getting by." This meant that they were relatively flexible in conflict situations and they maintained, even in the face of criticism of the state, a certain "reluctant loyalty"[67] to the regime. Ironically, work brigades, based on Soviet models, increased workers' negotiating powers and became an accepted forum for industrial and agricultural laborers as early as the 1950s.[68] They placed wage policies at the center of social issues. In a fragmented and unstable wage system, it seemed reasonable to look for solutions at the factory level, and to focus on agreements negotiated between managers and the brigades. In general these solutions were small-scale, individual compromises. The "widespread mentality of 'conformity and complaint'" may have functioned as a catalyst in this process.[69]

The lives of at least three different generations in the East were influenced either by the Nazi war economy or the SED planned economy. Despite obvious differences, these systems shared one important element – both regimes placed great demands on the industrial workforce, and they organized their labor policies accordingly.[70] In the "new federal states" no real labor market existed for over fifty years. What did exist (interrupted only shortly after the war) was widespread full employment. Relative job security was bought at the price of a "gradual loss of freedom."[71]

Sigrid Meuschel sees in this development a specifically twisted form of modernity. "One can speak of the GDR – if not in terms of an industrial society – then in terms of a worker's society with a high concentration in industrial production. In daily life and in leisure activities, in the organizational structure of the party, and also in collective and individual orientation and in the self-perceptions of workers themselves, the *Betrieb* occupied a central position. Self-perceptions were linked to individual qualifications and knowledge that were singular to a socialist planned economy and *Mangelwirtschaft*.[72] This constellation is "modern and yet a 'modernization trap,'" because "society in the GDR – undifferentiated and controlled by the party – was a stumbling block in the path of

all innovations the party sought to initiate." Recent economic studies and histories of technology support such findings.[73]

In an attempt to reconstruct mental structures of the period,
Rudolf Woderich has formulated four hypotheses:

1. The system's autarchy led to an increased isolation in "niches"
   and in the creation and strengthening of "separate spheres."
2. Convention and conformity determined social interactions in
   the GDR. Rather than pressure from the regime, accepted patterns of socialization led to a "search for the protection of the
   anonymous middle."
3. "The normality syndrome functioned as a binding strategy of
   rationalization for states of mind." In the center of all considerations was the GDR.
4. Ambivalences in the patterns of behavior or values were
   expressed on a practical level in the duality of "accommodation
   and obstinancy."[74]

This ambivalence was not only achieved by winning over the
workers politically. It was also a product of the egalitarian social
policies of the SED that led to the "excessive leveling of vertical
(class-specific) inequalities" within GDR society. Especially social
policy was meant to favor workers and collectivized farmers.[75] This
circumstance led in the first years after the war to a reconstitution
of the older workers' milieu that had existed between the wars,[76]
strengthening it, and ensuring its continued existence.[77] The SED's
social policies, with their characteristic "socialist paternalism"[78]
were a source of conservatism because they enabled workers to
enter relationships based on and furthering personal loyalty.

A high degree of stability in working conditions also strengthened
the social structures of the working class and shored up the staying
power of traditional proletarian milieus. Working and living conditions in many areas of East German industry remained unchanged
over long periods of time. A new milieu developed in new large factories (with housing developments), which was often more egalitarian than previous ones. We can distinguish between a "traditional
skilled labor milieu" and the "clientele of socialist big industry."[79]
The housing problem may also have contributed to the stability of
milieus. Even the building program initiated in the 1970s did little
to change the situation, and workers became even more tied to the
places of work.[80] In addition, social and geographical mobility was
limited by the deformation of age and sexual structures due to damage and exodus to the West. Family, coworkers, friends, and acquain-
tances thus remained relatively stable.[81]

Milieu stability should not be confused with stable social classes. The process of decoupling and dissolution of th main components of the workers' movement, initiated by Nazi policies,[82] was continued – mutatis mutandis – in the SBZ–GDR. The lack of independent interest groups and the impossibility of founding new ones beyond the reach of the party or the FDGB forced workers to improvise solutions within the system itself. Decentralized, and largely isolated from each other, laborers formed brigades or employees in smaller plants into relatively homogenous social groups that attempted to protect their interests within the factories. "Individual behavior, resulting from social conditions, was not only forced, and an expression of purposeful attempts to meet social demands – it was *counterproductive.*" The workplace became an arena for many actions – but not for fighting for better performance; low rents and prices did not inspire voluntary increases in achievement. "What was perceived of as 'socialist' was the removal of responsibilities or efforts." The result was a loss of individuality and a reliance on traditional social forms.[83]

Was this a return to the process of class formation begun in the nineteenth century? This process of a dissolution of corporatism[84] found a counterpart in socialist societies in the reliance of the "leading class" on structures outside of the "working class party" and its mass organization enforced by the dictatorship. Perhaps this development can be seen as a kind of re-corporization. Functionally, the development occurred in key positions within factories. As a result, the working class and the SED found themselves in a relationship in which the paradigm of labor served as a "hinge" between "system pressures and social perceptions."[85] It was this hinge that allowed for a political and social balance of interests. But real stability remained an elusive goal.

On balance, the workplace sheds an ambivalent light on the relationship between stagnation and dynamism in the GDR. At a very early stage, the East German working sphere developed a lasting discrepancy between the dynamics of change in property rights and the organization of the economy on the one hand and the continuity of technical, technological, and personnel factors on the other. The revolutionary demands of the SED resulted in a high degree of modernization, particularly due to increased numbers of women in the workforce. In other working areas and structures it had more conservative and limiting effects.

The extensive industrialization, nationalization and collectivization of the economy, carried out under centralized rule, the militarization of society, and the expansion of the ruling apparatus of the SED were interrelated, and had enormous social consequences. They formed the basis for a specific form of full employment that could only be sustained and balanced by massive social policies. This system not only swallowed up large amounts of economic resources, it also was a significant hindrance to modernization. The "real socialist" working world nevertheless also possessed some innovative potential, for example, when it was necessary to give up principles of planned development in favor of technical and technological catching-up. Improvisation resulted in dynamics of fragmentary innovation. Its limits were to be found in renewed calls for a return to a planned economy as well as in limited financial and material resources.

Notes

1. Sigrid Meuschel, *Legitimation und Parteiherrschaft in der DDR. Zum Paradox von Stabilität und Parteiherrschaft in der DDR 1945–1989* (Frankfurt, 1992); Harmut Kaelble, Jürgen Kocka, and Hartmut Zwahr, eds, *Sozialgeschichte der DDR* (Stuttgart, 1994); Jürgen Kocka and Martin Sabrow, eds, *Die DDR als Geschichte. Fragen – Hypothesen – Perspektiven* (Berlin, 1994); Richard Bessel and Ralph Jessen, eds, *Die Grenzen der Diktatur. Staat und Gesellschaft in der DDR* (Göttingen, 1996).

2. Johannes Berger, "Was bedeutet die Modernisierungstheorie wirklich – und was wird ihr bloß unterstellt?" *Leviathan* 24, no.1 (1996): 45–62.

3. Jeffrey Herf, *Reactionary Modernism. Technology, Culture, and Politics in Weimar and the Third Reich* (Cambridge, 1984).

4. Hans Mommsen, "Noch einmal. Nationalsozialismus und Modernisierung," *Geschichte und Gesellschaft* 21 (1995): 395.

5. Martin Kohli, "Die DDR als Arbeitsgesellschaft? Arbeit, Lebenslauf und soziale Differenzierung," in *Sozialgeschichte der DDR*, ed. Kaelble et al., 38.

6. Franz-Xaver Kaufmann, "Normative Konflikte in Deutschland: Basiskonsens, Wertewandel und soziale Bewegungen," in *Die Grenzen der Gemeinschaft. Konflikt und Vermittlung in pluralistischen Gesellschaften. Ein Bericht der Bertelsmann Stiftung an den Club of Rome*, ed. Peter L. Berger (Gütersloh, 1997), 155f.

7. Gerold Ambrosius and William H. Hubbard, *Sozial- und Wirtschaftsgeschichte Europas im 20. Jahrhundert* (Munich, 1986), 252–56.

8. Helmut Wollmann, "Der Systemwechsel in Ostdeutschland, Ungarn, Polen und Rußland. Phasen und Varianten der politisch-administrativen Dezentralisierung," *Aus Politik und Zeitgeschichte*, 1997, no. 5: 14; and Helmut Wiesenthal, "Die Transformation Ostdeutschlands. Ein (nicht ausschließlich) privilegierter Sonderfall der Bewältigung von Transformationsproblemen," in *Transformation sozialistischer Gesellschaften: Am Ende des Anfangs*, ed. Hellmut Wollmann, Helmut Wiesenthal, and Frank Bönker (Opladen, 1995), 134–59.

9. Kohli, "Die DDR," 39.

10. Horst Berger and Herbert F. Wolf with Arndt Ullmann, eds, *Handbuch der soziologischen Forschung. Methodologie, Methoden, Techniken* (Berlin, 1989), 1–8.

11. Christoph Kleßmann, *Die doppelte Staatsgründung. Deutsche Geschichte 1945–1955. 4th ed.* (Bonn, 1986), 262.

12. Mary Fulbrook, *Anatomy of a Dictatorship. Inside the GDR 1949–1989* (Oxford 1995).

13. Albrecht Ritschl, "Aufstieg und Niedergang der Wirtschaft der DDR: Ein Zahlenbild 1945–1989," *Jahrbuch für Wirtschaftsgeschichte* 2 (1995): 11.

14. Heike Solga, *Auf dem Weg in eine klassenlose Gesellschaft? Klassenlagen und Mobilität zwischen Generationen in der DDR* (Berlin, 1995), 215f.

15. Rainer Geißler, *Die Sozialstruktur Deutschlands. Zur gesellschaftlichen Entwicklung mit einer Zwischenbilanz zur Vereinigung*, 2nd ed. (Opladen, 1996), 174.

16. Manfred Lötsch, "Die Hofierung der Arbeiterklasse war nicht wirkungslos," *Frankfurter Rundschau* 14 November 1990; idem, "Sozialstruktur und Systemtransformation," in *Sozialer Umbruch in Ostdeutschland*, ed. Rainer Geißler (Opladen, 1993), 33.

17. Geißler, *Sozialstruktur*, 63.

18. Frank Adler, "Einige Grundzüge der Sozialstruktur der DDR," in *Projektgruppe SOEP* (Berlin 1991), 169.

19. Dietrich Storbeck, *Soziale Strukturen in Mitteldeutschland. Eine soziologische Bevölkerungsanalyse im gesamtdeutschen Vergleich* (Berlin, 1964), 153.

20. Ernst Beck, "Die Erwerbspersonen in der sowjetischen Besatzungszone nach der Stellung im Beruf," *Statistische Praxis* (hereafter SP) 3, no. 2 (1948): 43f.

21. In the Saxon plebiscite on 30 June 1946, 82.42 percent of the voters approved the "Law regarding the transfer of factories belonging to Nazis and war criminals into people's property." *Statistisches Jahrbuch der DDR 1955* (Berlin, 1956), 87.

22. Wolfgang Mühlfriedel and Klaus Wießner, *Die Geschichte der Industrie der DDR bis 1964* (Berlin, 1989), 212–58.

23. Wolfgang Fritz, "Die amtliche Erwerbstätigenstatistik in der DDR," *Historical Social Research* 22 (1997): 308.

24. Heinz Günter Steinberg, *Die Bevölkerungsentwicklung in Deutschland im Zweiten Weltkrieg mit einem Überblick über die Entwicklung von 1945 bis 1990* (Bonn, 1991), 154–60.

25. Ernst Beck, "Altersaufbau der Erwerbspersonen in der sowjetischen Besatzungszone," *Statistische Praxis* 4 (1949): 43f.

26. *Protokoll der Verhandlungen des III. Parteitages der SED*, vol. 2 (Berlin, 1951), 296f.

27. *Sozialreport 1990. Daten und Fakten zur sozialen Lage in der DDR* (Berlin, 1990), 15.

28. Statistisches Bundesamt et al., eds, *Datenreport 1992. Zahlen und Fakten über die Bundesrepublik Deutschland* (Mannheim and Bonn, 1992), 156.

29. Gunnar Winkler, ed., *Sozialreport '90. Daten und Fakten zur sozialen Lage in der DDR* (Berlin, 1990), 73.

30. *Datenreport 1992*, 539.

31. Werner Weidenfeld and Karl-Rudolf Korte, eds, *Handwörterbuch zur deutschen Einheit* (Bonn, 1991), 466.

32. Dietrich Mühlberg, "Überlegungen zu einer Kulturgeschichte der DDR," in Kaelble, *Sozialgeschichte*, 73.

33. *Gesetzblatt der DDR* (hereafter GBl.) 1949, no. 1: 7.

34. *GBl.* I/1961, no. 5: 29.

35. *GBl.* I/1968, no. 8: 210; Gbl. I/1974, no. 47: 440.

36. Hildegard Maria Nickel, "'Mitarbeiterinnen des Sozialismus' – Frauenarbeit in der DDR," in *Frauen in Deutschland: 1945–1992*, ed. Gisela Helwig and Hildegard Nickel (Berlin, 1993): 233–56, esp. 235–38.

37. Johannes Frerich and Martin Frey, *Handbuch der Geschichte der Sozialpolitik in Deutschland*, vol 2.: *Sozialpolitik in der DDR* (Munich and Vienna, 1993) 167–69.

38. *Datenreport 1992*, 455.

39. "Zur Alters- und Berufsstruktur der wirtschaftlich Tätigen," *Statistische Praxis* 22, no. 4 (1967): 216.

40. Horst Barthel, *Die wirtschaftlichen Ausgangsbedingungen der DDR. Zur Wirtschaftsentwicklung auf dem Gebiet der DDR 1945–1949/50* (Berlin 1979); Werner Matschke, *Die industrielle Entwicklung der Sowjetischen Besatzungszone Deutschlands (SBZ) 1945 bis 1948* (Berlin, 1988).

41. *Statistisches Jahrbuch der DDR 1955* (Berlin, 1956): 90.

42. Ritschl, "Aufstieg," 22.

43. Fritz Behrens, "Arbeitsproduktivität und Arbeitsintensität. Bemerkungen zu ökonomischen und politischen Problemen der Übergangsperiode," *Wirtschaftswissenschaft* 4, (1956): 384–401.

44. Behrens, "Arbeitsproduktivität," 398.

45. Fritz Behrens, "Einige Grundfragen der Arbeitsproduktivität im Lichte der Erfahrungen des ersten Fünfjahresplanes der DDR," *Wirtschaftswissenschaft* 4 (1956): 188–202.

46. Friedrich Haffner, "Die Transformation der Kommandowirtschaft in eine soziale Marktwirtschaft," in *Auf dem Weg zur Realisierung der Einheit Deutschlands,* ed. Alexander Fischer and Maria Haendcke–Hoppe–Arndt (Berlin, 1992), 11.

47. Lothar Baar, Uwe Müller, and Frank Zschaler, "Strukturveränderungen und Wachstumsschwankungen. Investitionen und Budget in der DDR 1949 bis 1989," *Jahrbuch für Wirtschaftsgeschichte* 2 (1995): 52f.

48. Paul Kennedy, *Vorbereitung auf das 21. Jahrhundert* (Frankfurt, 1997): 300.

49. Kurt Albrecht, "Die Auswirkungen des technischen Fortschritts auf die Art der Tätigkeit der Produktionsarbeiter in der Industrie," *Statistische Praxis* 17, no. 8 (1962): 199.

50. Winkler, *Sozialreport 1990,* 85.

51. André Steiner, "Beständigkeit oder Wandel? Zur Entwicklung der Industriestruktur der DDR in den sechziger Jahren," *Jahrbuch für Wirtschaftsgeschichte* 2 (1995): 101–18.

52. Hans-Günter Hockerts, "Grundlinien und soziale Folgen der Sozialpolitik in der DDR," in Kaelble, Kocka and Zwahr, *Sozialgeschichte:* 519–44.

53. Gunnar Winkler, ed., *Geschichte der Sozialpolitik der DDR 1945–1985* (Berlin, 1989), 14–17.

54. Gerhard Tietze and Gunnar Winkler, *Sozialpolitik im Betrieb. Soziale Erfordernisse des wissenschaftlich-technischen Fortschritts* (Berlin, 1988).

55. Ingrid Deich and Wolfhard Kohte, *Betriebliche Sozialeinrichtungen* (Opladen, 1997), 22.

56. For more information see Hockerts, "Grundlinien."

57. "Bericht des Zentralkomitees an den VIII. Parteitag der Sozialistischen Einheitspartei Deutschlands," in *Protokoll der Verhandlungen des VIII. Parteitages der SED* (Berlin, 1971), 1: 34, 61f.

58. Manfred Lötsch, "Zur Triebkraftfunktion sozialer Unterschiede," *Informationen zur soziologischen Forschung in der DDR* 17 (1981): 14–19.

59. Otto Reinhold, "Der Sozialismus als Leistungsgesellschaft," *Einheit* 44 (1989): 700.

60. Characteristic: Erich Honecker, *Aus meinem Leben* (Berlin, 1980), 250.

61. Heinz Hoffmann, *Die Betriebe mit staatlicher Beteiligung im planwirtschaftlichen System der DDR (1956–1972)* (Stuttgart, 1998).

62. Arnd Bauerkämper, Jürgen Danyel and Peter Hübner, "'Funktionäre des schaffenden Volkes'? Die Führungsgruppen der DDR als Forschungsproblem," in *Gesellschaft ohne Eliten? Führungsgruppen in der DDR,* ed. Arnd Bauerkämper et al. (Berlin, 1997), 11–86.

63. Klaus Helf, "Von der Interessenvertretung zur Transmission. Die Wandlung des Freien Deutschen Gewerkschaftsbundes (1945–1950)," in *Parteiensystem zwischen Demokratie und Volksdemokratie,* ed. Hermann Weber (Cologne, 1982), 339–66; Siegfried Suckut, *Die Betriebsrätebewegung in der sowjetisch besetzter Zone Deutschlands (1945–1948)* (Frankfurt, 1982).

64. See especially Manfred Hagen, *DDR – Juni '53. Die erste Volkserhebung im Stalinismus* (Stuttgart, 1992).

65. Peter Hübner, "Balance des Ungleichgewichtes. Zum Verhältnis von Arbeiterinteressen und SED Herrschaft," *Geschichte und Gesellschaft* 19 (1993): 15–28.

66. Peter Hübner, *Konsens, Konflikt und Kompromiß. Soziale Arbeiterinteressen und Sozialpolitik in der SBZ/DDR 1945–1970* (Berlin, 1995), 120–29.

67. Alf Lüdtke, "'Helden der Arbeit' – Mühen beim Arbeiten. Zur mißmutigen Loyalität von Industriearbeitern in der DDR," in *Sozialgeschichte,* ed. Kaelble et al., 188–213.

68. Wilfrid Döring and Günter Kemper, *Die Arbeitsbrigade im Volkseigenen Industriebetrieb* (Berlin, 1959).

69. Mary Fulbrook, "Herrrschaft, Gehorsam und Verweigerung – Die DDR als Diktatur," in *Die DDR als Geschichte. Fragen – Hypothesen – Perspektiven,* ed. Jürgen Kocka and Martin Sabrow (Berlin, 1994), 80.

70. Rüdiger Hachtmann, *Industriearbeit im "Dritten Reich." Untersuchungen zu den Lohn- und Arbeitsbedingungen in Deutschland 1933–1945* (Göttingen, 1989), 37–50; Storbeck, "Arbeitskraft und Beschäftigung," 49–61; Mühlfriedel and Wießner, 166–73.

71. Hansjoachim Henning, "Sozialpolitik III: Geschichte," in *Handwörterbuch der Wirtschaftswissenschaft* (Stuttgart, 1977), 7: 106.

72. Sigrid Meuschel, "Überlegungen," 9.

73. Jörg Roesler, "Einholen wollen und Aufholen müssen. Zum Innovationsverlauf bei numerischen Steuerungen im Werkzeugmaschinenbau der DDR vor dem Hintergrund der bundesrepublikanischen Entwicklung," in *Historische DDR-Forschung,* ed. Jürgen Kocka (Berlin, 1994), 263–85.

74. Rudolf Woderich, "Mentalitäten zwischen Anpassung und Eigensinn," *Deutschland Archiv* 25 (1991): 28–30.

75. Geißler, *Die ostdeutsche Sozialstruktur,*17.

76. Michael Hofmann and Dieter Rink, "Die Auflösung der ostdeutschen Arbeitermilieus," *Aus Politik und Zeitgeschichte,* 1993, no. 27: 31.

77. Christoph Kleßmann, "Die Beharrungskraft traditioneller Milieus in der DDR," in *Festschrift für Hans-Ulrich Wehler* (Munich, 1991), 146–54.

78. Gerd Meyer, "Sozialistischer Paternalismus. Strategien konservativen Systemmanagements am Beispiel der DDR," in *Politik und Gesellschaft in sozialistischen Ländern. Politische Vierteljahresschrift* 20 (1989): 426.

79. Hofmann and Rink, "Die Auflösung der ostdeutschen Arbeitermilieus," 31.

80. Wolfgang Junker, *Das Wohnungsbauprogramm der DDR für die Jahre 1976 bis 1990* (Berlin, 1973).

81. Winkler, *Sozialreport 1990,* 273–78.

82. Ulrich Herbert, "Arbeiterschaft im 'Dritten Reich': Zwischenbilanz und offene Fragen," *Geschichte und Gesellschaft* 15 (1989): 320–36.

83. Günter Kracht, "Die kulturelle Substanz der DDR-Gesellschaft," *Mitteilungen aus der kulturwissenschaftlichen Forschung* 16 (1993): 316f.

84. Jürgen Kocka, *Arbeitsverhältnisse und Arbeiterexistenzen. Grundlagen der Klassenbildung im 19. Jahrhundert* (Bonn, 1990), 3, 521, 525.

85. Winfried Thaa, "Die legitimatorische Bedeutung des Arbeitsparadigmas in der DDR," *Politische Vierteljahresschrift* 30 (1989): 99.

CHAPTER 16

THE HITLER YOUTH GENERATION IN THE GDR

INSECURITIES, AMBITIONS AND DILEMMAS

Dorothee Wierling

The label of "the reconstruction generation"[1] in the GDR refers mainly to the age group of those born in the 1920s. The older cohorts were too compromised by their affiliation with National Socialism, and lost most of their influence on public life in the Soviet Zone, apart from a small group of loyal communists returning from Soviet exile that comprised the "activists of the first hour." But those born in the twenties were young enough to be forgiven and old enough to be prepared for the new society, or to take over responsibility on the local level. They had experienced the Weimar Republic as children, the Third Reich as youths, and lived through often traumatic events at the end of the war. In contrast to their elders, whose support of the NSDAP was more pragmatic and opportunistic, the younger ones tended to be deeply fascinated by Nazi ideology and thus experienced the breakdown of the Third Reich as a painful shock.

For the West, the sociologist Helmut Schelsky has coined the label of the "skeptical generation" for this age group. He explains their apolitical attitude, their focus on private life and individual career as an answer to the experiences of mislead idealism, which the Hitler youth generation claimed for itself.[2] There is no reason why this attitude should not also have prevailed in the East, but given the low level of economic achievements on the one hand, and the powerful offer of a new world view on the other, an individualistic skepticism of the young obviously had less chance to develop in the Soviet Zone. A minority, although probably a large one, accepted the offer of re-education in the communist sense, and thus tried to give meaning to the past and gain hope for the future. Another minority, and again a large one, resisted the new order and either left for the West, or was disciplined by Stalinist rule.[3]

This essay will concentrate on those parts of the reconstruction generation which stayed in the GDR for good, tried to establish a new life and career, and were even eager to fit into its political framework. In looking at this generation, I try to understand what "history" meant for them, but also what they meant for the history of the GDR. I see them stuck in an ambiguous situation in many ways: when they were hit by the collapse of the Third Reich, they were adolescents, vulnerable and needy, but at the same time active and future-oriented; they were descendants of a weakened parent generation that was discredited, especially in moral respects – but among the elders there were also the heroes of antifascism, figures without fault. At the same time they were the educators of an even younger cohort, untouched by the war, national socialist dictatorship and even capitalism.

This puts the Hitler youth generation into an ambivalent relation towards "the past," but establishes a rather strong relation to "education." Ambivalence towards the past is due to the fact that, when being accepted into the socialist project, they had to confess and explain their youthful involvement in National Socialism as long as they lived in the GDR. And last but not least, they experienced a painful ambivalence in regard to their social achievements. No other generation in the GDR witnessed a similar upward mobility, but these accomplishments exacted a cost in the form of an extreme degree of political and social control, without the power or the privileges to compensate for it.

Patterns of Experience

The biographical background of this generation[4] reveals two prominent patterns of experience, following each other, or being intertwined in the same life story: there is a sense of crisis, mainly the economic crisis of the Great Depression, with mass unemployment at the end of the 1920s or beginning of the 1930s as its most dramatic feature. In addition, there is also the political crisis, accompanied by instability, constant conflicts and street violence by the radicals of the right as well as the left. All this created an atmosphere which was vaguely understood as dangerous, even by younger children. At the same time, there was another experience, a belief in the eventual stability and gradual improvement of one's social situation, a confidence that caused parents to invest in their children's education as a preparation for security and mobility. This outlook was a consequence of social democratic politics aiming at more social justice and better options for the working classes.

The young and active members of the reconstruction generation in the GDR typically came from skilled workers' background and less from lower middle class families. This was a milieu that offered some security with modest financial means and status, and a group which, especially in urban, nuclear families, would focus on the children's upbringing and future options. This private family program centered on an education which would enable the child to do better than his parents and even change from a blue to a white collar status. Even if wages were still low, and one's life style remained more or less the same, this change was regarded as an important step upward. As a rule, this achievement was more likely in a respectable and ambitious home, but it might even be possible in a subproletarian milieu, as the example of Frau Uhlig shows:

> Born in 1928 in Breslau, east of the Oder river, the oldest daughter of an unmarried woman, she grew up with an increasing number of siblings and a sequence of stepfathers in a one room apartment in a slum neighbourhood. Being a good pupil, she wanted to become a teacher, but the mother refused to send her to a Nazi teachers training school, which prepared high school students to become elementary school teachers. Her grades were so excellent that in 1943 she was admitted for an apprenticeship in a retail store – after finishing her *Pflichtjahr*, the mandatory year of social service the Nazis had introduced. In 1944, the family left Breslau, which was under heavy attack by the Soviet army, under dramatic circumstances. In the spring of 1945 they arrived in Gera, and the girl immediately managed to find a place where she could finish her apprenticeship. She entered the trade union and the Free German Youth, a youth organization that quickly came under the influence of the communists, and took a political training course. There, she was asked to become an assistant teacher, which turned out to be the beginning of her serious political commitment and her career. At the time of the interview in 1987, she had just asked to be suspended for health reasons from her position as a director for social affairs in one of the most important chemical companies of the GDR.[5]

Especially in the 1930s, and even well into the war, there was a growing hope among Germans that stability and mobility were within reach. Despite the Nazi dictatorship, these were the "good times,"[6] as many interviewees in the East and the West would later call them. These were also the times that the Hitler youth generation experienced as young people who prepared for an adult future. When the war came to an end, it, however, destroyed most of their hopes with it.

The war also offered different experiences as soon as young people got directly involved in it. On the one hand, it meant a positive challenge, and on the other, a traumatic shock. In both cases one effect was, nonetheless, the same: the sudden and dramatic end of childhood and the painful shift towards adulthood. This could and often did mean taking over adult responsibility: in the job, it brought challenges for which one was unprepared, for reasons of vocational training, former status, age, or gender; in or outside of the family, it could require filling adult roles, for instance, in the children's evacuation camps far from home. When the war came to its end, young people received little support from their parents and teachers, but also experienced little control.

In many cases, war meant violence and death. Encounters with death could happen even during the "normal" service in the Hitler Youth, where members were often used to clear the rubble after bombings and look for the wounded and dead. The closer war came to the German heartland, the more young people were directly involved in the fighting. A whole cohort of high school students were later labeled *Flakhelfergeneration*, after their service in air raid defense.[7] While these boys and girls were typically middle class kids, working class youth were in danger of being drafted up to the last minute, including those born in 1929. Many of them had positive fantasies and even experiences of heroism and comradeship, but for the most, feelings of extreme anxiety, shock and disillusionment were dominant. Often youths were completely on their own, when in the last days the military units dissolved and their officers left their posts.

Rudolf Kamp, born in 1929, was forced by German officers to leave his family on their flight from the East and the Soviet army towards the West. He was sent to a *Wehrertüchtigungslager*, a military training camp, and after some weeks marched with his unit south, "to defend Prague". On the day of Germany's defeat, his superiors left during the night, and the group of young privates was on their own, in the hostile surroundings of liberated Czechoslovakia. On their way to Germany, they tried to avoid the Czechs, but at the same time needed to come into the open for food. On one occasion, they were captured by a group of Czech officers who beat them, forced them to dig a large grave, and kneel down in front of it. But instead of being executed, they were confronted with Hitler portraits and forced to throw stones at them, before they were released. One day before his 16th birthday, Kamp reached the small town of Wurzen near Leipzig, where his parents were waiting for him.[8]

Among those who were fleeing the Russians at the end of the war, women, children and youth were clearly overrepresented.[9] Among our interviewees of the reconstruction generation, memories of flight or "resettling," as it was officially called in East Germany, were prominent, both in terms of the number of those who had been expelled, and the intensity of this formative experience. Although statistics are not available, all evidence suggests that these *Umsiedler* were quite eager to establish themselves under new circumstances and use the chances offered by the new authorities, after they had been forced to dissolve their traditional social and regional bonds. Even a strong wish to return to their homeland east of the Oder did not necessarily prevent the resettlers, especially the younger ones, from taking part in the reconstruction of their new home, for instance in Eisenhüttenstadt, the newly founded industrial town on the west bank of the Oder river.[10]

Again, the stories recalling flight combine positive challenges and negative traumas as contradictory experiences of the young. Often adolescents had to decide on the time to leave, the route to follow and the belongings to take with them, while the small children, the grandparents, and even the mothers, left the responsibility to them. At the same time, being lost, helpless, and disoriented was also part of their dramatic experience, where almost everything had to be left behind and the place where they would finally end up was still unknown. Memories of the lost war tend to stress outside events more than their inner effects; the narratives thus re-enact an almost manic concentration on survival under extreme and chaotic conditions. Young people were obviously more prepared to cope with the situation than their elders, who often sank into deep depression, although the young ones were also vulnerable.

There is a remarkable silence in the interviews on the complex emotions aroused by these experiences, but it is not difficult to imagine what those feelings must have been like. The huge relief that came with the end of the war must have been accompanied by an immense shock over the breakdown of personal, social, regional and ideological bonds. There must have been feelings of loss concerning people, home and homeland, ideals and beliefs, feelings of disappointment and despair, realizing the end of security and power, feelings of a loss of future perspectives, sadness about the shattered devotion to a beloved leader and a great cause, and finally feelings of humiliation facing the defeat and occupation, and perhaps a growing sense of shame and guilt after learning the truth about the Nazi crimes.[11]

The interviewees, men in particular, often allude to this confusing mixture of emotions with the stereotypical formula of "never again."[12] This phrase, or rather appeal, serves as an introduction to a story which one might read as a narrative of conversion. In most cases, it is not more than the image of an encounter with a victim of National Socialism: the antifascist fighter or liberated concentration camp inmate, identified by his striped uniform, who gives testimony of Nazi crimes, antifascist sacrifices, bystanders' guilt, the fight against evil and the moral victory of the good. Sometimes it is the former Russian slave worker, less often a Jewish Displaced Person,[13] in other cases an officer of the Soviet army, especially if the foreigner is highly educated, knows Goethe and Schiller, and impresses the young German with his generosity and manners. The encounter with one of these figures is interpreted as the turning point in the thinking of the narrator – it means a sudden insight and the chance to renounce the old ideals and be open and free for new ones. The higher the social status and the stronger the political involvement in the GDR, the more elaborate this story of conversion is likely to be. Its truth neither can, nor should, be in question here. What is important, is its centrality in the biographical design of a whole generation in the GDR. At times, even very careful narrators betray the ambiguity, even the cruelty of that experience.

> Konrad Naumann, born 1929, and at the time head of the most important SED district Berlin as well as member of the central committee of the communist party, gave a speech in front of that meeting in December 1965, when the plenary of the central committee condemned the liberal tendencies in cultural and youth politics and announced a harsher approach for the future. In comparing today's loose manners in youth with his own experience, he said: "It was in 1945, the comrades, who came home from Buchenwald, Dachau and Majdanek concentration camps grabbed us real tight, so that we almost couldn't breathe, and even without our consent, they put us where they wanted to put us and we grew up to be respectable, useful human beings."[14]

The Rebuilding Myth

When the war had ended, the first dangerous weeks of Red Army occupation passed, and the Americans had left Eastern Germany, an organized effort at rebuilding could finally begin in what was to become the Soviet zone. The reconstruction generation was then between fifteen and twenty-five years old. Women and expellees were overrepresented in it.[15] The immediate tasks were obvious: rejoining families, finding a place to live, getting a job, or obtaining a place in school. The interviews indicate that there were two very different reactions to the new situation: Some people showed a certain depressed passivity and lack of energy in the face of everyday challenges, as well as social activities and political orientation. This attitude could continue well into the 1950s and is reflected by a certain lack of stories, narrative flatness, or even silence in the accounts.

The other reaction was a manic, supposedly continuous activity aimed at resuming the life plan interrupted by the war, focused on going on. In the interviews this attitude is reflected by a narrative mode that shows the narrator in control of events in each and every situation: bold, witty, self-conscious and successful. Frau Hutter, an expellee born in 1929, talks about the first months after her arrival in the Soviet Zone in this way:

> We tried to find work. My siblings worked, they found a job in a film factory, that is my older siblings, my brother and sister. I took up work at an estate, and my younger sister worked as nanny in a family. My mother worked on a vegetable farm, so that we earned our living....When they announced the agrarian reform, I was asked if I wanted to become a farmer, and got an offer to take over a small farm, but I was not interested in such a thing in the long run, I wanted to go back to school, and so in November 1945, I applied for high school in Delitzsch and was admitted after I passed the exams....I wanted to continue on this path....[16]

While younger children focused on completing their school or vocational training, those who had been in the labor market already were eager to re-enter their prewar status as soon as possible. Their readiness meshed perfectly with the enormous need for personnel in fields like administration and education, which had been the most nazified and were, therefore, radically denazified in 1945. This demand could only be satisfied by rather old or rather young people, while the middle generation was compromised by their active support for the Nazis and had suffered most from the war, as reflected in the numbers of dead.

From the perspective of the authorities, it turned out to be easier to train the young than to cope with the old, whose views had been formed by their experiences in the Weimar Republic. The chosen candidates went through a crash course which provided the most basic knowledge and skills for their new task, together with some political schooling. This insufficient preparation had important political consequences, for it weakened the applicants, the new teachers or judges, often permanently, in relation to their clients or colleagues and made them structurally dependent upon the party. In 1945, there was a mass recruitment campaign, especially for teachers. The average age of these new teachers, *Neulehrer*, was twenty-five, but the majority was considerably younger, often just eighteen years old.[17]

The antifascist youth groups, out of which the FDJ grew in 1946, played an important role in mobilizing young people right from the start.[18] Initially, they attracted young people because they offered practical help, especially in searching for jobs or improving working conditions; but they also provided youths with many cultural opportunities as well as organizing dances and other social events. With the support of the Russian occupiers, they were one of the few institutions able to provide what young people so badly longed for right after the war. But the FDJ achieved influence over youth also by providing a new concept of meaning, a universal interpretation of history, a new *Weltanschauung*, which seemed powerful enough to explain the crimes and the defeat of the Nazis, remove the burden of guilt, give them hope for a planned future, offer identification with the Soviet victors and their leader, Stalin. It seemed to furnish them again with the secure framework of an organization, which became ever more authoritarian and hierarchical, including requiring members to wear a uniform. The FDJ was therefore able to offer continuity, while claiming to represent a radical breach with the past. To be sure, many young people were alienated by this attitude and opposed the organization. But others considered it more attractive, and it was those who would form a new type of FDJ youth, young men or women who, seemingly without major difficulties, were able to transform themselves into the New Man.

The 1950s were the most dramatic and dynamic phase in GDR history, since it was the time when the basic political, social, and economic changes took place. The nationalization of industry into so-called people's property, the collectivization of agriculture, the educational reforms and the creation of political mass organizations – this transformation which had an enormous impact on individual lives as well as social structure – was decided or begun at that time. Though these changes were part of a forced, authoritarian socialist modernization, compulsion alone does not describe their meaning for the population. It was impossible to create state socialism without the cooperation, if not support of many people, whose loyalty had to be secured, especially as long as the borders remained open. This was, however, only possible if the individuals involved would gain something from their engagement – there had to be hope for the satisfaction of personal desires, the pursuit of personal goals.

In 1950 the generation in question was between twenty and thirty years old. The GDR had been founded as a state and had developed political and administrative structures that allowed for a more systematic recruiting of a new elite. But East Germany was by no means a society where traditional milieus and structures had ceased to exist. The universities, which had gone through a brutal process of Stalinization, still contained a large number of students from middle class backgrounds.[19] Therefore, in the 1950s, the main conflicts with youth were going on in the universities, as well as in the high schools, which were also important middle class institutions.[20] On the one hand, the authorities relied on repression, causing many professors and students to leave the country for the West. The same was true for high school pupils who were not admitted to the universities because of their social background.[21] On the other hand, the party tried to educate a new and alternative intelligentsia, chiefly through the so-called "workers' and farmers' faculties" (ABF), whose symbolic meaning might surpass their material effect, even if from 9,000 to 12,000 students were trained there between 1950 and 1955. Eighty percent of these students came from working class or agricultural backgrounds.[22]

Through this and other measures, the authorities succeeded in forming a loyal, socialist elite, which already in the 1950s started to dominate the executive level in socialist industry, the professorships in the universities, and the local and district leadership of the communist party and its mass organizations.[23] For them, loyalty was easy, since they owed their position to the socialist character of the GDR. This experience created a widely accepted myth that in the GDR everybody, including those who had lived through the old society, had been given the chance to realize their personal dreams by building socialism.

The rebuilding myth not only referred to the experience of upward social mobility out of the working classes, but also glorified the reconstruction of the proletariat proper, i.e., the creation of a modern, socialist, industrial society. For example, large-scale national projects, like building a steel plant and new town on the Oder river in 1953, called Stalinstadt, attracted many young men and families. They had pragmatic reasons for coming, a well paid job, a new apartment, a better than average supply of consumer goods. But practical considerations did not exclude other attractions, which were less political than cultural: the heroic idea of building a plant and a town from scratch. Even if or because promises were not fully kept, expectations were not entirely satisfied, the challenge and the pathos of a new beginning under difficult circumstances remained vivid, and accounts of all the initial problems, hardships, and dangers make up numerous adventure stories in recollections from Eisenhüttenstadt.[24]

In order to build up an industrial sector that would make the GDR less dependent on the more industrialized West, the training of better skilled workers was a prime task. Not only did the majority of workers lack experience in heavy industry, since they came from agriculture or light industry, skilled workers were also overrepresented among those leaving for the West. The older generation often failed to obtain new qualifications in school or on the job. But for the younger generation this training program was a success which partly strengthened the positive image of the young male industrial worker, an ideal that stood for the whole project of reconstruction out of nothing – at least for a portion of the working class in the making. Many others preferred a proletarian existence under capitalism,[25] and another group which took part in the workers' uprising of June 1953, was taught the permanent lesson that political opposition was dangerous and doomed to fail. Nevertheless the biographical material shows that the bonding forces of the 1950s were not so much "politics," but the experience of taking part in a bold, challenging undertaking that was to pay off perhaps only several years ahead was still able to create feelings of satisfaction.

In the 1950s, the members of the Hitler youth generation seldom reached real power positions in industry. One exception is young Arenbeck, who became a leading manager in the Eisenhüttenkombinat Ost (EKO), although he had a middle class background and was a graduate of one of the infamous NAPOLAs, the Nazi elite schools.[26] In general, if "bourgeois" experts were needed, older and more experienced men were chosen. But for middle positions in industry, and political functions on the local or district level, the mobility of the younger generation was a widespread experience. Since advancement depended on proof of political loyalty, a growing number of SED members had, as can be concluded by their age and political socialization, no firsthand experience of and ties to the labor movement, but had to be educated to become communists in the party itself.[27] Their basic task in the new system was to execute central orders and impose strict discipline in their realm – an ambiguous experience from the start, which forced them to lean on higher authority to secure their own.

The subgroup which wanted to pursue political issues and ideals differed somewhat from the Hitler youth cohort as a whole that had returned life in the GDR to a degree of normalcy at the end of the 1950s. On the one hand, their social status and party affiliation offered a certain amount of protection and occasionally even power. On the other hand, they were subject to demands which could not be met under any circumstances. In every situation in life they had to give proof of deserving their status; their permanent role was that of a model citizen; they found themselves "sitting in a glass cage."[28] As party members, they were subject to education in the narrow sense of the word. They had to accept a strict system of rules and sanctions, relating also to their personal lives; they were under enormous group pressure, and had to follow so-called party orders in regard to which jobs to take, which tasks to fulfill and where to move. It was almost impossible to leave these structures if you did not want to risk your whole social existence or that of your family.

The party saw professional education and political training as a unit. The career level which required party membership was relatively low, and could sometimes include positions like foreman on the shop floor. Political training was required for certain positions, especially in education, where teachers had to take part in a party year, even if they were not members of the SED. It could be assumed that such a harsh discipline would favor a rather instrumental relationship to the party. But even if this were the case, it does not necessarily mean that the party was not able to create deeper ties. Sometimes such bonds were already a consequence of the social isolation of a party member in his family, neighborhood, or the workplace, which made him dependent on social contacts within the party, even if he might have joined just for opportunistic reasons. In the Hitler youth generation in particular, there was a strong desire for a clear system of beliefs, for a strict hierarchical order, and for a close community – all of which could be satisfied to a certain degree in the communist party.

Such satisfaction was, however, limited by the idol of the communist antifascist fighter who had given or at least risked his life for the cause of humanity and socialism. These were saintlike figures which could be only approached with the utmost respect and awe. Celebrated in a stylized narrative, they were far removed from complex reality and had become unassailable. This reverence applied not only to the loyal, but perhaps even more to the critical functionaries and intellectuals of this generation.[29] In contrast to these martyrs, all later communists were condemned to remain deficient and guilty, since in the GDR their utmost sacrifice could not be repeated, their ideal never be reached. Many stories about the 17 June 1953, when it was dangerous to confess publicly to party membership, contain an implicit message about such declarations as attempts to repeat an antifascist commitment to the final consequence.[30] But beyond dramatic situations, the loyal part of the Hitler youth generation had no alternative but to show their dedication to discipline, self-improvement and education, in order to prove a radical commitment to socialism and to compensate for their late birth.

The Failure of Education

The history of the GDR can also be interpreted as the story of a failed education project. Especially in the 1950s and 1960s education was a central topic, not only for state institutions or political mass organizations, but for political culture in general. One issue was the political re-education of those who had grown up under capitalism and National Socialism, that is, the Hitler youth generation itself. Another problem was the self-education of those who were to be the pillars of the system, not just the party members, but also the working classes. Thus, the workers' brigades that were propagated in the late 1950s were not only seen as units of collective work, but also as instruments of proletarian self-education and socialist culture.[31] Ultimately it was the whole population, every citizen of the GDR, which appeared in need of education, if only because they had not fought for socialism in a revolution, and it had been imposed on them by military force and repressive politics.

With those born after the war, education seemed a most promising project. The postwar generation had been kept away from hostile political influences and had gone through a party-controlled school system which dominated the lives of the young ever more effectively from the 1960s on. Ironically, the members of the Hitler youth generation, who themselves had gone through a most painful process of re-education, were now made the main agents of this education for the young. It was they who worked as teachers, headmasters, officials in departments of education, leaders of the children's organization Young Pioneers, or functionaries of the Free German Youth, in charge of youth clubs and summer camps. Through this educational role in the GDR, in particular, they shaped its history. For it was their success or failure that would decide whether the GDR would became a community of believers or a society held together mainly by force and fear. Here was their task. How was it to be fulfilled?

In the beginning, the results seemed rather encouraging. The childhood of the postwar generation in the 1950s gives an overwhelming impression of a smooth integration into the reformed school system as well as the children's organization. Founded in 1948, the Young Pioneers could claim to organize 80 percent of all children of the appropriate age at the end of the 1950s.[32] In the mid-1960s the socialist school reform was completed, the old generation of teachers was supplanted by the Hitler youth generation, and the last remnants of traditional education that had survived in small villages were ended. The pedagogical optimism which motivated theorists and practitioners in education seemed, therefore, totally justified. It was expressed in a nutshell by the Soviet theoretician Makarenko, who was convinced that "when a person is not well educated, it is the fault of his parents and educators and of nobody else, and when a child is good, it is also due to education...; no other education is as powerful as our Soviet pedagogy, because there are no obstacles whatsoever which would prevent anybody from developing into a full human being."[33]

The building of the Wall in 1961 also removed the circumstances from the GDR which could keep children from becoming socialist personalities. In the aftermath of this event, a cautious shift in the politics of education and the attitude towards youth took place. From a focus on control and discipline, the rhetoric as well as actual politics changed towards a more integrative, liberal discourse, which at least considered the interests and needs of young people as possibly different from those of adults. Young people's creativity and impatience should be used to further the socialist cause in the GDR. Since Walter Ulbricht backed these new ideas, they were written down in September 1963 as a Politburo declaration, under the heading: "Youth of Today – Masters [*Hausherren*] of Tomorrow. Trust and Responsibility for Youth."[34] The text, which became known as the "youth communiqué," dealt less with young people's claims than with the needs of the GDR, arguing that the tasks of modernization could only be fulfilled by mobilizing youthful energies and encouraging a more dynamic development of all levels of society. Still, the proclamation included some passages which recognized the rights of young people to act out their youthful desires, such as dancing to rock music, even if its origin was West of the Wall or the other side of the Atlantic.

The files on the huge FDJ-led campaign to propagate the communiqué among youths show that this was more than propaganda rhetoric. Instead, during discussions in schools, at universities and in the factories and offices, serious conflicts arose. While the young people often demanded more freedom in their realm and criticized their supervisors and elders, teachers especially were alarmed, worried, and offended. They protested against discipline violations which threatened their authority, and warned against the continuation of liberal policies which must end in chaos.[35] Overall, a liberal party faction, with the support of the highest functionaries, had joined forces with young activists on the local level against the more conservative agents of authority in the country. Their slogan of modernization through youth mobilization was based on the conviction that those born after the war were ready for such a project, that there were no "obstacles" to prevent it, aside from adult mistrust and doubts.

But a few years later, in 1965, the party course changed radically again towards more control and discipline instead of confidence in and freedom for youth. The project of educating youth to identify with socialist ideas and GDR politics, had, in effect, failed. On the contrary, young people had used the widened sphere of activities and expression to loosen their ties to the FDJ and to yield to what the authorities saw as the seductions of the West, namely popular culture, but also political ideas of liberalism. A major factor was the new media, such as transistor radios and television, which gave them free access to Western culture across the Wall and created new opportunities for a public sphere independent of what the political organizations were willing to offer. All over the GDR, young people formed rock bands with English names, singing English language songs. In a state of highly politicized paranoia, the authorities decided on harsh measures to enforce a socialist orientation and culture.[36]

The official interpretation of such youth rebellion saw the source of all evil in the West, which systematically tried to confuse, demoralize and disorient youth to prevent them from understanding their real interests and to prepare a third world war.[37] Although such an interpretation took the responsibility from the educators' shoulders, most members of the Hitler youth generation reacted with disappointment, envy, and hatred towards the young people, especially young male workers, who refused to follow those ideas of manliness which were associated with the concept of the socialist personality. This ideal was personified in the figure of the worker–fighter, whose prevailing characteristics were self-control and discipline as well as an uncompromising devotion to the communist cause. This model echoed those ideas of manliness that they themselves had grown up with during National Socialism. Their condemnation of the "effeminate" young men with their long hair and loose manners prove how important these ideals of manliness still were.[38]

The failure of the educational project was experienced as a shock in at least two ways: First, teachers were tied to their pupils through the type of pedagogical optimism which made their failure a sign of their own shortcomings. Second, the failure of educating the young generation untouched by the formative experiences of capitalism and imperialism must have nourished doubts. If their own re-education was more than superficial, they should have been able to convince others of its lasting success. The cultural crisis of the mid-1960s as well as later events such as the impact of the Czech invasion of 1968 and the protests against the expulsion of the critical singer Wolf Biermann in 1976,[39] shattered the hope for consensus and stability in the GDR. As a result, the loyal part of the Hitler youth generation sought to tie itself even more strongly to the authorities and hierarchical structures to which they belonged.

Cheated by History

The Hitler youth generation held its position in state and society until the very end, with only a few individuals reaching the highest level of real power. Of the seventy-one persons who had been candidates or members of the SED Politburo at some time during the existence of the SED, twenty-five were born between 1921 and 1930. Among these twenty-five, however, eight were just candidates, without ever reaching full membership. Three were members of this ruling body only in the short period of 8 November to 13 December 1989, that is from the resignation of the gerontocracy to the dissolution of the Politburo structure as such.[40] Some members of this cohort did gain considerable influence, such as Günther Mittag, in charge of the GDR economy, and Harry Tisch, the chairman of the official trade union (FDGB). Others were most prominent as SED reformers, such as Hans Modrow and Günther Schabowski, district secretaries in Dresden and Berlin. But forty years after its foundation, the GDR was essentially still ruled by their predecessor generation, standing for the same experiences and ideals: those born before and around the First World War and formed by the prewar communist movement.

In spite of its limited access to the central level of power, the Hitler youth generation was by no means without influence, nor has it been irrelevant throughout the GDR's history. As the only cohort of upward mobility in East Germany, disciplined by feelings of gratitude and guilt, the loyal, established part of that generation stood for the GDR's success as well as for its stagnation. From the later 1970s on, their prominence on the local, district and company level became a social and political problem, because they blocked the upward route for the next generation, and their perspective on their own past and the development of their society became ever more problematic.[41] The lessons of these histories pointed in a single direction: life was only secure under the guidance and shelter of those who held power, and this benevolence had to be earned by strict loyalty or it would be forfeited, and they would be lost. It was mainly due to their original weakness and ambivalence in the early postwar period that they had grown up unable to claim and live with autonomy.

In 1989, this group was between sixty and seventy years old. Many were still active in their jobs as well as in politics, and for their most prominent members, there had long been rumors of finally taking over actual political responsibility. For instance, Honecker's more liberal successor, Hans Modrow, was born in 1929, and looked back on the typical biographical experiences outlined above.[42] The end of the GDR therefore hit them particularly hard, not just through the loss of social status and security, but also through the negation of the lessons that they had drawn from their earlier lives. Many, therefore, experienced the societal breakdown as a repetition of the traumatic events of 1945, when for a short time they had been desperate and without perspective, until they had taken the healing hand of the rebuilding project and commu-

nist belief. Since it now seemed that this offer had turned out to be
an illusion, they relived desperation and depression in a strange
way, with those same feelings of guilt or denial that had already
characterized their response to the postwar beginnings.

Notes

1. The term "generation" is used according to the famous post-First World War
    essay of sociologist Karl Mannheim, "Das Problem der Generationen," in idem,
    Wissenssoziologie. Auswahl aus dem Werk (Neuwied, 1970): 509–65.
2. Helmut Schelsky, *Die skeptische Generation. Eine Soziologie der deutschen
    Jugend*, reprint (Frankfurt, 1975). The term Hitler youth generation refers to
    the important role of the Nazi youth organisation in the socialization of young
    people in the Third Reich.
3. Though not new, the problem of *Verwilderung*, i.e. the phenomenon of uncon-
    trolled, violent and unruly male youth in the cities, often organised in street
    gangs, was especially strong immediately after the war. Alfons Kenkmann,
    *Wilde Jugend: Lebenswelt großstädtischer Jugendlicher zwischen Weltwirtschafts-
    krise, Nationalsozialismus und Währungsreform* (Essen, 1996). See also Martin
    Goerner and Michael Kubina, "Die Phasen der Kirchenpolitik der SED und die
    sich darauf beziehenden Grundlagenbeschlüsse der Partei- und Staatsführung
    in der Zeit von 1945–1971/72," in *Materialien der Enquêtekommission: Aufar-
    beitung von Geschichte und Folgen der SED-Diktatur in Deutschland* (Frankfurt
    am Main, 1995), VI, 615–874.
4. The following examples come from a major oral history project conducted in
    1987 in the GDR that focussed on the reconstruction generation. See Lutz
    Niethammer, Alexander von Plato, and Dorothee Wierling, *Die volkseigene
    Erfahrung. Zur Archäologie des Lebens in der Industrieprovinz der DDR* (Berlin,
    1991). The patterns described are confirmed by the short biographies found in
    *DDR: Wer war wer? 2146 Biographien zur DDR-Geschichte. Ein elektronisches
    Lexikon unter windows*, ed. Bernd-Rainer Barth, et al. (Berlin, 1994).
5. From the interview with Bertha Uhlig (pseud.) see Dorothee Wierling, "Die
    älteste Schwester," in *Die volkseigene Erfahrung*, 478 ff.
6. Ulrich Herbert, "'Die guten und die schlechten Zeiten.' Überlegungen zur
    diachronen Analyse lebensgeschichtlicher Interviews," in *"Die Jahre weiß man
    nicht, wo man die heute hinsetzen soll." Faschismuserfahrungen im Ruhrgebiet*,
    ed. Lutz Niethammer (Bonn, 1983), 67–96.
7. Rolf Schörken, *Luftwaffenhelfer und Drittes Reich. Die Entstehung eines politi-
    schen Bewußtseins* (Stuttgart, 1984); and Heinz Bude, *Deutsche Karrieren.
    Lebenskonstruktionen sozialer Aufsteiger aus der Flakhelfergeneration* (Frank-
    furt am Main, 1987).
8. See his portrait "Gewalt und Gesetz" in *Die volkseigene Erfahrung*, 584 ff.
9. Alexander von Plato and Wolfgang Meinicke, *Alte Heimat – neue Zeit* (Berlin,
    1991).
10. The majority of our interviewees in Eisenhüttenstadt, situated right on the Pol-
    ish border, were expellees. Unfortunately, GDR statistics stopped registering
    expellees in 1950. See the catalogue of the Deutsche Historische Museum,
    *aufbau west – aufbau ost. Die Planstädte Wolfsburg und Eisenhüttenstadt in der
    Nachkriegszeit*, ed. Rosmarie Beier (Ostfildern–Ruit, 1997).
11. Alexander and Margarethe Mitscherlich, *The Inability to Mourn: Principles of
    Collective Behavior* (New York, 1975).

12. The slogan "never again" was already used after the First World War and is part of an often reprinted poster designed by communist artist Käthe Kollwitz.

13. Displaced Persons (DPs) is the postwar term for those millions of concentration camp inmates or slave laborers who often could or would not return to their previous homes.

14. Quoted from the protocol of the eleventh plenary session of the ZK in 1965, Stiftung Archiv der Parteien und Massenorganisationen im Bundesarchiv (SAPMO-Barch) IV 2/1/336: 198.

15. In 1950, women in the twenty-one to forty age group outnumbered men of their own age by 160 to 100. *Statistisches Jahrbuch der DDR 1955* (Berlin, 1956), 117 ff.

16. Interview with Frau Hutter, transcript p. 4. She later made it to the position of director of a company with 1700 employees. See *Alte Heimat – neue Zeit*, 165–83.

17. Brigitte Hohlfeld, *Die Neulehrer in der SBZ/DDR 1945–1953* (Weinheim, 1992), 70.

18. Ulrich Mählert, *Die Freie Deutsche Jugend 1945–1949. Von den 'Antifaschistischen Jugendausschüssen' zur SED–Massenorganisation* (Paderborn, 1995).

19. Christoph Kleßmann, "Relikte des Bildungsbürgertums," in *Sozialgeschichte der DDR*, ed. Hartmut Kaelble, Jürgen Kocka, Hartmut Zwahr, (Stuttgart, 1994) 254–70.

20. Christoph Kleßmann, "Zur Beharrungskraft traditioneller Milieus in der DDR," in *Was ist Gesellschaftsgeschichte?* ed. Manfred Hettling et al. (Munich, 1991), 146–54.

21. The denial of university admission for their children was among the main reasons which doctors mentioned for their flight to West Germany. Kleßmann, "Relikte des Bildungsbürgertums," 259.

22. Heike Solga, *Auf dem Weg in eine klassenlose Gesellschaft? Klassenlagen und Mobilität in der DDR* (Berlin, 1995), 104 ff.

23. Ralf Jessen, "Professoren im Sozialismus," in *Sozialgeschichte der DDR*, 217–53. See Hartmut Zimmermann, "Überlegungen zur Geschichte der Kader und Kaderpolitik in der SBZ/DDR," ibid., 322–56.

24. Alf Lüdtke, "'Helden der Arbeit' – Mühen beim Arbeiten. Zur mißmutigen Loyalität von Industriearbeitern in der DDR," in *Sozialgeschichte der DDR*, 188–213. "Stahnstadt" was changed to "Eisenhüttenstadt" in 1961.

25. For the dominance of economic reasons for leaving the country, see Viggo Graf Blücher, *Industriearbeiter in der Sowjetzone* (Stuttgart, 1959), 10f.

26. Jörn Schütrumpf, "KZ–Häftlinge, Parteilose und NSDAP–Mitglieder. Führungskräfte im entstehenden Eisenhüttenkombinat Ost," in *aufbau ost, aufbau west*, 171–80.

27. Lutz Niethammer, "Volkspartei neuen Typs? Sozialbiographische Voraussetzungen der SED in der Industrieprovinz," in *PROKLA 80* (September, 1990), a volume on political generations, 40–70. See also the main history textbook of the early years, *Geschichte der Kommunistischen Partei der Sowjetunion (Bolschewiki), Kurzer Lehrgang* (Berlin, 1946).

28. Hutter Interview, 32.

29. This attitude informs the works of almost all GDR writers of this generation, such as Günther de Bruyn, Christa Wolf and Franz Fühmann. For an attempt to destroy the saint-like image of these antifascists, see Monika Maron, *Stille Zeile sechs. Roman* (Frankfurt am Main, 1991).

30. Lutz Niethammer, "Where Were You on the 17th of June? A Niche in Memory," in *Memory and Totalitarianism, International Yearbook of Oral History*, ed. Luisa Passerini, (1992), 45–69.

31. Jörg Roesler, "Die Produktionsbrigaden in der Industrie der DDR. Zentrum der Arbeitswelt?" In *Sozialgeschichte der DDR*, 144–70; and Peter Hübner, *Konsens, Konflikt und Kompromiß. Soziale Arbeiterinteressen und Sozialpolitik in der SBZ/DDR 1945–1970* (Berlin, 1995), 223 ff.
32. Leonore Ansorg, *Kinder im Klassenkampf. Die Geschichte der Pionierorganisation von 1948 bis Ende der fünfziger Jahre* (Berlin, 1997), 173. See also Heinz-Elmar Tenorth, Sonja Kudella, and Andreas Paetz, *Politisierung im Schulalltag der DDR. Durchsetzung und Scheitern einer Erziehungsambition* (Weinheim, 1996), 99–174.
33. Quoted in Günther Schmid, "Die determinierende Rolle des Zieles im pädagogischen Prozeß," in *Makarenko heute*, ed. Alexander Bolz and Edgar Günthe (Berlin, 1973) 81–104.
34. "Jugend von heute – Hausherren von morgen. Der Jugend Vertrauen und Verantwortung. Kommuniqué des Politbüros des ZK der SED zu Problemen der Jugend in der DDR," *Schriftenreihe des Staatsrats der DDR* (Berlin, 1963).
35. Information of the Hauptschulinspektion Berlin for the Central Committee, SAPMO IV A2/16, vol. 9. See Monika Kaiser, *Machtwechsel von Ulbricht zu Honecker. Funktionsmechanismen der SED-Diktatur in Konfliktsituationen 1962–1972* (Berlin, 1997).
36. Günter Agde, ed., *Kahlschlag. Das 11. Plenum des ZK der SED 1965* (Berlin, 1991).
37. Dorothee Wierling, "Die Jugend, der Staat und der Westen. Texte zu Konflikten der 1960er Jahre," in *Akten, Eingaben, Schaufenster. Die DDR und ihre Texte, Erkundungen zu Herrschaft und Alltag*, ed. Alf Lüdtke and Peter Becker (Berlin, 1997), 223–40.
38. Dorothee Wierling, "'Negative Erscheinungen....' Zu einigen Sprach- und Argumentationsmustern in der Auseinandersetzung mit der Jugendsubkultur der DDR der sechziger Jahre," in *Werkstatt Geschichte* 5 (1993): 29–37. See also Michael Rauhut, *Beat in der Grauzone* (Berlin, 1993).
39. While the Biermann expulsion created only an intellectual stir, the bloody end of the Prague spring provoked workers' protests. See Monika Tantzscher, *"Maßnahme Donau und Einsatz Genesung": Die Niederschlagung des Prager Frühlings 1968/69 im Spiegel der MfS-Akten* (Berlin, 1994) and Manfred Krug, *Abgehauen. Ein Mitschnitt und ein Tagebuch* (Düsseldorf, 1998).
40. *DDR: Wer war Wer*, see fn. 4.
41. See Solga, *Auf dem Weg in eine klassenlose Gesellschaft?* passim.
42. Unpublished interview with Hans Modrow, conducted by Uwe Funk in 1993, transcript in author's possession. See also idem, *Ich wollte ein neues Deutschland* (Berlin, 1998).

CHAPTER 17

REFORMING SOCIALISM?

THE CHANGING OF THE GUARD FROM ULBRICHT TO HONECKER DURING THE 1960s

Monika Kaiser

An examination of the political landscape of East Germany in the 1960s reveals various distinct, and in part opposing, tendencies. These contradictions not only resulted from the changing structures of Eastern bloc politics, but also reflect tensions between two competing groups within the SED elite. Although they shared some basic beliefs and assumptions, these two factions differed considerably in questions of detail. Both constantly had to reach a consensus between themselves on the one hand and with the political interests of the Soviets on the other. Internally, these challenges centered on the question of whether in light of the evident backwardness and inflexibility of the inherited Soviet system the regime could be reformed, and whether this might be achieved without threatening the party's monopoly of power. While Ulbricht and his "reform strategists" believed change was possible and searched for ways to achieve it, party bureaucrats under the Honecker-led wing were from the outset much more skeptical of such a prospect.

The use of the term "reforms" – particularly in connection with Ulbricht's name – is contested, and indeed appears to some (as a few reactions to my book attest)[1] to be provocative and even absurd. This is in large part a result of the term's multiple meanings and connotations. In the West, the word has been used so indiscriminately that its meaning has been inflated,[2] and in the East, lay and professional discourses encompass definitions of the word that stray considerably from its root. In communist systems, measures and developments have been deemed "reforms" only when they "remove instruments of control from ruling authorities and allow society methods of control so that one can speak of a 'liberalization' of the system."[3] In this view, attempts by Eastern leaders to reduce bureaucratic waste or to curb unnecessary centralization can only be considered as "technocratic adjustments" – not as reforms. Such a narrow interpretation, while maintaining a certain inner logic, hinders an accurate assessment of the steps or phases of development within the socialist system.

In order to describe significant changes, transformations, and accommodations within "real socialism," a broadly defined concept of reform seems indispensable. If one proceeds from the actual meaning of the term, which was originally value-neutral and not directed at any particular social system (and it should not be), then one can define reform as the "planned transformation, improvement, or redefinition of the existing order." As such it is the "opposite of revolution."[4] Similar to state-led reform policies of other countries, the reform efforts of the GDR in the 1960s had "the goal of adapting the existing political system to changing political and social conditions."[5] In no way, however, were these attempts directed at any significant alteration of the foundations of the system – the unquestioned monopoly of the party – which a narrow application of the term to communist systems might suggest. Ulbricht, at least, pursued his reform policies with the goal of securing the continued existence and increased stability of the socialist system in the face of widely changing circumstances.

Ulbricht's Reform from Above

The "reform from above" initiated in the early 1960s unfolded before the backdrop of Ulbricht's unchallenged authoritarian rule. Aimed at increasing efficiency, these changes were meant to modernize the system and adapt it to the demands of a modern industrialized society in a period of scientific-technical revolution. As one of the first Eastern bloc party and state leaders, Ulbricht realized that the claimed superiority and ultimately even the survival of the socialist state depended on its ability to come to terms with what he called these "new challenges." Thus in contrast to the reform course set by Krushchev, the target of Ulbricht's ad hoc reform concept remained focused on the mechanisms of the economy. Step by step, organizational changes were to close the gap in work productivity[6] vis-à-vis Western countries (and particularly the

Federal Republic) in order to prove the supposed economic, political, social, and moral superiority of socialism.

Unlike earlier reform attempts, decided within the narrow confines of the ruling circle without the public's knowledge, the economic reforms initiated in 1962 under the title "Principles for the New Economic System of Planning and Management of the National Economy" (NÖSPL) were preceded by intense deliberations and experimental case studies. The first outlines of a reform course had been privately debated long before any official proclamations. Ulbricht, along with his personal assistant, the economist Dr Wolfgang Berger, was the leading force behind the proposals. He also included Dr Erich Apel and Dr Günther Mittag in his plans – both candidates of the Politburo nominated by Ulbricht to the party leadership in 1961 and 1962, respectively. These men were in large part responsible for the practical organization, preparation, and implementation of the reform plans, which began with the establishment of various working groups. Here, thousands of experts and scientists from all areas analyzed the state of society and discussed the economic changes needed.[7] The reform proposals were then tested for a period of six months in a series of small-scale experiments. Debated extensively both at the Sixth Congress of the SED in January 1963 as well as at the economic conference of the Central Committee, convened expressly for that purpose in June of the same year, NÖSPL finally became official policy in July 1963.

These plans, formulated at first by Ulbricht and his advisors (the "Group of Four") and then later discussed in public, proceeded from the premise that the economic system inherited from the Soviet Union suffered from serious shortcomings. "Appeals to morale and ideological consciousness" of the public could not, in the long run, mask deficiencies that stemmed from a basic disregard for material interests.[8] Ulbricht wanted to "move away from old dogmas" in his economic policies – not only from Stalinist orthodoxy but from the homemade version of GDR doctrinairism as well, both of which had stultified and damaged the economy.[9] Ulbricht's goal was the development of a national economic approach that would combine principles of economic planning with market-oriented strategies. By harmonizing social and personal interests, Ulbricht hoped to release forces within socialist society that would result in a faster and yet more balanced development than was possible in capitalist societies, which Marxism-Leninism saw as being primarily motivated by the search for maximum profit.

Several of these measures sought to increase production. These included a reduction of centralized economic planning; more independence for factories; a greater regard for economic criteria (such as value, currency-to-goods relationships, the market); and the application of so-called "economic levers" – monetary stimuli for both enterprises and workers in the form of profits, costs, bonus incentives, and wage differentials. Despite many inconsistencies, NÖSPL achieved many of its goals. Fundamentally, however, the plan represented a half-hearted attempt to turn back the clock and counter trends originating in 1945 that had reduced the influence of such economic factors as markets and currencies. Reforms were intended either to reverse these trends entirely, or to reintroduce market mechanisms on a new, social basis.

Rainer Lepsius has accurately depicted the bureaucratic character of the GDR in the 1970s and 1980s.[10] But it is important to note that there were also attempts to achieve more flexibility and move away from the closed "autarchic" economy of the GDR and to make advances towards the international market during the seventies. This was the aim of the reform of industrial prices[11] initiated in three different phases from 1964 to 1967. If Ulbricht had had his way, this reform would have led to a transition towards a "system of flexible prices" for industrial and economic goods as well as for service industries in 1969. The reforms also originally intended to grant different enterprises more freedom in determining how their profits should be invested; there was even some talk of eliminating inefficient enterprises altogether. In this light, Lepsius' claim that the GDR was marked by a lack of modernity remains open to question.

Even at the early stages of economic reform, it became clear that modifications in planning and management or the introduction of mechanical stimuli would be insufficient to increase productivity. The "human factor" had to be addressed and supported in other ways than just as a productive force. The January 1963 SED Party Congress therefore declared the "Education of Citizens of the Socialist Epoch" as another main goal, complementing material–technical and economic tasks. While the SED did not completely abandon its claims to political, ideological, and moral education of GDR citizens, it did modify its reform–pedagogical goals somewhat. In the face of the "scientific–technical revolution," levels of education and the "creativity of man" were therefore granted more significance.

The "new socialist man" was to be "a competent, well-educated personality who structures his life consciously and participates creatively in the development of our socialist democracy."[12] Criteria for the development of an appropriate consciousness were more than ever based on work: the "new man" was to be characterized by a strong work ethic, a desire to produce quality goods, a spirit of collectivism, and an "unflagging desire to learn." In addition, ideological principles such as "socialist patriotism" and internationalism or a "socialist attitude towards work and social property" continued to be emphasized as before. The SED leadership hoped to reach its pedagogical goals through a socialist reform of the educational system. It advocated the creation of a unified system that included kindergartens, universities, job training, and adult education, which remained in place until the demise of the GDR.

While the economy could be adjusted by the introduction of new mechanisms and economic instruments of control, changes in the nonmaterial world were much more dependent on an open discussion of the discrepancies between ideological claims and social realities. Ulbricht's ability to learn from and adapt to changing circumstances is demonstrated by his realization of the need for change, and attempts to use his authority to achieve it, in the early 1960s. This led, in the first half of the decade, to fitful attempts at liberalization, particularly in the area of cultural and youth policies, which allowed some room for individuality and for a critical appreciation of social problems. The youth communiqué,[13] released by the Politburo in September 1963 after months of intense debate, is especially important in this context. After numerous failed attempts by Ulbricht to prod Erich Honecker, the party member responsible for youth questions, toward a more flexible stance on policy questions, he dissolved the Politburo's Youth Commission and called a new committee into existence. He gave an "outsider," Kurt Turba,[14] leadership of this Commission, and asked him to appoint others from different organizations and institutions who would formulate a new youth policy.

This political change of course found expression in the youth communiqué. The declaration had significance beyond the narrow range of youth policy because it sought a broad transformation of the political and intellectual atmosphere of the GDR. Ulbricht knew from years of political experience that any attempt to solve social problems with administrative measures alone was doomed to failure. He attributed the stalemate in his reform program to bloated bureaucracy and believed that further progress would not be possible "without a broad discussion" in public. "The transformation cuts so deeply in society that it cannot be achieved by directives from above. And if these problems do not cause pain, there is no reason to discuss them. One thing has to be clear: what is at stake is a complete transformation, and not a mere correction!...After reading this communiqué, the worst bureaucrat must be moved to admit: 'Dammit, things are really going to have to change now.'"

The judicial ordinance released by the Ulbricht-led Council of State on 4 April 1963 should also be seen within this framework of attempted liberalization. It laid the foundation for the third reform of the judiciary which established social courts and led to a reformulation of the penal code,[15] as well as the passing of new laws (such as the Family Code of 1965). These and other measures resulted in a certain loosening of the dictatorship. As a corollary to the economic reforms, these legislative measures were designed to win public support for modernization measures and for increases in productivity. Unlike Krushschev's "thaw" or later Czechoslovakian visions of a "democratic socialism" and "socialism with a human face," the Ulbricht leadership did not want to allow a critical confrontation with the Soviet past, and was instead intent on maintaining the party's control. Its goal was not democratization in a Western sense; it intended merely to expand forms of participation in the party-controlled "socialist democracy" that was fundamentally different from bourgeois forms of democracy.

Ulbricht's goals to reform the party, which drew on Krushchev's measures, were also part of his plans for economic reform and liberalization. The party apparatus and most of the significant mass organizations were restructured along "production principles." while the authority of the main party apparatus – especially of the Secretaries and their divisions – was reduced at all levels.[16] The Politburo and other central party organs retained responsibility for "basic questions," while all other decisions were to be passed on to expert committees or panels. Party work was divided into different sections that addressed specific areas of social life and placed under special committees or bureaus that acted, for the most part, independently.[17] Specialists, rather than party hard-liners, increasingly received the opportunity to rise to positions of responsibility. During the reform era, hundreds of guests were often invited to attend the full meetings of the Central Committee and the Council of State, where they could openly voice their opinions. Party committees also increasingly included scientists and experts in decision-making processes.

Thus there is considerable evidence of a transformation within the SED regime towards what P. C. Ludz described in 1968 as "consultative authoritarianism."[18] Ludz, however, not only overemphasized the lasting effect of these developments, but he also simultaneously misjudged what he deemed the system's "long-term inability to resist the principles of participation" that resulted from the technical–economic constraints of a modern industrial society. Yet conservative elements within the system (and more specifically, the party's aspirations to maintain uniform and total control) proved to be much stronger than any attempts at modernization or reform. Even during the reform era, any shift toward "consultative authoritarianism" was countered by a trend towards "one man rule," typical of totalitarian regimes.

Ludz's second thesis regarding the rise of a "counter-elite," though convincing in some respects, misses the mark in others. He fails to prove, for example, that the political transformations occurring at the beginning of the 1960s resulted from pressures of a rising "counter-elite" that would oppose Ulbricht's ruling "clique." Conceptualizing the SED as two competing elite groups of "old cadres" and "technocrats" places too much emphasis on those elements that divided them, such as differing levels of education, while overlooking similarities and common traits, such as shared ideologies and political goals. Ludz's elite categories, then, do not adequately explain the political groupings in the GDR.

Ludz's contention that a "counter-elite" would win power and influence within the SED was unrealistic in 1968, when his work was published. It awakened false hopes for a convergence of industrial societies in East and West. In addition, the concept of a "counter-elite," based as it was on sociological categories, could not account for important aspects of the political system, such as the direct and indirect influence of the Soviet Union, the political organization of the GDR, and concrete, specific actions of the SED.

Still, one might, under certain circumstances, speak of the existence of a "strategic clique" and an "institutionalized counter-elite" within the SED leadership. However, I would define these two groups in a different way – namely in complete opposition to Ludz's terms. The "strategic clique" around Ulbricht consisted of those scientists and experts organized outside the traditional structures of the Soviet model. They met in small, informal circles, such as the Group of Four, or in working groups, or within special commissions or offices. After 1966 Ulbricht formalized this elite by creating a "strategic working group" directly under his authority which sought alternative solutions to the inefficient socialist system based on the Soviet model, and formed future visions that would address its shortcomings. The opposition to this group, the "institutionalized counter-elite," was comprised of anti-reform party members and bureaucrats who, in seeking to maintain their traditional positions of power, hindered or undermined the transformation process.

Honecker's Hardliner Backlash

In spite of the limited nature of the changes, these reform processes threatened to undermine the supremacy of the SED. Reform opponents around Honecker had to fear that they would be overtaken by the dynamic forces unleashed in the economy and society. They associated the decentralization that resulted from the introduction of the "production principle" with threats to the "unity of the party" – its ideological foundation and uniformity. In addition, they were smarting from their own loss of power, since important decision-making responsibilities had been passed on to the newly created expert panels. The original leadership offices of the party, the SED secretariats, were in danger of becoming entirely superfluous. Those functionaries, without specific expertise, who could previously justify their positions by pointing to years of party service, could no longer be assured of maintaining them. It is, therefore, not surprising that Honecker and other secretaries, as well as many others within the professional party apparatus, had a vested interest in hindering the reforms. At first this opposition was covert, occurring under the pretense of better serving the reform process itself. Objectively, however, it worked against the spirit of the reforms.

In the immediate aftermath of Krushchev's fall, anti-reform forces within the party and state apparatus (which, like all bureaucracies, were resistant to change) began to form under the direction of the Honecker-led Central Committee Secretariat. The fact that an oppositional course appeared so quickly after the tentative reforms in party structure, youth policies, and cultural and intellectual affairs, cannot be sufficiently explained by pointing to the inertia of a bureaucracy bent on resisting challenges to its rule. This resistance stemmed rather from power considerations and from an aversion to liberalization and its champions. On the one hand, resistance was directed at Ulbricht's men, such as Kurt Turba or Erich Apel, who had risen to the top as "outsiders" because of their professional qualifications or creativity, and were particularly enthusiastic about the new reform course. On the other hand, the bureaucracy's opposition was aimed at those segments of society supportive of the reform measures, especially scientific and artistic elites, as well as students.

The chemist Robert Havemann and the sculptor Fritz Cremer – both university professors – had used the new opportunities for discussion and raised eyebrows by asking critical questions in public. Honecker, Hager, and other functionaries saw this as a direct attack on the ideological monopoly of the SED leadership. They met this "transgression" with individual reprisals and with more general demands for a return to the "political–ideological directives" they felt had been neglected since the beginning of the reforms in 1963, and that had not been given their due, proper to Marxist–Leninist parties. This neglect was also traced to perceived "negative" trends within the youth movement and cultural life in general. In this area the limited liberalizing and democratizing trends had led to some unusual developments.

Newspapers and the youth radio station "DT 1964"[19] openly aired grievances, while criticizing leaders for their shortcomings or unwillingness to respond to reform suggestions. Amateur bands had sprung up in support of tolerance and the promotion of the interests and needs of young people. The international beat movement hit the GDR in full force, and many East German youths began to bring their looks in line with their Western idols. Many members of Honecker's founding generation within the FDJ looked at the new lifestyles of the younger generation with increasing incomprehension. They were disturbed by the loud, rhythmic music, by the critical distance from elders signaled by hair and clothing style choices, and by open talk of feelings and sexuality. They feared that the GDR's youth had been exposed to and seduced by the "American way of life," and were under the sway of "Western un-culture" and "decadence." Since reform opponents could not attack Ulbricht's party line openly, they had to find other scapegoats for the perceived "infiltration" of the "class enemy" into the safe world of socialist society. These were found in Turba's youth commission, and in the Ministry of Culture, in TV and the DEFA film studios, where functionaries, directors, authors, and screenwriters had embraced Ulbricht's declarations.

At the end of 1965, the Honecker-led wing succeeded in forcing through a first correction to Ulbricht's reform course with the help of methods peculiar to dictatorial bureaucracies, such as pointing out its dangers to the SED's monopoly of power. The liberalizing trends in cultural and intellectual life were rigorously curtailed, and the reform of the party was silently canceled, while the economic reforms were carried out in modified form under even more centralizing tendencies. Ulbricht tolerated these modifications after the party bureaucracy underscored the dangers of the new course by citing examples of transgressions, since he placed the monopoly of the party and his own personal political power above all other goals. In addition, concessions in the first two areas seemed to ensure the continuation of his planned economic reforms, which were very dear to him. Closing the economic gap with the highly developed industrial states, particularly the Federal Republic, remained for Ulbricht the foundation of all other developments. In contrast to the "reform communists," he considered the economic strength and resultant political stability of the state a necessary prerequisite for "democratization." Political freedoms, which might lead to a lessening of the party's power, could not be introduced due to the GDR's backwardness in comparison to the West. Such a course, Ulbricht believed, would lead to the end of socialism and the socialist dictatorship.

This shift of power and ideology within the GDR was accompanied and furthered by similar trends in the Soviet Union. In Leonid Brezhnev, SED leaders found a politician who came, like Honecker, from the party bureaucracy and who belonged to the military elite. At first his leadership led to a worsening of the foreign policy conditions needed for a continuation of economic reforms in the GDR. The new CPSU leaders looked to the support of their allies – particularly the relatively advanced economy of the GDR – to assist them in overcoming the crisis situation in the Soviet Union, and in forcing a new arms race. These demands undercut Ulbricht's plans to translate profits harvested in the course of reforms into benefits for workers. The slowness of the reforms in showing positive results also strengthened the hand of the dogmatic orthodox opponents, who could block the process of reform with increasing impunity. Rather than having to admit that the reform process had been only half-heartedly pursued, they could ascribe the lack of success to the reforms themselves.

The December 1965 plenary meeting which resulted in a cultural crackdown, a reversal of party reform measures, and a weakening of economic reforms, was the first real defeat of the Ulbricht-led reform wing. The unstable power relations within the SED led to a sort of "dual power" of the two wings, with Ulbricht on one side and Honecker and Stoph on the other. Ulbricht defined his role in terms of a visionary father who was working for the good of his country, and with the help of his advisors, he developed "strategies" or new approaches that were often quite far removed from reality. With the power of his office and the support of numerous other anti-reform bureaucrats behind him, Honecker opposed these policies by either ignoring or misapplying them. When Ulbricht finally became aware of this tactic in June–July 1970, he released Honecker from his offices and announced further personnel changes for the Eighth Party Congress.

After his dismissal, however, Honecker turned to the Soviet Union for support, and forced Ulbricht to revoke his earlier decision. In this endeavor he was able to use to his advantage the fact that Ulbricht had not only been trying to emancipate the GDR from the USSR domestically, but also to develop initiatives in foreign policy, especially regarding the question of the two German states. These challenged Brezhnev's new, ambitious plans for the Soviet Union within the Eastern Bloc. Ulbricht had wanted to reach an understanding between the FRG and the GDR without outside assistance. He was therefore more ready to make concessions to Bonn than the "security fanatics" in the SED and KPD were willing to allow. Honecker played to fears within Brezhnev's circle that an unstable situation similar to what had developed in Czechoslovakia would result if Ulbricht, who underestimated the existential dangers of a German–German rapprochement, continued to make concessions to "social democracy" and the Brandt government in the West. Honecker's intrigues hindered an understanding between the two Germanys and strengthened Soviet desires to make him Ulbricht's successor. The CPSU leadership in Moscow preferred a weak Honecker, dependent on their support, to an independent and confident Ulbricht. In addition, Honecker's policy of distancing the GDR from the West and his willingness to toe the Soviet line naturally spoke to Soviet interests. Therefore, the USSR supported the attempts of Honecker, Stoph, Axen, Verner, and others to slow down negotiations.

The undemocratic self-definitions of both the SED and the CPSU ruled out any public discussion of political alternatives. Since ruling groups within the two parties were legitimized through their own claims to infallibility, any attempt at discussing "both lines" or fronts would have damaged the "charisma of office" in a Weberian sense and might have had a destabilizing effect on the party itself and the system as a whole. Power struggles therefore had to be carried out behind the scenes. While Ulbricht used his authority to make idiosyncratic cadre appointments and created personal "staff organs" alongside regular structures, his opponents used the instruments and mechanisms of the established party apparatus to fight their battles. Their methods included intentionally misinterpreting directives, exaggerating unwelcome decisions, using Soviet pressure, or engaging in political intrigues and denunciations.

Ultimately the GDR had a subordinate position within the Soviet-led "socialist system," and was fundamentally dependent on the Soviet Union for its very existence. Therefore, it is not surprising that those groups within the SED that would carry the day were those most willing to promise obedience to leaders in Moscow, and more disposed to abandon policies that threatened to be potentially destabilizing in favor of toeing the Soviet line. The attempted reforms remained just that – a mere attempt at change that did not lead to a qualitative transformation of the system.

Blockages of Reform and Modernity

This evidence raises the broader theoretical question: Were communist dictatorships of the Soviet type in general, and the GDR in particular, capable of reform at all? There certainly was no dearth of attempted reforms in various East Bloc nations. Stalin's death led at first to attempts to initiate change at the political level. These were limited to self-criticisms by those in power, which were represented as transgressions of certain individuals and attributed to Stalinist crimes or dictatorial excesses that had come about as a result of intense class warfare. Later on, disillusionment and bottled-up frustrations led to spontaneous mass movements, such as in the GDR in 1953, Poland or Hungary in 1956. Because of their broad base support, Soviet leaders interpreted these mass protests as destabilizing threats to their own power, and accordingly, bloodily repressed them.

The leadership around Ulbricht had "learned" from these lessons and tried another path in the 1960s. They wanted to address deficiencies within the system with a "reform from above," while continuing to "move forward" without a potentially threatening discussion of past mistakes. At the center of their plans was the creation of an effective and functional economic system, which they could not initiate without first carrying out limited policies of liberalization and broadening participation. Although the East German reform program at no time seriously threatened the power of the SED (in contrast to the reforms carried out in Czechoslovakia),[20] its aims were never fully realized. This was less due to Soviet pressure than to opposition within the SED's own ranks which sought to regain lost authority and influence within the party and artificially exaggerated outside threats to achieve their aims. The fact that even the more technocratic developments could not be sustained seems to be proof that Soviet-style socialism was generally incapable of reform.

A lasting reform of socialism could have been possible – if at all – only in conjunction with the Soviet Union. The Brezhnev leadership, however, was neither willing nor ready for such a step. Brezhnev and his advisors had other goals for the USSR and its satellites: rearmament to achieve military superiority over the West, stabilization within the Soviet Union and thereby a consolidation of the party's power and a return to foreign policy predominance within the Eastern bloc.

Could or should the GDR be considered a "modern dictatorship"? The adjective "modern" and the even more diffuse term "modernization" are fraught with problems similar to those related to the concept of reform. Both are generally used in a normative context and applied exclusively to liberal democratic societies. If they are not restricted to certain political or social systems, they require new criteria in order to be applied. Besides those factors named by Jürgen Kocka[21] that distinguish modern dictatorships from older ones, some additional aspects seem relevant for modern dictatorial rule. The work of Mitchell G. Ash and others suggests that all varieties of state socialism contain "some basic components of the Enlightenment at least in their programmatic aspects."[22] Peter Sloterdijk's conclusions in his critique of modernity – that Marxism is part of a deluded modern dream of the endless possibilities of human control and exploitation of the material world – are convincing.[23] Hopes for liberation by transforming human circumstances, as well as an unshakable belief in progress, were characteristic of modernity in general.

The Ulbricht leadership in the 1960s combined its hopes for the creation of a "new socialist man" with an unswerving faith in the benefits of science and technology and the ability to plan production for reaching the highest levels of scientific and technological innovation. They were convinced of their ability to achieve their goals and hoped that the concentration of funds and materials in specific areas of the economy would result in "breakthroughs" that would function as "engines" of further development. By tapping into international trends and introducing them in the GDR, Ulbricht hoped to wean his country, with its lack of raw materials, from economic dependence on the Soviet Union and to transform it into a "high-tech" nation. At the same time, the Ulbricht leadership attempted – with an intensity unmatched before or since – to employ new scientific methods (such as cybernetics, heuristics, principles of scientific management, and computer technology) for its own rule. These scientific–technological delusions culminated in plans for a self-regulating "Economic System of Socialism."

Not only in programmatics and claims, but also in reality, a veritable push towards modernization can be observed during the 1960s. High accumulation rates in industry led to increased productivity and economic strength. But the GDR could not take full advantage of these advances, since the Soviet Union received their benefits by forcing the GDR into unfavorable trade and economic agreements, investing in new raw material storage facilities in the USSR, and buying increasingly expensive Soviet military equipment. Whatever advantages might have resulted from these modernizing trends were further weakened by Honecker's discontinuation of many new developments, ruinous social and credit policies in the 1970s.

The question raised by Konrad Jarausch as to whether there were phases within the SED dictatorship in which modernization was stronger than in others should be answered with a resounding yes for the 1960s. Although the designation "modern dictatorship" might be justified, when qualified as outlined above, it is also important to stress that modernization in this period was blocked by political interests – both internally and externally. Perhaps it would be most fitting to speak of the GDR dictatorship in terms of a failed attempt at an alternative modernity. In any case, the 1960s were a period marked by attempts to reach the levels of modernization in the West by different organizational means and on a different social basis.

Notes

1. Monika Kaiser, *Machtwechsel von Ulbricht zu Honecker. Funktionsmechanismen der SED-Diktatur in Konfliktsituationen 1962 bis 1972* (Berlin, 1997). For the subsequent facts and arguments see the extensive notes and sources of that monograph.
2. In Germany, proposed changes in health, pensions, taxes, or spelling have been debated so intensely that the word "reform" has lost almost all positive connotations.
3. Christoph Royen, *Reform und Wandel in Osteuropa. Erfahrungen und Aussichten* (Ebenhausen, 1987), 43–44.
4. *Brockhaus Enzyklopädie*, 19th rev. ed. (Mannheim, 1992), 18, 178.
5. Ibid.
6. One principle of Marxist–Leninist thought was that increases in work productivity were decisive for any victory or superiority of the new over older forms of society. In numerous internal conversations, Ulbricht estimated the FRG led the GDR by 20–25 percent.
7. For example, one central working group with 1,200 members under the leadership of Finance Minister Willy Rumpf was organized into 230 subgroups to formulate suggestions for price reform, the implementation of economic incentives, and factory investments.
8. Walter Ulbricht, "Das Programm des Sozialismus und die geschichtliche Aufgabe der Sozialistischen Einheitspartei Deutschlands," *Protokoll des VI. Parteitages*, vol. 1, 100.
9. See "Antwort auf Fragen der Delegierten," *Neues Deutschland*, 15 December 1962, 3. Ulbricht explained his program by referring to dogmas such as price stability or the so-called tonnage ideology, which valued quantitative over qualitative production criteria.
10. See M. Rainer Lepsius' keynote lecture at the Potsdam conference, December 1997.
11. In the first phase, all basic materials were revalued so as to allow a more exact accounting of production costs, while further steps would eventually approach real values.
12. "Programm der SED," *Protokoll des VI. Parteitages*, vol. 4, 376.
13. For the lively text, see "Der Jugend Vertrauen und Verantwortung. Kommuniqué des Politbüros des Zentralkomitees der SED zu Problemen der Jugend in der DDR," *Neues Deutschland*, 21 September 1963, 1–3. Reprinted in the brochure *Jugend von heute – Hausherren von morgen* (Berlin, 1963), 5–33.
14. After the June 1953 uprising, Turba had to leave the Honecker-led apparatus of the Central Committee of the FDJ and was transferred to the student newspaper *FORUM*. He came to Ulbricht's attention through his willingness to discuss controversial topics as editor.
15. See Thomas Klein's arguments in the present volume.
16. While the Politburo existed as the most important leading body of the SED on the central level, the secretariats were responsible for decisions related to eco-

nomic questions and regional issues on all lower levels. A Secretariat existed next to the Politburo on the central level that led and controlled the secretariats at the local and regional levels of the SED. After the 1950s Ulbricht no longer actively served in this function and delegated the office to Honecker.

17. At the central, district, and regional level, the following offices were created: 1. Industry and construction, 2. Agriculture, 3. Ideology, 4. Propaganda, 5. Western contacts, 6. Women, 7. Youth and sports. At the central level there was an additional commission for foreign policy.

18. Peter Christain Ludz, *Parteielite im Wandel. Funktionsaufbau, Sozialstruktur und Ideologie der SED-Führung. Eine empirisch-systematische Untersuchung*, 3rd rev. ed. (Cologne, 1970).

19. The program was created by Turba after the 1964 meeting of youths from all over Germany and was noted for its critical, humorous commentary as well as its "hot" music.

20. The "Prague Spring" of 1968 was also put down by Soviet troops and other Warsaw Pact armies (but without East German or Rumanian troops) because the USSR feared that the political reforms would result in the end of the dictatorship in Czechoslovakia.

21. See chapter 1 of this volume.

22. Mitchell G. Ash, "Wissenschaft, Politik und Modernität in der DDR – Ansätze einer Neubetrachtung," in: *Wissenschaft und Politik – Genetik und Humangenetik in der DDR 1949–1989. Dokumentation zum Arbeitssymposium in Münster*, 15–18 March 1995, ed. Karin Weisemann, Peter Kröner, and Richard Toellner (Münster, 1997), 2.

23. Peter Sloterdijk, *Eurotaoismus. Zur Kritik der politischen Kynetik* (Frankfurt, 1989), 59–60.

CHAPTER 18

MOBILITY AND BLOCKAGE DURING THE 1970s

Ralph Jessen

All modern societies are characterized to some degree by the tension between the promise of equality and the reality of social inequality. Which forms and what degree of inequality are considered legitimate within a particular society have varied greatly throughout history. While the West German market society of the 1990s accepts disparities based on private property, professional qualifications or employment, it views as problematic attempts to limit opportunity according to sex, ethnicity, or religious beliefs. In the GDR, the relationship between claims to legitimacy and promises of equality was much closer. The SED dictatorship based its rule on an ideology that categorically rejected market- and property-based inequality. The state's claims to superiority over the West rested on the party's promise to remove the "historically superfluous" and "unjust inequalities" of capitalist class society. The SED glorified the GDR as an egalitarian and open society on the path towards a communist utopia. Testimonies of many GDR citizens underscore the fact that openness and mobility were not merely constructs of communist propaganda, since they describe the early years of the "workers' and farmers' state" as a phase of unexpected opportunity in a "post-revolutionary mobile society."[1]

In the following, the development of social mobility in the GDR will be examined under three different aspects. The first question concerns how effective the SED was in the shaping of East German society along dictatorial lines in order to win acceptance for its totalitarian regime. Was GDR society largely the result of dictatorial construction, or were there limits to control and signs of autonomous developments? The second question examines the close relationship between the postulate of social equality and SED claims to legitimacy and asks in what manner the development of social mobility influenced the stability or instability of the dictatorship. The third question addresses social mobility in general as an important indicator of modernity, and asks whether mobility in the GDR can be termed "modern," and whether the social evidence supports the term "modern dictatorship."[2]

Post-War Mobilization

The establishment of the SED regime, founding of the GDR and constitution of a new "socialist" society east of the Elbe led to a broad and far-reaching mobilization of East German society in the 1940s and 1950s. This politically initiated and ideologically legitimated transformation was intended as social foundation of party rule while at the same time fulfilling one of its main programmatic goals. Nevertheless, this development cannot be explained as a result of inner developments within the SBZ–GDR. The Nazi regime and the war had loosened old ties and hierarchies, dislocated large segments of the population, and radically redistributed and destroyed property – whether in the shape of anti-Semitic terror or damage caused by the war.[3] Allied decisions regarding the future of Germany and Europe and Soviet occupation policies contributed to these processes – although with other motives and in different ways.[4] Less obvious, but just as significant were the effects of the Cold War division on the structure of East German society and the resultant mobilization of the GDR's populace.

Leaving aside the long-term "pre-conditions" stemming from the Third Reich, at least five different yet interrelated causes for the unusual degree of mobility in East Germany can be distinguished: first, the defeat of the Nazi regime also destroyed and removed from power the old ruling class and political elites. Almost the entire political and military elite, large portions of the upper levels of the civil service, judicial officials, teachers, and university professors lost their positions after 1945. Even if many highly qualified personnel were re-instated into their old jobs in the following years, the purges in the immediate aftermath of defeat meant social degradation and downward social mobility for many. The vacant positions they left behind were either occupied by politically reliable individuals, or by those not openly associated with the Nazi regime. The end of the Second World War had a greater lasting effect on the old elite than the First World War – and particularly in the Soviet-occupied zone, the impact was wide-reaching and long-lasting.[5]

Second, private property lost much of its significance for the structuring of society.[6] Proprietors of landed estates had been completely dispossessed as early as the fall of 1945. By the end of that year 6,330 large holdings of more than 100 hectares and 8,332 smaller farms had been confiscated and their owners expelled. By 1949 this land had been redistributed to more than a half million small holders, who until 1960 led an insecure existence as "new settlers" and farmers, when they were replaced by collective farms founded under massive pressure from the state.[7] Industrial plants, mines, banks, and insurance companies were also nationalized step by step after 1945 – at first with the justification that such measures were aimed at Nazi profiteers and collaborators. By 1950, state-owned factories produced half of the net GNP; and by 1956 83 percent of all industrial workers were employed in state-owned plants. By the beginning of the 1970s, with the exception of small artisans' shops, private ownership had practically disappeared from the industrial sector.[8] The property-owning middle-classes, the "bourgeoisie," had ceased to exist.

Third, the foundation and extension of the SED party apparatus brought many people, who had previously had little chance of upward social mobility, into mid-level or higher positions of power. They were employed in the state administration, education, large organizations run by the party, the press, the state-planned economic administration, as well as the military. These positions in the party and administrative apparatus were filled largely by young men and women who often came from the lower classes. Many had no higher degrees, and only a few years of schooling in the state- or party-sponsored crash courses. There were numerous quick careers to the top, often accompanied by moves from one position to another.[9]

Fourth, since political loyalty and protection could provide no solid basis for an effective administration, the SED and its administrative apparatus began to establish various training and educational facilities in 1946. These provided the next generation of qualified experts, largely bypassing more traditional paths of professional training. While professional barriers were lowered, the autonomy of experts was limited and political control over career choices increased. In so-called "preparatory institutes" and "workers' and farmers' faculties" young workers or employees prepared for university studies. "New teachers' courses" and "peoples' judges' schools" were meant to fill positions vacated by the denazification of schools and the judiciary; "social science faculties" at universities and a newly founded Administrative Academy trained a younger generation of party and state functionaries; new Ph.D. programs taught politically trained scientists; and "special courses" prepared university professors of ideologically sensitive disciplines for future tasks. Apart from their educational aspects, all of these institutions served as sites of political training, selection, and social privilege – they were politically controlled training grounds.

Fifth, the fluidity of East German society in the 1940s and 1950s was accompanied by a high rate of geographical mobility, accompanied by both upwards and downwards movement. Two larger dimensions need to be distinguished within this process. On the one hand were the "resettlers," as they were referred to the in the SBZ–GDR (or the expellees, as they were called in the West) – those German minorities from Poland, Czechoslovakia, and other Eastern European states that were forced to leave their homes because of Allied directives. The SBZ took in 4.3 million expellees, making up 24.2 percent of the entire East German population.[10] Having left behind all of their belongings, their homes, livestock, and livelihoods, these individuals experienced grave dislocation and loss of social status. Yet for this very reason they also were a highly motivated segment of society.[11] In addition to these expellees from the Eastern areas of Germany, there were, on the other hand, refugees who fled the GDR over the open border to the West. Between 1950 and 1961, 3.8 million people took this path when the Wall was built.[12]

Although the combination of political, economic, and personal motives for flight was extremely complex, as were the consequences of such action, at least three connections between expellee mobility and social mobility can be distinguished. Because a large portion of the dispossessed propertied classes and both conservative and liberal functional elites turned to the West, the GDR was relieved of a potentially politically disruptive class. In effect, the dispossessed disappeared from society.[13] Because many who left were younger people likely to be more active, enterprising, and willing to take chances than their elders, the GDR lost a great amount of mental capital. But the chances of upward mobility increased for passive and mediocre individuals who stayed behind. Especially hard to weather was the loss of highly qualified experts. This forced the SED to intensify training and education of the next generation, which translated into increased mobility. In order to halt further emigration, the SED also paid more attention to the material and career interest of these groups, which slowed down the leveling of society.

The limits of the transformation process became most apparent in academic professions farthest from the political arena – such as the natural sciences, engineering, and medicine.[14] Because the knowledge of these professionals was essential and could not be "dispossessed" as factories had been, the SED had to accept them, for better or worse, in spite of the fact that they might have been opposed to the regime, based on their origins, habitus, and political beliefs. In fact, because every scientist lost to the West was seen as part of a larger brain drain, the party used every means at its disposal to keep such professionals – from monetary incentives to honorary titles. The influential group of university professors, especially, made up a traditionalist block that slowed down and distorted the general transformation of society.

In 1962, only 13.3 percent of professors in the natural sciences came from working class families; in the technical sciences, this number was 13.2 percent; in the medical sciences only 5.1 percent were of proletarian origin. Such numbers were far removed from the goal of "proportional recruitment" relative to the structure of society as a whole. Only 22.5 percent of the natural scientists belonged to the SED, while 31.7 percent had previously been members of the NSDAP. Among engineers, there were 27.6 percent SED members as opposed to 37.4 percent one-time Nazis, and in the medical sciences the distribution was 25.3 percent to 31.3 percent.[15] The limits of change were also evident in the continued female underrepresentation in the workforce. Despite their increased numbers at the university level, women had to content themselves with lower- and mid-level positions.[16]

In spite of these limitations, the SBZ–GDR of the late 1940s and 1950s remained a society mobilized by the results of war and the communist revolution. At greatest risk of downward mobility were private entrepreneurs and high-level officials of the old regime. Those in the best position to maintain their status were members of the indispensable technical, scientific, or medical professions.[17] The best chance for upward mobility was enjoyed by young adults from the working class, who were willing to conform to the party's demands for loyalty and could take advantage of the numerous possibilities for advancement. The politics of dictatorial counter-privilege can be seen most clearly in the universities, where the numbers of students from the working classes increased from 4 percent in 1945–46 to 53 percent in 1958.[18] The basis of social inequality had been fundamentally altered: private property lost its significance, cultural capital was marginalized, while expertise retained its relatively high value. Membership in the lower social classes could be used as social capital to provide entrance into the party apparatus.

Above all, political loyalty – in the form of party membership or positions of responsibility – became a prerequisite for upward mobility. Despite the legend of the GDR's "good beginnings" of a society on the way to a more just world, it should be emphasized that mobility for some segments of the populace did not only occur at the cost of the middle classes who had been dispossessed, degraded, and discriminated against, but also went hand in hand with the very construction of the dictatorship. Those who profited from the openness and opportunities of the early years had contradictory experiences. While they could enjoy possibilities previously denied them, they discovered how much their lives and careers depended on their political behavior, and quickly learned that political loyalty was the price of advancement. Much speaks for the argument that it was this "mobile generation" that had the greatest loyalty to the SED state.[19]

The Blockage of Mobility

In the 1960s, the patterns of mobility within East German society began to change considerably. The dynamic associated with the first decade slowed markedly. As this trend continued during the following decades, the GDR became a stagnating society in two different ways. It was blocked from without by the Wall, and blocked from within by a frozen, rigid social structure. Before 1989 Western observers could only make out the outlines of this development, because the SED buried the results of studies carried out by East German sociologists. Until the very last moment of its existence, the SED state maintained the myth of a just, open society. Scholars are now able to describe in some detail the processes by which the "channels of mobility"[20] were closed. The most thorough examinations of social mobility in the GDR have been carried out in the past few years at the Max Planck Institute for Educational Research in Berlin, as part of the research project "Individual lives and historical change in the GDR." Karl-Ulrich Mayer, Heike Solga and others have published numerous works on the subject.[21] Their results, which are based on representative and retrospective surveys, show that social mobility had come to an almost complete halt at all levels by the 1970s. Social mobility between the generations was also on the wane.

The "socialist service class," which included not only top party functionaries, but all party cadres at mid-level managerial positions, and experts such as teachers, doctors, and engineers,[22] increasingly recruited new members from within its own ranks. If one excludes farmers from the analysis, this service class was the most open of all groups during the 1950s, while in the 1980s it had become the most closed. In the 1950s, sons of working class families had the same chance of mobility as those belonging to the service class. In the 1960s and 1970s, the chances for sons of functionaries tripled, and in the 1980s, they were seven to eight times higher than working class sons.[23] A look at intragenerational mobility reveals similar results, with career opportunities declining with every successive generation. While those born around 1930 had the best chances for a rapid career, those born around 1960 were greeted with closed doors and forced to make do with subordinate positions.[24] Marriage behavior also reveals similar tendencies. Daughters from families of the functionary class born after 1950 were five times more likely to marry someone from the service class than daughters from other groups.[25]

Finally, these developments can be seen most clearly in the dramatic transformation in the social composition of universities. While the number of working class students fell from 53 percent in 1958 to 7–10 percent at the end of the 1980s, the number of students from families of the "intelligentsia" rose during the same period from 14 percent to 78 percent. The universities had returned to self-recruitment of the educated classes.[26]

According to both external and internal reports, the actual social makeup of the universities was veiled by an arbitrary definition of the category "working class child," so that the SED could maintain the myth of equal educational opportunities for all. A 1976 directive regarding the social origins of applicants included as "workers" those individuals active in transport and the media, as well as the service industry; young people raised in state homes; recognized victims of the Nazi regime and their children; full-time political employees of the state; officials of the SED and the mass organizations; and career soldiers and officers. Thus the statistical category "worker" was opened wide for all members of the political service class.[27]

Increased social closure was accompanied by certain, if limited, variations in opportunities. Higher social groups within the "intelligentsia" and the functionary class had above-average incomes, more savings, and comfortable furnishings; they could generally afford a car and a telephone and could participate more frequently in elite cultural activities such as visits to the theater or museums. But other indicators of living standards had little or no relationship to social position. Whether or not someone had Western currency, owned an apartment or a weekend house, had a larger flat or access to expensive or "exotic" consumer goods such as televisions, refrigerators, computers, dishwashers, or video recorders was relatively independent of one's position within the social hierarchy.

Opportunities such as travel to or contacts with the West were also generally evenly distributed.[28] At least in regards to consumption, social inequalities had few dramatic consequences. In sum, the result was a paradoxical society, characterized both by static hierarchies and egalitarianism.

Why did this remarkable reversal of the trend towards opening occur? Various causes must be considered. For instance, one important element was the demographic transformation associated with the previous phase of increased mobility. The revolutionary break of 1945 removed old elites from power, and the expansion of the party and state apparatus meant that large numbers of the generational cohort born around 1930 were placed in positions of power. The new service class was therefore extremely homogenous – in its loyalty to the SED, social origins, and age structure. Once in power, these new office holders displayed great tenacity in maintaining their positions, even when it became obvious in later years that younger competitors were more qualified. The extreme closure of the 1970s and 1980s was also in some measure a demographic echo of the previous opening of society and the resultant asymmetries in the age structure of cadres. In this sense one could argue that the politically motivated mobility of the Ulbricht years led perforce to the social stagnation of the Honecker era.

The closing of the border in 1961 with the erection of the Wall also played an important role in this development. The GDR lost on average 320,000 – mostly young – people per year between 1950 and 1961; the number had sunk to only 27,000 per year between 1962 and 1969 – mostly retirement age people.[29] This meant that the demand created by abandoned positions in the economy and administration markedly declined, but also that competition between possible applicants for these positions increased as the Western market became closed to them. In this competition, individuals of the educated classes with personal connections to the functionary elites fared better. Whereas the years before 1961 saw increased geographical mobility linked to intense social mobility, the Wall became a real hurdle to upward movement within society.

Less spectacular than the Wall, but probably more significant for the social stagnation of East German society was the fact that the socialist functionary class had reached its limit of growth by the end of the 1960s. During the latter part of the Ulbricht era, GDR leaders had set their hopes on the "scientific–technical revolution" that would spur expansion in research and science. Students increased by 61 percent between 1960 and 1972. But the transition to the Honecker era was accompanied by different priorities. Instead of vague technical utopias, the regime put its money into practical politics of social policy and housing. The demand for scientific and technical experts waned; their positions were frozen or abolished. The number of university students decreased by 20 percent between 1970 and 1976 and remained at that level.[30] Whereas in West Germany the universities saw incredible expansion and experienced a process of social opening, universities in the East shrank and closed their doors to outsiders.[31]

Educational policies of the 1970s had similar effects. Step by step officials canceled various measures aimed at including the underprivileged in schools and universities, after having successfully recruited the first loyal functionary generation. Performance became a more important element in education. While workers' and farmers' faculties were closed, students with special abilities were placed in advanced courses and special schools. Because the uniform school system guaranteed equal chances for children from all social strata, compensatory measures aimed at helping less advantaged groups no longer played a significant role. Educational policies bid a silent farewell to earlier models aimed at creating a student body composed of all social groups. Inequalities in educational opportunities based on different socialization were no longer addressed politically, and became more pronounced – children from the educated classes brought with them a different cultural background, other motivational resources, and the support of their parents. Their increased number in subsequent cadres became less problematic for the SED, as more such children came from politically correct families of the socialist intelligentsia.[32]

Positions were, nonetheless, not awarded on the basis of merit, because careers became increasingly dependent on political criteria. Particularly in the face of shortages, political capital (such as party membership or functionary duties) became an important criterion for selection.[33] In the 1970s and 1980s, those with the best chances of entering the service class were themselves children of functionaries, or individuals who had already proven their loyalty to the system by entering the party or assuming duties at an earlier age. While in the 1950s, proximity to the system had compensatory effects for upwardly mobile workers, in the last two decades of SED rule it became the leading selection criterion for aspirants from the service class.[34] Under these circumstances it is not surprising to note that the percentage of loyal service class members in the Max Planck study stayed constant at 55 percent, while the number of loyal workers decreased from 27 percent in the group born around 1930 to 16 percent in the group born in 1960.[35] It also should be noted that career advancement did not always occur in the open. Backstage politicking and personal connections aided system insiders.[36] While political reduction of the performance principle as a criterion for the academic professions worked to the advantage of lower social groups in the early years, it became an obstacle to mobility in the last two decades of SED rule.

Finally, it was not only the presence of differential chances but also the selective willingness to take advantage of such opportunities that determined upward mobility. Many GDR citizens were wary of assuming higher positions. Low rates of mobility therefore also reflected an unwillingness to be upwardly mobile. This had many causes – higher positions often brought little prestige and many problems. In positions without any real autonomy, office-holders found themselves sandwiched between unpredictable authorities and unaccommodating subjects. Also, gestures of political conformity were not willingly performed by all. Official support for the social prestige of workers compared to the precarious prestige of the "intelligentsia" also did not necessarily make upward mobility an attractive goal.[37]

Upward mobility also meant less in the face of relatively equal incomes, little chance for the purchase of consumer goods, and the leveling effects of social policies which reduced any chance of raising one's living standards. Instead, due to increased political controls, functionaries were threatened with the loss of private contacts in the West and the DM shadow economy. Lower social groups felt that the costs of a move up were hardly worth the effort, especially when not connected to increased material benefits, while those milieus near the party and educational elites were generally not motivated by material concerns.[38] In this area as well it becomes evident that the homogenizing policies of the "welfare dictatorship"[39] – in the form of leveled living standards – unwittingly resulted in social differentiation, since different milieus reacted in quite different ways to the politically given opportunities.

(Im-)Mobility and (Un-)Modernity

What significance do these results have for the picture of the GDR as a "modern dictatorship," and how are they related to the problems of the SED regime's relative stability? It is hard to reach clear conclusions, since the processes of social mobility and blockage described above were only one aspect of East German society and their significance is difficult to isolate from all the other factors at work. The following points are meant to serve as interpretative suggestions, without promising to provide a complete explanation of this phenomenon.

First, this development cannot be described as "modern" in the manner suggested by functionalist theories of inequality. In the 1980s some educational sociologists, such as Manfred Lötsch, argued that social inequalities lead to greater performance, and therefore more economic efficiency.[40] Self-recruitment within the intelligentsia, therefore, made good sense, because certain cultural resources related to performance could be passed on internally. By urging that performance be rewarded, these sociologists demanded a more differentiated pay structure that would favor experts and decision-makers in positions of power. With this theory, Lötsch and others turned against what they perceived as a harmful downward leveling of society and economy in the GDR. They interpreted this excess of equality as one of the causes for the chronic lack of innovation and performance in the GDR economy.[41]

According to this theory, it might seem that the GDR was on the right track after the 1970s. Western commentators have also interpreted these weak signs of declining mobility as growing modernization and convergence. They meant that such developments translated into "a clear orientation towards the efficiency criteria of industrial societies and a 'politics of modernization,'" that would "further analogies with developments in West German society."[42] There is, however, little evidence for such a modernization. There is no proof that the closed society of the 1970s and 1980s was becoming more technologically or economically efficient, in fact, the opposite was true. Even if privilege no longer weighed more heavily than performance-based criteria, individuals were still under such pressure of political conformity that it is impossible to speak of the triumph of meritocracy. GDR society became less equal, but not more meritocratic.

The evidence presented above naturally raises the question of the character of GDR society anew. Was East Germany really an undifferentiated, "classless" society, as Sigrid Meuschel claimed?[43] Or did the "closing of channels of upward mobility" mirror the formation of the functionary elites as a new class? This is the argument put forward by Heike Solga of the Max Planck Institute: "There can be very little doubt...about the existence of classes as social constructions that differ according to opportunities and self-perceptions."[44] Though plausible before the backdrop of decreasing mobility, this interpretation suffers from a purely economic definition of class. In the tradition of leftist critiques of real-existing socialism she argues that even under socialism class was based on the unequal distribution of "property." Property is defined here as control of the means of production and resultant goods, since the legal fiction of the "people's property" said little about true conditions. Solga argues that class membership in state socialism was based on the amount of control any given individual possessed over these resources.[45]

This argument is not persuasive either, since the idea of a propertied class rests on the supposition that inequality is a result of the economic processes of the market. Economic classes are market classes. But state socialist societies were characterized by their very lack of market mechanisms. The socially structured power of the market and property was overshadowed by political considerations. It is, therefore, difficult to base the significance of the "service class" (made up of middle and upper echelon functionaries in the party, state, economy, culture, and police apparatus) on its relationship to the means of production. This approach might be plausible when speaking of the political ruling class in the narrower sense, the Politburo, the circle around the ZK, heads of the mass organizations, and the SED regional party secretaries, who had control over the economy, and for company directors or functionaries within the ministries of industry and the planning commission. But what is to be gained from deducing the class membership and privileges of Stasi officers, representatives of the Kulturbund, FDJ secretaries, university rectors, institute directors, theater directors, and authors from the degree of their control over the means of production? These professionals and others based their social position on their expertise, function, political loyalty, and perhaps on their relationship to their clients or their own social origins, but not on the relative control of state-owned property.

Whether these groups can be deemed "classes" or not, an analysis of mobility reveals a degree of social structuration that is difficult to reconcile with the idea of an undifferentiated, classless society. During the 1970s, an unplanned interaction between dictatorially determined conditions and individual actions resulted in the formation of new structural inequalities that need further study. Neither the undifferentiated classless society, nor the immobile "class society" are necessarily "modern" in the sense implied by the term "modern dictatorship". While the idea of the former implies a close link between dictatorship and social blockage, another perspective is possible, based on the recognition that social mobility and blockage stem from two very different causal sources. Mobility in the GDR's early years was ideologically legitimized and consciously initiated in order to meet the SED's interests as well as the economic demands of a developing economy. The blockage of the 1970s and 1980s went against the party's own claims, had ambiguous economic consequences and was not – as far as can be determined – politically intended. Although decisions regarding education and cadre policies eventually led to stagnation, there was never any official change in policies like in the 1950s and 1960s heralding the creation of the workers' and farmers' cadres. The replacement of the old elites at the GDR's inception was an act of political violence against the social logic of the old system, while the mobility blockage of later years occurred as the result of social processes that were part of the internal political logic of the new system.

Closer inspection reveals that developments within East German society were only partially a result of dictatorial planning, and partly also the unintended consequences of the regime.[46] While the massive flight of the 1950s, resulting from the regime's repressive measures, sped up mobility, it limited the state's ability to interfere in many professions; the fluidity of the early years paved the way for the stagnation of the next generation; the leveling policies indirectly led to a social re-differentiation; career interests of the loyal service class proved stronger than abstract claims for equality that served to legitimate the system; conflict between the criteria of performance versus loyalty were decided in favor of the latter, which meant that short-term stability was bought at the cost of long-term threats to the system itself. These developments raise the question of the nature of the regime. Even if one might interpret the closing of the privileged service class as a further step in the consolidation of dictatorial rule, it should be emphasized that this did not occur as a result of any direct political action, but rather came about as a consequence of social processes. Because the SED's claims to rule extended ever further into all areas of society, they provoked unforeseen reactions that contradicted the party's own goals.

Stagnation and Destabilization

A final interpretation of the problem also depends on the social and political consequences of inequality and stagnation. Were the patterns of mobility mere constructs of the socialist state with no real meaning for the self-perceptions and actions of the populace, or were they significant? Did they serve perhaps as a decisive "endogenous cause for the fall of the GDR," as Karl-Ulrich Mayer and Heike Solga argue?[47] To answer these questions two separate developments need to be differentiated.

First, one should practice caution when examining the linkage between position and consciousness so as not to repeat the false inferences of vulgar Marxist critiques of capitalism. Several arguments speak against overestimating the relevance of blockage and interpreting the oppositional movements of the late 1980s mainly as an expression of frustration felt by aspirants to higher positions, thwarted in achieving their goals. First, no discursive or action groups formed on the basis of common "class interests" (if one could call it that) – there was, in short, no class consciousness. Even the social closure of the service class did not remove the dichotomy between rulers and ruled which was the main axis of inequality that outweighed all social differences. The majority of the "functional service class" (engineers, doctors, teachers, and scientists) hardly participated in the mechanics of rule. Material conditions and concrete opportunities were not markedly different between the upper, middle, or lower levels of society. The GDR remained largely a "society of individuals,"[48] and social closure remained generally inconsequential in the face of the power structure – at least when considering the collective action of social groups. In this sense it is possible to describe the GDR as a "classless" society, since it never possessed classes as units of collective agency.

Second, the forms of social and cultural differentiation that possessed political relevance in the GDR's later years were only tangentially related to the structures of vertical inequality. One gets the impression instead that the phenomena of horizontal differentiation followed different directions than the described patterns of inequality.[49] Not unlike pluralization in modern Western societies, milieus of different lifestyles and values became the basis of common action, and served as abstract "class positions."[50] What connected the nonconformist youth culture of the punk bands or the skinheads to the small group of activists interested in civil rights and the environment, or to the members of church organizations who sought possibilities for independent action was the conscious renunciation of the chances offered by the SED.

Few of these dissidents chose nonconformity because their path upwards on the social ladder was blocked, but rather they became nonconformists because they did not wish to enter into or advance within the system. Particularly the active members of the peace movement, the civil rights movement, and the environmental movement cultivated an ascetic, anti-materialist life-style. They placed little or no stock in their careers or material comforts, and instead sought personal autonomy and self-determined community.[51] If these milieus did possess a common denominator around which they could communicate and organize, it was not a common "class," but rather the Protestant Church, the only institution not under control of the party.[52]

These objections need to be considered when weighing those arguments aimed at uncovering the relationship between large structural change and the end of the SED dictatorship. The increasing blockage of society rendered the regime's claims to legitimacy less and less believable. Since its inception the SED tried to justify its rule with the promise of social equality in an attempt to distinguish itself from West German "class society." The more these claims diverged from reality, the less effective they were as substitute legitimization. How sensitive the populace was to apparent inequality became clear in winter 1989–90, when GDR citizens became incensed over the "luxurious" lives of SED elites (admittedly quite humble by Western standards). But if the experience of mobility was central for the loyalty of the *Aufbau* generation, and only an exception limited to the regime's early years, then the "normalization" under the protection of the Wall triggered a creeping process of erosion of the foundation of old loyalties. This raises the basic question of whether dictatorships can possess something like a "normal state," or whether any attempt at normalization results in destabilization.

Declining mobility is a strong indicator for the reduction of integration within GDR society. The SED regime had always placed great emphasis on the loyalty of its citizens, but stagnation showed the limits of integration through individual advancement. Even those willing to make their peace with the regime were rewarded less for their efforts. The younger generation saw itself in a position of "multiple relative deprivation"[53] and looked towards an ever bleaker future. Since loyalty of the founding generation had been linked to the possibility of advancement, one could make the reverse inference that blocked career opportunities resulted in increased alienation. As far as can be ascertained, this feeling of exclusion had its greatest impact on the desire to emigrate, which led to the uncontrolled mass exodus in the last months of the regime's existence. The cohort of eighteen to twenty-nine year olds, which had the lowest chances of mobility, was precisely overrepresented in the exodus of 1989. In the weeks before the border was opened in November 1989, this group supplied 46.3 percent, and in the following three months 55.9 percent, of all emigrants, although it made up only 25 percent of the entire GDR adult population.[54] For those segments of the population unable to rise socially, leaving the country could become, in some circumstances, the "only attractive path to mobility."[55]

The small oppositional minority of civil rights, peace, women's and environmental groups, who were unwilling to turn their backs on the GDR and instead wanted to reform it from the ground up, faced another set of circumstances linking blocked mobility and possible action. As interviews show, many dissidents came from families that had experienced the transformation of the early Ulbricht era as a social step downwards, but who nevertheless chose to stay in the East.[56] Parents of these activists had often belonged to professions, such as doctors, scientists, or artists, that granted them a certain protection due to their indispensability. Yet because of their bourgeois habitus, elite perceptions of culture, and Christian beliefs, these professions lived at the margins of socialist society. In their niches at the edge of the SED system these bourgeois families kept alive the values and cultural capital of civil society that inspired the next generation of oppositional circles. In other cases, the parents of these activists belonged to the dispossessed, propertied middle class who passed their distaste for the regime on to their children.

In the succession of generations, the experience of social deprivation and marginalization combined with gestures of cultural superiority and a Christian rigorism to form a nonconformist habitus typical of the oppositional movement. It was not the social blockage of the Honecker era, but the mental distance caused by loss of status and social exclusion of the 1950s that became the catalyst of the dissident movement which demanded radical changes in the GDR in the 1980s.

Both the radical opening of GDR society in the 1950s and its slow closure in the last two decades of the regime would therefore have contributed to the downfall of the GDR dictatorship. This argument, however, should not be carried too far, since experiences of blockage were only one element among many that lined the path to collapse. One ought to be careful not to downplay the original political impetus of the East German revolution and the desire of the populace for freedom and democracy by overemphasizing the significance of abstract structural developments. But if one is looking for deeper causes of the escalation of inner opposition and flight that led to the collapse of the SED regime in 1989, the question of generation-specific experiences that link exit and voice with advancement and exclusion must be addressed.[57]

Notes

1. Lutz Niethammer, Alexander von Plato, and Dorothee Wierling, *Die volkseigene Erfahrung. Eine Archäologie des Lebens in der Industrieprovinz der DDR. 30 historiographische Eröffnungen* (Berlin, 1991), 44–45; see also Dorothee Wierling's article in the present volume.

2. Cf. Jürgen Kocka in this volume and Hartmut Kaelble, *Historische Mobilitätsforschung. Westeuropa und die USA im 19. und 20. Jahrhundert* (Darmstadt, 1978).

3. Michael Prinz and Rainer Zitelmann, eds, *Nationalsozialismus und Modernisierung* (Darmstadt, 1991); and David Schoenbaum, *Hitler's Social Revolution* (Garden City, 1967).

4. Norman M. Naimark, *The Russians in Germany: A History of the Soviet Zone of Occupation, 1945–1949* (Cambridge, 1995).

5. Helga A. Welsh, *Revolutionärer Wandel auf Befehl? Entnazifizierungs- und Personalpolitik in Thüringen und Sachsen (1945–1948)* (Munich, 1989); Clemens Vollnhals, ed., *Entnazifizierung. Politische Säuberung und Rehabilitierung in den vier Besatzungszonen 1945–1949* (Munich, 1991); Arnd Bauerkämper, Jürgen Danyel and Peter Hübner, "' Funktionäre des schaffenden Volkes?' Die Führungsgruppen der DDR als Forschungsproblem," in *Gesellschaft ohne Eliten? Führungsgruppen in der DDR*, ed. Arnd Bauerkämper (Berlin, 1997), 11–86, esp. 46–52.

6. Arnd Bauerkämper, "Die Neubauern in der SBZ/DDR 1945–1952. Bodenreform und politisch induzierter Wandel der ländlichen Gesellschaft," in *Die Grenzen der Diktatur. Staat und Gesellschaft in der DDR*, ed. Richard Bessel and Ralph Jessen (Göttingen, 1996), 108–36; Rainer Karlsch, *Allein bezahlt? Die Reparationsleistungen der SBZ/DDR 1945–1953* (Berlin, 1993); Matthias Judt, "Aufstieg und Niedergang der 'Trabi-Wirtschaft,'" in *DDR-Geschichte in Dokumenten. Beschlüsse, Berichte, interne Materialien und Alltagszeugnisse*, ed. idem (Berlin, 1997), 87–164.

7. Bauerkämper, "Neubauern," 109.

8. "Wirtschaft," in *DDR-Handbuch*, ed. Hartmut Zimmermann, 3rd ed., 2 vols (Cologne, 1985), vol. 2, 1485–503; "Wirtschaftspolitik," in *So funktionierte die DDR*, ed. Andreas Herbst, Winfried Ranke, and Jürgen Winkler, 3 vols (Reinbek, 1994), vol. 2, 1159.

9. Waldemar Krönig and Klaus-Dieter Müller, *Anpassung, Widerstand, Verfolgung. Hochschule und Studenten in der SBZ und DDR 1945–1961* (Cologne, 1994), 442–90.

10. Alexander von Plato and Wolfgang Meinicke, *Alte Heimat – neue Zeit. Flüchtlinge, Umgesiedelte, Vertriebene in der Sowjetischen Besatzungszone und in der DDR* (Berlin, 1991), 25.

11. Detailed studies concerning the *Vertriebene* in the GDR are lacking.

12. Hartmut Wendt, "Die deutsch-deutschen Wanderungen – Bilanz einer vierzigjährigen Geschichte von Flucht und Ausreise," *Deutschland Archiv* 24 (1991): 386–95.

13. Albert O. Hirschman, "Exit, Voice, and the Fate of the GDR: An Essay in Conceptual History," *World Politics* 45 (1992–93): 173–202.

14. Ralph Jessen, "Professoren im Sozialismus. Aspekte des Strukturwandels der Hochschullehrerschaft in der Ulbricht-Ära," in *Sozialgeschichte der DDR* (Stuttgart, 1994), ed. Hartmut Kaelble, Jürgen Kocka, and Hartmut Zwahr (Stuttgart, 1994), 217–53; Christoph Kleßmann, "Die Beharrungskraft traditioneller Milieus in der DDR," in *Was ist Gesellschaftsgeschichte? Positionen, Themen, Analysen*, ed. Manfred Hettling et al. (Munich, 1991), 146–54.

15. The rates apply to professors at universities and other institutions of higher learning. BAP R-3, 6060. Cf. Ralph Jessen, *Akademische Elite und Kommunistische Diktatur. Die ostdeutsche Hochschullehrerschaft in der Ulbricht- Ära* (Göttingen, 1999); Ralph Jessen, "Diktatorischer Elitenwechsel und universitäre Milieus. Hochschullehrer in der SBZ/DDR (1945–67)," *Geschichte und Gesellschaft* 24 (1998): 24–54; Anna–Sabine Ernst, *'Die beste Prophylaxe ist der Sozialismus.' Ärzte und medizinische Hochschullehrer in der SBZ/DDR 1945–1961* (Münster, 1997).

16. Gunilla-Friederike Budde, "Paradefrauen. Akademikerinnen in Ost- und Westdeutschland," in *Frauen arbeiten. Weibliche Erwerbstätigkeit in Ost- und Westdeutschland nach 1945*, ed. Gunilla-Friederike Budde (Göttingen, 1997), 183–211.

17. Christoph Kleßmann, "Zur Sozialgeschichte des protestantischen Milieus in der DDR," *Geschichte und Gesellschaft* 19 (1993): 29–53.
18. Rainer Geißler, *Die Sozialstruktur Deutschlands. Ein Studienbuch zur gesellschaftlichen Entwicklung im geteilten und vereinten Deutschland* (Opladen, 1992), 227.
19. Cf. Niethammer et al., *Volkseigene Erfahrung;* Gerd Dietrich, "Karriere im Schnellverfahren: die HJ-Generation in der frühen DDR," *Hochschule Ost* 2 (1996): 25–34; Erika M. Hoerning, "Aufstieg und Fall der 'neuen' Intelligenz," *Berliner Debate. Initial* 2 (1996): 21–23.
20. Wolfgang Engler, *Die zivilisatorische Lücke. Versuche über den Staatssozialismus* (Frankfurt, 1992), 88–99.
21. Heike Solga, *Auf dem Weg in eine klassenlose Gesellschaft? Klassenlage und Mobilität zwischen Generationen in der DDR* (Berlin 1995); Johannes Huinink et al., *Kollektiv und Eigensinn. Lebensverläufe in der DDR und danach* (Berlin, 1995).
22. Solga, *Klassenlose Gesellschaft*, 78.
23. Heike Solga, *"Systemloyalität" als Bedingung sozialer Mobilität im Staatssozialismus, am Beispiel der DDR* (Berlin, 1994), 18f.
24. Johannes Huinink, Heike Solga, "Occupational Opportunities in the GDR: A Privilege of the Older Generations?" *Zeitschrift für Soziologie* 23 (1994): 237, 253, esp. 251.
25. Solga, *Klassenlose Gesellschaft*, 175; Cf. Iris Häuser, "Lebensstile und politische Kultur in der DDR-Gesellschaft der achtziger Jahre," in *Gesellschaftliche Differenzierung und Legitimitätsverfall des DDR-Sozialismus. Das Ende des anderen Weges in die Moderne,* ed. Winfried Thaa et al. (Tübingen, 1992), 123–240, esp. 180.
26. Geißler, *Sozialstruktur*, 227.
27. "Hinweise für die soziale Einstufung von Bewerbern für ein Hoch- und Fachschulstudium, Berlin, 15 September 1976," in *Die Praxis der Hochschulen bei der sozialen Zuordnung der Studienbewerber und Aspekte der sozialen Herkunft von Hochschuldirekt- und Fernstudenten,* Rainer Fritsch and Erika Rommel (unpubl. MS of the Zentralinstitut für Hochschulbildung der DDR, Berlin, 1987). Cf. Edeltraud Schulze, "Jugend in der DDR – ausgewählte Zahlen und Fakten," in *Jahresbericht 1993. Institut für zeitgeschichtliche Jugendforschung* (Berlin, 1993), 171–224.
28. Martin Diewald and Heike Solga, "Soziale Ungleichheiten in der DDR: Die feinen, aber deutlichen Unterschiede am Vorabend der Wende," in Huinink et al., *Kollektiv und Eigensinn*, 261–305.
29. Wendt, *Wanderungen*, 388, 391.
30. Staatliche Zentralverwaltung für Statistik, ed., *Statistisches Jahrbuch der DDR* 31 (1986): 303.
31. Cf. Geißler, *Sozialstruktur*, 229–30.
32. Erika M. Hoerning, "Vertikale Mobilität in der DDR. Der Typus des Aufsteigers," in *BIOS Zeitschrift für Biographieforschung und Oral History* 7 (1994): 255–69.
33. Engler, *Zivilisatorische Lücke*, 94–98.
34. Solga, *Systemloyalität*, 26ff.
35. Ibid., 23f.
36. Matthias Wagner, "Gerüst der Macht. Das Kadernomenklatursystem als Ausdruck der führenden Rolle der SED," in *Gesellschaft ohne Eliten*, 87–108.
37. Günter Gaus, *Wo Deutschland liegt. Eine Ortsbestimmung* (Hamburg, 1983), 90–92; and Rudolf Woderich, "Mentalitäten im Land der kleinen Leute," in *Abbruch und Aufbruch: Sozialwissenschaften im Transformationsprozeß: Erfahrungen – Ansätze – Analysen,* ed. Michael Thomas (Berlin, 1992), 76–90.

38. Geißler, *Sozialstruktur*, 230; Astrid Segert and Irene Zierke, *Sozialstruktur und Milieuerfahrungen. Empirische und theoretische Aspekte des alltagskulturellen Wandels in Ostdeutschland* (Opladen, 1997), 95f; Häuser, *Lebenstile*, 199f.

39. See Konrad Jarausch's contribution in the present volume.

40. Rainer Geißler, "Sozialstrukturforschung in der DDR – Erträge und Dilemmata. Eine kritische Bilanz zur Triebkraft-Debatte und Mobilitätsanalyse," in *Berliner Journal für Soziologie* 4 (1996): 517–40; Manfred Lötsch, "Arbeiterklasse und Intelligenz in der Dialektik von wissenschaftlich-technischem, ökonomischem und sozialem Fortschritt," in *Deutsche Zeitschrift für Philosophie* 33 (1985): 31–41; idem, "Konturen einer Theorie der Sozialstruktur," *Berliner Journal für Soziologie* 1 (1991): 195–202; idem, "Ungleichheit – materielle, politische und soziale Differenzierung und ihre gesellschaftlichen Konsequenzen," in *Eine Deutsche Revolution. Der Umbruch in der DDR, seine Ursachen und Folgen*, ed. G.-J. Glaeßner (Frankfurt, 1991), 126–38.

41. See Katharina Belwe, "Annäherung von Arbeiterklasse und Intelligenz. Eine 'Nivellierung nach unten,'" *Deutschland-Archiv* 16 (1983): 161–67.

42. Rüdiger Thomas, "Sozialer Wandel in der DDR – Transformation oder Modernisierung," in *"Modernisierung" versus "Sozialismus," Formen und Strategien sozialen Wandels im 20. Jahrhundert,* ed. Ruffmann and Altrichter (Erlangen, 1983), 282f.; idem, "Aspekte des sozialen Wandels in der DDR," in *Sozialstruktur und sozialer Wandel in der DDR*, ed. H. Timmermann (Saarbrücken, 1988), 27–55; Rainer Geißler, "Bildungschancen und Statusvererbung in der DDR," *Kölner Zeitschrift für Soziologie und Sozialpsychologie* 35 (1983): 767; Hans-Georg Wehling, "Sozialstruktur und soziale Schichtung," in *Bundesrepublik Deutschland und DDR. Die beiden deutschen Staaten im Vergleich* (Berlin, 1980), 359–66.

43. Sigrid Meuschel, *Legitimation und Parteiherrschaft. Zum Paradox von Stabilität und Revolution in der DDR 1945–1989* (Frankfurt, 1992); idem, "Überlegungen zu einer Herrschafts- und Gesellschaftsgeschichte der DDR," *Geschichte und Gesellschaft* 19 (1993): 5–14.

44. Diewald and Solga, *Soziale Ungleichheiten*, 303.

45. Solga, *Klassenlose Gesellschaft,* 63–91.

46. Detlef Pollack, "Die konstitutive Widersprüchlichkeit der DDR. Oder: War die DDR-Gesellschaft homogen?" *Geschichte und Gesellschaft* 24 (1998): 110–31; Ralph Jessen, "Die Gesellschaft im Staatssozialismus. Probleme einer Sozialgeschichte der DDR," *Geschichte und Gesellschaft* 21 (1995): 96–110.

47. Karl-Ulrich Mayer and Heike Solga, "Mobilität und Legitimität. Zum Vergleich der Chancenstrukturen in der alten DDR und der alten BRD oder: Haben Mobilitätschancen zu Stabilität und Zusammenbruch der DDR beigetragen?" *Kölner Zeitschrift für Soziologie und Sozialpsychologie* 46 (1994): 206.

48. Thomas Schmid, *Staatsbegräbnis. Von ziviler Gesellschaft?* (Berlin, 1990): 16.

49. Dieter Rink, "Das Leipziger Alternativmilieu. Zwischen alten und neuen Eliten," in *Soziale Milieus in Ostdeutschland. Gesellschaftliche Strukturen zwischen Zerfall und Neubildung*, ed. Michael Vester, Michael Hofmann, and Irene Zierke (Cologne, 1995), 228.

50. Segert and Zierke, *Sozialstruktur und Milieuerfahrungen*: 30ff; Peter A. Berger and Peter Sopp, "Dynamische Sozialstrukturanalysen und Strukturerfahrungen," in *Sozialstruktur und Lebenslauf,* ed. idem (Opladen, 1995), 9–24.

51. Ehrhart Neubert, *Geschichte der Opposition in der DDR 1949–1989* (Berlin 1997), 421–63.

52. Mary Fulbrook, *Anatomy of a Dictatorship. Inside the GDR 1949–1989* (Oxford, 1995), 203–6.

53. Mayer and Solga, *Mobilität und Legitimität*, 206; Häuser, *Lebensstile*, 224f; see also Michael Hofmann and Dieter Rink, "Mütter und Töchter – Väter und Söhne. Mentalitätswandel in zwei DDR-Generationen," *BIOS Zeitschrift für Biographieforschung und Oral History* 6 (1993): 199–223.

54. Dieter Voigt, Hannelore Belitz-Demiriz, and Sabine Meck, "Die innerdeutsche Wanderung und der Vereinigungsprozeß. Soziodemographische Struktur und Einstellungen von Flüchtlingen/Übersiedlern aus der DDR vor und nach der Grenzöffnung," *Deutschland Archiv* 23 (1990): 734.

55. Frank Adler, "Der DDR-Realsozialismus und sein Ende (Strukturen – Erosion – Zusammenbruch)," in *Die Revolution in Mittel- und Osteuropa und ihre Folgen* (Bonn 1991), 41.

56. Segert and Zierke, *Sozialstruktur und Milieuerfahrungen*, 190–96; cf. Rink, *Alternativmilieu*, 227; and Michael Hofmann, "Bürgergeist in Ostdeutschland. Konfliktlinien im Transformationsprozeß," *Hochschule Ost* 2 (1996): 71–84.

57. Cf. Hirschman, *Exit, Voice, and the Fate of the GDR, passim.*

POSTSCRIPT

CHAPTER 19

RETHINKING THE SECOND GERMAN DICTATORSHIP

Christoph Kleßmann

It is one of the ironies of GDR history that its final chapter has been preserved in popular memory as the *Wende* or "course change." Seeking to imply that the SED regime could be reformed and improved, Egon Krenz, the youngest member of a rather fossilized Politburo, coined this term to designate his pragmatic reform-communism. That one of the newest representatives of the Old Guard could shape the consciousness of his former subjects so permanently needs some explanation, especially since the expression *Wende*, borrowed from the world of sailors and surfers, generally refers to a shift in direction, but not a change of crew or boats.

The "heroes of [the] Leipzig" demonstrations also desired a better GDR – not reunification with the FRG by any means. They saw the events of the fall of 1989 as part of a peaceful revolution, the first successful popular rising in German history. But were these momentous events not something more than a mere "turn about"? Those who had been politically persecuted have once again become marginalized, although they provided the impetus that led to the fall of the GDR. The revolution they instigated in 1989 did not so much stall as develop in an initially unintended direction that was determined by those who wanted to see events portrayed as a mere change of course. But in the meantime the factors that made the collapse of the old system seem inevitable have become more visible.

It has proven quite difficult for scholars to settle on one single conceptual term for the GDR or its demise. The attempt to find a single expression is complicated by the fact that every successful revolution – if it is to be more than a putsch – is linked to a collapse of the old system. The GDR's end can, according to one's point of view, be characterized as a collapse or as an implosion. Konrad Jarausch has discussed the difficulties involved in developing an adequate terminology through historical comparison in a volume on the inner erosion of the East German state.

The GDR was born in the wake of a revolution, which although real, could not be called by this word due to political considerations. Only later would GDR historians and Marxist theoreticians attempt to make the term fashionable. The first GDR constitution of 1949 was outwardly bourgeois – yet despite its preservation of parts of the Weimar constitution, it codified the results of the people's revolution that had swept through all of Central and Eastern Europe. What was distinct about the SBZ was one reservation: the constitution had as its goal a united Germany, and saw the GDR as the better half of a now divided nation.

In 1949 few people believed that Germany would remain permanently divided, or that a state lacking democratic legitimation could survive for any period of time. Founded with some difficulty, shored up by the political and military support of the Soviet Union, the East German state achieved relative stability in 1961 and, after it had obtained international recognition in 1971, even became an established player on the stage of postwar European politics. The strategy of "change through detente" (*Wandel durch Annäherung*) showed some success, and offered long-term possibilities within a power constellation that appeared carved in stone. Political observers could hardly imagine that this dictatorship would one day collapse and lead to the founding of a re-unified German state. It was only after the regime's demise that those elements leading to its fall became more apparent.

Whether one views the regime from its beginning or from its end, the GDR has always seemed somewhat provisional. At its inception, East Germany was seen in the West as "a state that should not exist" (Ernst Richert) and as a totalitarian dictatorship. After its passing, the regime appeared for many commentators as an entity doomed from the start to "failure in stages" (Mitter/Wolle). But beginning in the 1970s, some scholars took a different interpretative tack. The term totalitarian dictatorship began to disappear from use. Book titles such as "The GDR is no longer merely a zone" (Hans Werner Schwarze), "The Calculated Emancipation" (Rüdiger Thomas), or the GDR as a "German Alternative" (Hermann Rudolph), signaled new ways of looking at the GDR that came under fire after 1990 as attempts to gloss over harsh realities.

Placing the GDR within the larger context of German history presents special difficulties, because the evaluation of the East German record is more heavily determined by past reception and interpretation than that of other periods. Discussions of GDR development therefore mirror different stages and approaches within German historiography.

GDR Peculiarities

Although the GDR was an integral part of the Soviet system in post-war Europe, it also represented a special case within the Eastern Bloc. In order to understand the unique nature of the GDR, scholars must employ a variety of approaches to its past. Many features of the regime, previously ignored or disregarded, only became visible after 1990. Competing explanations seem to agree that GDR history can be characterized by three systemic elements that have possessed varying degrees of significance during different stages of its development.

First, the GDR's dependence on the Soviet Union was of immense importance. Although the regime could gain a degree of independence during the 1950s, East Germany had less room for political maneuvering than other East European states that were based upon prior nations.

But overemphasizing the regime's nature as a Soviet satellite (a regular scholarly practice in the 1950s) runs the risk of overlooking another important feature of the GDR – the German communists. It was this group which supported the regime and forced the populace to follow its will. Yet the SED was also ready to make numerous compromises and concessions, because, unlike the Nazi rulers, it could not assume popular support but instead had to win or coerce it. An exclusive focus on the role of the GDR as a Soviet satellite (or on the omnipotence of the USSR) disregards those elements of grudging loyalty that were central to the state's existence. Indeed, such an approach comes close to exonerating the GDR and its citizens. It does little to explain the long duration and relative stability of the GDR as a socialist system "in half a country" (Dietrich Staritz). It is therefore essential to emphasize the relative external independence and voluntary internal subordination as necessary elements of the GDR. This view also opens the possibility of exploring longer lines of continuity within the history of the German *Obrigkeitsstaat* in the twentieth century.

The third element I would like to examine is so specific and unique to the GDR that it has made many authors hesitant to consider East Germany within the comparative perspective of Eastern

Bloc countries – the regime's relationship to its other half in the West. The "distancing [from] and intertwining" with the FRG (*Abgrenzung und Verflechtung*) are topics that belong to the most interesting, but also contested and complicated issues of the GDR's past. Although the significance of the relationship between the two different German states can hardly be overstated, more empirical research is needed before its true impact can be determined.

West Germany was omnipresent in GDR politics and society, either directly or indirectly. Its influence constantly pressured the SED either to confront the West directly or to isolate the East from its perceived threat. Isolation proved the only way to achieve legitimization as an independent East German state. Even without socialism Poles and Czechs could still consider themselves Poles and Czechs; but without socialism a GDR that lacked political legitimacy risked immediately falling prey to the bigger and richer Federal Republic as representative of the German nation.

Any consideration of the GDR dictatorship therefore ought to occur within the framework of these three different elements. This would avoid a resuscitation of older totalitarianism theories and reduce the danger of subsuming the GDR under the history of the eastern bloc. It also allows scholars to complement concrete social historical case studies with an analysis of larger political structures, while guaranteeing a certain amount of skepticism towards attempts to integrate GDR history seamlessly into a master narrative of postwar German development. Although political leaders continued to pay lip service to the ideal of a German nation, and demonstrators in 1989 made appeals to the same, Germans had more difficulties imagining themselves as part of a "nation without a house" (Adolf Birke) the longer political division lasted. The fact that this was so is proven by the enormous social and psychological difficulties that have stood in the path towards inner unity.

Such a multi-dimensional perspective can help to explain the stability as well as the rapid dissolution of the GDR, and its various ruptures, continuities, loyalties, and disloyalties.

The Issue of Modernity

Unlike in Poland or other socialist countries, Soviet communism, by aiming at forced industrialization and social egalitarianism, brought few modernizing advances to the GDR and Czechoslovakia, both highly developed industrial states. Therefore, the concept of "modern dictatorship" seems quite problematic and the term's applicability rather limited. No doubt there was a real intention to modernize the GDR that did not remain without results. This became especially clear in the 1960s. But in general, the GDR dictatorship cannot be understood in such terms. Modernizing forces hardly influenced its political, economic, or cultural developments, even if many areas of development remain unexamined and unclear.

Labor historians, for instance, have hardly addressed the SED's central claim to be the standard bearer of the German socialist workers' movement. The significance of the party's programmatic goals cannot be grasped by pointing to the ideological rhetoric of the "workers' and peasants' state." The "leading class" in many ways tried to live up to such propaganda claims. From education to labor law, it made a real difference whether one belonged to the proletariat or not. In this sense, the progressive and "modern" goals of the labor movement were not merely empty promises. And the possibility of upward mobility for the previously excluded created certain loyalties beyond the influence of Soviet control or the imposition of a "dictatorship of the proletariat" from above. But was this particularly "modern"? Forced social emancipation went hand in hand with open discrimination against the former elites. By barring entrance into universities to children from bourgeois families, the SED helped fuel an exodus to the West, especially among the former intelligentsia, and thereby created enormous difficulties for the state. Educational policies were therefore highly ambivalent in regards to their relative modernity, and calls for egalitarianism constantly undermined attempts to create a more merit-based economy.

Perhaps more importantly, modernization as an emancipatory social movement quickly ran into artificial limits within the GDR. The SED's definition of the "working class" was part of an ideological attempt to halt a development sweeping across all industrialized economies, namely the shift from blue to white collar work, from physical labor to service. In this regard the GDR seemed quite antiquated until its end, since it conserved and justified structures that could be maintained only through complete isolation. The service sector remained utterly underdeveloped. This made the social rupture after 1990 more severe and inevitable. It has meant, as well, that only about one fourth of those employed today in East Germany are presently working in the same sector as before 1990. Workers are, therefore, also over-represented within the ranks of the unemployed.

Similar developments can be ascertained within the SED's policies towards women that stemmed from older labor traditions, but were often overridden by the demands of the labor market. In many respects GDR gender policies were more "modern" than those of the FRG: women were included in the workforce as a matter of course; they were guaranteed legal and economic equality; they possessed easy access to divorce, and enjoyed a highly developed infrastructure to support families. Yet the East developed no women's movement comparable to that of the West, which in turn led to complications and difficulties after 1990. The SED was as unsuccessful as its neighbors to the West in generating family policies that addressed men as caregivers. Moreover, men dominated in the political sphere, and were over-represented within the upper levels of the Politburo, ZK, and the Stasi. In this respect the GDR strongly resembled the Federal Republic of the 1950s and 1960s. The GDR was, therefore, everything but modern in regard to its lack of social differentiation, even if the thesis of a homogenization of society is only partly correct, since under the surface of an apparently "frozen" society other forms of differentiation slowly developed.

The near perfection of the state security system on the other hand – which the SED believed was vital to its continued existence – was modern in a most macabre fashion. The refinement of the Stasi's methods reveals the pathological elements of modernity as expressed in the GDR dictatorship. While accentuating those elements of modern social policy that were characteristic of the GDR, Konrad H. Jarausch's concept of "welfare dictatorship" expressly links them to the traditional paternalistic claims of an absolutist state. Although the Stasi's methods of surveillance and control in the regime's final phase came frighteningly close to Orwell's vision, they should nevertheless not be placed within the totalitarian tradition, which bears the heavy traces of Stalinist influence. One of totalitarianism's most striking features – mobilization for utopian goals – occurred only partially in the GDR, or was not achieved at all. Instead, it was stagnation, carelessness, and apathy that were much more typical of East German society. Permanent revolution was not the GDR's problem, but, as Jürgen Kocka has correctly pointed out, "advancing sclerosis" was the cause of the state's continuing crisis. Simultaneously, the regime's attempts to provide all-encompassing social care for its subjects took the socialist project of the social welfare state to a new level of absurdity because of the state's complete inability to cover its own costs.

What remains, then, of the so-called "modern dictatorship"? In many respects, the discussion about the term echoes earlier debates concerning modernity and modernization under National Socialism. And yet the differences between the two are considerable.

At the heart of the often quite heated controversy about the Third Reich has been the difference between intent and effect. Undoubtedly, Nazi policies did have modernizing effects, especially in the wake of social and economic ruptures caused by the Second World War. Ralf Dahrendorf noted as much more than three decades ago.

It is also undeniable that certain modern elements were present in the ideology and practice of the NS state, something younger scholars, most notably Rainer Zitelmann, have maintained. This is evident in areas such as the Nazi fascination with technology, or policies related to architecture and urban planning, as well as the possibilities for upward social mobility. The Nazi regime was in many respects a highly developed "modern dictatorship." Skilled use of modern methods of communication, technology, and mass mobilization combined with ideological deception, made the Hitler state the prototype of a successful modern dictatorship with totalitarian aims, an incredible degree of energy and broad public acceptance and support.

Yet recognition of the regime's modern aspects cannot refute the criticism voiced by the regime's socialist and liberal opponents – that it was a counter-revolutionary, reactionary movement based on an atavist utopia of biological racism. As David Schoenbaum noted years ago, when speaking of the Nazi regime, its methods and goals must be distinguished. The Nazi revolution was a movement directed at dismantling bourgeois society, carried out with the most modern methods available to that very society. Thereby, the regime unleashed effects that collided with its own goals in the long run. In addition, the dictatorship's relative modernity cannot be established without a consideration of the calculated murder of millions of victims. If the concept of modernization is to have any meaning, the NS regime was everything *but* modern.

The postwar communist dictatorships – at least those in Europe —seemed to present themselves quite differently. Ideologically, their emancipatory goals and calls for social equality place them within the enlightenment tradition. It is for this reason that supporters of "real existing socialism" often have difficulties with diachronic comparisons between dictatorships. Important socialist and communist goals are quite compatible with modernization processes, such as the fascination with industrial society, an orientation towards unbridled growth, socially determined rationalization, the destruction of older traditions, and political and social emancipation. The methods employed to achieve these goals were also initially modern, but their terrorist elements set free pathological aspects of modernity, typical of the twentieth century.

Especially the regime's last phase exemplifies the darker side of the modern – the ruthless exploitation of resources without concern for the consequences, the using-up of existing stocks and the general deterioration. Many of these developments can be explained by economic constraints. Yet the most important element is not economic, but rather the regime's inability to make corrections which seems inherent in all political systems. Only with Gorbachev were attempts at reform made, but they came too late. In a period of global change involving a "scientific-technological revolution" as well as new forms of communication, all communist regimes proved to be backward, non-competitive, and certainly not at all modern. This was not clear at their inception, and so in this sense one might speak of modernization in the earlier rather than later stages of their development.

Besides modern technical possibilities that many dictatorships have at their disposal, two other elements are typical of such regimes. They are plebiscitary approval via fake elections, and more importantly, the replacement of normal political legitimization by social gratification. Tim Mason saw the trauma of the November Revolution as one of the main motivating factors behind Nazi social policy up to the outbreak of the war. This suggests structural parallels for the postwar period. After the defeat of socialist alternatives, (briefly attempted in Hungary and Poland in 1956 and in Prague in 1968) and the failure of economic reforms with the NÖSPL, Honecker's social concessions offered a timely and in many ways "necessary" way out. Social policy became preventative crisis management, meant to avert crises like the "revolt on the coast" in Poland during the winter of 1970, or even a repeat of the events of the 17th of June. The "soft stabilizing factors" (K. D. Henke) of such an expansive social policy render Konrad Jarausch's term of a "welfare dictatorship" plausible. The somewhat more unwieldy concept suggested by Klaus Schroeder – "a late totalitarian welfare and surveillance state" – goes in a similar direction and highlights important themes. Both aspects in their most excessive form are more applicable to the regime's later phase and therefore offer little help in categorizing and analyzing earlier periods that were in many instances more modern.

For these reasons, the explanatory power of the term "modern" is even more limited than Jürgen Kocka has surmised, largely because it does not sufficiently capture the complexity of developments within the later decades.

East German Dynamics

An examination of GDR development reveals the picture of a contradiction-ridden socialist experiment conceived as an alternative to the FRG and accepted as such by a small, loyal minority. During the 1950s and 1960s the majority undoubtedly experienced the GDR brutally and openly as a modern dictatorship. But until the completion of the Wall, the East German populace could always choose flight to the West over staying and dealing with the harsh realities of life within the GDR. After the Wall's completion, not only the outward possibilities changed, but people's experiences as well. They developed a broad-based, if somewhat unwilling loyalty that rested on an "acceptance of necessity" combined with increasing signs of outward decline and inward erosion.

While the picture of a "niche society" has been criticized by some that point to the Stasi's penetration into even the most remote corners, the actual experiences of the regime's citizens seem to reaffirm it in part. The GDR was not just an albeit "dictatorial safe-haven" (*heile Welt der Diktatur*) (Stefan Wolle) for those critics who now look back upon its past. A changing foreign policy climate also made the "limits of the dictatorship" more apparent and more usable. The populace developed a will of its own in dealing with the institutions and political demands of the state in all areas – in literary, cultural, and scientific life, the churches, and the factories. The SED tolerated such assertiveness as long as it did not assume political dimensions. In its later stages, the GDR therefore presented a diffuse mixture of forms of accommodation, partial resistance, and widespread political apathy. The lines of social tension that Detlef Pollack accurately describes continued to exist and eventually led to a decline in loyalty, without actually resulting in open confrontation.

A deep chasm, therefore, separates the dynamic beginnings of the GDR, characterized by mobilization and optimism, from its final phase, which was marked by insecurity, defensiveness, and an increasing inability to recognize reality. This gulf makes it difficult to develop a single, overarching concept to characterize the entire course of the GDR dictatorship.

SELECTED BIBLIOGRAPHY

1. Handbooks, Memoirs and Sources

Badstübner, Rolf and Loth, Wilfried, eds, *Wilhelm Pieck – Aufzeichnungen zur Deutschlandpolitik 1945–1953* (Berlin, 1994).

Baumgartner, Gabriele and Hebig, Dieter, eds, *Biographisches Handbuch der SBZ/DDR 1945–1990* (Munich, 1996–97), 2 vols.

Die Biermann-Ausbürgerung und die Schriftsteller. Ein deutsch-deutscher Fall. Protokoll der ersten Tagung der Geschichtskommission des Verbandes deutscher Schriftsteller (VS) vom 28.2. bis 1.3.1992 in Berlin (Cologne, 1994).

Bonwetsch, Bernd, Bordjugow, Gennadij and Naimark, Norman N., eds, *Sowjetische Politik in der SBZ 1945–1949. Dokumente zur Tätigkeit der Propagandaverwaltung (Informationsverwaltung) der SMAD unter Tjul'-panov* (Bonn, 1998).

Broszat, Martin and Weber, Hermann, eds, *SBZ–Handbuch. Staatliche Verwaltungen, Parteien, gesellschaftliche Organisationen und ihre Führungskräfte in der Sowjetischen Besatzungszone Deutschlands 1945–1949* (Munich, 1993²).

Diedrich, Torsten, Ehlert, Hans and Wenzke, Rüdiger, eds, *Im Dienste der Partei. Handbuch der bewaffneten Organe der DDR* (Berlin, 1998).

Dokumente zur Deutschlandpolitik. Deutsche Einheit. Sonderedition aus den Akten des Bundeskanzleramtes 1989/90 (Munich, 1998).

Eppelmann, Rainer et al., eds, *Lexikon des DDR-Sozialismus* (Paderborn, 1998²).

Fricke, Karl-Wilhelm, *MfS intern. Macht, Strukturen, Auflösung der DDR-Staatssicherheit. Analysen und Dokumentation* (Cologne, 1991).

Gerlach, Manfred, *Mitverantwortlich. Als Liberaler im SED-Staat* (Berlin, 1991).

Hager, Kurt, *Erinnerungen* (Leipzig, 1996).

Henke, Klaus-Dietmar et al., eds, *Anatomie der Staatssicherheit. Geschichte, Struktur und Methoden. MfS-Handbuch* (Berlin, 1995 ff.).

Herbst, Andreas, Ranke, Winfried and Winkler, Jürgen, eds, *So funktionierte die DDR* (Reinbek, 1994), 3 vols.

Idem, Stephan, Gerd-Rüdiger and Winkler, Jürgen, eds, *Die SED. Geschichte, Organisation, Politik. Ein Handbuch* (Berlin, 1997).

Hoffmann, Dierk, Schmidt, Karl-Heinz and Skyba, Peter, eds, *Die DDR vor dem Mauerbau. Dokumente zur Geschichte des anderen deutschen Staates 1949–1961* (Munich, 1993).

James, Harold and Stone, Marla, eds, *When the Wall Came Down: Reactions to German Unification* (London, 1992).

Jarausch, Konrad H. and Gransow, Volker, eds, *Uniting Germany: Documents and Debates 1944–1993* (Providence, 1994).

Judt, Matthias, ed., *DDR-Geschichte in Dokumenten. Beschlüsse, Berichte, interne Materialien und Alltagszeugnisse* (Berlin, 1997).

Klemperer, Victor, *So sitze ich denn zwischen allen Stühlen. Tagebücher 1945–1959*, ed. Walter Nowojski (Berlin, 1999), 2 vols.

Kleßmann, Christoph and Wagner, Georg, eds, *Das gespaltene Land. Leben in Deutschland 1945 bis 1990. Texte und Dokumente* (Munich, 1993).

Krenz, Egon, *Wenn Mauern fallen. Die friedliche Revolution* (Vienna, 1990).

Mählert, Ulrich, ed., *Vademekum DDR-Forschung. Ein Leitfaden zu Archiven, Forschungseinrichtungen, Bibliotheken, Einrichtungen der politischen Bildung, Vereinen, Museen und Gedenkstätten* (Opladen, 1997).

Materialien der Enquete-Kommission "Aufarbeitung von Geschichte und Folgen der SED-Diktatur in Deutschland" (12. Wahlperiode des Deutschen Bundestages), ed. Deutscher Bundestag (Baden-Baden, 1995).

Mitter, Armin and Wolle, Stefan, eds, *"Ich liebe Euch doch alle!" Befehle und Lageberichte des MfS Januar–November 1989* (Berlin, 1992²).

Modrow, Hans, *Ich wollte ein neues Deutschland* (Berlin, 1998).

Philipsen, Dirk, ed., *We Were the People: Voices from East Germany's Revolutionary Autumn of 1989* (Durham, 1993).

Potthoff, Heinrich, *Bonn und Ost-Berlin 1969–1982. Dialog auf höchster Ebene und vertrauliche Kanäle. Darstellung und Dokumente* (Bonn,1997).

Przybylski, Peter, *Tatort Politbüro* (Berlin, 1991-92), 2 vols.

Reiher, Ruth et al., eds, *Mit sozialistischen und anderen Grüßen. Porträt einer untergegangenen Republik in Alltagstexten* (Berlin, 1995).

Schabowski, Günter, *Das Politbüro. Ende eines Mythos* (Reinbek, 1990).

Scherstjanoi, Elke, ed., *Das SKK-Statut. Zur Geschichte der Sowjetischen Kontrollkommission in Deutschland 1949 bis 1953. Eine Dokumentation* (Munich, 1998).

Suckut, Siegfried, ed., *Das Wörterbuch der Staatssicherheit. Definitionen zur "politisch-operativen Arbeit"* (Berlin, 1996).

Weber, Hermann, ed., *DDR. Dokumente zur Geschichte der Deutschen Demokratischen Republik 1945–1985* (Munich, 1987³).

Weidenfeld, Werner and Korte, Karl-Rudolf, eds, *Handbuch zur deutschen Einheit* (Frankfurt, 1996²).

Idem and Zimmermann, Hartmut, eds, *Deutschland-Handbuch. Eine doppelte Bilanz 1949–1989* (Munich, 1989).

Wolf, Markus, *The Man Without a Face* (New York, 1997).

Zimmermann, Hartmut et al., eds, *DDR-Handbuch* (Cologne, 1985³), 2 vols.

2. Secondary Works

Ansorg, Leonore, *Kinder im Klassenkampf. Die Geschichte der Pionierorganisation von 1948 bis Ende der fünfziger Jahre* (Berlin, 1997).

Ash, Timothy Garton, *In Europe's Name. Germany and the Divided Continent* (New York, 1993).

Barck, Simone, Langermann, Martina and Lokatis, Siegfried, *"Jedes Buch ein Abenteuer" Zensur-System und literarische Öffentlichkeiten in der DDR bis Ende der sechziger Jahre* (Berlin, 1998²).

Bathrick, David, *The Powers of Speech: The Politics of Culture in the GDR* (Lincoln, 1995).

Bauerkämper, Arnd et al., eds, *Gesellschaft ohne Eliten? Führungsgruppen in der DDR* (Berlin, 1997).

Bender, Peter, *Episode oder Epoche? Zur Geschichte des geteilten Deutschland* (Munich, 1996).

Besier, Gerhard, *Der SED-Staat und die Kirche* (Munich, 1993–95), 3 vols.

Bessel, Richard and Jessen, Ralf, eds, *Die Grenzen der Diktatur. Staat und Gesellschaft in der DDR* (Göttingen, 1996).

Childs, David and Popplewell, Richard, *The Stasi: The East German Intelligence and Security Service* (New York, 1996).

Eckert, Rainer and Faulenbach, Bernd, eds, *Halbherziger Revisionismus. Zum postkommunistischen Geschichtsbild* (Munich, 1996).

Idem, Kowalczuk, Ilko-Sascha and Stark, Isolde, eds, *Hure oder Muse? Klio in der DDR* (Berlin, 1994).

Idem, Küttler, Wolfgang and Seeber, Gustav, eds, *Krise, Umbruch, Neubeginn. Eine kritische und selbstkritische Dokumentation der DDR-Geschichtswissenschaft 1989–90* (Stuttgart,1992).

Engler, Wolfgang, *Die Ostdeutschen. Kunde von einem verlorenen Land* (Berlin, 1999).

Fischer, Andreas, *Das Bildungssystem der DDR. Entwicklung, Umbruch und Neugestaltung seit 1989* (Darmstadt, 1992).

Fricke, Karl Wilhelm, *Die DDR-Staatssicherheit. Entwicklung, Strukturen, Aktionsfelder* (Cologne, 1989³).

Fulbrook, Mary, *Anatomy of a Dictatorship. Inside the GDR, 1949–1989* (Oxford, 1995).

Furet, Francois, *Das Ende der Illusion. Der Kommunismus im 20. Jahrhundert* (Munich, 1998).

Geschichte der deutschen Einheit in vier Bänden. vol 1. Korte, Karl Rudolf, *Deutschlandpolitik in Helmut Kohls Kanzlerzeit*; vol 2. Grosser, Dieter, *Das Wagnis der Währungs-, Wirtschafts- und Sozialunion*; vol 3. Jäger, Wolfgang, *Die Überwindung der Teilung*; vol 4. Weidenfeld, Werner, *Außenpolitik für die deutsche Einheit* (Stuttgart, 1998).

Goeckel, Robert F., *The Lutheran Church and the East German State* (Ithaca, 1995).

Gotschlich, Helga, ed., *"Links und links und Schritt gehalten..." Die FDJ: Konzepte, Abläufe, Grenzen* (Berlin, 1994).

Häder, Sonja, *Schülerkindheit in Ost-Berlin. Sozialisation unter den Bedingungen der Diktatur 1945–1958* (Cologne, 1998).

Henkel, Rüdiger, *Im Dienste der Staatspartei. Über Parteien und Organisationen der DDR* (Baden-Baden, 1994).

Herf, Jeffrey, *Divided Memory: The Nazi Past in the Two Germanies* (London, 1997).

Hertle, Hans-Hermann, *Der Fall der Mauer. Die unbeabsichtigte Selbstauflösung des SED-Staates* (Opladen, 1996).

Idem and Stephan, Gerd-Rüdiger, eds, *Das Ende der SED. Die letzten Tage des Zentralkomitees* (Berlin, 1997).

Hoffmann-Pawlowsky, Jutta, and Voigt, Freya, *Lebenslinien. Geschichte von Frauen aus der DDR* (Frankfurt/Oder, 1995).

Holzweißig, Gunter, *Zensur ohne Zensor. Die SED-Informationsdiktatur* (Bonn, 1997).

Hübner, Peter, *Konsens, Konflikt und Kompromiß. Soziale Arbeiterinteressen und Sozialpolitik in der SBZ/DDR 1945–1970* (Berlin, 1995).

Huinink, Johannes et al., *Kollektiv und Eigensinn. Lebensläufe in der DDR und danach* (Berlin, 1995).

Hurwitz, Harold, *Die Stalinisierung der SED. Zum Verlust von Freiräumen und sozialdemokratischer Identität in den Vorständen 1946–1949* (Opladen, 1997).

Iggers, Georg G. et al., eds, *Die DDR-Geschichtswissenschaft als Forschungsproblem* (Munich, 1998), Beiheft 27 of the *Historische Zeitschrift*.

Jarausch, Konrad H., *The Rush to German Unity* (New York, 1994).

Idem, ed., *Zwischen Parteilichkeit und Professionalität. Bilanz der Geschichtswissenschaft der DDR* (Berlin, 1991).

Idem and Middell, Matthias, eds, *Nach dem Erdbeben. (Re-)Konstruktion ostdeutscher Geschichte und Geschichtswissenschaft* (Leipzig, 1994).

Idem and Siegrist, Hannes, eds, *Amerikanisierung und Sowjetisierung in Deutschland 1945–1970* (Frankfurt, 1997).

Joas, Hans and Kohli, Martin, eds, *Der Zusammenbruch der DDR. Soziologische Analysen* (Frankfurt, 1993).

Kaelble, Hartmut, Kocka, Jürgen and Zwahr, Hartmut, eds, *Sozialgeschichte der DDR* (Stuttgart, 1994).

Kaiser, Monika, *Machtwechsel von Ulbricht zu Honecker. Funktionsmechanismen der SED-Diktatur in Konfliktsituationen 1962 bis 1972* (Berlin, 1997).

Keßler, Mario, *Die SED und die Juden – zwischen Repression und Toleranz. Politische Entwicklungen bis 1967* (Berlin, 1995).

Kleßmann, Christoph, *Die doppelte Staatsgründung. Deutsche Geschichte 1945–1955* (Göttingen, 1991[5]).

Idem, *Zwei Staaten, eine Nation. Deutsche Geschichte 1955–1970* (Bonn, 1997[2]).

Kocka, Jürgen, ed., *Historische DDR-Forschung. Aufsätze und Studien* (Berlin, 1993).

Idem and Sabrow, Martin eds, *Die DDR als Geschichte. Fragen, Hypothesen, Perspektiven* (Berlin, 1994).

Kowalczuk, Ilko-Sascha, Mitter, Armin and Wolle, Stefan, eds, *Der Tag X – 17. Juni 1953. Die "Innere Staatsgründung" der DDR als Ergebnis der Krise 1952/54* (Berlin, 1995).

Lemke, Michael, *Die Berlinkrise 1958 bis 1963. Interessen und Handlungsspielräume der SED im Ost-West-Konflikt* (Berlin, 1995).

Lüdtke, Alf and Becker, Peter, eds, *Akten. Eingaben. Schaufenster. Die DDR und ihre Texte. Erkundungen zu Herrschaft und Alltag* (Berlin, 1997).

Mählert, Ulrich, and Stephan, Gerd-Rüdiger, *Blaue Hemden – Rote Fahnen. Die Geschichte der Freien Deutschen Jugend* (Opladen, 1996).

Maier, Charles S., *Dissolution: The Crisis of Communism and the End of East Germany* (Princeton, 1997).

Markovits, Inga, *Die Abwicklung. Ein Tagebuch zum Ende der DDR-Justiz* (Munich, 1993).

Meuschel, Sigrid, *Legitimation und Parteiherrschaft in der DDR. Zum Paradox von Stabilität und Revolution in der DDR 1945–1989* (Frankfurt, 1992).

Mitter, Armin and Wolle, Stefan, *Untergang auf Raten. Unbekannte Kapitel der DDR-Geschichte* (Munich, 1993).

Naimark, Norman M., *The Russians in Germany: A History of the Soviet Zone of Occupation, 1945–1949* (Cambridge, 1995).

Naumann, Klaus, ed., *NVA. Anspruch und Wirklichkeit. Nach ausgewählten Dokumenten* (Hamburg, 1996²).

Neubert, Ehrhart, *Geschichte der Opposition in der DDR 1949–1989* (Berlin, 1997).

Niemann, Heinz, *Meinungsforschung in der DDR. Die geheimen Berichte des Instituts für Meinungsforschung an das Politbüro der SED* (Berlin, 1994).

Niethammer, Lutz, Plato, Alexander von and Wierling, Dorothee, *Die volkseigene Erfahrung. Eine Archäologie des Lebens in der Industrieprovinz der DDR* (Berlin, 1991).

Pirker, Theo et al., eds, *Der Plan als Befehl und Fiktion. Wirtschaftsführung in der DDR. Gespräche und Analysen* (Opladen, 1995).

Podewin, Norbert, *Walter Ulbricht. Eine neue Biographie* (Berlin, 1995).

Pollack, Detlef, *Kirche in der Organisationsgesellschaft. Zum Wandel der gesellschaftlichen Lage der evangelischen Kirchen in der DDR* (Stuttgart, 1994).

Poppe, Ulrike, Eckert, Rainer and Kowalczuk, Ilko-Sascha, eds, *Zwischen Selbstbehauptung und Anpassung. Formen des Widerstands und der Opposition in der DDR* (Berlin, 1995).

Potthoff, Heinrich, *Die "Koalition der Vernunft." Deutschlandpolitik in den 80er Jahren* (Munich, 1995).

Rüddenklau, Wolfgang, *Störenfried. DDR-Opposition 1986–1989* (Berlin, 1992²).

Sabrow, Martin, ed., *Verwaltete Vergangenheit. Geschichtskultur und Herrschaftslegitimation in der DDR* (Leipzig, 1997).

Idem and Walther, Peter, eds, *Historische Forschung und sozialistische Diktatur. Beiträge zur Geschichtswissenschaft der DDR* (Leipzig, 1995).

Schroeder, Klaus, *Der SED-Staat. Partei, Staat und Gesellschaft 1949–1990* (Munich, 1998).

Solga, Heike, *Auf dem Weg in eine klassenlose Gesellschaft? Klassenlagen und Mobilität zwischen Generationen in der DDR* (Berlin, 1995).

Staadt, Jochen, *Die geheime Westpolitik der SED 1960–1970. Von der gesamtdeutschen Orientierung zur sozialistischen Nation* (Berlin, 1993).

Staritz, Dietrich, *Geschichte der DDR* (Frankfurt, 1996²).

Steiner, André, *Die DDR-Wirtschaftsreform der sechziger Jahre. Konflikt zwischen Effizienz und Machtkalkül* (Berlin, 1999).

Walther, Joachim, *Sicherungsbereich Literatur. Schriftsteller und Staatssicherheit in der Deutschen Demokratischen Republik* (Berlin, 1996).

Weber, Hermann, *Die DDR 1945–1990* (Munich, 1993²).

Weitz, Eric D., *Creating German Communism, 1890–1990. From Popular Protests to Socialist State* (Princeton, 1997).

Werkentin, Falco, *Politische Strafjustiz in der Ära Ulbricht. Vom bekennenden Terror zur verdeckten Repression* (Berlin, 1997²).

Whitney, Craig, *Spy Trader* (New York, 1993).

Wolle, Stefan, *Die heile Welt der Diktatur. Alltag und Herrschaft in der DDR 1971–1989* (Berlin, 1998).

Zelikov, Philip and Rice, Condoleezza, *Germany Unified and Europe Transformed. A Study in Statecraft* (Cambridge, MA, 1995).

NOTES ON CONTRIBUTORS

Leonore Ansorg, member of the ZZF in Potsdam, is a former dissident who has worked on the indoctrination of East German youth through the Young Pioneers.

Simone Barck, researcher at the ZZF, is an accomplished literary scholar who has commented on East German literature as well as the censorship system.

Arnd Bauerkämper, member of the ZZF, is a productive social historian who is working on the transformation of East German agriculture and the process of collectivization.

Burghard Ciesla, research fellow at the ZZF, is an economic historian with interests in the development of technology and transportation policy.

Christoph Classen, doctoral student at the ZZF, is preparing a dissertation on East German radio policies during the 1950s.

Jürgen Danyel, researcher at the ZZF, is an imaginative cultural historian who has written on anti-fascism and is working on the leadership style of the GDR elite.

Thomas Heimann, researcher at the ZZF, is a media historian who is currently analyzing the development of GDR television and film production.

Peter Hübner, project leader at the ZZF, is an authority on the development of the East German labor movement and is presently working on the transformation of political and economic elites.

Renate Hürtgen, member of the ZZF, is an erstwhile labor organizer who is investigating the internal structure of the East German trade union movement.

Konrad H. Jarausch, Lurcy Professor of History at the University of North Carolina and co-director of the ZZF, has written most recently on Americanization and Sovietization, the post-unification debates about German identity and on East German historiography.

Ralph Jessen, research fellow at the Free University of Berlin, is a rising social historian who has just finished a major study on the transformation of the GDR professoriate.

Monika Kaiser, researcher at the ZZF, is a former archivist with particular expertise in the SED apparatus and currently is writing a biography of Walter Ulbricht.

Mario Keßler, member of the ZZF, is a scholar with wide-ranging interests in topics such as the Bolshevik Revolution, Communist dissidents, and GDR Jewish policy.

Thomas Klein, researcher at the ZZF, is a former dissident who is focusing on opposition currents within the SED as well as the periodic efforts to repress them.

Christoph Kleßmann, professor of history at Potsdam University and co-director of the ZZF, is a well-known contemporary historian who has produced comparative studies of the two Germanys and is currently writing on East German labor history.

Sylvia Klötzer, member of the ZZF, is a literary scholar interested especially in satire and cabaret as tolerated forms of regime criticism within the GDR.

Jürgen Kocka, professor of history at the Free University of Berlin and founding director of the ZZF, is one of the leading historians of modern Germany, with broad interests in labor history, comparative theory, and the development of the GDR.

Dagmar Langenhan, research fellow at the ZZF, is a sociologist specifically interested in the transformation of rural society and the development of women's work.

Jochen Laufer, researcher at the ZZF, is a former opposition member who is the editor of important documents on postwar German policy from the Soviet Foreign Ministry.

Michael Lemke, project leader at the ZZF, is a diplomatic specialist who has written extensively on GDR efforts to establish an independent foreign policy and the Berlin crisis.

Thomas Lindenberger, project leader at the ZZF, is an unconventional everyday historian who investigates the interaction between the SED and the populace through the people's police.

Siegfried Lokatis, member of the ZZF, is a historian of publishing who has written much on the development of East German censorship and the book production system.

Detlef Pollack, professor of sociology at the University of Frankfurt-Oder, has published extensively on the Protestant Church in East Germany as well as the development of resistance within the GDR.

Patrice G. Poutrus, doctoral student at the ZZF, is working on a dissertation about the problem of East German food policy.

Sabine Roß, researcher at the ZZF, is a social science historian and computer specialist interested in quantitative remains of the GDR and women's careers.

Martin Sabrow, project leader at the ZZF, is an innovative cultural historian who has written on the Rathenau murder and now works on the legitimizing role of East German historiography.

Dorothee Wierling, fellow at the Essen institute for cultural history, is an oral historian who is investigating the impact of generation and gender on East German lives.

INDEX

A

Abschnittsbevollmächtigte, See ABV
ABV, 7, 128–140
Adenauer, Konrad, 50, 102
Agricultural Production
    Cooperative, *See* LPG
Alltagsgeschichte, 125
Americanization, 95, 333
Ansorg, Leonore, 7, 163
Apel, Erich, 327, 332
Arendt, Hannah, 23, 52–53, 200,
    207, 286
Ash, Mitchell, 336
Axen, Hermann, 335

B

Baltic states, 74, 79
Barck, Simone, 7, 213
Bauerkämper, Arnd, 7, 265
Beck, Ulrich, 48
Becker-Schmidt, Regina, 168
Behrens, Friedrich, 293–94
Benjamin, Walter, 232
Berend, Ivan, 19
Berger, Wolfgang, 327
Berlin Wall, 33–34, 139, 348, 371
Berlin, 76, 82, 99, 102–103, 199,
    249
Biermann, Wolf, 245, 320
Birke, Adolf, 366

Bokov, F.E., 113
Bourdieu, Pierre, 175
Brandt, Willy, 51, 335
Braun, Volker, 258
Brezhnev, Leonid, 253, 334, 336
Brie, Michael, 36
Broszat, Martin, 5
Brzezinski, Zbigniew, 23

C

cabaret, 199, 241–251, 260
cadres, 183, 187, 189, 217, 265–77,
    331, 335, 346–49, 353
censorship, 199, 201, 214–19,
    227, 230, 241, 246, 249–60
Central Institute for History, 199
Central Party Control Commission,
    See ZPKK
Cibulka, Hans, 36
Ciesla, Burghard, 7, 143
Classen, Christoph, 7, 213
Cockburn, Cynthia, 166
collectivization, 10, 33, 99, 128,
    130–32, 135, 138, 143, 148,
    287, 298, 301, 314
COMECON, 10, 149
COMINFORM, 81, 114
Communist Party of Germany,
    See KPD
Communist Party of the Soviet
    Union, *See* CPSU

consumerism, 7, 144, 153, 157
CPSU, 334–335
Cremer, Fritz, 332
Creuzberger, Stefan, 73
currency reform, 73, 79, 80–85
Czechoslovakia, 254, 320, 335–36, 344

D

Dahlem, Frank, 265
Dahrendorf, Ralf, 368
Danyel, Jürgen, 7, 265
DEFA, 219, 226–30, 242, 333,
  See also film
Democratic Women's League,
  See DFD
denazification, 268
de-Stalinization, 6, 115, 242, 254,
  See also Stalinism; post-Stalinism
Deutsche Film Aktiengesellschaft,
  See DEFA
DFD, 179
dictatorship,
  approaches to, 6–8, 17
  modern, 6, 17–19, 21–24, 47,
    55–56, 163, 169, 171, 175,
    178, 189, 197, 213, 233, 273,
    285, 300, 336, 342, 350–52,
    366–370
  welfare, 6, 17, 47, 59–62,
    64–65, 146, 173, 274, 277,
    297, 350, 368, 370
discourse, 195, 198, 199–208
dismantling, 6, 73–78
Dölling, Irene, 167
Dörner, Diedrich, 146
Dorothee Wierling, 307
Dresden, 36, 249, 250
Düdder, Heinz, 244

E

Eckermann, Walther, 198
economy,
  Mangelwirtschaft, 144, 299
  planned economy, 143–58, 171,
    270–73, 288–95, 299–302
education, 317–20, 329, 349
Eigen-Sinn, 9, 125, 140

Eisler, Gerhart, 223
elites, *See* cadres
Engler, Wolfgang, 54
Ensikat, Peter, 9

F

FDGB, 164, 171–72, 270, 301, 321
FDJ, 256, 270, 314, 319, 333
Fechner, Max, 115
film, 214, 218–19, 223, 225–30,
    233, 242–44, 333, *See also*
    DEFA
Flora, Peter, 59
Foucault, Michel, 7, 126, 161
Free German Trade Union
  Federation, *See* FDGB
Free German Youth, *See* FDJ
FRG (Federal Republic of
  Germany),
  comparisons with the GDR,
    167–68, 293, 367–68
  influence on the GDR, 214,
    220–222
  policies toward the GDR, 50–51
Friedrich, Carl, 23, 53
Fürsorgediktatur, *See* dictatorship,
  welfare

G

Gauck, Joachim, 195
Gaus, Günter, 48
GDR (German Democratic
  Republic),
  attitudes toward the West, 95,
    98, 102, 276, 286, 320
  founding of, 84–85
  homogeneity of, 27, 267, 268,
    275, 299, 368
  interpretations of, 4–6, 10, 18,
    23–24, 47, 49, 50, 364, 371
  legitimacy of, 4, 32, 36–37, 126,
    132, 177, 195–97, 207–208,
    287, 341–42, 355, 364, 366
  limited autonomy of, 93, 96,
    104, 365
  relations with the FRG, 196,
    204, 221, 327, 333–35, 366
  stagnation of, 285–86, 294–302

generations, 174, 180–81
  Flakhelfergeneration, 310
  founding generation, 180–81
  reconstruction generation,
    180–81, 307–322
German-Soviet Non-Aggression
  Pact, 206
Glasnost, 229, 249
Goldhammer, Bruno 115
Gorbachev, Michail, 119, 370
governmentality, 126–127, 134,
  138–140
Grass, Günter, 59
Grotewohl, Otto 3, 98–99, 113

H

Haftendorn, Helga, 92
Hager, Kurt, 196, 198, 202, 206,
  332
Hallstein doctrine, 51
Hamburg, 199
Harich, Wolfgang, 260
Havemann, Robert, 332
Heiduczek, Werner, 36
Heimann, Thomas, 7, 213
Hein,Christoph, 36
Henrich, Rolf, 58
Herrschaftsdiskurs, See discourse
historicization, critical 5
Honecker, Erich, 6, 8, 58, 61, 63,
  127, 144, 259, 295, 321, 325,
  329, 331–37, 370
Honecker, Margot, 183
Hübner, Peter, 7, 285
Huinink, Johannes, 28
Hungary, 24, 75, 254, 336
Hürtgen, Renate, 7, 163

I

Industrial Feeding Farm, *See* KIM
Institute for Marxism-Leninism,
  199, 252, 255

J

Jahn, Günter, 248
Janka, Walter, 260
Jarausch, Konrad, 17, 47, 274, 297,
  337, 364, 368, 370

Jesse, Eckhard, 53
Jessen, Ralph, 8, 28, 341–42
Jews, 6, 63, 118, 119

K

Kaiser, Monika, 8, 325
Kennedy, Paul, 294
Keßler, Mario, 6, 109
KIM, 147, 150
Klein, Thomas, 6, 109
Klötzer, Sylvia, 7, 241
Knyshevskji, Pavel, 76
Kocka, Jürgen, 6, 15, 55, 336, 368,
  370
Koestler, Arthur, 195
Koselleck, Reinhart, 48
Koval, Konstantin, 77
KPD, 51, 78, 80, 84, 112–114, 276,
  334
Kremlin, 73
Krenz, Egon, 363
Krushchev, Nikita, 114, 326, 330,
  332

L

labor, 286, 288–93, 298–302
Land, Rainer, 36
Lange, Ingeburg, 177
Langenhan, Dagmar, 7, 177
Laufer, Jochen, 6, 73
Leipzig, 216, 229, 363
Lemke, Christiane, 54
Lemke, Michael, 6, 91
Leonhard, Wolfgang, 195
Lepsius, Rainer, 328
Lindenberger, Thomas, 7, 125
Linz, Juan, 54
literature, 199, 217–18, 225–33,
  241, 243, 251–60
Lokatis, Siegfried, 7, 241
Loth, Wilfried, 73
Lötsch, Manfred, 297, 351
LPG, 128, 136–137, 148, 151, 185
Lüdtke, Alf, 125
Ludz, Peter Christian, 55, 274,
  330–31
Lutheran Church, 36, 354

M

Magdeburg, 36
Malenkov, Georgij, 75
Maletin, Pavel, 80
Mannheim, 3
Marshall, George 81
Mason, Tim, 370
Matern, Hermann, 113
Mayer, Karl-Ulrich, 28, 346, 353
media, 213–234, 243, 246, 248,
    319–320
Meier, Artur, 54
Merker, Paul, 115
Meuschel, Sigrid, 9, 27–28, 54,
    299, 351
Mielke, Erich, 195
Ministry for State Security, *See* Stasi
Ministry of Culture, 217–219, 242,
    252, 255, 257, 260, 333
Mittag, Günther, 61, 321, 327
Mitter, Armin, 364
modern dictatorship, *See* dictator-
    ship, modern
Modrow, Hans, 249–50, 321
Mohr, Hubert, 198
Molotov, Wjatscheslaw M., 79–81
Morgner, Irmtraud, 36
Moscow, 10–11, 73–74, 78, 80–83,
    92, 98–100, 104, 252–53
Mückenberger, Christiane, 229
Müller, Heiner, 36

N

Naimark, Norman, 73
National Socialism, *See also*
    denazification
GDR comparisons to, 5, 196, 285,
    See also totalitarianism
    historical memory of, 311–312
    influences on the GDR, 10, 290,
    299, 342
Neues Forum, 58
Niethammer, Lutz, 135, 205–06

O

Oelßner, Fred, 96, 115
Okun, Bernd 36
Ostpolitik, 51, 62

P

People Owned Factory, *See* VEB
People Owned Estate, *See* VEG
perestroika, 62, 119, 204
Pieck, Wilhelm, 3, 98, 82–83, 113,
    120
Poland, 24, 74, 79, 118, 254, 336,
    344
police, *See Volkspolizei*
Pollack, Detlef, 6, 27, 55, 56, 58,
    371
post-Stalinism, 8, 17, 22, 24, 109,
    111, 116, *See also* Stalinism;
    de-Stalinization
post-totalitarian, 6, 22, 24, 54,
    see also totalitarianism
Potsdam Conference, 75–76
Potsdam, 248, 249, 251
Poutrus, Patrice, 7, 143
Prague Spring, 119, 217

R

real existing socialism, 5, 9, 17,
    48, 62–63, 117, 168, 182,
    188, 275
reform, 295, 325–331
    blockages against, 331–338
    definitions of, 325–326
Reich, Jens, 207
Reinhold, Otto, 297
Renate Hürtgen, 163
Richert, Ernst, 364
Ristock, Inge, 245
Ritschl, Albrecht, 293
Rosenau, James, 92
Roß, Sabine, 7, 177
Rudolph, Hermann, 364
Rytlewski, Ralf, 54

S

Sabrow, Martin, 7, 195
SAG, 78, 79
SBZ, 50, 76–85, 112, 115, 152,
    312, 364
SCC, 94, 99, 103
Schabowski, Günther, 321
Scheddin, Uwe, 247
Schelsky, Helmut, 307

Schirdewan, Karl, 115
Schlotterbeck, Anna and Friedrich, 115
Schmidt, Werner, 34
Schoenbaum, David, 369
Schrecker, Hans, 115
Schroeder, Klaus, 17, 370
Schwarze, Hans Werner, 364
SED,
    Central Committee, 177, 218–29, 227, 229, 271, 297, 327, 330, 332, 352, 368
    central rule of, 29
    founding of, 113–114
    Politburo, 195, 219, 245, 252–53, 321, 329–30, 352, 363, 368
    purges within, 114–115
Segert, Dieter, 36
Selbmann, Fritz, 115
Semenov, Vladimir, 82
Semirjaga, Michail, 73
Simonow, Konstantin, 101
Slánský trial, 118
Sloterdijk, Peter, 337
Social Democratic Party of Germany, *See* SPD
social cleavages, 28–29, 39, 288, 290
social mobility, 342–356
Socialist Unity Party of Germany, *See* SED
Sokolovskij, Vasliley, 81
Solga, Heike, 28, 287, 346, 353
Sonderweg, 275, 277
Soviet Control Commission, *See* SCC
Soviet Military Administration of Germany, *See* SVAG
Soviet Occupied Zone, *See* SBZ
Soviet Stock Company, *See* SAG
Soviet Union, 18, 48, 73, 79, 81, 112, 249, 327, 331, 334–37, 364–65
Sovietization, 6, 85, 93–95, 98–100, 102–104
SPD, 3, 112–114
Sperling, Fritz, 115

SRK, 215
Srubar, Ilja, 35
Stalin, Josef, 18, 19, 74–76, 81, 83, 95–99, 101, 112, 117, 119, 205–06, 260, 265, 314, 335
Stalinism, 6, 8, 17, 22–24, 52, 60, 95–96, 98, 103, 109–119, 215, 227, 254, 265, 308, 315, 327, 368 *See also* de-Staliniza-tion; post-Stalinism
Staritz, Dietrich, 365
Stasi, 4, 6, 38, 60, 116, 118, 127, 206, 214, 217, 226, 230, 248–51, 368, 317
State Radio Committee. *See* SRK
Stoph, Willi, 334–335
Strittmatter, Erwin, 258
SVAG, 74, 77–85, 113, 178, 214

T

Thalheimer, August, 119
Thälmann, Ernst, 199, 219
Third Reich, *See* National Socialism
Thomas, Michael, 54
Thomas, Rüdiger, 364
Tisch, Harry, 321
totalitarianism, 196–97, 214, 233, 207, 364, *See also* post-totalitarian
    alternatives to, 55–56, 64–65, 109, 366
    critique of, 4, 6, 10, 18, 22, 49, 52–56, 91, 368
    definitions of, 23, 52
Trotsky, Leo, 52
Turba, Kurt, 329, 332–333

U

Ulbricht, Walter, 6, 8, 63–64, 98, 100, 102, 113, 143, 148, 199, 201, 252, 255, 259, 269, 274, 295, 319, 325–338
Union of People Owned Companies, *See* VVB
Unrechtsstaat, 3, 17, 47, 63
Upper Silesia, 76
Uschkamp, Irma, 183

V

Varga, Eugen, 74
VEB, 79, 270
VEG, 185
Verner, Paul, 335
Volkseigene Betriebe, See VEB
Volkspolizei, 125–128, 130, 139
VVB, 147, 150

W

Wander, Maxie, 36
Wandlitz, 275
Warsaw Pact, 10
Weber, Max, 21, 54, 196
Weimar Republic, 10, 58, 64, 285,
     296, 307
welfare dictatorship, *See* dictator-
     ship, welfare
Wierling, Dorothee, 7, 307
Woderich, Rudolf, 300
Wolf, Christa, 36, 231, 245, 258
Wolf, Konrad, 229
Wolle, Stefan, 58, 364, 371
Wollweber, Ernst, 115
women,
     emancipation of, 163–169, 172,
          174, 178
     female labor, 163–89, 288–92,
          345, 367–68
     legal equality, 178–79
     liberation of, 4
     reproduction, 167, 170, 179,
          181, 186–87,
     self-perceptions, 165, 167,
          171–75, 180–81, 188

Y

Yalta Conference, 75

Z

Zhukov, Gregory, 80
Ziller, Gerhart, 115
Zitelmann, Rainer, 369
ZPKK, 114